Mexican
Light

Exciting, Healthy Dishes
from the Border and Beyond

Mexican
Light

Exciting, Healthy Dishes
from the Border and Beyond

Martha Rose Shulman

WILLIAM MORROW AND COMPANY, INC.
New York

MEXICAN LIGHT

Library of Congress Cataloging-in-Publication Data

Shulman, Martha Rose.
Mexican light : exciting, healthy dishes from the border and
beyond / Martha Rose Shulman.
        p.   cm.
    Includes index.
    ISBN 0-688-17466-3
    1. Cookery, Mexican.   2. Low-fat diet—Recipes.   I. Title.
TX716.M4S48   2000
641.5'638—dc21   99-39648
                                                          CIP

Printed in the United States of America

First Edition

1 2 3 4 5 6 7 8 9 10

Drawings by Lisa Ryan

www.williammorrow.com

To Mary Shulman,
my wise and loving stepmother,
who taught me to cook

Contents

Acknowledgments

First of all I'd like to thank my editor, Frances McCullough, who knew that this was the project for me and got me going on it as soon as she found out that I would be moving to California from France.

Two people have been particularly generous and helpful. Carmen Ramírez Delgollado of Mexico City took me under her wing right after I met her, introducing me to the marvelous cuisine of her native Veracruz and taking me all over the state to taste it. She also taught me many dishes in her fantastic Mexico City restaurant, El Bajio. Thank you, Carmen, for sharing your passion for Mexican food and art with me.

Chicago chef Rick Bayless, author of *Authentic Mexican,* offered me the use of his extensive library before I'd even begun work on the book, and although I never could find the time to take him up on that, I had the great good fortune to participate in a weeklong culinary and cultural adventure that he and his wife, Deann, organized in Oaxaca. I am grateful to you, Rick, for helping me master many techniques used in Mexican cooking and for so generously sharing your knowledge of Mexican food. Also, thanks for the wonderful meals at Topolobampo.

I have been grateful to Diana Kennedy ever since her first cookbooks appeared in the 1970s. I so desperately wanted to cook the wonderful food I had begun to discover on my trips to Mexico, and there were the recipes, every one I wanted and more. Anyone who walks into an American kitchen hoping to produce Mexican food with an authentic taste owes Diana Kennedy, who brought real Mexican food into the American kitchen, a huge debt.

My heartfelt gratitude to Frederick Hertz of Oakland, California, for making our move to Berkeley so easy, for being such a good friend, and for being a taster—and tester—so often.

Thanks to Lorraine Battle for her expert assistance and good company in the kitchen.

Thanks to Anne Trager and Debra Valentine for their expert, helpful recipe testing.

Thanks to the Greenblatt family—Stephen, Ellen, Aaron, and Josh—for letting me come *with* dinner so often during my intense recipe-testing periods and for being such enthusiastic eaters.

As always I am grateful to my agent, Molly Friedrich, for her constant support.

And, of course, thanks to my husband, Bill, who has eaten Mexican food almost every night for two years.

Preface

A Rich, Full Circle

Mexican food came into my life when I was 18 and spent the summer working with Chicano migrant farmworkers in Michigan. Part of my job entailed visiting families in the migrant camps every night, and I became friendly with several of them. I had been to Mexico when I was 13 and loved the tacos, so I asked one family to teach me how to make them. On a hot, humid evening, in a stifling shack housing a family of eight, Señora Saenz and two of her daughters showed me how to refry beans and make enchiladas filled with seasoned ground beef. And I taught the Saenz girls how to make a cake . . . from a mix.

At summer's end I went back to my comfortable student life on the East Coast, but I couldn't get the Mexican-American culture out of my head. I made tacos and enchiladas for my friends, studied Spanish, wore "Boycott Grapes" buttons to support the striking United Farmworkers led by César Chávez, and returned to Michigan the following summer. One of the high points was a large organizing meeting held by the Colorado Migrant Council, where for two or three days we ate incredible meals, prepared by the farmworkers' wives in the camp kitchen. I watched and helped where I could, enjoying every minute. There was singing and dancing after every meal, and the grand finale was a Mexican barbecue—barbacoa—which entailed digging a big pit to barbecue the entire head of a steer. (I have to admit I never liked this fiesta dish, even in those days, when I was a more enthusiastic meat eater.)

That conference hooked me, so I followed the people I worked with back to Texas, specifically the Rio Grande Valley. A planned semester off from school turned into a 12-year stay.

I can't imagine a place more different from the New England I grew up in than that valley, a flat, fertile area stretching from Brownsville to Laredo. Mexico is just across the river from where we lived, and that is where I'd go, several times a week, to buy onions, carrots, beans, and garlic.

Mexico is also where my friends and I would go for dinner, most often to the border town of Reynosa. What I really loved to eat, in a little restaurant on the main square, were the beans, cooked in a pot with lots and lots of cilantro and served in a big bowl with an endless supply of enormous homemade tortillas, both flour and corn. My friends and I still talk about those beans and their heavenly broth.

I lived with the family of a woman I worked with, Alma Canales. From Alma I learned how to make a good pot of pinto beans and to make guacamole in a molcajete, the basalt mortar and pestle commonly used in Mexico for making salsas, guacamole, and grinding spices. I learned to make tamales, too. Just before Christmas the pig owned by the extended family was slaughtered, and for the next few days, every night the family sat around the table preparing tamales, singing and gossiping. What a thrill! I also got fat on the flour tortillas, made with quite a bit of lard every morning by Alma, her two sisters, and her mother.

Whenever I traveled I headed south. In three different trips I spent several weeks learning to weave, living with the family of Don Isaac Garcia in the beautiful Zapotec Indian village near Oaxaca called Teotitlán del Valle. As soon as it was light enough to see, I would begin weaving, and about an hour later one of the Garcia girls would bring me breakfast, invariably the yellowest eggs I had ever seen, a sweet roll or corn tortillas, and black beans or a soup. As I wove I would hear the local women grinding corn on a stone metate, then, at about 11:00, the pat-pat-pat of tortillas being made. Soon afterward the smells of food being cooked would begin. If only I had known then that I was going to be a cook, not a weaver, I would have spent more time in the kitchen!

At about 3:00 I would have my lunch—tortillas, soup, possibly an egg. When I asked why I kept getting soups and eggs, Don Isaac replied, "We were told that gringos can't digest anything else." The soups, particularly the rich black beans, were wonderful—a tomato-based tortilla soup and one with vermicelli in it, a very light leek soup, and my favorite, a turkey stock with vegetables and pieces of turkey mixed with beaten egg, called higaditos.

Still, I *could* digest other foods, like the exotic-tasting chicken with mole at the food stalls in the Oaxaca market and the fantastic Oaxacan moles (there are seven different moles from this region) prepared for fiestas and weddings, usually a dark brown one or a mole negro served with turkey.

It was at the fiestas that I also discovered mezcal, an agave-based drink like tequila that is much loved in Oaxaca but was then unavailable north of the border. Fortunately times have changed on both sides of the border. Teotitlán del Valle now boasts a fantastic restaurant called Tlamanalli, owned and operated by Abigail Mendoza. When I lived in the village in the early seventies, there was not even running water! And mezcal, happily, is now available in the United States, a particularly fine one from Oaxaca called Encantado imported by Mezcal Importers Inc.

Eventually I fell in love with France, and after several years in Austin I moved to Paris in 1981. But I never really left Mexico behind. I filled my car with as many cooking utensils, cookbooks, and Mexican cooking ingredients as I could fit into the trunk and took it on the ship. With me came a heavy tortilla press and comal (a griddle for baking the tortillas), a bean pot, a few packs of Ziploc bags for making tortillas, several bags of masa harina (the flour used for corn tortillas), a year's supply of chiles and cumin seeds, and several pounds of black beans.

That first year in Paris I shared a large apartment with two friends from Texas; we always entertained with Mexican food, and we entertained a lot. Our debut was a brunch, which my friends Maggie and Steve called a migathon for the main dish, migas, scrambled eggs with crisp tortillas, onions, tomatoes, and chiles. Accompanied by black bean nachos, stuffed jalapeños, homemade tortillas, and, of course, margaritas, the brunch was such a hit that a day later I got a call for a catering job. The editor of the *International Herald Tribune* was turning 40, and his wife wanted to surprise him with a Mexican dinner party. Before I knew it I was in business in Paris—as Yellow Rose Catering—making Tex-Mex and Mexican food. I also began giving monthly paying dinners in my apartment, and I opened every season with Mexican food. That those dinners filled faster than any others and were by far the most festive confirmed my feeling that no food is more fun than Mexican food; a Mexican dinner is always a party.

Meanwhile, I continued to read new Mexican recipes and try new dishes, though I had to depend on Asian markets for cilantro, chiles, avocados, and limes and on visiting friends, who were always instructed to bring chiles or Mexican chocolate. As I studied and cooked the cuisines of the Mediterranean and my beloved Provence, I developed techniques for keeping the fats down in my cooking without sacrificing flavor, and those techniques inevitably made their way into my Mexican cooking.

When I returned to California in 1993, I rekindled my love affair with Mexico, and my passion is stronger than ever. Latino culture had made a huge mark on this country during my 12-year absence. I was astounded and delighted by the availability of Mexican ingredients and the quality of produce in general, especially in California. It was easy to plunge right in, to learn as much as I could about chiles and other ingredients, to master authentic recipes and experiment with the ideas that they inspired.

In the two years that I have been working on this book, I have made only a small dent in the cuisines of Mexico. My travels are far from over. I look forward to expanding my repertoire with dishes from areas that I have yet to explore in depth, such as the Yucatán and the Pacific states. My goal here was not so much to compile a definitive Mexican cookbook as to give you a medium-size collection of recipes that bring you some of the essential flavors of Mexico.

As I began to cook for this book, I was struck by similarities between Mexico's produce markets and the ones that had thrilled me in the Mediterranean. I found myself using, over and over again, the foods that were unknown in Europe before the discovery of the Americas—beans, squash, corn, tomatoes, potatoes, and chiles. But I also found myself cooking dishes based on foods that reminded me of the Mediterranean Basin, which I found piled high in Mexican markets as well—wild mushrooms, fava beans, lentils, chickpeas, greens, and, of course, garlic.

I was particularly inspired by the cuisine of the state of Veracruz and was lucky enough to have Carmen Ramírez Delgollado, a native of Xalapa and owner of El Bajio Restaurant in Mexico City, as my guide there. All of the cuisines of Mexico reflect a melding of Old and New World gastronomic cultures, but none has retained Spanish flavors and techniques to the extent that the cuisine of Veracruz has. Olive oil is used widely, and capers, olives, almonds, and raisins come up again and again in recipes. Just consider the regional dish that is most widely known in our country, huachinango a la Veracruzana. Red snapper is cooked in a richly flavored tomato sauce that contains olive oil, onions, garlic, green olives, capers, parsley, rosemary, thyme, oregano, and bay leaves. It also contains pickled jalapeño peppers (named for the capital of the state, Xalapa, or Jalapa): that's what makes it taste Mexican.

Indeed, chiles, tomatoes, and other special ingredients such as corn, tomatillos, and various herbs like cilantro and epazote, as well as particular cooking techniques—griddle-toasting, blending, searing—make Mexican food unique. These are the techniques and the ingredients that give the cuisine its own authentic taste, a taste that has been in no way hampered by a lighter touch.

In addition to my trips to Mexico, I've visited Texas several times during these last two years, and I'm happy to report that there is more good Mexican food than ever in Austin. Fonda San Miguel, the first really fine Mexican restaurant in that city, is as wonderful as ever under the guidance of its chef/owners, Miguel Ravago and Tom Gilliland. I always love seeing them, and their food remains impeccable. New, since I left, is Las Mañitas, on South Congress Avenue, where I would be happy to eat breakfast every day. It was there that I first ate one of my favorite dishes, Yucatecan huevos motuleños—fried eggs with black beans, tortillas, salsa, and cheese.

I've also spent a lot of time in Los Angeles, which will be my new home by the time this book comes out. There I have been particularly impressed by chef Jose Rodriguez, at the restaurant La Serenata de Garibaldi, on East First Street. Jose is a genius with fish and sauces. He has a light hand, and his cuisine is magical; my recipes for fish with spicy vegetable salsa and fish with green tomatillo mole were inspired by the food I've eaten at his restaurant.

Los Angeles sometimes feels almost like Mexico to me. Even on the West Side, which is not particularly Latino, the supermarkets all sell Mexican ingredients—tomatillos, cactus paddles, tortillas, dried chiles, and Mexican cheeses. And if I really want to "go to Mexico," I drive east on First Street to El Mercado, the big Mexican market. There I drink fresh carrot and orange juice, just as in the Oaxaca market, and eat quesadillas and guacamole in market stalls. I can find any Mexican cheese or chile I want in this market and buy hot, fresh tortillas. The market is bustling, especially on Saturdays, and filled with music, color, and spirit—everything I love about Mexico. You can have the same experience in other American cities, particularly Chicago and San Francisco.

I hope that the recipes in this book will bring you some of this spirit, which so touches me. Mexico has one of the world's greatest, brightest cuisines. With this book—and a light hand—I have tried to capture its essence.

Martha Rose Shulman
September 1995
Berkeley, California

Introduction: Mexican Light

This is a book for people who love the vibrant flavors of Mexican food and also want to keep their dietary fats low. Light Mexican food may seem like an oxymoron, but the authentic cuisines of Mexico—a vast country with a cuisine that is at least as varied as that of France—are not really so high-fat, certainly not overall. Yes, lard is an important ingredient in Mexican cooking. But in Mexico you never find the kind of heavy, calorie-laden "combination plate" that we associate with border-Mex food. Nor do you find vast quantities of bright yellow cheese piled onto everything from tacos to salads. Cheese is sprinkled over enchiladas or into tacos or quesadillas with a light hand in Mexico, and many of the cheeses are lower-fat varieties. Every tortilla casing is not deep-fried south of the border. What we call *nachos* in Tex-Mex cooking are called *tostadas* in Mexico, because the tortilla pieces topped with something luscious (never melted Colby or process cheese) are toasted, not fried. Quesadillas are often cooked on a griddle, as are tacos. When tortillas for tacos are fried, they're *never* deep-fried into the half-moon-shaped taco shells that we use in this country. As for high-protein foods, although pork and beef are used widely, poultry is used even more; chicken and turkey are incredibly lean and tasty in Mexico. And with its enormous coastline—Gulf, Caribbean, and Pacific—Mexico is a treasury of fish dishes. The really rich food in Mexico is reserved for fiestas and weddings; we think of these dishes when we think of Mexican food because these are the items that tend to appear on American restaurant menus. But everyday Mexican food is a much simpler affair.

I've written *Mexican Light* for a wide range of cooks, experienced or beginners, for people who love Mexican food so much they could eat it every day, for those who like to cook this kind of food occasionally, and for people who are somewhere in between. Most of the recipes are for no-nonsense dishes that are quick and easy for after-work, family cooking; many are perfect for entertaining at a dinner party, brunch, or buffet (many of these recipes are also quick enough for everyday cooking). There are also some more time-consuming, complex dishes for weekend cooking.

Many of the dishes are authentic and remain unaltered. In some traditional dishes, however, oil is reduced, lard eliminated, or a high-fat ingredient like whole milk replaced by its low-fat equivalent. Other recipes are dishes I developed in my kitchen to showcase a flavor or an ingredient prevalent in Mexican cooking. Rather than a compendium of authentic Mexican food, then, this is a collection of delicious, healthful recipes *inspired* by the cuisines of Mexico and the border states, dishes full of color and flavor, spice and spirit, freshness and life.

How have I lightened the cuisine? First, as I always do, I have chosen recipes that are inherently low in fat. Mexican salsas, for example, require little if any fat, and they are often what defines a dish. The majority of the dishes in this book are vegetarian. I have emphasized fish as well, and as for meat, I've stuck to skinless chicken, mostly chicken breasts, which are the lowest-fat part of the bird. The collection reflects the diet that I like to eat every day.

With the exception of one bread recipe, I have made one significant change in some of the recipes in this book: I've omitted lard, not because I am against the use of this ingredient but because I prefer to work with mono-unsaturated fats like olive and canola oil. According to my nutrition tables, lard has no more total fat than canola or olive oil (.7 gram less, in fact). But a much greater percentage of lard's fat is saturated (39 percent as opposed to 14 percent in olive oil, 6 percent in canola), and lard contains 13 milligrams of cholesterol, whereas the vegetable oils contain none. A diet too high in saturated fat and cholesterol is thought to increase the risk for heart disease and other obesity-related illnesses. Canola and olive oil are both high in mono-unsaturated fats, which, research has found, help *lower* blood cholesterol levels. My decision not to use lard means that a key Mexican flavor is absent from some of the recipes, most notably refried beans. So I can't claim authenticity here, but with the addition of other good things to these dishes—garlic and onion, herbs and spices and chiles—I can claim great flavor.

Some dishes, unfortunately, just won't work without lard. There is no way, for example, to make a light tamale dough without fat. The lard-free tamales such as those I've eaten in the Oaxaca Valley require very fresh masa made from local corn. With so many other delicious dishes to make, I didn't find tamales an essential inclusion. The same goes for flour tortillas. All of the nonfat varieties I've found in supermarkets have the texture of rubber when heated, so I've decided to stick with corn and leave burritos at the burrito stands. Other dishes that must be deep-fried have been passed over in favor of easy tortilla dishes made with soft, hot tortillas filled or topped with something fresh and lively.

I have, however, retained one high-fat food that is a staple in Mexican cooking: the avocado. Avocado is high in fat, but it's mostly monounsaturated, and there's no cholesterol. Avocados are also high in fiber and a good source of vitamins A, B$_6$, C, E, and folic acid. Fortunately, a little goes a long way. So while you won't find a traditional guacamole here, you will find a traditional blend of tomatillos and avocado, and avocado adds richness, flavor, and depth to some of my salsas, tacos, sandwiches, and soups.

My biggest accomplishment in the fat-reducing department was figuring out how to make really crunchy tortilla chips in the microwave. This little trick also allows me to give you a terrific selection of tostadas (nachos) and chilaquiles.

As for cheese, obviously the cheese enchiladas and burritos you may be accustomed to are not in these pages. But I have worked out an excellent low-fat quesadilla with 10 different fillings. And again, in real Mexican food delicious, milky-white fresh cheese or dried crumbly cheese is sprinkled over dishes with a light hand.

Generally I use less fat for frying than traditional recipes call for. This means cooking in heavy nonstick skillets over slightly lower heat than is usual. Sticking and burning shouldn't be a problem because so many foods here are cooked with blended tomatoes, leaving plenty of liquid in the pan. Much of the Mexican repertoire is cooked on a grill or a griddle or simmered in a rich-tasting broth—cooking methods that are not fat-dependent.

As for desserts, although traditional Mexican sweets are descended from rich Spanish treats, what we really want to eat after a Mexican meal is something light and fruity. You'll find plenty to choose from in that department.

All in all, there are enough tantalizing choices here to allow you to cook and eat healthy Mexican food every day.

Equipment

Most of the necessary equipment is standard, but I find a few items particularly useful.

Some Useful Items for Preparing Mexican Food

BLENDER   The blender is much better suited to making many Mexican sauces than the food processor because the small blades and narrow jar more evenly puree chiles, tomatoes and tomatillos, and other mixtures. Sauces pureed in a food processor often have an uneven texture. In fact, my food processor hardly gets used when I'm cooking Mexican food.

MEDIUM-MESH WIRE STRAINER   Many of the mixtures that are pureed in a blender are then strained through a medium-mesh strainer. A fairly large one that sits on a bowl is most convenient. The type sold at most supermarkets is fine.

RUBBER GLOVES   Buy a box of latex surgical gloves, at a medical supply store or a drugstore. These thin gloves are perfect protection when you work with chiles. You don't want to seed chiles without them. One box costs about the same as two pairs of kitchen gloves, which are much clumsier to work with.

ELECTRIC SPICE MILL   This is exactly the same gadget as an electric coffee grinder and may be sold under that name. Don't use your coffee grinder for spices, however, because the coffee beans will eventually pick up the spicy residues in the plastic top. It's worth investing in a separate spice mill so that your cumin and other spices can be as fresh as possible. Some of the recipes in this book begin by asking you to grind up peppercorns, cloves, cinnamon, and cumin. These inexpensive gadgets are also useful for grinding up toasted tortillas, used for thickening soups and stews.

MORTAR AND PESTLE   You can also use a mortar and pestle for grinding spices. I use mine mostly for pounding garlic to a paste for certain dishes and for pounding garlic and chipotle chiles together. The mortar is also very useful for mashing avocados. In Mexico heavy, three-legged basalt molcajetes are in every kitchen for making salsas and guacamole and grinding spices, and other foods. Rather than lug one back from Mexico, I've continued to use my olive-wood mortar and pestle with success. Stone, wood, and earthenware are all suitable, but if you use earthenware, make sure it's heavy enough to withstand pounding. If you buy a Mexican molcajete, make sure it is not too porous. *To cure a molcajete:* Place about ¼ cup of uncooked rice in the molcajete and grind with the pestle. The ground rice will be gray. Remove the rice, rinse the molcajete, and dry. Repeat four or five times, until the ground rice is just about clear. Rinse and dry the molcajete.

CITRUS PRESS   Powered by hand or electricity, this is handy for the lime juice called for often in Mexican cooking.

CAST-IRON GRIDDLE OR SKILLET   Old-fashioned cast-iron pans are perfect for toasting quesadillas, chiles, and garlic and for making and heating tortillas. If you happen to be in a Mexican market, an excellent minor investment is a sheet-metal comal, a thin flat griddle that is very efficient for quickly toasting dried chiles and garlic.

METAL SPATULA   You'll use this tool every time you toast dried chiles, to press them down on the hot comal or skillet.

TONGS   Useful for manipulating garlic cloves and chiles when you're toasting them and for grilling peppers over a flame.

BAKING SHEETS   You will begin many of the recipes in this book by roasting tomatoes under a broiler. A jelly-roll type of baking pan, covered with foil, is the best vessel.

TORTILLA PRESS   Useful if you want to try making your own tortillas or for making plantain pancakes. The presses are sold in Mexican markets. It's easiest to find aluminum tortilla presses, but hold out for a heavy iron one, which is much more effective. If you go to Mexico, you might want to bring back one of the lovely wooden ones commonly used there.

ZIPLOC SANDWICH BAGS   Heavy-duty Ziploc bags come in very handy for making tortillas, empanadas, or plantain pancakes. Regular heavy-duty plastic wrap works too, but not as well as the bags.

KITCHEN SCALE   I always use mine to weigh the vegetables for a recipe. A simple scale with a fairly large bowl is all you need.

Pots, Pans, and Serving Dishes

HEAVY-BOTTOMED NONSTICK SKILLETS   These get better and better. The nonstick material is now high-quality, and the pans are much better heat conductors than they used to be. Make sure the pan is fairly heavy. Have one that is at least 12 inches in diameter and a 10-inch one if you wish, for cooking smaller quantities.

LARGE HEAVY-BOTTOMED FLAMEPROOF CASSEROLE For soups, beans, and stews you'll need a large, slow-simmering pot. In Mexico earthenware cazuelas and ollas are used. But I use the same heavy enameled cast-iron Le Creuset that I use for all my cooking. They hold the heat very well.

LARGE STOCKPOT I use mine not just for stocks but also for beans, when my heavier casserole is in use, for cooking pozole (hominy), and for steaming corn.

SAUCEPANS You'll need one or two $1^{1}/_2$- to 2-quart saucepans, for steaming, cooking rice, steam-heating tortillas, and some salsas. I use heavy-bottomed Le Creuset saucepans for most cooking, but for steaming and heating water or stock I use lightweight enameled saucepans.

BAKING DISHES There are some vegetable gratins and puddings in this collection, for which I use 2- to 3-quart gratin dishes, either earthenware or Le Creuset. You will also need them for heating enchiladas.

TWO-QUART CERAMIC SOUFFLÉ DISH Necessary equipment if you plan to make sweet potato soufflé or flan. You could substitute $^{1}/_2$- or 1-cup ramekins.

COLORFUL PLATTERS, BASKETS, AND SERVING DISHES Mexican food is made to be presented on colorful earthenware platters and in pretty bowls. They don't have to be from Mexico. You'll also want a nice pitcher for drinks.

Utensils

KITCHEN KNIVES A lot of chopping is required in this cuisine, so make sure you have a good sharp chef's knife, a stone for sharpening, and a steel for honing. You'll be amazed at how much more quickly the work will go with good knives. I use an 8-inch stainless-steel chef's knife, and I have several stainless-steel paring knives. For cutting cilantro it helps to have a thin-bladed knife, such as a fish-filleting knife.

MEASURING SPOONS Have two sets, one for dry ingredients and one for wet.

WOODEN SPOONS AND SPATULAS These are essential for cooking in nonstick skillets.

BEAN MASHER For mashing beans as you refry them. What a difference this tool has made in my life! It's a flat meshed disk on the end of a handle and is much more efficient than a potato masher.

STEAMING BASKET OR POT   For steaming vegetables and steam-heating tortillas.

SKIMMER OR SLOTTED SPOON   For skimming stocks, chicken water, and bean broth.

BOX GRATER   Particularly useful for crumbling hard Mexican aged cheese (queso añejo or cotija). Use the large holes.

GARLIC PRESS   This is optional, since chopping is more efficient than using a poor-quality garlic press. However, a good one, with a deep cylinder for housing the garlic and holes that are flush against the surface, is very handy. It should press the garlic through the holes, pureeing the garlic as it does so, not crushing the garlic.

CHEESECLOTH   For straining stocks.

PASTRY BAG WITH STAR TIP   Not essential, but it will come in handy if you make chocolate meringue cookies or little almond cookies.

Ingredients

This list includes only the ingredients that come up in these recipes. Since I use only a handful of dried and fresh chiles, it would be silly to confuse you with a complete list (and there is so much conflicting information out there that, I assure you, it would be confusing). Other products, such as pork products commonly used in Mexican cooking, don't occur in these pages. Spanish names are listed in parentheses for foods that are often sold under these names in Mexican and Latin markets. For a more extensive glossary of Mexican ingredients, see the bibliography at the end of this book.

Avocados

Look for the dark, thick, gnarly-skinned Hass (sometimes spelled *Haas*) variety. These are grown in California, and soon we will have imports from Mexico. They are richer—twice as high in fat—and less watery than their brighter green, thin-skinned Florida cousins. Since we are using a very small amount here, I'd rather use the avocado with the nuttiest, most delicious flavor, the Hass. In the recipes I leave the choice to you. I always call for small or medium avocados, which weigh 6 ounces maximum (with the pit in; a quarter of a medium avocado, peeled and pitted, weighs about 1 ounce).

To keep avocado slices from discoloring, toss them with lime or lemon juice. Cover cut avocados tightly with plastic wrap and don't remove the pit, to delay discoloration. Ripe California avocados will keep for a week in the refrigerator. If you buy unripe avocados (they will be hard and a brighter green), put them in a paper bag to hasten ripening.

Bitter Orange

Also called *Seville orange* and *sour orange*: The juice of the bitter orange is used widely in the Yucatán, where it grows abundantly. Bitter oranges have a rough, gnarly skin and an acidic, slightly bitter taste. You can use lime juice instead, since it's difficult to find bitter oranges here.

Black Beans
(frijoles, frijoles negros)

These are the beans used most extensively in southern Mexico and throughout Central America. They have a marvelous rich flavor and texture and yield a thick, savory broth. They're delicious simply simmered in water with garlic, onion, and cilantro or epazote or refried. Often called *black turtle beans,* dried black beans are available in most supermarkets, whole foods stores, and, of course, in Latin American markets. I've indicated in recipes where canned black beans can be substituted for dried. The brands I recommend are S&W and Progresso and any organic brands sold at whole foods stores. Make sure the can contains nothing but beans, water, and salt.

Cactus Paddles
(nopales or nopalitos)

These are the broad teardrop-shaped leaves of the prickly pear cactus. They have a crunchy texture and a tart, pickly taste that I love—too bad it took me so long to discover how easy it is to prepare them. By the time they reach the supermarket shelves, most of the spines have been removed and only the eyes that the spines grew from remain.

Cactus paddles are always cooked, and unfortunately they lose their bright green color when exposed to heat. There seems to be no way around this. If you boil them for a while they will lose the mucilaginous substance (similar to that in okra) that flows from them when cut.

Canola Oil

This oil, made from rapeseeds, has come into use in recent years. I like it because it has practically no flavor, so it doesn't alter the taste of my dishes. It has the highest ratio of unsaturated to saturated fat of any oil, and along with olive oil it is recommended because it has a very high percentage of cholesterol-lowering monounsaturated fats.

Chayote

Chayote is a light-green pear-shaped vegetable related to squash. It has a squashlike taste but unlike squash maintains a lively, crunchy texture even after being stewed. To prepare it, peel the chayote and cut it in half, then remove the pit from the middle and slice or chop.

Cheese (queso)

The cheeses used in Mexico are for the most part fresh, white farmer cheeses made from part-skim cow's milk. Most are crumbling cheeses like ricotta, feta, or goat cheese, although there are some marvelous string cheeses (quesillo) from Oaxaca and melting cheeses from the north of Mexico. In this book I call mainly for queso fresco, literally fresh cheese that is moist and light, or a harder, saltier aged crumbling cheese called either *queso añejo* or *cotija* (because it comes from the town of Cotija). Queso fresco, which is also called *queso ranchero,* and queso cotija are increasingly available in supermarkets in cities where there is a Mexican community (I can always get Doña Rosa brand queso ranchero and queso cotija in Los Angeles, for example). Mexican markets are the place to look if you can't get these cheeses in the supermarket. Queso fresco (or ranchero) has a high water content and is not a great keeper. But the hard, crumbly aged cotija will keep for weeks, wrapped in foil or a Ziploc bag, in the refrigerator.

Substitutes for Mexican Cheeses

For queso fresco and añejo you can substitute Parmesan, feta, or goat cheese. If you are going to use feta, you might want to soak it for an hour or two before using, to leach out some of its brine. You can also use dry-curd cottage cheese (add some salt to it) and farmer cheese. For string cheese, use domestic or Italian string cheese. For my quesadillas I use a mix of nonfat cottage cheese and either Monterey Jack, mild or sharp white Cheddar, and/or Parmesan.

Chiles

In the last five years it has become much easier to find dried chiles in supermarkets, and fresh serranos and jalapeños are almost ubiquitous. Many stores also stock poblano chiles and banana (guëro) chiles. Canned chiles are stocked on the foreign-food shelves, and you can usually find pickled jalapeños and sometimes chipotles canned in adobo sauce, which are called for in these pages. You will find the chiles you can't find in the supermarkets in Mexican and imported food markets and some whole foods stores.

Briefly, chiles are all in the *Capsicum* genus of plants. The heat in hot chiles comes from the chemical capsaicin, which is concentrated in the veins and seedpod of the chile. Remove these parts and your chile will be milder. To tell how hot a chile is, taste a small sliver; your tongue will tell you at once. When very hot small whole chiles such as jalapeños or chipotles are stuffed, the chiles are first soaked in heavily salted water, or a mixture of coffee grounds, sugar, and water, to leach out some of the heat. When you work with hot chiles, always wear rubber gloves. It's impossible to avoid coming into contact with the veins and seeds of the chile, and you will get capsaicin on your hands when you do. This element isn't water soluble, so merely washing your hands won't be enough to remove it. It can sting your hands, and definitely it will sting your eyes if you happen to rub them. Anyone who has ever had this excruciating experience knows to wear gloves.

The following list includes only those called for in this book. See the bibliography if you want to consult a more complete listing. When I say a chile is medium-hot or medium-picante, to me it's still picante, so beware. These terms are relative. The degree of heat in chiles is widely disputed. Tasting is the best way to tell.

Dried Chiles

Store dried chiles in tightly sealed plastic bags in the freezer or in glass jars in a cool, dark place. They will keep for a year if stored properly. Many dried chiles are brittle, but try to find chiles that are not so brittle as to be fragile. They should be in one piece.

CHILE ANCHO Also called *pasilla* in California (but it's a completely different chile from the pasilla listed here), this is the dried poblano chile. The name means "wide," and these are wide, thick, dark burgundy chiles. They are usually about 2 to 2½ inches wide at the top and taper down to a point. They're about 3 to 4 inches long. Ancho chiles are quite sweet and rich, yielding more pulp than any other dried chile. I think they're mild, though others describe them as moderate. They're the main chile in adobo sauce, the Mexican barbecue sauce. Their skin is wrinkled and should not be brittle. Like many other dried chiles, they have a slightly bitter edge to their flavor.

CHILE DE ÁRBOL This thin red-orange chile averages about 3 inches long and tapers to a sharp point. It is very hot and is usually soaked and used in sauces.

CHILE CHIPOTLE Chipotles are smoke-dried jalapeños. The word comes from the Nahuatl words for "smoked chile." Jalapeños do not air-dry well, which is why smoke is used to force-dry them after they ripen. There are a few different types of smoked jalapeños. The chipotle meco is the most prized. It averages about 2½ inches long, is dark brown, wrinkled, and brittle, and has light brown leathery striations. It has a complex smoky taste and is extremely picante, but not astringent. The chipotle mora, which is sometimes simply called *chipotle* or *chilpotle* and other times called *chile mora,* or *mora,* is smaller, averaging 1½ to 2 inches long, and has a redder hue and slightly less heat than the meco. It is more pliable than the meco and has a sweeter dried chile flavor. Although dried chipotles are much easier to find than they were even a few years ago, their canned counterparts, usually packed in a spicy barbecue-type adobo sauce, are more widely available. This is the type that most of the recipes in this book will call for. Their heat spreads quickly through a dish, so they are often added at the very end of cooking.

CHILE GUAJILLO   This is a smooth-skinned, dark red chile that averages about 4 inches in length and 1 to 2 inches at the top in width. It tapers to a blunt point. Guajillos have a slightly bitter, fairly picante flavor and are used in many sauces and salsas. Guajillos are light and have a smaller ratio of flesh to skin than anchos. The two are often used together.

CHILE PASILLA   In its fresh form this is the chile chilaca, a long, narrow, dark green chile. Pasillas average 4 to 6 inches and are almost black. They have wrinkled skin and a complex mild to moderately hot astringent flavor. Do not confuse this chile with the pasilla de Oaxaca, which is a smoke-dried, *much* hotter chile.

DRIED CHILE POWDER   Pure chile powder is usually made from New Mexico red chiles in this country, which are mild to moderately hot. In Mexico powdered chile is made from chile de árbol and from chile piquín (both of which are extremely hot and should not be used as the chiles in this book). Pure New Mexico chile powder has none of the preservatives, salt, and flavors added to commercial "chili powder." Use it for the southwestern-style chilies in this book. Store ground chile in a tightly sealed jar or bag in the freezer.

Fresh Chiles

The fresh chiles used in most of these recipes (jalapeños and serranos) are easy to find in most supermarkets. Poblanos, habaneros, and banana peppers can be found in Mexican markets if not in the supermarkets. Keep chile peppers in the produce drawer of your refrigerator, but don't seal them tightly in plastic. They will keep for several weeks.

ANAHEIM   These chiles, named after Anaheim, California, can be used interchangeably with New Mexico red and green chiles and long green chiles. They're sold in both their green and ripe (red) states, the red ones being sweeter. They are usually slightly picante, although sometimes they can be quite hot, and make an excellent spicy addition to vegetable dishes and salads. The pretty chiles are long and thin-skinned, about an inch wide at the top, tapering down to a point.

CHILE GUËRO   (Also called *banana chile* and *Hungarian wax* and, in Veracruz, sometimes *chile largo*.) This pale green to yellow chile—literally *blond*—can be similar in shape and size to a jalapeño, about 2½ inches long and

1 inch wide at the top, or it can be about 4 to 5 inches long, tapering to a blunt point. It's used in sauces and yellow moles, and in many Veracruzana dishes. The chiles are moderately hot, with a juicy texture and a very fresh taste.

CHILE JALAPEÑO   Jalapeños are among the most familiar chiles in the United States. They are a beautiful dark green color and average about 2 inches long and 1 inch wide at the top. The flesh is medium-hot to hot (though they can also be annoyingly mild), juicy, and complex. Jalapeño literally means "from Jalapa" (or Xalapa), the capital of the state of Veracruz, and the peppers are found in many Veracruzana dishes. Jalapeños are used interchangeably with serrano chiles in many of the salsas in this book. In Mexico jalapeños often go by the name *cuaresmeños* or *huachinangos.*

CHILE POBLANO   This beautiful, shiny, dark green, medium to large chile (they average 3 to 4 ounces) comes from the state of Puebla (Poblano means "from Puebla"). They are the chiles used in Mexico for most chiles rellenos (stuffed chiles) and for the strips of roasted chiles called *rajas.* The flesh is mild to medium-hot and not particularly juicy. Their flavor is complex, made all the more so by roasting. In California this chile is sometimes called *chile pasilla* or *ancho.*

CHILE SERRANO   This delicate-looking bright green chile is the one I use most in my salsas and sauces. Smaller than a jalapeño, the serrano is only about $1/2$ inch wide and about 2 inches long. It has a very fresh flavor that Mexican cooking authority Rick Bayless describes very accurately as "grassy," and is moderately hot.

CHILE HABANERO   These small orange or yellow-orange chiles, shaped like miniature bell peppers, are extremely hot. They are used widely in the Yucatán. Sometimes they're confused with *Scotch bonnets,* a different chile.

Canned Chiles

The two types of canned chiles called for in this book are pickled chiles, either jalapeños, serranos, or chipotles, and canned chipotles in adobo. I have provided recipes for the pickled chiles, but as a time-saver some of the commercial brands are quite good. They are easily found in most supermarkets and all Mexican markets.

PICKLED CHILES   (chiles en escabeche, chiles escabechados, or chiles encurtidos). They are usually jalapeños, although sometimes the jalapeños are mixed with serranos. In Mexico guëros—largos—are also pickled. Once you open the can, transfer the chiles to a glass jar and make sure they are covered with brine (you can add 2 parts vinegar to 1 part water to top up the marinade). Pickled chiles have a very special acidic/picante flavor and add a very interesting dimension to many Veracruzana dishes.

CHIPOTLES EN ADOBO These incredibly complex, smoky-hot chiles add a wonderful dimension to any number of dishes, from sauces to soups to salads to vegetable stews. Adobo sauce here is a spicy, sweet and sour tomato-based barbecue-type sauce. There are several brands of chipotles en adobo. They vary in quality; generally, look for all-natural sauces without too much sugar added, such as the San Marcos brand. Once opened, transfer chiles en adobo to a glass jar and keep refrigerated for two to three weeks.

PICKLED CHIPOTLES (chipotles en escabeche or escabechados). These are harder to find than adobo-packed chipotles, so I've given you a recipe for them. They keep for weeks in the refrigerator as long as they're covered in brine, and they are absolutely marvelous if you like a picante seasoning on a sandwich or in a salad.

Mexican Chocolate

Although chocolate isn't exactly a low-fat ingredient, I've included it in two of the desserts in this collection. Mexican chocolate is blended with ground cinnamon, sugar, and almonds so that it has a special flavor. The texture is grainy. It's used in Mexico exclusively for hot chocolate, but I use it here for a sorbet and grate it into a meringue for a delicious, light cookie. You can find Mexican chocolate in Mexican markets and in some supermarkets on the imported-food shelves. Keep it well wrapped in the freezer; it will keep for a year.

Cilantro (fresh coriander)

This pungent herb is essential in fresh tomato salsas and many cooked salsas and is ubiquitous as a garnish. It's found in most supermarkets, at any time of year. To store, cut the ends of the stems off and wrap a damp piece of paper towel around the bottom, then seal this with foil. Place in a plastic bag and refrigerate. Or wash, shake dry, and wrap the bunch in a paper towel. Place in a plastic bag and refrigerate. The cilantro should keep for a week if there are no rotting wet leaves on the inside of the bunch.

Cinnamon

Mexican cinnamon (which also comes from Ceylon) is different from the hard sticks we find in supermarkets. The sticks are long, wide, shaggy, and crumbly.

The layers of cinnamon bark are much softer than the cassia cinnamon sticks and more aromatic. They are easy to grind in a spice mill. This type of cinnamon can be found in Mexican markets.

Corn

In Mexico the corn used for tortilla dough (masa) is dried field corn. The hard, starchy kernels are soaked in water mixed with slaked lime, which causes the hard kernel shells to loosen from the grain. This is also the corn from which pozole, or hominy (see listing for pozole), is made. When I call for corn in this book, I mean sweet summer corn; it's not what you find in Mexico, but it's an irresistible late-summer vegetable here.

Corn Husks

These can be found in any store that sells Mexican ingredients. They are used as tamale wrappers in traditional Mexican cooking, but here I've used them for fish. Corn husks are soaked in boiling water for an hour or two to make them pliable before using. Keep them sealed in a plastic bag in a cool, dry place. They'll be good for a year.

Epazote

This is the one herb I call for in several recipes that isn't readily available in supermarkets. It can be found in some Mexican markets, and it's very easy to grow. The little plant I put in my herb garden last year is now a bush. It grows wild, in urban as well as rural environments. The herb has a jagged, feathery leaf that grows on sprigs of about seven leaves. The plants can grow 2 to 3 feet high, and they're perennials. Epazote has a very pungent, sort of musty aroma. In and of itself it isn't appealing in the way that, say, basil or tarragon is. But simmer it with a pot of beans or add it to a soup or a mushroom stew toward the end of cooking, and it adds a deep, earthy dimension that is uniquely Mexican. If you can't find this herb, don't despair. Wherever I call for it, I tell you what to use for a "big taste" if you can't find it or not to bother with any substitute. Cilantro or parsley is the usual replacement. The taste is not similar at all, but cilantro gives a big Mexican taste of its own, and parsley gives a very herbal taste.

Hibiscus (Jamaica)

These look like red flowers, but they're actually the dried calyxes of the flowers from the hibiscus or Jamaica plant. They are brewed into a tart red herbal tea (the red in Red Zinger tea), which is sweetened and chilled to make a wonderfully refreshing drink.

Hoja Santa

This large green leaf is used throughout southern Mexico in any number of dishes. I rarely call for it in this book, because I've never seen it in this country. When I do list it, I also list a substitute combination of basil, fennel tops, mint, and tarragon (a combination of three of the four is also fine). Hoja santa, also known as *acuyo* and *hierba santa,* has a strong anise flavor that calls to mind sarsaparilla (the flavor of root beer), mint, tarragon, and basil, so a combination of these herbs can be used as a substitute. It's used in green moles and stews; in Veracruz fish and vegetables are wrapped and cooked in the leaves, and it's also the basis of a wonderful green fish sauce.

Jícama

This is a turniplike root vegetable with coarse brown skin and pulpy white flesh. The texture is like that of a juicy, crisp radish, but jícama isn't pungent. It's somewhat sweet and applelike at its best. It is served sprinkled with lime juice and chile powder in Mexico and minced and mixed with orange and chile in the salsa/salad called *pico de gallo.* Choose smaller jícama if you can, as it tends to be less woody than large ones. Increasingly available in supermarkets, it will keep for several weeks, unwrapped, in the refrigerator.

Limes

Limes, which are called *limones* but should not be confused with lemons, are used widely in Mexican cooking. A squeeze of lime juice is the finishing touch in many soups, and lime juice is essential for seviche, where it cooks the raw fish, and many other fish dishes, salads, and desserts. The limes used in Mexico are for the most part small greenish yellow limes that we call *Key limes.* The small size is particularly convenient if you happen to have a Mexican lime squeezer, which is too small to work well with our larger Persian limes. In the Yucatán there is a particular bitter lime that gives the dishes of that region a special flavor. I've tested all of the recipes in this book with our larger seedless limes.

Mangoes

I once spent a month in Cuernavaca, and I'll never forget the incredibly ripe and juicy mangoes, which fell to the ground throughout the day from trees in the parks. Small yellow mangoes are the most widely available in Mexico. Here I find the larger reddish yellow mangoes more often. If they are truly ripe, the two types are equally luxurious. They should give when you press on them and should smell like mangoes. They're very juicy and a bit messy to work with. This intensely flavored, juicy fruit is extremely high in vitamin A, beta-carotene, and vitamin C. Though mangoes taste incredibly rich, a 7-ounce mango has no more calories than a banana.

Masa

Masa is the dough used for corn tortillas, tamales, and thickening soups and stews. It's made from lime-soaked ground field corn and water and can sometimes be purchased from tortilla factories or Mexican markets. If you buy masa for tortillas, the dough should be refrigerated and used within a day. In this book masa is never required; you have the option of using masa harina (see next entry), which is now easy to find in supermarkets, or ground toasted tortillas.

Masa Harina

This dried, powdered, processed masa flour is ready to be reconstituted with warm water for making tortillas, tamales, and the like. Masa harina is sold in many supermarkets; look for it in the Mexican section or with the other flours. The two commonly available brands are Quaker and Maseca. Stored in the refrigerator or freezer, masa harina will keep for a year.

Olive Oil

Although we associate this oil with Mediterranean cooking, not Mexican, it is used in the state of Veracruz, where the cuisine has many Spanish overtones. I also take the liberty of using it for many of the dishes in this book that might otherwise call for a different oil. I use a fairly mild-flavored olive oil, such as the widely distributed Colavita, for my Mexican food. In Mexico Spanish oil is used. The olive oil produced in Mexico is unimpressive.

Onions

The onions used in Mexican cooking are white, which have a stronger, cleaner taste than the sweeter yellow onions, which are not grown in Mexico. That said, I tested many of the recipes in this book with the less expensive yellow onions with excellent results. But use white onions for garnishing dishes, and in dishes where the onion is not cooked.

Pozole (and Dried Chiles)

The pozole (also spelled *posole,* especially in New Mexico) that you buy in the United States, mostly from New Mexico, is hominy: field corn that has been soaked in water with slaked lime so that the husks come loose from the kernels, then dried. In Mexico the treating and drying step hasn't been taken, so dried field corn must first be treated with lime before pozole can be made. That's why I never made pozole until I went to New Mexico and came home with several pounds of this wonderful grain. The corn and its broth are very fragrant and flowery after simmering for a few hours; the grains even look like flowers after a while, as the kernels splay and open out. Pozole is the basis for several stews, which are also called *pozoles.* In Mexico it is usually cooked with pork, tripe, or a combination of pork and chicken, though vegetarian pozoles do exist. I've developed recipes for low-fat green and red pozoles, some with chicken, a few with no meat at all, and one with rabbit. The hearty one-dish meal is now one of my favorite dishes for entertaining. You can substitute canned hominy for pozole, but you won't get the benefit of the wonderful broth that results from slowly cooking dried field corn. Markets and mail-order houses that sell southwestern foods sell pozole. I have bought white, blue, and yellow pozole in New Mexico.

Sources for pozole include the following:

M&S Produce
PO Box 220
Alcalde, NM 87511
(505) 852-4368
Price list available

Los Chileros
PO Box 6215
Santa Fe, NM 87501
(505) 471-6967
Price list available

Casados Farms
PO Box 1269
San Juan Pueblo, NM 87566
(505) 852-2433
Price list available

Piloncillo

This unrefined brown sugar is sold in hard cylinders, pyramids, cones, or disks in Mexican markets. It has a rich molasses flavor. The cones are quite hard and must be sliced with a sharp or serrated knife before being chopped. They can also be grated. Store it in a cool, dry place, well wrapped, and it will last indefinitely.

Plantain

Plantains look like oversize bananas, and when they're ripe they taste like a rather starchy banana. The skin is thick, and unless the plantains are very ripe it does not come away from the flesh easily. When ripe, plantains turn almost black and become soft and sweet. They reflect the Caribbean influence on the cuisines of the east coast of Mexico, most notably that of Veracruz. When called for in these recipes, plantains should be completely ripe.

Pumpkin Seeds

Hulled green pumpkin seeds are used widely throughout Mexico. They are the basis for the nut-thickened sauces called *pipians* and are essential in some of the green moles. You can find hulled pumpkin seeds in most whole foods stores and in Mexican markets. Store them in a jar or bag in the freezer for several months.

Rice

Rice is a staple in Mexican cooking. It's usually fried in oil first, then simmered in broth, often with the addition of green herbs for green rice (arroz verde) or with tomatoes for red rice (arroz rojo). I fry the rice in much less oil than is traditionally used. Use medium-grain or long-grain rice for these recipes.

Salt

This is one of the most important ingredients in Mexican cooking—or any cooking for that matter. There is no substitute. You can follow a recipe exactly, but if you undersalt the dish, it will be disappointing. It's such a simple thing, but it can make or break a recipe. It's especially important in Mexican cooking, because a balance of flavors is created when salt is combined with chiles so that the picante elements are not overpowering. I make suggestions in most of the recipes for quantities, but I am giving you the low end of what's required. If I suggest, say, $1/2$ teaspoon of salt, begin with that, then taste and add more if you think the flavor of the dish is not vivid enough. I use sea salt. It's more expensive than regular salt, but I think it has a better flavor, and in the end you'll use less.

Squash Blossoms

In Mexico the blossoms used are pumpkin squash blossoms. In this country it's easier to find zucchini blossoms in season, and although they're different— zucchini blossoms are softer than pumpkin blossoms and have less flavor— they work for the recipes in this book. Choose long fresh blossoms, and if they're attached to the zucchini, use the zucchini in your recipe or for another dish. They will keep for a day in the refrigerator but are best used right away, especially for stuffing.

Sweet Potatoes

These are often called *yams* in markets. I mean the orange sweet potatoes when I call for them in recipes.

Tomatillos

Although their name makes them sound like little tomatoes, tomatillos come from a different family of fruits altogether, the same family as the husk-wrapped gooseberry. Tomatillos look like small hard green tomatoes wrapped in a papery husk. The husk is removed and the tomatillos are usually simmered or roasted before being used for salsas and sauces. Most Mexican green sauces are based on tomatillos. They have a wonderful tart flavor and a high pectin content, so that sauces made with them thicken beautifully. Canned tomatillos are acceptable for the recipes in this book, but fresh ones are preferable and are to be found wherever Mexican produce is sold, including many supermarkets. They should be firm and smooth under the husks; feel the part around the stem to make sure there are no soft spots or spoilage. Sizes of tomatillos vary, but on average they weigh about $1^{1}/_{2}$ to 2 ounces.

Tomatoes

Tomatoes are used throughout this book, probably more than any other ingredient. In Mexico they're called both *jitomates* and *tomates*. In some recipes I specify plum (or Roma) tomatoes, which are more pulpy and suitable for cooked sauces, though ordinary tomatoes can be substituted (plum tomatoes are, however, usually available year-round). For uncooked salsas I use round, juicy tomatoes, and of course you want to use them in season. If you are making salsa out of season, you'll have to sweeten it with balsamic vinegar. Not authentic, but it really does help bring out any residual sweetness. In many of the recipes the tomatoes are roasted before being blended or chopped, a technique that yields a marvelous, particularly Mexican taste. Canned tomatoes, such as Muir Glen brand, may be substituted in many dishes.

Tortillas (Corn)

Available in most supermarkets, in a range of brands and quality. Local brands will be freshest. As a rule, I try to buy the lightest-colored corn tortillas I can find. A whiter masa (the dough used for the tortilla) is an indication that the slaked lime used to treat the corn has been rinsed off thoroughly (sometimes, though, the tortillas are yellower because they're made from yellow corn). I also prefer the thin ones to thick tortillas. For making chips in the microwave or oven, thin tortillas work best. Homemade corn tortillas are not as flexible as commercial tortillas, so they're difficult to manipulate for quesadillas and enchiladas, and they don't work well for making chips. They are fine for soft tacos, and for serving at the table they can't be beat. When I buy tortillas, I take the package and bend it a little in my hands to ascertain how flexible the tortillas are. If they are very dry, they won't bend easily.

Vinegar

The vinegars used in Mexican pickles and other dishes are mild, often made from pineapple and other tropical fruits. Our apple cider vinegar is usually called for in Mexican recipes here, but I think rice wine vinegar is the closest to the vinegar used in Mexico, because it's very mild (about 4.4 acidity). My second choice is low-acidity champagne vinegar, and third choice is apple cider vinegar.

WHAT TO BRING BACK FROM MEXICO

I always travel to Mexico with an extra bag—or I pick up a Mexican market bag while I'm there (see list)—so that I can bring back cooking ingredients and equipment from the markets. Here are some suggestions for items that will come up in the recipes in this book.

Dried chiles: Particularly harder-to-find varieties like the chile meco and the chile pasilla de Oaxaca.

Dried beans: You will find such a wide variety in the markets—white, black, red, yellow, chickpeas, and on and on—at a terrific price. I always bring back black beans and yellow favas for soup.

Coffee honey: This is a dark honey with a wonderful flavor. I use it in rice pudding and as a topping for bread and toast.

Mexican chocolate: For hot chocolate and desserts.

Pumpkin seeds: For thickening sauces like green tomatillo mole.

Dried corn husks: Used for tamales; I use them for wrapping fish fillets.

Vanilla: Mexican vanilla is not pure vanilla, but it has a very nice flavor, and the price for a large bottle is fantastic.

Vanilla beans

Garlic: The garlic in Mexico has a marvelous, pungent flavor.

Oregano: A different variety from Greek oregano, Mexican oregano is in the verbena family.

Cinnamon

Dried mushrooms: For mushroom stews.

Hibiscus flowers (jamaica):   For making marvelous iced drinks.

Masa harina: For tortillas and thickening stews.

Tortilla press

Lightweight sheet-metal comal

Lime press: Press limes with the rounded side *up* and cut side down.

Molcajete

Large plastic market bag: These tightly woven plastic-handled bags are incredibly strong, just right for bringing it all home.

$\mathcal{P}$RONUNCIATION GUIDE

Añejo: an-<u>yay</u>-ho

Cazuela: ca-<u>sway</u>-lah

Chipotle: chi-<u>poat</u>-lay

Comal: co-<u>mahl</u>

Cotija: co-<u>tee</u>-hah

Escabeche: es-<u>cah</u>-<u>bech</u>-ay

Frijoles: free-<u>ho</u>-lays

Guëro: (g)<u>where</u>-o

Habanero: ah-bah-<u>nay</u>-ro

Hoja: <u>o</u>-ha

Jalapeño (Xalapeño): hah-lah-<u>pen</u>-yo

Jamaica: hah-<u>mah</u>-eeca

Jícama: <u>hee</u>-cah-mah

Jitomates: hee-to-<u>mah</u>-tays

Molcajete: mol-cah-<u>het</u>-ay

Nopales: no-<u>pah</u>-lays

Oaxaca: wah-<u>hah</u>-cah

Olla: <u>Oy</u>-ya

Pasilla: pah-<u>see</u>-yah

Piloncillo: pil-on-<u>see</u>-yo

Piquín: Pee-<u>keen</u>

Pozole: po-<u>so</u>-lay

Quesillo: kay-<u>see</u>-yo

Queso: <u>kay</u>-so

Rajas: <u>rah</u>-hahs

Relleno: re-<u>yay</u>-no

Tomatillo: to-mah-<u>tee</u>-yo

Introduction to the Recipes

Making It Easy

Mexican food may *seem* complicated, but the cuisine is actually a very easy one to master. There are two reasons that the cuisine appears to be difficult. The first is that, before you actually begin to cook a dish, the ingredients require different and perhaps unfamiliar types of preparations, such as roasting and blending. But once these techniques are mastered, you'll see that the actual cooking is quite fast and often largely unattended.

The other reason Mexican food appears to be complex is that many dishes consist of several elements, such as a salsa, a tortilla, and a filling; or fish and a salsa, or eggs and beans. But it's the fact that the cuisine *does* consist of several elements that makes seemingly complicated dishes quite simple—because the same elements come up again and again. They're easy to make, easy to keep on hand, and easy to mix and match. Once you've become familiar with the salsas, for example, they should become a regular part of your repertoire. Then you won't think twice about making a Mexican meal. Poached, shredded chicken breasts, chicken and vegetable stocks, beans and refried beans are also a snap and freeze well. With salsas, chicken breasts, and beans under your belt, you'll find a huge variety of Mexican dishes at your fingertips.

Techniques and Tips

I've reiterated instructions for these new techniques in footnotes to the recipes, but you'll soon find that you don't have to read them, because roasting tomatoes, toasting dried chiles and garlic on a griddle, pan-searing blended sauces, and heating tortillas will have become second nature to you.

But just so you can get an idea of what's ahead, here is a list of the techniques that are most often repeated. The directions here are detailed. They're abbreviated in many of the recipe footnotes, so I advise you to refer to this section if Mexican cooking is new to you. Once I mastered these techniques I understood dimensions of Mexican flavors that can't be achieved any other way.

Also included here are a few little tricks that I learned in Mexican kitchens that help to speed the process.

Rinsing Raw Onions

This will prevent the raw onion taste from lingering in your mouth. Once sliced or chopped either rinse with cold water or with water acidulated with vinegar; or soak for a few minutes in hot tap water and drain; or toss with vinegar.

Heating Tortillas

How you heat tortillas depends in part on what you are heating them for.

STEAM-HEATING   This is a good way to heat tortillas for serving at the table, for soft tacos, and also for enchiladas and enfrijoladas. However, I find that the tortillas can become a bit fragile for enchiladas when heated this way, so if you have a microwave oven, use it.

To steam: Wrap 14 tortillas in a kitchen towel or heavy cloth napkin. Bring $1/2$ inch of water to a boil in a lidded saucepan fitted with a steamer. Place the tortillas on the steamer, cover, and steam for 1 minute. Remove from the heat and let sit, covered, for 10 to 15 minutes. Serve wrapped in the towel in a basket. Or proceed with your recipe. Discard the top and bottom tortilla if they break.

IN THE OVEN   This is a good way to heat tortillas for serving at the table or for soft tacos. Preheat the oven to 350 degrees. Wrap the tortillas in aluminum foil and heat through for 15 minutes. For fresh homemade tortillas, wrap the tortillas as you make them in a towel, then wrap the towel in foil and heat. To keep the tortillas warm for several hours, turn the oven to the lowest setting.

IN A DRY SKILLET   This is a good method for quesadillas and for soft tacos. Heat a heavy-bottomed skillet, griddle, or comal over medium-high heat and heat the tortillas, a couple at a time, turning them every 30 seconds or so, for 2 to 3 minutes, until flexible and warm. Wrap in a clean kitchen towel or aluminum foil if you aren't using them right away.

IN THE MICROWAVE   I use this method most often for enchiladas or enfrijoladas, before dipping the tortilla in the sauce. When you heat tortillas in a microwave, they lose moisture (which is why the microwave works so well for toasting them), so for table serving I don't recommend this method, which can make the tortillas rubbery. But for enchiladas they're dipped in sauce and hold together well. For quesadillas and tacos the method works if they are filled or topped right away. Wrap four at a time in wax paper or a damp towel and heat in a microwave for 1 minute at HIGH (100 percent) power.

Toasting Dried Chiles

Wearing rubber gloves, break the stem ends off the chiles and shake out the seeds. Open the chiles out flat and remove the veins. Tear the chiles into large flat pieces; I usually just break them in half or, for smaller chiles, leave them in one piece, opened out flat. Heat a dry skillet, griddle, or comal over medium to medium-high heat. Toast the chiles, one piece at a time. Place a piece on the hot surface and press down with a metal spatula. It will begin to crackle, blister, and change color in a matter of seconds. It will also smell toasty (if you're toasting several chiles, you will probably find the chile fumes irritating to the throat; turn on the exhaust fan if you have one). Turn the chile immediately and repeat on the other side. Toasting chiles goes quickly because they toast so fast. The smell and the blistering are the key signs that it's time to turn them and remove from the heat. Try to avoid blackening the chile, since this will result in a bitter taste. Transfer immediately from the griddle to a bowl or plate.

Toasting Fresh Chiles

Heat a dry skillet, griddle, or comal over medium heat. Toast whole small fresh chiles, laying them on the hot surface and turning them often until the skin is charred in spots and the chile has softened. This should take 10 to 15 minutes. Remove from the heat and proceed with the recipe.

Roasting Poblano Chiles

Poblano peppers are roasted and peeled before being cut into strips, called *rajas,* stuffed, or used for other recipes. You can do this directly over a gas flame, or you can roast the peppers under a broiler.

ROASTING ABOVE A GAS FLAME   Flame-roasted peppers will be firmer than broiler-roasted peppers, because they cook less. I recommend this method if you are going to stuff the peppers. To roast above a gas flame, light a burner and place the chiles directly above the flame. Turn the chiles often, using tongs, until charred uniformly. Place in a bowl covered tightly with a plate and allow to sit for 5 minutes to further loosen the skin. Remove the charred skin and rinse under cold water. I use the running water to help remove the skin, but some cooks say that flavor is lost when you do this. Pat dry with paper towels and proceed with the recipe.

ROASTING UNDER A BROILER   This goes faster than flame roasting, but the chiles cook more, which may be undesirable, depending on how firm you want them to be. Preheat the broiler and line a baking sheet with foil. Place under the broiler at the top rack setting, 2 to 3 inches from the heat. Check after 1 minute to see if the peppers are charred on one side (they can have uneven surfaces, which will result in variations in the timing). Cooking under an electric broiler is slower than cooking under gas, so the chiles may take up to 4 or 5 minutes to grill. Check every minute. When charred on one side, turn them over and grill on the other side. Continue to turn the peppers until they are charred all over. Place in a bowl covered tightly with a plate and allow to sit for 5 minutes or until cool enough to handle, to further loosen the skin. Remove the charred skin and rinse under cold water if necessary. Pat dry with paper towels and proceed with the recipe.

Seeding Fresh Chiles

This tip comes from the March/April 1994 issue of *Cook's Illustrated.* Holding the pepper by its stem, slice off at the tip, about 1/8 inch from the bottom. Stand on a cutting board on the cut end and, holding the pepper by the stem, slice off the sides. You will be left with the stem, seeds, and inner membranes. If you want the chile to taste even milder, slice the veins away from the sides of the chiles.

Toasting Unpeeled Garlic

Toasting garlic on a griddle gives the garlic a very special grilled flavor that is uniquely Mexican. Do not peel the cloves. Heat a dry skillet, griddle, or comal over medium heat. Place the garlic cloves on the hot surface and turn every few minutes, until they are blackened in places and the garlic is soft, with a toasty smell. You'll have to test by gently squeezing the clove. It doesn't have to be as soft as long-cooked oven-baked garlic, but it should give. This should take 10 to 15 minutes. Remove from the heat and, when cool enough to handle, peel. If some spots on the garlic are hard, like charcoal, cut those bits away.

Peeling Tomatoes

Bring a pot of water to a boil. Meanwhile, core the tomatoes. Drop the tomatoes into the water and boil for 30 seconds. Transfer immediately to a bowl of cold water. Drain, rinse again with cold water, and slip off the skins.

Seeding Tomatoes

Cut the tomatoes in half crosswise. Hold the tomato half over a bowl or the sink and gently squeeze out the seeds.

Roasting Tomatoes

This step comes up again and again in the recipes. Preheat the broiler. Line a baking sheet with aluminum foil. Place the tomatoes on the baking sheet, stem side down, and place the baking sheet 2 to 3 inches from the heat (at the highest rack setting). Broil 2 to 5 minutes, until the tomatoes are charred on one side (electric heat is slower than gas). Turn the tomatoes over and grill on the other side for 2 to 5 minutes, until blackened. Remove from the heat and transfer the tomatoes to a bowl. Tip any juice that may have accumulated on the baking sheet into the bowl. Using the foil means that you won't have to clean the baking sheet. Allow to cool until you can handle them, then core and peel and proceed with the recipe.

Preparing Tomatillos

First remove the husk and rinse the tomatillos, which have a sticky surface. Either roast, as above for tomatoes, or simmer. Bring a saucepan of water to a boil, drop in the tomatillos, and turn the heat to medium-low. After 5 minutes, flip the tomatillos over if the tops look like they aren't cooking and simmer for another 5 minutes, 10 minutes in all. Gently drain the tomatillos or remove from the water with a slotted spoon. They will be a darker, more olive green color and soft. When tomatillos are simmered they become more acidic than when roasted.

Preparing Cilantro

I used to spend a great deal of time preparing cilantro, because I thought I had to pick the leaves off every stem as I do with other herbs. I have since learned that stems are not unwelcome in salsas and other dishes, so you can work with cilantro without separating the bunch. But you do have to be sure to get the sand out first. The following method works very well.

CLEANING CILANTRO   Fill a deep bowl with cold water. Hold the bunch of cilantro at the end of the stems and vigorously plunge into the bowl of water several times. The water will fill with sand. Change the water and repeat the process, plunging the cilantro up and down in the water. If the water again fills with sand, change it again and repeat the process until no more sand comes off the cilantro. Some bunches of cilantro have little pebbles hidden in the middle. To make sure all are dislodged, once the water runs clean, stick your fingers down into the bunch and feel around for pebbles. Spin the bunch in a salad spinner or shake the cilantro dry. If you live in a house with a yard, go out back and swing the cilantro around to get rid of excess water. Then wrap the cilantro in several thicknesses of paper towel. Refrigerate in a plastic bag if not using right away. Cilantro will keep for a week if it isn't wet.

CHOPPING CILANTRO   This is how they do it at Frontera Grill, Rick Bayless's restaurant in Chicago. Clean the cilantro as directed, then dry it well and lay the bunch on a cutting board. Hold the stems with one hand and, using a very sharp, thin-bladed knife (such as a fish filleting knife), cut the bunch crosswise from the top in thin slivers. If you don't want pieces of stem included (if, for example, you are using the cilantro as a garnish), with dry hands lift the cut cilantro and let the stems fall through your fingers. Place the cut cilantro on several layers of lightly dampened paper towel, then cover with plastic, roll up the paper towel, and refrigerate. The cilantro will keep for a few days.

Preparing Cactus Paddles

Carefully hold the end where the paddle has been cut from the plant, watching out for spines, and, using a sharp paring knife, trim off the outer edge of the paddle. Using a potato peeler or a sharp knife, scrape off all of the spiny nodes. Cut into $1/2$-inch dice (or as directed). Bring a large pot of water to a rolling boil and add a tablespoon of salt and $1/4$ teaspoon baking soda (to help retain *some* color). Add the diced cactus and boil uncovered until tender, about 15 minutes. Drain and proceed with the recipe.

Preparing Shrimp

The recipes here all call for shrimp to be shelled and deveined. To shell, pull off the legs, then pull off the shell, which will come loose easily. To remove the vein that runs down the back of the shrimp, using a paring knife, make a shallow slit down the back of the shrimp. You will see a vein, which is usually black. Remove it with the tip of your knife and quickly rinse the shrimp.

Crumbling Aged Mexican Cheese

You can do it with your hands, but a box grater is a useful item. Use the big holes. It goes quickly.

Peeling Avocados

Cut the avocado in half and remove the seed. If the avocado is to be diced, cut the avocado from the cut side, up to but not through the skin. Using a soup spoon, scoop out the avocado, which will come out easily, ready cut. If it is to be sliced, cut through the skin, then just peel off the skins if you are using Hass avocados. Use the dicing method for thin-skinned varieties.

Searing Blended Sauces

This is a key technique in Mexican cooking. Mexican sauces are in a way twice cooked. The elements, like tomatoes, are grilled or boiled and blended with other ingredients, then the puree is cooked quickly in a hot pan. It sears the sauce, which thickens and cooks down quickly. Liquid may then be added and the sauce simmered until it reaches the desired flavor and consistency. Make your puree as directed in the recipe. Heat the oil in a heavy-bottomed sauce-pan, casserole, or nonstick skillet over medium-high heat. Drizzle a bit of the puree into the pan. It should sizzle loudly. If it doesn't, wait a couple of minutes and try again. When the pan is quite hot, pour in the sauce. You want a loud sizzling "whoosh." Stir constantly with a wooden spoon for 1 to 8 minutes, until the mixture thickens, changes color, and begins to stick to the bottom of the pan. Proceed with the recipe.

Adding Salt

When you salt a dish depends on what you are cooking. Never salt beans or pozole until they're soft, because the salt hardens the cellulose casing. Once they have softened I like to simmer beans in a salted broth, because I think they absorb the salt better than if they are salted at the very end of cooking. With many of the vegetable dishes here I ask you to salt early on in the cooking, because the salt will bring out the natural juices of the vegetables, creating a simmering medium and eliminating the need to add oil. It's important to taste what you cook so that you can determine whether the dish needs more salt. This final tasting and salting should be done at the end of cooking.

Preparing Mangoes

Cut down the flat side of the pit on both sides so that you have two large flat pieces with the peel on. Using a small sharp knife, slice lengthwise from the cut side, down to the skin but not through it. Slice crosswise, down to the skin but not through it. Now press the skin side of the halves with your thumbs to turn inside out (it looks like the mango served in restaurants now). Slice off the little squares from the skin. For the rest of the mango, slice down the remaining sides of the pit and peel away the skin from these strips. There will still be some flesh adhering to the pit. Hold the mango over a bowl while you slice it off (or indulge; lean over the sink and eat what's left adhering to the pit).

Grinding Whole Spices

In the recipes that follow, both whole and ground measures are listed for spices in the ingredients lists. Spices like cumin seeds, pepper, cinnamon, cloves, and coriander taste much more vivid if you grind them whole just before you work with them. It doesn't take long at all in an electric spice mill (which is the same thing as a coffee mill). Measure in the spice and grind, beginning by pulsing the mill several times, then grinding for several seconds. If you are grinding cinnamon stick, break it up into small pieces first so it won't jam the blades. Stop and start the spice mill a few times to get a finely ground spice. You can also pound spices in a molcajete or mortar and pestle to grind them.

Cleaning the Blender Jar

If a stock or water is to be added to the puree, run $1/2$ cup of it in the blender to get the last bits of puree off the blades. To wash the blender jar, fill one-third full of soapy water and run at high speed.

Menu Planning

One of the aspects of Mexican food that makes menu planning fun is the ease with which elements of a dish can be recycled. Once you get used to making a variety of Mexican preparations, such as salsas, beans, shredded poached chicken, toasted tortillas, and soup stocks, you'll see how easy it is to recycle one preparation into another dish. For example, whenever I poach chicken breasts for one dish, I use the stock for a soup, such as simple chicken consommé with tomato, mint, chile, and avocado; or for a salsa like cooked green tomatillo sauce or green tomatillo mole. If I have leftover green tomatillo mole from the hors d'oeuvre or the enchiladas I served last night, you can be sure I'll go out and get some shrimp or salmon to cook in the sauce for tonight's dinner. Leftover refried black beans will top nachos or tostadas or will go into Veracruz-style scrambled eggs with refried black beans. Chicken left over from one dish will be shredded into a delicious chicken salad with chipotle chiles, added to a soup, or tossed with a salsa and used as a filling for quesadillas or a topping for soft tacos. As for leftover toasted tortillas, they will be used up in chilaquiles or sprinkled onto soups.

I usually plan my menus around one particular dish. It may be a soup, tacos, quesadillas or enchiladas, a fish or a chicken dish, or even eggs or chilaquiles. Every recipe in Chapters 6 and 8–12 can be served as the focus of a simple meal, accompanied by rice, potatoes, steamed vegetables, and/or a salad. I usually serve hot corn tortillas when I'm serving Mexican food, but any bread will work. Many of the heartier salads in Chapter 5 can also be served as a main dish, with tortillas or bread. Even beans or beans and rice can make a great meal with a green salad and hot tortillas. The vegetable dishes in Chapter 13, as well, can be used to top or fill tortillas. Sprinkle on a bit of cheese or serve with rice, and you've got a delicious vegetarian main dish.

On the other hand, you may wish to try a selection of these dishes. When I was testing recipes for this book, we often ate two or three salads or a salad and a rice dish plus a soup as a meal. But don't feel you have to make more than one Mexican dish to have a great meal with Mexican flavors; a simple green salad and some fresh fruit for dessert is often all you will need or want to complete a menu. For more complex menus, designed for entertaining, see the menu section at the end of the book.

Simple Weekday Menus

Mexican food is synonymous with "filling food" to many people, but that's because most Tex-Mex restaurants customarily overfeed their customers. There is no reason you can't eat this great cuisine every day without coming away from the table feeling sleepy and full. The portions of many of the tortilla-based dishes like quesadillas and soft tacos that I've allotted—two per person—may seem small if you compare them to typical "combination plate" servings. But two quesadillas or soft tacos, with rice, beans, or a vegetable side dish and a green salad—or even with just a green salad—makes quite a satisfying plate of food. These are manageable menus, for feeding your family after work and school. They're light by Tex-Mex standards, but nobody will be

ℳIXING AND MATCHING

Master the basic sauces, learn to make a good pot of beans and shredded poached chicken breasts, and you'll have a variety of dishes at your fingertips. Here's how you can mix and match. All the recipes listed are in this book.

Salsa Fresca

Black Bean Nachos
Black Bean Tostadas (aka Chalupas)
Quesadillas with Potatoes and Sorrel
Quesadillas with Broccoli and Garlic
Garlicky Zucchini Quesadillas
Swiss Chard Quesadillas
Grilled or Panfried Chicken Breasts with Salsa
Grilled Tuna with Tomato and Corn Salsa (or any cooked fish fillet)
Mussels on the Half-Shell with Salsa Fresca
Bite-Size Cornmeal Pancakes with Tomato-Corn Salsa

Salsà Ranchera

Chicken Entomatadas
Mushroom and Garlic Enchiladas with Chipotle Tomato Sauce (just add chipotles to the ranchera sauce)
Basic Cheese Quesadillas
Fried Eggs with Spicy Cooked Tomato Sauce (Huevos Rancheros)
Red Chilaquiles
Red Chilaquiles with Zucchini, Tomato, and Egg
Fried Eggs with Black Beans, Tortillas, and Salsa

Salsa Verde Cruda

Soft Tacos or Tostadas with Chicken and Tomatillo Salsa
Chicken and Tomatillo Quesadillas
Grilled or Panfried Chicken Breasts with Salsa

Cooked Green Tomatillo Salsa

Pan-Cooked Salmon Fillets with Tomatillo Salsa
Green Enchiladas with Chicken Filling
Green Enchiladas with Spinach and Corn Filling
Green Chilaquiles
Green Chilaquiles with Chicken, Corn, and Squash

A Great Pot of Beans

Black Bean Nachos
Black Bean Tostadas (aka Chalupas)
Veracruz-Style Scrambled Eggs with Refried Black Beans
Fried Eggs with Black Beans, Tortillas, and Salsa
Refried Black Beans with Plantain Pancakes
Squash Blossoms Stuffed with Refried Black Beans
Black Bean Chili
Black Bean Salad
Enfrijoladas
Black Bean and Greens Stew
Black Bean Chilaquiles

Shredded Poached Chicken Breast

Veracruz-Style Chicken Picadillo
Green Chilaquiles with Chicken, Corn, and Squash
Soft Tacos or Tostadas with Chicken and Tomatillo Salsa
Soft Tacos or Tostadas with Chicken, Corn, and Avocado
Green Enchiladas with Chicken Filling
Chicken Entomatadas
Chicken and Tomatillo Quesadillas
Chicken Salad with Chipotle Chiles
Chicken and Potato Soup with Lime
Chickpea and Vegetable Soup with Chicken, Lime, and Chipotles

walking away from the table hungry. Serve additional corn tortillas or crusty whole-grain bread with soups and with the salad if you wish. For dessert, just add fresh fruit.

Soft Tacos with Chicken and Tomatillo Salsa
White Rice with Herbs
Tossed green salad

Soft Tacos with Oyster Mushrooms and Tomatoes
Rice or Refried Beans
Green Bean Salad or Baby Lettuces with Lime and Balsamic
  Vinaigrette

Chicken Salad with Chipotle Chiles
Jícama and Orange Salad
Corn tortillas

Corn, Tomato, and Poblano Soup or Late-Summer Vegetable Soup
Baby Lettuces with Lime and Balsamic Vinaigrette
Corn bread or corn tortillas

Black Bean Soup with Tomatoes and Cumin or Veracruz-Style Fava
  Bean Soup
Tossed green salad
Corn bread or corn tortillas

Quesadillas with Broccoli and Garlic
Potatoes with Rajas or simple steamed potatoes
Tossed green salad or Nasturtium and Watercress Salad

Swiss Chard Quesadillas
Rice (either plain rice or Red Rice with Peas and Carrots) or beans (A
  Great Pot of Beans or Refried Beans)
Tossed green salad

Red Chilaquiles with Zucchini, Tomato, and Egg
Refried Beans
Tossed green salad

Grilled Swordfish or Halibut with Mango Mint Salsa
Steamed green vegetable or corn on the cob
Baby Lettuces with Lime and Balsamic Vinaigrette

Grilled or Panfried Chicken Breasts with Salsa
Corn off the Cob with Mexican Herbs or corn on the cob or Baked
    Sweet Potatoes with Lime
Tossed green salad

Chili sin Carne
Corn bread or corn tortillas
Tossed green salad

Roasted Yellow Tomato Soup
Vinegar-Bathed Shrimp
Green Rice with Cilantro and Spinach or Parsley, or plain rice

WHAT TO DRINK WITH MEXICAN FOOD

Both beer and wine go well with Mexican food. Beer is what most people choose, but wine makes a perfect accompaniment when you choose the appropriate type. You also have a wide range of nonalcoholic drinks to choose from in Chapter 1, as well as cocktails like Mexican sangria and margaritas, both of which I have sipped pleasurably throughout Mexican meals.

Wine and Mexican Food

You don't want to choose a subtle, complex wine like an aged Bordeaux, Cabernet Sauvignon, or Burgundy, nor will a delicate white wine stand up to the robust flavors in Mexican dishes. Spicy food likes spicy wines, so I choose wines that also accompany other gutsy cuisines. Reds include Rhône wines and wines from Provence and southwestern France and California wines made from some of the same grapes, Syrah and Mourvèdre. Chiantis go well for the same reason; they are hearty and fruity. I also think light, fruity wines go very well with Mexican food, so I often serve Zinfandel, Beaujolais or Gamay, or Merlot. The Spanish wines made by Torres go well with Mexican meals. My house wine, a cabernet franc from Mas Chichet in the Rousillon, is also a good choice. As for white wines, I think Alsatian wines can make fantastic mates for Mexican food. Gewürztraminer, in particular, is a spicy wine that is marvelous with moles and with fish or chicken with salsa. I would also serve an Alsatian

Riesling (California Rieslings are too sweet), a white Côtes-du-Rhône, a Viognier, a sturdy Sauvignon Blanc, or a Marsanne.

Beer

Beer is what I drink with Mexican food most often when I'm in Mexico. My favorite Mexican beers are Bohemia, Dos Equis (the dark one, not the lager), and Negro Modelo. Bohemia is a light amber not-too-bitter beer with a wonderful clean hops taste. Dos Equis is a dark beer with a rich, complex, caramel-inflected taste. Dos Equis also makes a lager now, which is very bright and refreshing. Negro Modelo is a dark beer, very rich and caramel-inflected, with a strong hops taste. Superior is also popular, a lighter lager with a good full-bodied flavor. I also order Tecate, which is a slightly bitter, lighter-colored beer; it's not a great beer, but I like it better than other Mexican lagers like Corona and Carta Blanca. The custom is to drink Tecate with lime; it becomes a sort of ritual.

We have so much good beer now in the United States that there's no real *need* to buy Mexican beer to drink with the food in this book. It just adds to the atmosphere. But any of the fantastic microbrews that are appearing across the nation will be most welcome with this food. Whether you drink lager or a darker beer is really a matter of taste. It all goes well.

About the Nutritional Data

The recipes in this book have been analyzed by Hill Nutrition Associates for calories, fat, saturated fat, protein, carbohydrates, fiber, and sodium. If an ingredient in a recipe is optional, that ingredient is not included in the analysis. Also, where a fixed quantity of an ingredient, such as salt, is not specified, the ingredient will not be included in the analysis. If you are concerned about your sodium intake, know that the salt you add to a dish will increase the sodium content shown in the data. When a recipe gives a range of servings, it has been analyzed for the smaller number of servings.

About total fat and saturated fat. Each gram of fat contains 9 calories. To calculate the percentage of calories from fat (or saturated fat) in a recipe, multiply the number of grams by 900, then divide by the number of calories. You will see that in some of the recipes, more than 30% of the calories come from fat. However, you'll also see that the total number of calories in these recipes is low, and that the percentage of calories from saturated fats, the fats that cause cholesterol to build up in the bloodstream, is *very* low. I believe that if a delicious dish is nutrient-rich and low in calories and saturated fats, you should not be overly concerned if the total fat is higher than 30%.

Chapter
One

Drinks

Fresh Fruit Waters
Cantaloupe-Seed Horchata
Sparkling Limeade
Iced Hibiscus Tea
Licuados: Mexican Smoothies
Tequila with Sangrita Chaser
Margaritas
Mexican Sangria
Pot-Brewed Coffee with Cinnamon and Brown Sugar

Mexico loves its drinks. The juicers and blenders in Mexican markets are always whirring. In the Camino Real Hotel in Oaxaca the selection of morning fruit and vegetable juices is astounding: orange, grapefruit, papaya, tangerine, carrot, pineapple, guava, and celery!

One of the most tempting sights in a Mexican market, or on a Mexican street for that matter, is the display of large glass jars filled with colorful drinks. They are aguas ("waters"), made by combining blended fruit, sugar, and water. Tamarind water is made from soaked tart tamarind pods, water, and lots of sugar. The bright red drink—not the watermelon water, but the other one, without the seeds in it—is iced hibiscus tea, agua de jamaica. And the pale green one will be limeade. There will also no doubt be a rich, milky horchata made from almonds and rice and possibly one made from melon seeds. These drinks couldn't be more refreshing, and they go well with Mexican food. But in Mexico, unless I'm absolutely sure that the drinks are made with bottled water and purified ice (as they are in the better restaurants), I usually look but don't touch. At home it's another story. I much prefer these wonderful cold drinks to bottled juices. They're very easy to make and keep well in the refrigerator for a couple of days.

Licuados—Mexican smoothies—always seem safer to me as long as I ask for them to be made without ice, sin hielo, and I've never had a problem. What a satisfying, filling breakfast, quick lunch, or snack they make.

Then there are the alcoholic drinks. You just can't beat a good margarita; I remain faithful to the recipe I've been using for years. I've also given you a recipe for a marvelous chaser, called *sangrita,* which is meant to be sipped along with a copita (a little cup) of high-quality tequila or mezcal.

On my most recent trip to Mexico I was introduced to Mexican sangria, which is much different from (and I think preferable to) its Spanish counterpart. Mexican sangria is made with red wine, lime juice, sugar, and sparkling water. You can't get a better wine cooler.

Mexico loves delicious hot beverages too. The hot chocolate is world renowned. That doesn't quite fit into my low-fat parameters, but another sweet and wonderful hot drink, café de olla, does. This is pot-brewed coffee sweetened with brown sugar and cinnamon. I never thought I liked sweetened coffee until I tasted this. I could begin or end my day with this luscious beverage, which has also inspired a dessert.

This chapter is just a sampling of the large repertoire of Mexican drinks. There are many more, punches and atoles (masa-thickened drinks), fruit drinks, fermented drinks, and cocktails. But this will give you a start. More than any other cuisine, Mexico provides drinks for every occasion. For those who don't drink alcohol, this chapter provides a wide range of beverage choices for serving with Mexican food.

Aguas Frescas: Fresh Fruit Waters

Makes 8 servings

Aguas frescas are light, refreshing, thirst-quenching drinks made by blending together fresh ripe fruit and water. Sweeten them with sugar as desired and add a little lime juice for flavor. The key is to begin with very sweet, juicy fruit. My favorites are pineapple, cantaloupe, and watermelon.

2½   **pounds peeled ripe pineapple, seeded cantaloupe, or watermelon**
 1   **quart water**
 1   **to 2 tablespoons fresh lime juice to taste**
 1   **to 2 tablespoons sugar to taste**

Finely chop and set aside 2 cups of the fruit.

Puree the remaining fruit together with the water in a blender. Strain through a medium-mesh strainer into a large glass or earthenware jug or a wide-mouthed pitcher. Taste and add lime juice and sugar as desired. Stir in the chopped fruit. Cover and chill for an hour or more. Ladle into glasses, over ice if desired, and serve.

Advance Preparation: Although fruit drinks are best served the day they are made, I've enjoyed this for a day or two, cold from the refrigerator.

PER PORTION (PINEAPPLE)

Calories	45	Protein	0
Fat	.01 g	Carbohydrate	11 g
Saturated Fat	0	Fiber	0
Cholesterol	0	Sodium	1 mg

PER PORTION (CANTALOUPE)

Calories	28	Protein	0
Fat	.14 g	Carbohydrate	7 g
Saturated Fat	0	Fiber	0
Cholesterol	0	Sodium	5 mg

PER PORTION (WATERMELON)

Calories	35	Protein	0
Fat	.34 g	Carbohydrate	8 g
Saturated Fat	0	Fiber	0
Cholesterol	0	Sodium	2 mg

CANTALOUPE-SEED HORCHATA

Makes 1 large or 2 small servings

Horchata is a milky drink, very refreshing and sweet, often made with soaked rice and almonds. This one is absolutely delicious. Once you know how much flavor is hidden in cantaloupe seeds, you'll save the seeds and membranes for this drink every time you cut open a melon. The best formula I've found for melon-seed horchata is Diana Kennedy's (*Mexican Regional Cooking,* Harper Perennial, 1990), which this recipe is almost identical to, except for slightly less sugar.

1   cup cantaloupe seeds, stringy membranes, and juice, from about
      2 cantaloupes, depending on size
1   cup cold water
1   tablespoon sugar
1   to 2 teaspoons fresh lime juice to taste

Combine all of the ingredients in a blender and blend until smooth. Transfer to a jar, cover, and refrigerate for 5 hours or more. Strain through a fine-mesh strainer and serve, over ice cubes if desired.

Advance Preparation: This must be made 5 hours before serving and can be made a day ahead.

SPARKLING LIMEADE

Makes 5 to 6 servings

None of the so-called flavored mineral waters compare with real fresh limeade, and I've come across no better formula than Rick Bayless's, in his book *Authentic Mexican* (William Morrow, 1987). This makes a great nonalcoholic cocktail and goes well with everything in this book.

1$\frac{1}{3}$ **cups fresh lime juice, from 8 to 10 limes or more if small**
$\frac{1}{2}$ **cup sugar**
1   **quart sparkling water**

Combine the lime juice and sugar in a bowl. Stir until the sugar is dissolved. Transfer to a pitcher or a carafe, add the sparkling water, and stir together. Pour over ice and serve.

Advance Preparation: The sweetened lime juice can be kept in the refrigerator for several hours before adding the mineral water.

PER PORTION

Calories	79	Protein	0
Fat	.05 g	Carbohydrate	22 g
Saturated Fat	0	Fiber	0
Cholesterol	0	Sodium	1 mg

ICED HIBISCUS TEA

Makes 6 servings

Keep this cooling and refreshing drink on hand in the refrigerator during hot spells. You can find dried hibiscus flowers in whole foods stores, where herb teas are sold in bulk, and in many Mexican markets.

2   quarts water
2   cups (about 2 ounces) dried hibiscus flowers
²/₃   cup sugar or more to taste

Bring 6 cups of the water to a boil in a large saucepan and add the hibiscus flowers and sugar. Stir for 1 minute, until the sugar is dissolved. Remove from the heat.

Transfer the mixture to a stainless-steel or glass bowl (the tea will stain plastic) and allow to steep for 2 hours. If you can't wait, allow to steep for 15 minutes for a weaker tea.

Strain the tea into a pitcher, pressing on the flowers with the back of a spoon to extract all of the water. Add the remaining 2 cups water and chill. Pour over ice cubes to serve.

Advance Preparation: This will keep for a couple of days in the refrigerator.

Variation: Pour two thirds of a glass of the iced hibiscus tea and top up with sparkling mineral water.

PER PORTION

Calories	91	Protein	0
Fat	.01 g	Carbohydrate	23 g
Saturated Fat	0	Fiber	0
Cholesterol	0	Sodium	2 mg

$\mathcal{L}$ICUADOS: MEXICAN SMOOTHIES

Makes 1 large serving

These filling fruit milk shakes make a great breakfast or a light lunch or snack on a hot summer day. In Mexico licuados are made with milk, fruit, and sugar. I've broken with tradition and used yogurt, buttermilk, or juice in some. In recipes that call for juice you can boost protein if you like by replacing the juice with the same quantity of milk, buttermilk, or yogurt.

Banana Licuado
- 1   cup cold skim milk
- 1   large ripe banana
- 1   teaspoon sugar or honey or more to taste, optional

Banana-Strawberry Licuado
- 1   small or $^1/_2$ large ripe banana
- 1   heaped cup (about 8 large) strawberries, hulled
- $^1/_2$ cup skim milk or plain nonfat yogurt plus $^1/_2$ cup apple
          juice or 1 cup milk or yogurt
- 1   teaspoon honey

Mango Licuado
- 1   cup (1 medium) ripe mango
- $^1/_2$ cup fresh orange juice
- $^1/_2$ cup low-fat (1%) buttermilk
- 1   tablespoon fresh lime juice

Peach Licuado
- 2   medium sweet, juicy ripe peaches, peeled and pitted
- $^1/_2$ cup fresh orange juice
- $^1/_2$ cup plain nonfat yogurt or low-fat (1%) buttermilk
- 1   teaspoon honey

Pineapple-Mint Licuado
- 1   heaped cup chopped (about $^1/_4$ large or $^1/_2$ small) fresh ripe
          pineapple

$^1/_2$ **cup fresh orange juice**
$^1/_2$ **ripe banana**
1 **tablespoon (about 6) fresh mint leaves**
$^1/_2$ **cup plain nonfat yogurt**

Place all the ingredients in a blender with 2 or 3 ice cubes and blend at high speed until smooth. Pour into a tall glass and serve.

PER PORTION (BANANA)

Calories	222	Protein	10 g
Fat	1 g	Carbohydrate	47 g
Saturated Fat	.53 g	Fiber	2 g
Cholesterol	5 mg	Sodium	129 mg

PER PORTION (BANANA-STRAWBERRY)

Calories	263	Protein	6 g
Fat	1 g	Carbohydrate	61 g
Saturated Fat	.36 g	Fiber	7 g
Cholesterol	2 mg	Sodium	71 mg

PER PORTION (MANGO)

Calories	227	Protein	6 g
Fat	2 g	Carbohydrate	49 g
Saturated Fat	.88 g	Fiber	2 g
Cholesterol	8 mg	Sodium	180 mg

PER PORTION (PEACH)

Calories	253	Protein	9 g
Fat	.67 g	Carbohydrate	57 g
Saturated Fat	.21 g	Fiber	4 g
Cholesterol	2 mg	Sodium	88 mg

PER PORTION (PINEAPPLE-MINT)

Calories	275	Protein	8 g
Fat	1 g	Carbohydrate	58 g
Saturated Fat	1.3 g	Fiber	3 g
Cholesterol	7 mg	Sodium	83 mg

Tequila and Mezcal

Mexico's agave distillates, the well-known tequila and its lesser-known cousin mezcal (sometimes spelled *mescal* in the United States), can be as smooth and as pleasant to drink as the best cognacs or single-malt whiskeys. Once you discover the finer tequilas and mezcals, you may find yourself, as I have, choosing these spirits above all others for sipping before or after a meal.

Both tequila and mezcal come from the heart (called the *piña*) of the huge, spiky agave plant, which is also known as the *maguey*. The difference between the two lies in the variety of agave used, the place in which they are made (all tequila must be made in a designated area; thus all tequila is mezcal but not all mezcal is tequila), and the methods and equipment used in the baking, fermenting, and distilling.

Tequila is made from only one species of agave, the agave tequilana Weber, blue variety, commonly known as the *blue agave*. It is produced from agaves grown in only five central Mexican states: all of Jalisco and designated areas of Guanajuato, Michoacán, Nayarit, and Tamaulipas. Most tequila is produced in two areas of the west-central state of Jalisco and has been since the seventeenth century. This is where the well-known tequila producers, José Cuervo and Sauza, have their distilleries, in the town of Tequila. Tequila production by the larger producers is highly mechanized. The better tequilas are aged in oak barrels or tanks. Though the spirit is clear by nature, colorings— caramel for the most part—can be added.

There are four categories of tequila. White or silver tequila—tequila blanco—is legally defined as fresh from the still. It does not benefit from aging, but the tequilas made from 100 percent agave can have a very fresh taste. This is the kind I often use for margaritas. Gold tequila—tequila joven abocado—is silver tequila with the addition of colorings and flavorings to mellow the flavor. This may exist purely as a marketing device, since the tequila is essentially the same as silver tequila. Tequila reposado, or rested tequila, has been aged for two months to a year in oak tanks or barrels. Flavorings and coloring agents are usually added. These tequilas have mellowed and are fine for sipping; they can also be used for margaritas. But the best tequilas, in my opinion, are the aged tequilas, tequilas añejos. These have been aged for at least one year in government-sealed oak barrels. They also contain flavorings and colorings. They are smooth and complex, like good single malts or cognacs. I reserve these tequilas for sipping (slowly; *not* drinking in one shot) and use the younger, less expensive tequilas for mixed drinks like margaritas.

The brands of tequila most widely sold in the United States are Cuervo, Sauza, and Herradura. They each come in the four types; Sauza has five grades—Tres Generaciones (the highest), Conmemorativo, Hornitos, Extra, and Blanco. Cuervo's highest (and my favorite to date) is 1800, then Centenario, Especial, and Blanco. Herradura distributes Añejo, Reposado, Blanco Suave, and Blanco.

Mezcal, my current favorite spirit, is produced on a much smaller, artisanal scale, in tiny rural distilleries called *palenques.* Oaxaca is designated as the principal denomination of origin for mezcal, as Jalisco is for tequila. Good mezcal has a smokier flavor than tequila and a complexity that I find very interesting.

The piñas from 7- to 10-year-old agaves are roasted in underground, stone-lined ovens over charcoal made from local woods. It is at this stage that mezcal is imbued with its smoky nuances and smoothness. Once the piñas have been roasted, they are crushed with hand-hewn mallets or in mills with grindstones and transferred to open wooden vats for fermentation, which takes 8 to 15 days. The fermented juice, or tepache, is then distilled twice, first in earthenware jugs called *ollas,* which are also thought to contribute to mezcal's flavor, then in alembic stills.

Until recently I had drunk good, high-quality mezcal only in Oaxaca. Happily, there is now a very fine, super-premium mezcal being imported from Oaxaca, called Encantado. When I sip this delicious, evocative eau-de-vie, I am always transported to the quiet, mystical valley of Oaxaca.

TEQUILA WITH SANGRITA CHASER

Makes 4 servings

Good aged tequila, like Cuervo 1800 or Herradura Añejo, is as fine a drink as a good cognac or an aged single malt. It is wonderful drunk alongside a shot of sangrita, a spicy-sweet mixture of orange juice, grenadine (a syrup made from pomegranates), tomato juice, lime juice, and cayenne, Tabasco, or salsa. I sipped the best sangrita I've ever tasted one afternoon in the courtyard of the Posada Coatepec, a luxurious hotel built in the wealthy coffee town of Coatepec, in the Veracruz highlands. I've tried to duplicate it here.

- 1/2 **cup fresh orange juice**
- 1 **tablespoon grenadine syrup**
- 1/4 **cup tomato juice**
- 1/4 **cup fresh lime juice**
- 1/2 **teaspoon Tabasco sauce or** 1/8 **teaspoon cayenne pepper or more to taste**
- **salt to taste**
- 4 **shots good aged tequila**
- **lime wedges for serving**

Mix together the orange juice, grenadine, tomato juice, lime juice, Tabasco, and salt. Refrigerate for 1 hour or place in the freezer for 30 minutes. Stir and pour into small shot glasses.

Serve the tequila in shot glasses, each one accompanied by a glass of sangrita. Pass lime wedges.

Advance Preparation: You can make the sangrita hours ahead of serving and keep it covered in the refrigerator.

PER PORTION

Calories	112	Protein	0
Fat	.07 g	Carbohydrate	7 g
Saturated Fat	0	Fiber	0
Cholesterol	0	Sodium	60 mg

MARGARITAS

Makes 8 servings

The secret to the margaritas I've been serving for years is a simple formula: 1 part fresh lime juice to $1^1/_2$ parts tequila and $^2/_3$ to $^3/_4$ part triple sec or Cointreau, depending on how sweet (and strong) you want your margaritas. I usually go for the $^3/_4$ proportion, because it's so easy to work out those quantities for a crowd. To make the drinks a little less lethal, while retaining the balance of flavors, I blend my margaritas in a blender with ice.

1	cup fresh lime juice
$1^1/_2$	cups tequila
$^3/_4$	cup Cointreau or triple sec
2	cups ice cubes
	coarse sea salt and 1 lime, cut into quarters, for the glasses, optional

Combine the lime juice, tequila, and Cointreau in a pitcher and stir together.

Place the ice cubes in a blender and pour in the margarita mix. Blend until the ice cubes are well chopped. Transfer to the pitcher.

Prepare the glasses if you are salting them. Grind the salt medium-coarse in a spice mill. Place it on a plate. Rub the rim of your glasses with the cut lime and very gently dip in the salt. It should not be caked. If you aren't sure that your guests want salt, dip only one side of the rim.

Pour the margaritas and enjoy!

Advance Preparation: Lime juice is always best when freshly squeezed, but I usually have to get a head start when I'm serving this for a crowd. The juice doesn't suffer too much if mixed at once with the alcohol. Mix the lime juice with the tequila and Cointreau or triple sec and refrigerate for up to 2 hours. Blend with the ice just before serving.

PER PORTION

Calories	184	Protein	0
Fat	.04 g	Carbohydrate	10 g
Saturated Fat	0	Fiber	0
Cholesterol	0	Sodium	0

MEXICAN SANGRIA

Makes 6 servings

This is dangerously quaffable. Mexican sangria isn't anything like the Spanish drink, which can be quite strong and cloying. The Mexican version is really a red wine and lime spritzer, one of the most refreshing accompaniments I can think of to a Mexican meal. It makes a great cocktail as well.

- ²/₃ **cup fresh lime juice**
- ¹/₂ **cup sugar**
- ¹/₄ **cup water**
- 1 **bottle dry, fruity red wine such as Beaujolais, Gamay, or Zinfandel**
- 1 **cup sparkling water**
- **ice and slices of lime for garnish**

Mix together the lime juice, sugar, and water and stir until the sugar is dissolved.

Pour the wine into a pitcher and stir in the lime syrup and sparkling water. Add ice or place ice in each glass and serve. Garnish each glass with a slice of lime.

Advance Preparation: You can mix up the lime syrup a few hours before mixing the sangria, but lime juice always tastes better the fresher it is.

PER PORTION

Calories	162	Protein	0
Fat	.02 g	Carbohydrate	21 g
Saturated Fat	0	Fiber	0
Cholesterol	0	Sodium	7 mg

POT-BREWED COFFEE WITH CINNAMON AND BROWN SUGAR

Makes 4 to 6 servings

I don't usually drink coffee after a meal, but I love Mexican café de olla, coffee brewed, campfire style, in a pot and sweetened and spiced with brown sugar and cinnamon. To me it's like dessert. Use less sugar if you wish.

1 quart water
¼ pound Mexican piloncillo sugar, roughly chopped, or ½ cup brown sugar plus, if desired, 1 teaspoon molasses
4 inches Mexican cinnamon stick
⅔ cup (2 ounces) Viennese roast or French roast coffee, regular or decaffeinated, medium to coarse grind for pot-brewed coffee, finely ground for filter coffee

In a 2- or 3-quart noncorrosive saucepan, combine the water, sugar, and cinnamon. Simmer for 5 minutes. Stir in the coffee, remove from the heat, cover, and let steep for 5 minutes.

Line a strainer with a dampened double layer of cheesecloth and place over a pitcher or strain directly into mugs. Strain in the coffee and serve.

DRIP COFFEE WITH CINNAMON AND BROWN SUGAR

If you don't like the texture of pot-brewed coffee, place the coffee in a drip filter over a measuring cup. Bring the water to a boil and pour 2 cups of the water slowly over the coffee. Dissolve the sugar in the remaining water, add the cinnamon sticks, and simmer for 10 minutes. Stir into the coffee and serve.

Advance Preparation: This should be made just before serving.

PER PORTION

Calories	91	Protein	0
Fat	.01 g	Carbohydrate	23 g
Saturated Fat	0	Fiber	0
Cholesterol	0	Sodium	13 mg

Chapter
Two

Sauces and Condiments

Salsa Fresca
Tomato, Avocado, and Corn Salsa
Salsa Ranchera
Cooked Tomato and Black Bean Salsa
Roasted Tomato and Chile Guajillo Salsa
Salsa Verde Cruda
Cooked Green Tomatillo Salsa
Chipotle and Tomatillo Salsa
Green Tomatillo Mole
Mango Salsa
Adobo Sauce
Red Chile Paste (Adobo)
Chipotle Salsa
Creamy Chipotle Dip
Pickled Chiles with Carrots, Onion, and Garlic
Pickled Chipotle Chiles
Homemade Chile Powder
Chile Salt

No hay mejor salsa que un buen apetito.
There's no better sauce than a good appetite.

Salsas—sauces—are the backbone of Mexican cooking. They're present in one form or another throughout the meal. When you sit down at a table, small bowls of salsa—red and green, cooked and uncooked, fiery hot and mild, will be there for dipping toasted or fried tortillas and for spooning onto antojitos—tacos, quesadillas, tostadas, empanadas. The main course may revolve around a richer, more complex sauce, an adobo or mole, in which meats, fish, or vegetables are stewed. Here the sauce defines the dish.

Indeed the ethnicity of a meal can be determined by the presence of a Mexican sauce. A simple grilled fish or chicken breast becomes a Mexican dish when served with tomato, corn, and avocado salsa, as does corn on the cob served with creamy chipotle dip or pan-cooked salmon with salsa verde. Perhaps this dish won't be an authentic Mexican recipe, but the flavors of Mexico and the border will be unmistakable.

One of the great things about salsas is that so many of them are fat-free. The uncooked sauces are made with vegetables or fruit and chiles. How convenient for us—without altering a thing, you can create incredibly healthy low-fat meals just by combining these salsas with fish or chicken or grains and vegetables. The cooked sauces here require a minimum of oil. In Mexico they are made with a bit more, but they don't require a lot of fat to bring out the flavors of the herbs, chiles, spices, and vegetables.

With the exception of the green tomatillo mole, I have not included any of the marvelous nut-thickened pipians and moles that are an important part of Mexico's sauce repertoire, because they're too high in fat for our purposes. My green tomatillo mole has fewer pumpkin seeds than an authentic green mole, but it's rich and delicious and goes a long way. For a green mole with no pumpkin seeds at all, see the Oaxacan green herb mole with white beans and vegetable in chapter 12.

For the most part, Mexican sauces rely on tomatoes or tomatillos, chiles, onions, and garlic or some combination thereof. The most intense sauce in this collection is the chipotle salsa, which is actually a paste, made with smoky-hot chipotles, garlic, and water. It's meant to be spread in the thinnest film, onto tortillas or empanadas, tacos or corn. The degree to which the other sauces burn is left to the discretion of the cook. I often give a range of chiles or the choice to seed fresh chiles to lower the heat. Where there is no range, as in the roasted tomato and chile guajillo salsa or the adobo sauce, the heat of the dried chiles, while prominent, is rounded out with other flavors.

The basic cooked red and green sauces here come up in recipes in subsequent chapters. The cooked tomato sauce, for example, is the beautiful red sauce in huevos rancheros; crisp tortillas are cooked in the same sauce for red chilaquiles, and it's the basic sauce for the tomato-sauced enchiladas called *entomatadas.* A tart and savory, mildly picante cooked green salsa goes into many tacos and enchiladas, and green chilaquiles depend on it. I repeat these recipes when they recur, partly because I don't want you to have to turn back to another page, and partly because they may be altered slightly (stretched, perhaps, with a bit of stock or water).

Most of the recipes here are authentic, although I've made up a few of the tomato salsas, inspired by the late-summer harvest here in northern California (the red and yellow salsa fresca and the tomato, corn, and avocado salsa). I also made up the low-fat creamy chipotle dip; this cottage-cheese-based version of chipotle mayonnaise, which I've enjoyed in the Veracruz highlands of Mexico as well as in California, has become an indispensable dish in my repertoire.

Hand in hand with table salsas go the pickled chiles and vegetables that are used as condiments in Mexico. They are available here in cans, but when you make them yourself you'll see how much richer they can taste. The canned versions are often quite harsh. As for pickled chipotles, if you have a taste for the picante, you might get hooked on these. I add them, just a sliver or two, to sandwiches and salads, to quesadillas, and even to soups when I want to spice things up. Make one recipe, and you'll have the condiment in your refrigerator for months.

A note on the number of servings: The number of servings for some of these salsas can vary depending on what the sauce is used for. If a given salsa is to be used as a table salsa for dipping chips or garnishing tostadas, it will go further than it will if it's to be used as a sauce for a main dish. For this reason I give a range for the number of servings, along with the yield, with many of the recipes. The nutritional analysis is based on the smaller number of servings throughout.

SALSA FRESCA

Makes about 2 cups, serving 6 to 8

I have been making this salsa for years. In summer, when tomatoes are wonderful, a day rarely goes by that I don't make it. I serve it with grilled fish and chicken, with tacos and quesadillas of all kinds, I dress salads with it and even toss it with pasta. In winter and spring, when good tomatoes are unavailable, a little balsamic vinegar adds to the sweetness of the tomatoes. Of course this is not a Mexican ingredient, but I find that most insipid tomatoes need it.

Try the salsa with half red and half yellow tomatoes—beautiful with grilled salmon or halibut.

1	to 1¼ pounds (4 medium or 2 large) tomatoes, finely chopped,
½	small red onion, minced and rinsed
2	to 3 jalapeño or serrano chiles or more to taste, seeded for a milder salsa and minced
¼	cup chopped fresh cilantro or more to taste
1	to 2 teaspoons balsamic vinegar, rice wine vinegar, or fresh lime juice to taste, optional
	salt to taste, about ½ teaspoon

Mix together all the ingredients. Let sit for about 15 minutes before serving.

Advance Preparation: This should be made on the day you serve it, but it will hold for several hours in the refrigerator. The salt will draw juice out of the tomatoes, making the salsa more watery, but this doesn't bother me.

PER PORTION (¼ CUP)

Calories	18	Protein	1 g
Fat	.21 g	Carbohydrate	4 g
Saturated Fat	.03 g	Fiber	1 g
Cholesterol	0	Sodium	144 mg

Tomato, Avocado, and Corn Salsa

Makes about 2³/₄ cups, serving 6 to 8

This salsa has a wonderful play of textures and flavors. The small amount of avocado adds a creamy quality, and the corn is crunchy and sweet. Naturally you want the best, sweetest white corn you can get. Serve this salsa with grilled tuna or swordfish, with grilled chicken breasts, or with chips. I sometimes make a meal of it with soft corn tortillas.

1	to 1¹/₄ pounds (4 medium or 2 large) tomatoes, finely chopped
¹/₂	small red onion, minced and rinsed
2	to 3 jalapeño or serrano chiles to taste, seeded and minced
¹/₄	cup chopped fresh cilantro or more to taste
1	tablespoon rice wine vinegar, balsamic vinegar, or fresh lime juice, optional
¹/₂	small ripe avocado, peeled, pitted, and minced
1	ear white corn, steamed for 5 minutes and kernels removed salt to taste, about ¹/₂ teaspoon

Mix together all the ingredients. Let sit for 15 minutes, in or out of the refrigerator, before serving.

Advance Preparation: This should be made on the day you serve it, but it will hold for several hours in the refrigerator.

PER PORTION

Calories	72	Protein	2 g
Fat	3 g	Carbohydrate	11 g
Saturated Fat	.53 g	Fiber	2 g
Cholesterol	0	Sodium	196 mg

Salsa Ranchera

Makes about 2 cups, serving 4 to 8

This classic cooked tomato-chile sauce is terrific with eggs, like huevos rancheros, with chips, as a base for chilaquiles or enchiladas, and with grilled fish and chicken. If your tomatoes are very pulpy, thin out the sauce with water.

2   pounds (8 medium or 4 large) tomatoes, roasted*
2   to 3 serrano or 1 to 2 jalapeño chiles or more to taste, seeded for a milder sauce and chopped
¼   to ½ small onion, coarsely chopped (about 2 to 4 tablespoons), to taste
2   garlic cloves, minced or pressed
1   tablespoon canola oil
    salt to taste, about ½ teaspoon or more
    water as needed

Place the tomatoes, along with any liquid that has accumulated in the bowl, the chiles, onion, and garlic in a blender and puree, retaining a bit of texture.

Heat the oil in a large heavy nonstick skillet over medium heat. Drop a bit of puree into the pan and, if it sizzles loudly, add the rest (wait another minute or two if it doesn't). Cook, stirring, for about 10 to 15 minutes, until the sauce darkens, thickens, and begins to stick to the pan. Add salt and thin out with water as necessary. Remove from the heat.

Advance Preparation: This will keep for 4 to 5 days in the refrigerator. It can be frozen for 3 months.

Variations: For a smoky, hot taste, add a canned chile chipotle en adobo and simmer with the tomatoes. Remove from the sauce when it is cooked. For a very hot version, add an habanero chile, slit down the middle, with the tomatoes. Remove from the sauce when it is cooked.

---

* *To roast tomatoes:* Preheat the broiler. Line a baking sheet with foil and place the tomatoes on it. Place under the broiler, about 2 to 3 inches from the heat (at the highest rack setting). Turn after 2 or 3 minutes, when the tomatoes have charred on one side (this may take longer in an electric oven), and repeat on the other side. Remove from the heat and transfer to a bowl. When the tomatoes are cool enough to handle, peel and core.

For a milder onion taste and a bit of texture, do not add the onion to the blender. Sauté in the oil until tender—about 5 minutes—before adding the tomato mixture.

PER PORTION (¹/₄ CUP)

Calories	42	Protein	1 g
Fat	2 g	Carbohydrate	6 g
Saturated Fat	.17 g	Fiber	2 g
Cholesterol	0	Sodium	147 mg

COOKED TOMATO AND BLACK BEAN SALSA

Makes 3 cups, serving 8

The idea for this salsa with black beans comes from Trader Joe, a California discount supermarket. My mother, who lives in Los Angeles, always has it in her refrigerator; it's one of her favorite lunches. Eat this with tortillas or chips, with bread, as a sauce for grilled chicken or fish, or just as is.

1¹/₂   **pounds (5 medium or 3 large) tomatoes, roasted***
2   **garlic cloves, toasted***
2   **teaspoons canola oil**
1   **onion, chopped**
³/₄   **to 1 teaspoon cumin to taste**
   salt to taste, ¹/₂ to 1 teaspoon
2   **to 3 serrano or 1 to 2 jalapeño chiles to taste, seeded if desired and chopped**
2   **tablespoons chopped fresh cilantro**
1   **cup cooked black beans (canned are fine)**

* To roast tomatoes: Preheat the broiler. Line a baking sheet with foil and place the tomatoes on it. Place under the broiler, about 2 to 3 inches from the heat (at the highest rack setting). Turn after 2 or 3 minutes, when the tomatoes have charred on one side (this may take longer in an electric oven), and repeat on the other side. Remove from the heat and transfer to a bowl. When the tomatoes are cool enough to handle, peel and core.

* To toast garlic: Heat a heavy skillet or comal over medium-high heat and toast the garlic in its skin, turning or shaking the pan often, until it smells toasty and is blackened in several places, about 10 minutes. Remove from the heat and peel.

Puree the tomatoes, along with any liquid that has accumulated in the bowl, and the garlic coarsely in a blender or in a food processor fitted with the steel blade.

Heat the oil over medium heat in a heavy saucepan or nonstick skillet and add the onion. Cook, stirring, until tender, about 5 minutes. Add the tomato puree, cumin, salt, and chiles. Cook, stirring, for 15 to 20 more minutes, until the mixture is thick and aromatic. Stir in the cilantro and black beans. Taste and adjust seasonings. Remove from the heat and allow to cool or serve hot.

Advance Preparation: This will keep for about 4 days in the refrigerator.

PER PORTION

Calories	67	Protein	3 g
Fat	2 g	Carbohydrate	11 g
Saturated Fat	.15 g	Fiber	2 g
Cholesterol	0	Sodium	215 mg

ROASTED TOMATO AND CHILE GUAJILLO SALSA

Makes 1$^1/_2$ cups, serving 8 to 10

This is a great table salsa for dipping chips and is also good with grilled chicken and fried or scrambled eggs. It has a very deep, toasty flavor; it's also very slightly bitter and quite picante but not mouth-searing. You can experiment with other chiles here, using the same tomato base. Try pasillas or, for a very hot sauce, pasilla de Oaxaca (one will suffice) or chipotles.

- 1   **pound (4 medium or 2 large) tomatoes, roasted***
- 4   **guajillo or pasilla chiles, toasted***
- 2   **large garlic cloves, toasted***
       salt to taste, about $^1/_2$ teaspoon
- $^1/_4$ **cup water**

Transfer the tomatoes, along with any liquid that has accumulated in the bowl, toasted chiles, garlic, and salt to a blender and puree at high speed until smooth. Strain through a medium-mesh strainer into a bowl. Add the water to the blender and turn on to clean the sides of the jar. Strain the water into the sauce. Let stand at room temperature for 30 minutes, then taste and adjust salt.

Advance Preparation: I have served this sauce after a week in the refrigerator, and everybody loved it. But the fresher it is, the better. It will become hotter by the day.

PER PORTION

Calories	15	Protein	1 g
Fat	.18 g	Carbohydrate	3 g
Saturated Fat	.02 g	Fiber	1 g
Cholesterol	0	Sodium	142 mg

* *To roast tomatoes:* Preheat the broiler. Line a baking sheet with foil and place the tomatoes on it. Place under the broiler, about 2 to 3 inches from the heat (at the highest rack setting). Turn after 2 or 3 minutes, when the tomatoes have charred on one side (this may take longer in an electric oven), and repeat on the other side. Remove from the heat and transfer to a bowl. When the tomatoes are cool enough to handle, peel and core.

* *To toast chiles:* Wearing rubber gloves, tear the chiles into flat pieces and remove the seeds and veins. Heat a heavy skillet or comal over medium heat and toast the chiles on both sides, pressing them down with a metal spatula and turning them as soon as they sizzle and blister, in a matter of seconds. Remove from the heat at once and transfer to a bowl or plate.

* *To toast garlic:* Heat a heavy skillet or comal over medium-high heat and toast the garlic in its skin, turning or shaking the pan often, until it smells toasty and is blackened in several places, about 10 minutes. Remove from the heat and peel.

SALSA VERDE CRUDA

Makes 2¹/₂ cups, serving 8 as a table salsa,
4 as a sauce with tacos, fish, or chicken

This classic, lively, bright green tomatillo salsa is easy to make and useful for more than just dipping tortilla chips. If you have it on hand, a quick taco is at your fingertips; it's also a wonderful sauce for vegetables (especially potatoes), meat, and fish.

1   pound (about 8 large) tomatillos, husked and rinsed, or two 13-ounce cans, drained
2   to 5 jalapeño or serrano chiles to taste, seeded for a milder salsa and coarsely chopped
¹/₂   medium onion, roughly chopped and rinsed if blending, finely chopped and rinsed if stirring in
2   large garlic cloves, roughly chopped, optional
     salt to taste, about ¹/₂ teaspoon
¹/₄   cup fresh cilantro or more to taste
¹/₄   to ¹/₂ cup water as needed

If you're using fresh tomatillos, either roast under a broiler, following the directions on page 31, or simmer in water to cover for 10 minutes. Drain and place in a blender or a food processor fitted with the steel blade. If you're using canned tomatillos, drain and place in the blender. Add the chiles, onion if desired, garlic, salt, and cilantro. Blend to a coarse puree. Transfer to a bowl and thin as desired with water. Taste and adjust seasoning. Let stand for 30 minutes or longer to allow the flavors to develop before serving.

Alternate Method: Stir the onion (finely chopped) into the puree.

Advance Preparation: This will hold for a few days in the refrigerator, but the fresher it is, the more vivid the flavors.

PER PORTION

Calories	40	Protein	2 g
Fat	.55 g	Carbohydrate	8 g
Saturated Fat	0	Fiber	0
Cholesterol	0	Sodium	275 mg

Variation

TOMATILLO AND CILANTRO SALSA: For an emerald-green sauce that rings with the flavor of cilantro, use 2 whole bunches of cilantro, washed and stems trimmed. You should have about 2 cups cilantro, tightly packed. Blend as above.

PER PORTION

Calories	42	Protein	2 g
Fat	.58 g	Carbohydrate	8 g
Saturated Fat	0	Fiber	0
Cholesterol	0	Sodium	417 mg

COOKED GREEN TOMATILLO SALSA

Makes 2¹/₂ cups, serving 4 to 8

This tangy salsa, thinner than the uncooked tomatillo version, has all sorts of uses beyond its excellent one as a table salsa. I use it for chilaquiles, in many vegetable and chicken taco toppings, as a simple sauce for chicken or fish (it's especially beautiful against a pink salmon fillet), and for my green enchilada sauce.

1   pound (about 8 large) tomatillos, husked and rinsed, or two 13-ounce cans, drained
2   to 5 jalapeño or serrano chiles to taste, seeded for a milder salsa and coarsely chopped
¹/₂   small white onion, chopped (about ¹/₄ cup)
1   large garlic clove, roughly chopped
    salt to taste, ¹/₂ to 1 teaspoon
8   fresh cilantro sprigs or more to taste
2   teaspoons canola or safflower oil
2   cups vegetable, garlic, or chicken stock

If you're using fresh tomatillos, simmer in water to cover for 10 minutes. Drain and place in a blender or a food processor fitted with the steel blade. If you're using canned tomatillos, drain and place in the blender. Add the chiles, onion, garlic, salt, and cilantro. Puree the mixture.

Heat the oil in a heavy saucepan or a nonstick skillet over medium heat. Drizzle a bit of the tomatillo mixture into the pan and, if it sizzles loudly, add the rest (wait a bit if it doesn't). Cook the tomatillo puree, stirring, until it thickens and begins to stick to the pan, about 5 minutes. Add the stock, stir together, and bring to a simmer. Simmer for 15 to 20 minutes, stirring occasionally, until the mixture is thick enough to coat the front and back of your spoon. Remove from the heat, taste, and adjust salt.

Alternate Method: For a milder onion flavor and a bit of texture, don't blend the onion with the tomatillos. Sauté in the oil until tender before adding the puree, then proceed with the recipe.

Advance Preparation: This will hold for 4 days in the refrigerator and can be frozen.

PER PORTION

Calories	66	Protein	2 g
Fat	3 g	Carbohydrate	9 g
Saturated Fat	.15 g	Fiber	1 g
Cholesterol	0	Sodium	652 mg

CHIPOTLE AND TOMATILLO SALSA

Makes 1 cup, serving 6 to 8 as a table sauce

I learned to make this toasty, smoky, picante table salsa in Oaxaca with chef Rick Bayless. In Oaxaca Rick used small purplish tomatillos, which I've never seen in the markets here. But the sauce is delicious made with the larger green tomatillos that are readily available wherever Mexican ingredients are sold.

- **2 dried chipotle chiles, seeded and toasted***
- **½ pound (about 4 large) tomatillos, husked and roasted,* or one 13-ounce can, drained**
- **2 medium garlic cloves, toasted***
- **½ cup water as needed**
- **salt to taste**

Transfer the toasted chiles to a bowl and cover with boiling water. Weight with a plate to keep the peppers submerged and soak for 30 minutes.

Transfer the tomatillos to a blender along with any juice that has accumulated in the bowl. Drain the chipotles, rinse briefly, and add to the blender along with the toasted garlic. Blend the mixture until fairly smooth, leaving a bit of texture. Transfer to a bowl and thin out as desired with water. Season to taste with salt.

Advance Preparation: This will keep for a couple of days in the refrigerator, but it will become hotter. The fresher it is, the better.

PER PORTION

Calories	12	Protein	1 g
Fat	.18 g	Carbohydrate	2 g
Saturated Fat	0	Fiber	0
Cholesterol	0	Sodium	0

GREEN TOMATILLO MOLE

*Makes 3¹/₂ to 4 cups, serving 8 as a main-dish sauce,
20 as a dip or hors d'oeuvre topping*

I've been making this luxurious mole for years, combining it most often with chicken, rabbit, or potatoes and corn. In this book I use it as a sauce for salmon or shrimp. It makes a great topping for yeasted cornmeal pancakes or dip with chips. The mole is made with pumpkin seeds and tomatillos and has a marvelous rich flavor. I've been steadily reducing the amount of pumpkin

* *To toast chiles:* Heat a heavy skillet or comal over medium heat and toast the chiles on both sides, pressing them down with a metal spatula and turning them as soon as they sizzle and blister, in a matter of seconds. Remove from the heat at once and transfer to a bowl or plate.

* *To toast garlic:* Heat the same skillet over medium-high heat and toast the garlic in its skin, turning or shaking the pan often, until it smells toasty and is blackened in several places, about 10 minutes. Remove from the heat and peel.

* *To roast tomatillos:* Preheat the broiler. Line a baking sheet with foil and place the tomatillos on it. Place under the broiler, about 2 to 3 inches from the heat (at the highest rack setting). Turn after 2 or 3 minutes, when the tomatillos have charred on one side (this may take longer in an electric oven), and repeat on the other side. Remove from the heat and transfer to a bowl. When the tomatillos are cool enough to handle, peel.

seeds; a ground toasted tortilla helps to thicken the sauce, and you still get that rich nutty flavor.

2	ounces (¹/₃ cup) hulled pumpkin seeds
3	cups chicken, vegetable, or garlic stock
1	pound (16 medium or about 8 large) tomatillos, husked and rinsed, or two 13-ounce cans, drained
2	to 4 jalapeño or serrano chiles to taste, seeded
5	large romaine or leaf lettuce leaves
¹/₂	medium onion, roughly chopped
3	large garlic cloves, roughly chopped
8	fresh cilantro sprigs
¹/₄	teaspoon ground cumin
³/₄	teaspoon ground cinnamon
	pinch of ground cloves
1	corn tortilla, toasted,* crumbled and ground in a spice mill (2 tablespoons)
1	tablespoon canola oil
	salt to taste, about ¹/₂ teaspoon

Toast the pumpkin seeds in a dry skillet over medium-high heat, shaking the pan or stirring constantly until they have browned and popped, about 5 to 8 minutes. Remove from the heat and transfer to a bowl. Pulverize in a spice mill in batches and sift into a bowl. Stir in ³/₄ cup of the stock and mix well. Set aside.

If you're using fresh tomatillos, simmer in water to cover for 10 minutes, until soft. Drain and place in a blender. If you're using canned tomatillos, just place them in the blender. Add the chiles, lettuce, onion, garlic, cilantro, spices, and toasted tortilla. Blend until the mixture is smooth, stopping and starting the blender and stirring if necessary.

Heat the oil in a heavy saucepan or casserole over medium-high heat. Drizzle in a bit of the pumpkin seed mixture and, if it sizzles, add the rest (wait

---

* *To toast tortilla:* To bake the tortilla, preheat the oven to 325 degrees. Place the tortilla on a baking sheet and bake for 20 to 30 minutes, until light brown and crisp, shaking the baking sheet every 10 minutes. Allow to cool on a rack. To microwave, place on a plate or on the plate in your microwave oven. Microwave on HIGH (100%) power for 1 minute. If the tortilla is not crisp, turn it over and microwave for another 40 seconds. If still not crisp and are just beginning to brown, microwave for another 20 to 30 seconds or until crisp. Cool on a rack or in a basket.

a minute or two if it doesn't). Cook, stirring constantly, until the mixture thickens, about 5 minutes. Add the tomatillo mixture and cook again, stirring, for about 5 to 10 minutes, until the mixture thickens. Stir in the remaining 2¼ cups stock, bring to a simmer, add salt, cover partially, and simmer for 20 minutes, stirring often, or until the sauce is thick. It should coat the front and back of a spoon like cream. Taste and correct seasonings. Remove from the heat.

Advance Preparation: This sauce will keep for 3 days in the refrigerator and freezes well. Whisk after thawing to restore its consistency.

PER PORTION

Calories	98	Protein	3 g
Fat	6 g	Carbohydrate	9 g
Saturated Fat	.74 g	Fiber	1 g
Cholesterol	0	Sodium	352 mg

MANGO SALSA

Makes 1 cup, serving 4

This is a heavenly salsa. It's best when the mango is really ripe, which means you may have a puree rather than a dice. That's why I mix in a little jícama—for texture without introducing another big flavor. Serve this with grilled or steamed halibut, swordfish, snapper, or sea bass or with grilled chicken breasts.

1   **large ripe mango**
2   **serrano chiles, minced**
1   **tablespoon chopped fresh cilantro**
¼   **cup minced peeled jícama**
     juice of 1 medium lime

Peel, pit, and finely chop the mango. Toss with the remaining ingredients. Let sit for 1 hour before serving, in or out of the refrigerator. Serve at room temperature, with grilled fish or chicken breasts.

Advance Preparation: This can be made a few hours before serving and held in the refrigerator.

RED CHILE PASTE (ADOBO)

Makes 1¹/₄ cups, serving 6

The advantage that this paste has over adobo sauce is that it keeps indefinitely in the refrigerator. It's used mostly as a marinade to smear on meat and sometimes fish, which is in turn roasted, broiled, grilled, or baked. It has a roasted, slightly bitter taste. Since I prefer the sweet-and-sour, smoother-tasting sauce, I often turn this one into a sauce or sweeten it with a bit of sugar. It's convenient to have on hand for both sauces and marinades.

8   medium ancho chiles, toasted*
8   garlic cloves, toasted*
¹/₂   teaspoon ground cinnamon
1   clove, ground (a pinch)
2   large bay leaves, ground
¹/₈   teaspoon cumin seeds, ground, or heaped ¹/₈ teaspoon ground
       cumin
¹/₄   teaspoon freshly ground black pepper
¹/₂   teaspoon dried oregano, preferably Mexican
¹/₂   teaspoon dried thyme
1¹/₂ teaspoons salt or more to taste
¹/₄   cup cider vinegar
¹/₄   cup water or more as needed

* *To toast chiles:* Wearing rubber gloves, tear the chiles into flat pieces and remove the seeds and veins. Heat a heavy skillet or comal over medium heat and toast the chiles on both sides, pressing them down with a metal spatula and turning them as soon as they sizzle and blister, in a matter of seconds. Remove from the heat at once and transfer to a bowl or plate.

Pour boiling water to cover over the toasted chiles. Weight with a plate so the chiles stay submerged. Soak for 30 minutes, then drain. Place in a blender or food processor fitted with the steel blade, with the toasted garlic.

Add the remaining ingredients. Blend the mixture until smooth, starting and stopping the blender or food processor and stirring down the sides.

Strain the paste through a medium-mesh strainer into a bowl, transfer to a jar with a tight-fitting lid, cover, and refrigerate.

PER PORTION

Calories	56	Protein	3 g
Fat	.56 g	Carbohydrate	13.3 g
Saturated Fat	.03 g	Fiber	1 g
Cholesterol	0	Sodium	558 mg

Variation

QUICK ADOBO SAUCE: Heat 1 tablespoon canola oil in a heavy saucepan over medium heat. Add a bit of the paste and, if it sizzles, add the rest (if not, wait a minute or two). Cook, stirring constantly with a long-handled spoon (the paste will sputter), for 5 to 10 minutes, until the paste is thick and dark burgundy-orange. Stir in 1 cup chicken, vegetable, or garlic stock, 1 cup fresh orange juice, and 1 tablespoon sugar. Simmer over low heat, stirring often, for 20 to 30 minutes, until thick and fragrant.

PER PORTION

Calories	109	Protein	3 g
Fat	3 g	Carbohydrate	21 g
Saturated Fat	.20 g	Fiber	1 g
Cholesterol	0	Sodium	651 mg

* To toast garlic: Heat a heavy skillet or comal over medium-high heat and toast the garlic in its skin, turning or shaking the pan often, until it smells toasty and is blackened in several places, about 10 minutes. Remove from the heat and peel.

ADOBO SAUCE

Makes a bit more than 2 cups, serving 8 as a marinade or sauce

You could call adobo sauce Mexican barbecue sauce. This recipe, based on one by Rick Bayless, is one of several I've found. Sometimes the sauce is more like a paste, to be kept indefinitely in the refrigerator and used to coat fish or chicken before grilling or cooking in corn husks. I like this one because the orange juice and sugar with the vinegar give it an appealing sweet-and-sour quality that contrasts nicely with the hot, slightly bitter chiles. This makes a wonderful marinade for meaty fish like tuna and can also be used with firm-fleshed white fish like cod, monkfish, or catfish. Traditionally it is served with pork, but it serves equally well as a marinade for chicken and turkey. A food processor can be used instead of a blender here, with good results.

8	medium ancho chiles, toasted*
2	tablespoons canola oil
$\frac{1}{2}$	medium onion, diced
3	large garlic cloves, peeled
2	to $2\frac{1}{2}$ cups chicken, vegetable, or garlic stock as needed
$\frac{1}{2}$	teaspoon ground cumin
1	bay leaf, ground in a spice mill
$\frac{1}{2}$	teaspoon dried oregano, preferably Mexican
$\frac{1}{4}$	teaspoon dried thyme
$\frac{1}{4}$	cup cider vinegar
1	cup fresh orange juice
1	tablespoon sugar
	salt to taste, $\frac{1}{2}$ to 1 teaspoon

Cover the toasted chiles with boiling water and weight with a plate so they will remain submerged. Let soak for 1 to 8 hours to draw out harshness.

Heat 1 tablespoon of the oil in a nonstick skillet over medium heat, add the onion and garlic, and cook, stirring often, until browned, about 5 to 8 minutes. Remove from the heat and place in a blender or a food processor fitted with the steel blade.

* *To toast chiles:* Wearing rubber gloves, tear the chiles into flat pieces and remove the seeds and veins. Heat a heavy skillet or comal over medium heat and toast the chiles on both sides, pressing them down with a metal spatula and turning them as soon as they sizzle and blister, in a matter of seconds. Remove from the heat at once and transfer to a bowl.

Drain the chiles, rinse with cold water, and gently squeeze out the soaking liquid, which will be bitter. Add the chiles to the blender or food processor along with ²/₃ cup of the stock. Add the ground cumin and bay leaf, the oregano, thyme, and vinegar. Blend until smooth. Strain into a bowl through a medium-mesh strainer. You should have about 1¹/₂ cups of puree.

Heat the remaining oil in a heavy saucepan over medium-high heat and add the chile paste. It should sizzle. Cook, stirring constantly with a long-handled spoon, for 5 to 8 minutes, until it is quite thick and dark and beginning to stick to the pan. Stir in 1 cup of the remaining stock and the orange juice, cover partially, reduce the heat to medium-low, and simmer for 45 minutes, stirring occasionally, until the sauce is thick like barbecue sauce and a deep red-brown color. A small film should be forming on the top by this time. Stir in the sugar and salt, adjust the seasonings, and remove from the heat. Thin as desired with the remaining stock.

Advance Preparation: This will keep for at least 2 weeks in the refrigerator and can be frozen.

PER PORTION

Calories	114	Protein	2 g
Fat	6 g	Carbohydrate	16 g
Saturated Fat	.70 g	Fiber	0
Cholesterol	0	Sodium	367 mg

CHIPOTLE SALSA

Makes 1 scant cup, serving 20

This thick, concentrated salsa appears in a much oilier version, on every table in the state of Veracruz. It is meant to be spread ever so thinly onto empanadas or trickled into soups or onto tacos. The flavor is deep and complex, and the salsa will burn your lips if you aren't careful. Make sure you wear rubber gloves when you seed the chiles.

2   ounces (about 1 cup) dried chipotle chiles, stemmed and
        toasted,* seeded and deveined
¾   to 1 cup water as needed
5   large garlic cloves, peeled
2   tablespoons canola or sunflower oil
    salt to taste

Cover the toasted chiles with boiling water. Weight with a plate so the chiles
stay submerged and let sit for 30 minutes. Drain and remove the seeds and
veins (wear rubber gloves). Transfer to a blender or a food processor with the
steel blade, and add about ¾ cup water and the garlic. Blend until smooth,
stopping and starting the blender and stirring several times. Add more water
if absolutely necessary. Strain into a bowl.

Heat the oil in a small heavy nonstick skillet or saucepan over medium-
high heat and add a little bit of the puree. If it sizzles loudly, add the rest (wait a
few minutes if it doesn't). Stir the sauce and turn the heat to medium. Cook, stirring often with a long-handled wooden spoon (it sputters a lot), until thick and
beginning to stick to the bottom of the pan, about 10 minutes. Remove from the
heat, add salt to taste, and allow to cool. Transfer to a jar and refrigerate.

Advance Preparation: This will keep for several weeks in the refrigerator.

PER PORTION

Calories	21	Protein	0
Fat	2 g	Carbohydrate	2 g
Saturated Fat	.17 g	Fiber	0
Cholesterol	0	Sodium	1 mg

* *To toast chiles:* Heat a heavy skillet or comal over medium heat and toast the chiles on
both sides, pressing them down with a metal spatula and turning them as soon as they sizzle and blister, in a matter of seconds. Remove from the heat at once and transfer to a bowl
or plate.

CREAMY CHIPOTLE DIP

Makes 1¹/₂ cups, serving 16 as a dip

In the state of Veracruz, where chipotle chiles are beloved, you will often find a sort of chipotle mayonnaise on restaurant tables, to be eaten with chips. It has a heavenly smoky hot, garlicky flavor and makes a great dip for shrimp and vegetables. It's also great on a sandwich. But my absolute favorite use for this is as a replacement for butter, with corn. See the recipe for grilled corn for a real treat.

2   **to 3 large garlic cloves to taste, peeled**
    salt to taste, about ¹/₂ teaspoon
2   **canned chipotles en adobo, rinsed and seeded**
1   **cup nonfat cottage cheese**
¹/₄ **cup plain nonfat yogurt**
¹/₄ **cup mayonnaise, Hellmann's or Best Foods or homemade**

Place the garlic cloves in a mortar and pestle with half the salt and pound and mash until the mixture is smooth. Add the chipotles and continue to pound and mash to a paste.

Place the cottage cheese in a food processor fitted with the steel blade and blend until smooth. Add the yogurt and mayonnaise and continue to blend until the mixture is very smooth. The cottage cheese should not be grainy at all. Add the garlic and chipotle paste and blend in. Taste and adjust salt. Refrigerate in a covered container until ready to use.

Advance Preparation: This will keep for a couple of days in the refrigerator, but the garlic will become more pungent and the chipotles will get hotter, so you may want to use less of both.

PER PORTION

Calories	41	Protein	2 g
Fat	3 g	Carbohydrate	2 g
Saturated Fat	.40 g	Fiber	0
Cholesterol	3 mg	Sodium	156 mg

PICKLED CHILES WITH
CARROTS, ONION, AND GARLIC

Makes about 3 cups, serving 16 to 20

Of course canned pickled chiles (chiles en escabeche) are easy to find, but these are so much better. Pickled chiles, especially jalapeños, are used frequently in Veracruz dishes. The escabeches in Veracruz are much less acidic than the ones we are used to, because a lovely mild pineapple vinegar is used there. I suggest you use rice wine vinegar—other possibilities are champagne vinegar and cider vinegar. These make a great condiment. Keep them on hand for making quick salsas.

- 1/2 **pound firm, unblemished jalapeño or serrano chiles or a mixture**
- 2 **tablespoons olive oil**
- 5 **large garlic cloves, peeled and slightly crushed**
- 1 **medium onion, thinly sliced**
- 1 **large carrot, peeled and sliced 1/4 inch thick**
- 3/4 **cup rice wine vinegar, champagne vinegar, or apple cider vinegar, plus more as needed**
  water as needed, about 3/4 cup
- 1/2 **teaspoon salt**
- 10 **peppercorns**
- 3 **cloves**
- 5 **bay leaves**
- 1 **fresh rosemary sprig**
- 1/2 **teaspoon dried oregano**

Using a toothpick, a skewer, or the tip of a sharp knife, pierce the chiles in a few places so that they absorb the marinade.

Heat the oil over medium heat in a heavy saucepan large enough to hold all the chiles. Add the garlic, onion, and carrot and cook, stirring, until the onion is tender, about 5 minutes. Add the chiles and cook, stirring, for 5 minutes, until they soften slightly. Add the vinegar and enough water to cover the chiles. Add the remaining ingredients and bring to a boil. Reduce the heat to low, cover, and simmer for 10 minutes, turning the chiles over halfway through. The chiles should be olive green at the end of the cooking time. Remove from the heat and allow to cool. Remove the rosemary.

Transfer the chiles and vegetables with their marinade to glass jars. Top up with equal parts vinegar and water if they are not submerged in the marinade. Cover and refrigerate. Wait a day or more before using.

Advance Preparation: These will keep for several weeks in the refrigerator if submerged in the marinade.

PER PORTION

Calories	31	Protein	0
Fat	2 g	Carbohydrate	4 g
Saturated Fat	.23 g	Fiber	0
Cholesterol	0	Sodium	72 mg

PICKLED CHIPOTLE CHILES

Makes 2 cups, serving about 32

These fiery-hot chipotles en escabeche make a marvelous condiment for all those who love very picante food. Even for moderate chile lovers a strip of one of these pickles in a soup, sandwich, or salad adds many dimensions of smoky picante flavor. These chiles are a must for the sensational sandwiches made in Puebla called *cemitas.*

- ¼ **pound dried chipotle chiles or moras**
- 2 **tablespoons canola or olive oil**
- 2 **large garlic cloves, thinly sliced**
- 1 **medium onion, thinly sliced**
- 1 **large carrot, thinly sliced**
- 2 **bay leaves**
- 2 **fresh oregano sprigs or ¼ teaspoon dried**
- 2 **fresh thyme sprigs or ¼ teaspoon dried**
- 1¼ **cups rice wine vinegar, apple cider vinegar, or champagne vinegar or more as needed**
- 3 **tablespoons dark brown sugar or grated piloncillo**
  salt to taste, about ¾ teaspoon
- 1 **cup water or more as needed**

Rinse the chiles if they're dusty and pat dry. Pierce in several places with the tip of a sharp knife so that they absorb the marinade.

Heat the oil over medium heat in a heavy saucepan large enough to hold all the chiles. Add the garlic, onion, and carrot and cook, stirring, until the onion is tender, about 5 minutes. Add the chiles and cook, stirring, for 5 to 8 minutes, until they soften slightly. Add the herbs, vinegar, sugar, salt, and water and bring to a boil. Reduce the heat to low, cover, and simmer for 15 minutes, stirring often. The chiles should be soft at the end of the cooking time. Remove from the heat and transfer to a nonreactive bowl. Allow to cool, cover, and refrigerate. Stir a few times every day for a few days.

Transfer the chiles and vegetables with their marinade to glass jars. Top up with 2 parts water to 1 part vinegar if they are not submerged in the marinade. Cover and refrigerate.

Advance Preparation: These will keep for several weeks in the refrigerator if submerged in the marinade.

PER PORTION

Calories	29	Protein	1 g
Fat	1 g	Carbohydrate	4 g
Saturated Fat	.17 g	Fiber	0
Cholesterol	0	Sodium	54 mg

HOMEMADE CHILE POWDER

Makes $^1/_3$ cup

Pure ground chile powder isn't as easy to find as whole dried California and New Mexico chiles. So here's a recipe for making it at home. It's *very* easy. The chiles must be toasted in a low oven to dry them out. Then they'll blend up to a nice dry, fresh-tasting powder. I buy Mojave Foods packaged dried chiles at my local supermarket for this. California chiles are mild, and New Mexico chiles are usually hot. It's nice to have both on hand.

2 ounces dried chiles, about 6 California chiles for mild or 8 New Mexico chiles for hot

Preheat the oven to 250 degrees. Brush any dust off the chiles. If you are going to make both the mild and the hot chile powder, toast each type of chile on a separate baking sheet. Place the chiles on a baking sheet and bake for 20 to 40 minutes for the California chiles, 20 to 30 minutes for the New Mexico chiles, which are thinner skinned. The chiles will begin to give off a chile aroma after about 15 minutes. They are done when they are noticeably more brittle than when you put them in the oven. They don't need to be hard when you touch them, but they do need to harden as they cool. Check them after 20 minutes, pressing on one to see how much it gives. If it is still very flexible, almost moist, bake for another 5 minutes and check every 5 minutes. Don't let them turn black, or they'll taste bitter.

Remove the chiles from the heat and allow them to cool completely on a rack.

Wearing rubber gloves, break the tops off the chiles and shake out all the seeds. Break the chiles up into small pieces and transfer, in batches, to an electric spice mill. Grind to a fine powder. Transfer to a bowl and let the powder cool completely (it is warmed by the action of the spice mill). Transfer to small jars or Ziploc bags and, if not using up quickly, store in the freezer.

Advance Preparation: The chile powder lasts several months in the freezer, but at room temperature it will lose its freshness after a few weeks.

PER PORTION (1 TEASPOON)

Calories	10	Protein	0
Fat	.55 g	Carbohydrate	2 g
Saturated Fat	.10 g	Fiber	0
Cholesterol	0	Sodium	1 mg

CHILE SALT

Makes about $^1/_3$ cup (1 standard-size spice jar)

This seasoning is nice to have on hand for sprinkling onto sliced jícama or griddle-toasted fava beans. You can vary the proportions, using less chile for a saltier chile salt and more for a stronger chile taste.

2 tablespoons fine sea salt
3 to 4 tablespoons mild or hot pure chile powder to taste

Mix the salt and chile powder together and combine well. Keep in a jar in a cool, dry place.

Advance Preparation: This will keep for a month in a cool, dry place or for several months in the refrigerator or freezer.

PER PORTION ($^1/_3$ TEASPOON)

Calories	5	Protein	0
Fat	.27 g	Carbohydrate	1 g
Saturated Fat	0	Fiber	1 g
Cholesterol	0	Sodium	568 mg

Chapter
Three

Tortillas, Breads, and Sandwiches

Corn Tortillas Made from Masa Harina
Chips Without Oil
White Sandwich Rolls (Bolillos)
String Cheese Sandwiches from Puebla (Cemitas)
Flaky Rolls from Veracruz (Pambazos)
Filled Pambazos
Mexican Beans on Toast (Molletes)
Corn Bread
Yeasted Cornmeal Pancakes

The Indians had corn and tortillas. The Spanish brought wheat, and when the French came, in the mid–nineteenth century, they brought a tradition of bread baking and pastry that has remained throughout Mexico. In addition to wonderful corn tortillas, Mexico has a tremendous variety of yeast breads. Some are simple, hard-crusted French-type breads, shaped into small rolls called *bolillos* and used for sandwiches and as table bread. There are also many, many rich egg breads, descended directly from the French brioche. These are higher-fat breads, containing quite a bit of butter or lard, so I haven't included them here. The breads made for the Day of the Dead, at the beginning of November, are especially rich and wonderful.

Sandwiches are one of the big surprises of Mexican food. Each is made on a particular bread, and the fillings vary from sandwich to sandwich. They are a far cry from the tortas of my early travels in Mexico, the ones that small children sell on buses. In Xalapa in the Veracruz highlands chicken sandwiches are served on delicious flaky rolls called *pambazos*. The typical sandwich served in bustling cafés in the city of Veracruz is like a club sandwich, filled with various meats, tomatoes, onion, and lettuce. That sandwich is called a *media-noche* because people eat them in the bars, late at night.

In Puebla—and nowhere else—there are incredible string cheese sandwiches made on crusty sesame seed rolls, called *cemitas*. They're packed with avocado, tomatoes, pickled chipotle chiles, and a magical cresslike herb called *papaloquelite*. And in Oaxaca there are molletes, a sort of Mexican version of beans on toast; but in this case it's luscious refried black beans spread onto toasted hard-crusted bolillos or the flatter hard-crusted white rolls called *teleras*.

But corn remains the main breadstuff of Mexico. Many parts of Mexico *smell* of fresh masa (dough for corn tortillas). The Indian women who arrive at the Oaxaca market from the villages before dawn, with their market wares, their hot tortillas, and their masa, smell like masa, like fresh tortillas—a clean, earthy, comforting smell that I will always associate with small local Oaxacan buses.

Corn tortillas are the building blocks for the most well-known Mexican dishes—enchiladas, tacos, quesadillas, tostadas, nachos. Happily, commercial tortillas are now easy to find in supermarkets. These are more suitable for making enchiladas than thicker homemade tortillas. But there is nothing like a fresh tortilla for eating at the table, so I urge you to try making them.

As for fried tortilla chips, you won't find them in these pages. Instead I have a recipe for microwave-toasted chips, which are crisp and have a marvelous flavor. It's worth getting a microwave oven just to be able to have these chips without oil.

I've also included some border food here, like Texas corn bread, which goes so well with Mexican food. And there's a yeast-raised cornmeal pancake that makes a delicious unique hors d'oeuvre or an accompaniment to stews.

Sadly, sliced soft white bread (as well as fast-food pizza) has been making inroads into Mexico for decades, just as it has everywhere else. It seems so strange. When I lived in Teotitlán del Valle, on Sundays Don Isaac's daughter would come to bring me lunch with a big smile on her face. "Today we have pan Bimbo," she would say, handing me a plate of expensive packaged white bread with storebought jam. I accepted it gracefully, yearning for the hot corn tortillas that I knew the family was eating for lunch.

CORN TORTILLAS MADE FROM MASA HARINA

Makes about 15 tortillas

Homemade tortillas are unbelievably good, and the packaged masa harina—the treated powdered ground corn from which they're made—is available in more and more supermarkets. The trick to making good tortillas from powdered masa harina is to have a dough that is neither too dry (or the tortillas will be dry and cracked), nor too wet (or it will be difficult to manipulate the dough). The dough should be soft without being sticky; it is often described as having the texture of soft cookie dough. You will get the knack after a few times at the tortilla press. To make homemade tortillas, you'll need a heavy griddle or cast-iron skillet, a tortilla press, and a few small Ziploc bags or 2 squares of heavy plastic, cut to fit your tortilla press. Because homemade tortillas are thicker than store-bought ones, they are not as pliable to use in enchiladas and quesadillas. Serve them hot, as an accompaniment to all Mexican dishes.

If you have access to masa dough—a local tortillería, for instance—buy some and make tortillas at home.

1³/₄   **cups masa harina**
1¹/₈   **cups hot tap water or more as needed**

In a bowl, or in a food processor fitted with the steel blade, combine the masa harina and water. Knead until smooth. Add a bit more water if the dough doesn't feel soft (though it should not be sticky); it shouldn't crumble at all. Wrap in plastic, a plastic bag, or a damp towel and let sit for 30 minutes.

Begin heating your griddle over medium heat (heat two if you have them; the process will go twice as fast). It should be hot when you put the first tortilla on it. Knead the tortilla dough for a few seconds and add a bit of water, a teaspoon at a time, if it has dried out since mixing. Divide into 15 pieces slightly smaller than a golf ball and cover with a damp towel or place again in the plastic bag.

Place a piece of plastic wrap or a Baggie on the bottom plate of your tortilla press. Place a ball of dough in the center and cover with the second piece of plastic. Gently press down with your hand, then place the plate of the tortilla press over the top. Press down gently but firmly. Open the tortilla press and turn the tortilla 180 degrees so that it will flatten out evenly, then press again. Don't press too hard, or the tortilla will be difficult to remove from the plastic. It should be about $1/16$ inch thick.

Peel the top piece of plastic away from the tortilla with a slow, even motion. Flip the tortilla onto the peeled-away piece of plastic and peel away the bottom piece. Now gently turn the tortilla on your free hand, peel away the plastic that is now on top, and gently lay the tortilla onto the hot baking surface. You should hear it start to cook, a very low sizzle. If you don't, the heat is too low; turn it to medium-high and wait a minute. Flip the tortilla over after 20 seconds, when it has loosened itself from the bottom but before the edges begin to brown or curl. Cook for 20 to 30 seconds on the other side and flip back onto the first side. It should be very lightly browned in spots, and on this third turn it should begin to puff. Cook for 20 to 30 seconds, until lightly browned in spots, and remove from the heat. Wrap in a clean kitchen towel. Make all of the tortillas in this way, stacking them in the towel as they are finished. Keep well wrapped and let the tortillas rest for 15 minutes before serving. They will finish their cooking in the towel and will become pliable. The tortillas can be kept hot in a low oven for about an hour. Wrap the towel tightly in foil and place in the oven.

TO REHEAT COLD TORTILLAS: Wrap the tortillas in a clean kitchen towel and set in a steamer above $1/2$ inch of water. Bring the water to a boil, cover, and boil for 1 minute. Remove from the heat and let stand, covered, for 15 to 20 minutes.

Advance Preparation: The fresher the better, but well wrapped these will keep for a day. Reheat cold tortillas as described.

Calories	49	Protein	1 g
Fat	.51 g	Carbohydrate	11 g
Saturated Fat	.07 g	Fiber	1 g
Cholesterol	0	Sodium	1 mg

CHIPS WITHOUT OIL

Makes 6 servings

There are two ways to make chips without oil: bake them in the oven or crisp them in the microwave. I prefer the microwave. For the same reason that microwaves aren't suitable for breads or crusts—they draw out moisture—they are perfect for making chips. The chips come out crisp rather than hard, as they can when you use the oven. However, for making dishes like chilaquiles or tortilla soups, where chips are cooked into a dish, the texture isn't quite as important. And the oven is much more convenient, since with the microwave you have to stand by and turn the chips. No matter which method you use, it's best to use thin rather than thick tortillas because the thicker tortillas make harder chips.

One thing to consider when choosing between the microwave and the oven: do you really need a clean wedge or strip for your chip? If broken or crumbled crisp tortilla pieces will suffice, then use the microwave, following the instructions for crisp whole tortillas for tostadas. The texture will be excellent, and whole tortillas are toasted quickly in the microwave.

**12   store-bought corn tortillas, cut into sixths, eighths, strips, or
        small squares
        salt, optional**

This step is optional. For best results, the tortillas should be somewhat dry. However, I've had perfectly good results without letting the tortillas dry out for an hour. Spread the tortilla pieces on a rack and leave to dry for 1 hour or more.

USING THE OVEN: Preheat the oven to 325 degrees. Place the tortilla pieces on a baking sheet and crisp and brown in the oven for 20 to 30 minutes, until light brown and crisp, shaking the baking sheet every 10 minutes. Allow to cool on a rack.

USING THE MICROWAVE: Every microwave is different, so you will have to experiment with yours. Place about 6 to 10 pieces at a time on a plate or on the plate in your microwave. Microwave for 1 minute on HIGH (100%) power. If the pieces are not crisp, turn them over and microwave for another 40 to 60 seconds. They will be moist on the bottom. If the pieces are still not crisp and are just beginning to brown, cook for another 20 to 30 seconds, until crisp. Cool on a rack or in a basket.

NOTE: Once you've tried this set of directions for microwaving you might want to experiment. The time on mine varies, depending on how many tortillas I have in it at once and how moist they were to begin with. But it always works well, whether it takes 1, 2, or 3 minutes.

Advance Preparation: If you make your chips in the microwave, the chips will hold for several hours. If you're using the chips in a soup or in chilaquiles, where they will be bathed in a liquid medium, they can be made a day ahead of time whether you toast them in the oven or in the microwave. They are always best when eaten on the day and soon after you make them, however.

Variation
CRISP WHOLE TORTILLAS FOR TOSTADAS: Use the same method. The microwave works best, and it's quick.

If a recipe calls for crumbled toasted tortillas, toast whole tortillas as directed for chips because it goes so quickly.

PER PORTION

Calories	112	Protein	2 g
Fat	1.25 g	Carbohydrate	24 g
Saturated Fat	.16 g	Fiber	2 g
Cholesterol	0	Sodium	80 mg

White Sandwich Rolls (Bolillos)

Makes twenty-four 2-ounce or sixteen 3-ounce rolls

These are as marvelous as any good French baguette. The dough is a slow-rising one, and the resulting bread has a deep, complex flavor. Unfortunately, today in Mexico bolillos are often puffed up and without character. But when they are crusty and good, they are wonderful. They make terrific sandwich rolls.

For the Starter:
- 1/4   teaspoon active dry yeast
- 1/2   cup lukewarm water
- 6   ounces (1 1/4 cups) unbleached white flour

For the Bread:
- 2   teaspoons active dry yeast
- 2   cups lukewarm water
- 1 1/2 pounds (5 cups) unbleached white flour, plus up to 2 ounces (scant 1/2 cup) for kneading
- 2   teaspoons salt

MAKE THE STARTER: The day before you bake, make the starter. Dissolve the yeast in the water in a medium bowl or in the bowl of your electric mixer. Stir in the flour with a wooden spoon or with the beater attachment of your mixer. If you're making this by hand, scrape out onto a lightly floured surface and knead until you have a uniform, slightly tacky dough. Return the dough to the bowl. If you're using an electric mixer, change to the dough hook and knead at low speed for 2 minutes, until the dough is uniform and slightly sticky. Transfer to a medium bowl. Cover the bowl tightly with plastic wrap. It helps to seal the plastic with a rubber band.

MAKE THE DOUGH: Dissolve the yeast in the water in a large bowl or in the bowl of your electric mixer. Stir in the starter and combine well.

Kneading the dough by hand: Mix together all but 1/4 pound (heaped 3/4 cup) of the flour and the salt and gradually fold into the yeast mixture. As soon as you can, scrape the dough out onto a lightly floured kneading surface. Knead, adding unbleached white flour as necessary, for 10 minutes. The dough will be sticky at first but will become very elastic, though it will remain tacky on the surface. Shape into a ball.

Kneading with an electric mixer: Mix together all but 4 ounces (heaped ³/₄ cup) of the flour and the salt and add all at once to the bowl. Mix together with the paddle, then change to the dough hook. Mix at low speed for 2 minutes, then at medium speed for 8 to 10 minutes. If the dough seems very wet and sticky, sprinkle in the remaining flour as necessary. Scrape out the dough onto a lightly floured surface and knead for a minute or so by hand. Shape into a ball.

Rinse out the bowl, dry, and brush lightly with olive or canola oil. Place the dough in the bowl, seam side up first, then seam side down. Cover with plastic wrap and set in a warm place to rise for 3 hours or longer, until the dough has nearly tripled in size.

Punch down the dough, turn it out of the bowl, and knead for a minute. Shape into a tight ball. Return to the bowl, cover again, and let rise another 2 hours, until again nearly tripled.

Turn out the dough onto a lightly floured surface and moisten your hands slightly. Divide the dough in half and shape into 2 long sausage shapes about 2 inches in diameter. Cut each sausage into 12 pieces weighing about 2 ounces each for small rolls, 8 pieces weighing 3 ounces for larger rolls. Shape each piece into a round ball by rolling it under cupped hands on your work surface or by folding the dough and pulling it under itself and pinching the bottom all the way around.

Lightly oil 2 or 3 baking sheets and sprinkle with cornmeal.

Shape the bolillos. Take a ball of dough and flatten it to an oval shape using the heel of your hand or a rolling pin. Fold one third of the dough along a long side over toward the center, as if you were folding a letter, and flatten with the heel of your hand. Now take the dough along the folded side and fold over to meet the other edge, as if you were completing the letter folding (except the edges will be curved, since you began with an oval shape), and flatten the edges together using the heel of your hand, then roll gently back and forth under the palms of your hands and pinch the ends so that the rolls taper to a point. Place the shaped bolillos, seam side up, on the baking sheets. Let rise for 1 hour while you preheat the oven to 400 degrees.

Just before baking, use a moistened razor blade to make a lengthwise slash, slightly off-center, in each bolillo. Bake in the upper part of the oven for 20 to 30 minutes, until they are golden and sound hollow when tapped. Cool on a rack.

Variations

TELERAS: These are flatter bread rolls made from the same dough as bolillos. They are like squat bolillos with one or two indentations down the middle.

Follow the instructions for bolillos up to shaping them. Flatten each piece of dough into an oval shape about ½ inch thick. Using the side of your hand or a pastry scraper, press either 1 or 2 lines down the length of the dough. Press down hard, stopping just short of cutting the dough. Gently turn the dough flat side up onto the prepared baking dishes and let rise for 1 hour, until it almost doubles. Meanwhile, preheat the oven to 400 degrees.

Flip the rolls over and bake for 20 to 30 minutes (do not slash), until they are golden and sound hollow when tapped. Cool on a rack.

CEMITAS: These are sandwiches from Puebla, made on a similar roll. For more authentic cemitas, when you shape the rolls, brush with water and sprinkle with sesame seeds, about ½ to 1 teaspoon per roll, before the final rising.

PER PORTION (2-OUNCE ROLL)

Calories	142	Protein	4 g
Fat	.73 g	Carbohydrate	29 g
Saturated Fat	.10 g	Fiber	1 g
Cholesterol	0	Sodium	184 mg

STRING CHEESE SANDWICHES FROM PUEBLA (CEMITAS)

Makes 1 sandwich

Cemitas are special sandwiches made in the city of Puebla. I'd been to that city a few times, for the mole and for the chiles en nogada, a rich stuffed chile dish, before I was introduced to this luscious sandwich. It's the crusty bread studded with sesame seeds, the pickled chipotles, and the herb called *papaloquelite* that make these so wonderful. Papaloquelite tastes like a sort of cross between watercress, cilantro, and tarragon. It looks like a cress on a long stem. Accordingly I am using a combination of these three ingredients here. Pickled chipotles make this quite hot; pickled jalapeños can be substituted, though the flavor will be different. Bolillos work perfectly; so would any good-quality crusty roll. I have reduced the amount of cheese in mine, and my avocado slices are thinner than the ones in Puebla, but the pickled chipotles and the combination of flavors taste authentic, and the sandwiches taste quite rich. My father once told me that when he was a child avocados were referred to as "poor man's butter," and indeed here the avocado is spread on the bread just like butter. I think the 2-ounce bolillo makes a good portion.

1	2- or 3-ounce good-quality hard-crusted sandwich roll, preferably one with sesame seeds, cut in half
1/4	medium-size ripe avocado, peeled and cut into very thin slivers salt to taste
1/2	ounce string cheese or part-skim mozzarella cheese, shredded (about 1/8 cup)
1	small or 2 or 3 slices of pickled chipotle chiles, canned or homemade
1	thin slice red or white onion, separated into rings and rinsed
1/4	cup watercress leaves
4	fresh cilantro sprigs, or more to taste, chopped
1/2	teaspoon chopped fresh tarragon
1/2	tomato, sliced

Spread the top and bottom halves of the roll with the avocado. Sprinkle with salt. Make a layer of half the cheese on the bottom half of the roll. Top the cheese with chile slices. Then make another layer with the remaining cheese. Layer the onion over the top.

Toss together the cress, cilantro, and tarragon and top the onions with this. Lay the tomato slices on top, sprinkle with more salt, close the sandwich with the top half of the bread, press down hard, and serve.

Advance Preparation: There's nothing much to do in advance here, except pickle the chiles, which last for weeks in the refrigerator. The sandwiches are best assembled and served right away.

PER PORTION

Calories	483	Protein	14 g
Fat	26 g	Carbohydrate	52 g
Saturated Fat	5 g	Fiber	5 g
Cholesterol	7 mg	Sodium	686 mg

FLAKY ROLLS FROM VERACRUZ (PAMBAZOS)

Makes 16 rolls

These flaky rolls are used for marvelous sandwiches of the same name that are a specialty of Xalapa in the state of Veracruz. The sandwiches are spread with beans and filled with lettuce, tomato, and shredded chicken, chorizo, or sardines, which my Mexico City restaurateur friend Carmen says is the most traditional. In Mexico the fat used in the bread is always lard, but I'm taking liberties here. The version I make with butter tastes and feels like a pambazo to me.

1	tablespoon active dry yeast
1½	cups lukewarm water
1	pound (about 3⅓ cups) unbleached white flour, plus 2 to 3 ounces (up to ½ heaped cup) for kneading and 2 to 3 ounces (½ cup) for dipping
½	teaspoon sugar
4	tablespoons vegetable shortening, lard, or softened unsalted butter
1½	teaspoons salt

MAKE THE STARTER: Dissolve 1 teaspoon of the yeast in ½ cup of the water in a medium bowl or in the bowl of your electric mixer. Stir in 1 to 1¼ cups of the flour with a wooden spoon or with the beater attachment of your mixer, enough to make a soft dough. If you're making this by hand, scrape out onto a lightly floured surface and knead until you have a uniform, slightly tacky dough. Return the dough to the bowl. If you're using an electric mixer, change to the dough hook and knead at low speed for 2 minutes, until the dough is uniform and slightly sticky. Transfer to a medium bowl. Cover the bowl tightly with plastic wrap. It helps to seal the plastic with a rubber band. Let rise for 2 hours or until doubled.

MAKE THE DOUGH: Dissolve the remaining yeast in the remaining water in a large bowl or in the bowl of your electric mixer. Stir in the starter, sugar, and shortening or butter and combine well.

Kneading the dough by hand: Mix together the remaining flour (except the flour set aside for kneading and dipping) and the salt and gradually fold into the yeast mixture. As soon as you can, scrape the dough out onto a lightly floured kneading surface. Knead, adding unbleached white flour as necessary, for 10 minutes. The dough will be sticky at first but will become very elastic, though it will remain tacky on the surface. Shape into a ball.

Kneading with an electric mixer: Mix together all the remaining flour (except the flour set aside for kneading and dipping) and the salt and add all at once to the bowl. Mix together with the paddle, then change to the dough hook. Mix at low speed for 2 minutes, then at medium speed for 8 to 10 minutes. If the dough seems very wet and sticky, sprinkle in the remaining flour as necessary. Scrape out the dough onto a lightly floured surface and knead for a minute or so by hand. Shape into a ball.

Rinse out your bowl, dry, and brush lightly with oil. Place the dough in the bowl, seam side up first, then seam side down. Cover with plastic wrap and set in a warm place to rise for 3 hours or longer, until the dough has nearly tripled in size.

Punch down the dough, turn out of the bowl, and knead for a minute. Shape into a tight ball. Return to the bowl, cover again, and let rise for another 2 hours, until again nearly tripled.

Turn out the dough onto a lightly floured surface and moisten your hands slightly. Divide the dough in half and shape into 2 long sausage shapes about 2 inches in diameter. Cut each sausage into 8 pieces. Shape each piece into a round ball by rolling them under cupped hands on your work surface or by folding the dough and pulling it under itself and pinching the bottom all the way around. Quickly dip the rounded side of each roll into the 1/2 cup flour you set aside for dipping so that the surface is lightly dusted.

Lightly oil 2 baking sheets and sprinkle with cornmeal. Set the rolls on the baking sheets and let rise for 1 hour, until doubled. Meanwhile, preheat the oven to 350 degrees.

Slash the rolls in the middle with a sharp moistened knife or razor blade, place in the oven, and bake for 20 to 30 minutes, until light brown on the surface. Remove from the heat and cool on a rack.

Advance Preparation: These will keep for about 3 days, though they get drier each day. They freeze well.

PER PORTION

Calories	173	Protein	4 g
Fat	4 g	Carbohydrate	28 g
Saturated Fat	.99 g	Fiber	1 g
Cholesterol	0	Sodium	207 mg

FILLED PAMBAZOS

Makes 1 sandwich

Pambazos are easy to throw together. These sandwiches are typically filled with chicken or chorizo, and the bread is spread with beans. Tomato and avocado complete the filling. The sardine filling is the one that my friend Carmen Ramírez Delgollado remembers from her childhood. It's also the one you are least likely to be served today in a restaurant in Xalapa or Cordova. The sardines used were always canned, says Carmen. They reflect the Spanish influence in Veracruzana cuisine. She would have had olive-oil-packed sardines, but here I'm using the water-packed variety, which is much lower in fat and has good flavor.

1	**Pambazo**
1	**heaped tablespoon pureed black beans, canned or homemade, at room temperature**
	ground cumin to taste
	salt to taste
¼	**small avocado, peeled, pitted, and thinly sliced, optional**
	about ¼ cooked chicken breast, shredded (1 ounce meat) (page 312), or 1 whole water-packed canned sardine, filleted (about ½ can)
	a few slices of pickled chipotle chile, canned or homemade, optional
1	**small leaf romaine lettuce, shredded**
½	**tomato, sliced**
	vinegar to taste

Cut the roll in half horizontally. Thin out the beans with water if necessary so that they have a spreadable consistency. Season them with cumin and salt to taste. Spread both halves of the bread with the beans. Top with the avocado, shredded chicken or sardine fillets, and sliced chiles. Add the lettuce and tomato, sprinkle with vinegar and salt, and cover with the top half of the pambazo.

Advance Preparation: All of the elements can be ready hours or a day before you assemble this, but you should serve right after assembling so that the bread doesn't fall apart.

PER PORTION (WITH CHICKEN)			
Calories	252	Protein	15 g
Fat	6 g	Carbohydrate	35 g
Saturated Fat	1 g	Fiber	3 g
Cholesterol	24 mg	Sodium	309 mg

PER PORTION (WITH SARDINE)			
Calories	481	Protein	21 g
Fat	27 g	Carbohydrate	45 g
Saturated Fat	7 g	Fiber	6 g
Cholesterol	120 mg	Sodium	521 mg

MEXICAN BEANS ON TOAST (MOLLETES)

Makes 1 sandwich

A bolillo or telera—the hard-crusted Mexican roll—is lightly toasted, slathered with refried black beans, sprinkled with cheese, and toasted. Traditional molletes are spread with oil or butter before being slathered, almost stuffed, with the beans. But I find my reduced-fat version wonderful to eat without even the cheese—or the salsa, for that matter. The beans alone and the quality of the bread make the dish.

1 **Bolillo or good-quality crusty roll, cut in half horizontally**
⅓ **cup black Refried Beans (page 193) at room temperature, moistened with some of the bean-cooking liquid**
1 **tablespoon grated medium-sharp Cheddar or Monterey Jack cheese, optional**
¼ **cup Salsa Ranchera (page 63), Salsa Fresca (page 61), or Salsa Verde Cruda (page 67), optional**

Toast the halved roll lightly in a toaster oven or in a 375-degree oven (10 minutes in the oven).

Spread both halves with the beans. Using the back of your spoon, press the beans into the bread so that they are almost stuffing the half-roll. Sprinkle on the cheese. Return to the oven or toaster oven and heat through until the cheese has melted and the beans are crusty on the surface, about 5 to 10 minutes in the oven. Serve with the salsa of your choice.

Advance Preparation: Refried beans will keep for a few days in the refrigerator, and this is a great way to use them up.

PER PORTION

Calories	299	Protein	11 g
Fat	5 g	Carbohydrate	54 g
Saturated Fat	.48 g	Fiber	7 g
Cholesterol	0	Sodium	667 mg

Variation
QUICK VERSION USING CANNED BEANS: No reason to think you can't make these without cooking and refrying beans first. Open a can of cooked black beans and coarsely puree them in a food processor with 1 teaspoon ground cumin and 1 teaspoon ground chile powder. Use as is or, if you wish, fry for 15 minutes in 2 teaspoons canola oil.

CORN BREAD

Makes 1 loaf, serving 8 to 10

This is a rich, moist corn bread with a grainy texture. It's slightly sweet and goes beautifully with hearty soups, chilies, and stews. You can also make it with blue cornmeal.

1	cup stone-ground yellow or blue cornmeal
1/2	cup whole wheat or whole wheat pastry flour
3/4	teaspoon salt
1	tablespoon baking powder
1/2	teaspoon baking soda
1	cup plain nonfat yogurt
1/2	cup skim milk

1   **tablespoon mild honey**
2   **large eggs**
2   **tablespoons unsalted butter**

Preheat the oven to 425 degrees.

Sift the cornmeal, flour, salt, baking powder, and baking soda into a large bowl. Beat together the yogurt, milk, honey, and eggs in another bowl.

Put the butter in a heavy 9-inch square baking dish, a 2-quart enameled gratin dish (such as a Le Creuset), or a 9-inch cast-iron skillet and place it in the oven for about 3 minutes, until the butter melts. Remove from the heat, brush the butter over the sides and bottom of the pan, and pour the remaining melted butter into the yogurt and egg mixture. Stir together well, then fold the liquid mixture into the dry mixture (or vice versa). Do this quickly, being careful not to overwork the batter. A few lumps are okay.

Pour the batter into the hot buttered pan, place it in the oven, and bake for 30 to 40 minutes, until the top is golden brown and a toothpick inserted in the center comes out clean. Let the loaf cool in the pan or serve it hot.

Advance Preparation: Although this is best served the day it's made, and it's so easy to throw together that it shouldn't pose a problem, it is also moist enough to keep for a day if wrapped in foil as soon as it cools.

PER PORTION

Calories	145	Protein	6 g
Fat	4 g	Carbohydrate	22 g
Saturated Fat	2 g	Fiber	1 g
Cholesterol	55 mg	Sodium	457 mg

Yeasted Cornmeal Pancakes

Makes 20 larger or 60 small pancakes,
serving 12 to 15 as an appetizer or 6 as a main dish

These rich-tasting pancakes have a grainy texture and a sweet, earthy flavor. They make a marvelous hors d'oeuvre, topped with a dollop of any number of salsas. I also serve them as an elegant bed for shredded chicken with green mole.

1	teaspoon active dry yeast
2	tablespoons lukewarm water
1/4	teaspoon sugar
1 1/8	cups lukewarm low-fat (1%) or skim milk
1/4	pound (2/3 cup) stone-ground yellow cornmeal
1/4	pound (heaped 3/4 cup) unbleached white flour
1	teaspoon salt
1/2	cup low-fat (1%) buttermilk or plain nonfat yogurt
2	large eggs, separated

Dissolve the yeast in the water in a bowl. Stir in the sugar and milk and let sit for 5 minutes.

Combine the cornmeal, flour, and salt, and gradually add to the milk. Mix together well. Stir in the buttermilk. Beat in the egg yolks. Cover with plastic wrap and let sit in a warm place for 2 hours, until the batter is quite bubbly and spongy.

Beat the egg whites to soft peaks and gently fold into the batter.

Lightly grease a heavy griddle or a heavy nonstick skillet or crêpe pan and heat over medium heat. Ladle on several small spoonfuls of batter, about 1 tablespoon per miniature pancake, 2 or 3 for larger pancakes. Hors d'oeuvre–size pancakes should be about 2 inches in diameter, main-dish pancakes 3 or 4 inches, as desired. Cook for about 1 minute for smaller pancakes, 2 for larger, until bubbles break through and you can turn the pancakes without breaking them. Using a metal spatula, turn the pancakes and brown on the other side for about 30 seconds to a minute. Transfer to a plate.

Continue to cook the pancakes in this fashion. Overlap them on the plate as you transfer them from the pan. If they are stacked, they will become too soggy. If you're not serving them right away, wrap in a kitchen towel or aluminum foil and keep warm in a 300-degree oven. If you're serving them much later, stack between pieces of wax paper or parchment and wrap in foil. Reheat for 30 minutes in a 325-degree oven.

Advance Preparation: The pancakes will keep in the refrigerator for 3 days and freeze well. Transfer directly from the freezer to a 350-degree oven and bake for 30 minutes. Unfrozen pancakes will reheat in 20 minutes in a 325-degree oven and can also be reheated for 1 minute in a microwave.

PER PORTION (LARGE PANCAKE)

Calories	64	Protein	2 g
Fat	1 g	Carbohydrate	10 g
Saturated Fat	.44 g	Fiber	0
Cholesterol	22 mg	Sodium	132 mg

Chapter *Four*

Hors d'Oeuvres and Finger Foods

Griddle-Toasted Fava Beans
Jícama Slices with Lime Juice and Chile Powder
Shrimp with Creamy Chipotle Dip
Crudités with Creamy Chipotle Dip
Tomatillo Guacamole
Nachos (Tostadas) with Tomatillo Guacamole
Shrimp and Lime Nachos (Tostadas)
Crabmeat Tostadas or Tacos
Black Bean Nachos (Tostadas)
Filled Masa Cups
Bite-Size Cornmeal Pancakes with Tomato-Corn Salsa
Mussels on the Half-Shell with Salsa Fresca
Stuffed Jalapeño Peppers
Stuffed Chipotle Chiles

No le tengan miedo al chile aunque lo vean colorado.
Don't be afraid of the chile pepper, even though it's so red.

Hors d'oeuvres that taste of Mexico are always the ones I remember from a party. They're lively, and they can be very light. Many of the recipes you'll find here are classic Mexican dishes, snacks like the black bean nachos (tostadas), the stuffed jalapeño chiles and chipotle chiles, and the picadas, little masa containers filled with salsa or black beans. I've changed some of the traditional recipes to make them low-fat. Other dishes are my own inspiration, or they're based on ideas I've picked up, mostly at cocktail parties. I had a cornmeal "blini" topped with salsa at a cocktail party in the Hamptons a few years ago, and it stuck in my mind. I've been serving green tomatillo mole on polenta or cornmeal pancakes for quite some time, because the corn and the mole go together so well. Mussels on the half-shell, tossed with a salsa or a cilantro pesto, make a surprising, delicate hors d'oeuvre. All of these awaken the taste buds without killing the appetite, and they're all easy to eat with one hand, one of my main requirements for an hors d'oeuvre.

A WORD ABOUT NACHOS: Most authorities on Mexican cooking will not even use the word *nacho* and are indignant when they see this word applied to Mexican food. What we call *nachos* are in fact *tostadas,* toasted tortilla chips with a topping. Be that as it may, *nachos* is their name in much of the United States, so that's what I use here (with *tostadas* in parentheses) so that the recipes are recognizable to readers.

GRIDDLE-TOASTED FAVA BEANS

Makes 4 servings

I was so happy when I found fava beans in the Oaxaca market. Just like the Mediterranean, I thought. And just as in the South of France, in Mexico fava beans make a popular before-meal snack. The beans are toasted on a griddle, giving them a special roasted flavor, and guests peel away the skins and eat the tasty beans, sprinkled with salt or chile salt.

2 pounds fava beans, removed from their pods
salt or Chile Salt as desired

Heat a heavy skillet or comal over medium heat. Toast the beans for 3 to 5 minutes on a side. They should brown or blacken in spots. Transfer to a bowl. The beans should be peeled and eaten as they are cooked and dipped or sprinkled with salt.

Advance Preparation: These are best warm, but I have served them an hour after toasting and had no complaints. If you wait too long, the skins will toughen and they will become difficult to peel.

PER PORTION

Calories	159	Protein	12 g
Fat	1 g	Carbohydrate	26 g
Saturated Fat	0	Fiber	0
Cholesterol	0	Sodium	110 mg

Jícama Slices with Lime Juice and Chile Powder

Makes 12 servings

These bulbous brown-skinned tubers are white and crunchy on the inside, with a texture somewhat like radish but a much sweeter flavor. Unfortunately, the jícama I've encountered lately has very little character. Good jícama has more than a crunchy texture; it should have an almost appley flavor. This is the simplest way to serve jícama—an easy hors d'oeuvre that never fails to please. Use pure chile powder like the one on page 81 for these.

> 1   **medium jícama, peeled, quartered, and sliced about ¼ inch thick**
> **juice of 2 limes**
> **ground mild red chile powder to taste**
> **salt to taste**

Arrange the jícama on a platter and douse with the lime juice. Sprinkle with chile powder and salt and serve.

Advance Preparation: The jícama can be tossed with the lime juice, chile powder, and salt in a bowl and refrigerated for several hours before arranging on a platter. Cover with plastic so the jícama doesn't dry out. Sliced jícama can also be held in a bowl of water in the refrigerator for a couple of days. For the variation, the jícama salad needs at least 2 hours and will keep for a day in the refrigerator, though it's best to add the orange on the day you are serving.

PER PORTION

Calories	12	Protein	0
Fat	.05 g	Carbohydrate	3 g
Saturated Fat	0	Fiber	0
Cholesterol	0	Sodium	2 mg

Variation

Jícama Slices Topped with Spicy Pico de Gallo: Make the jícama and orange salad in the next chapter. Add to it 2 finely chopped serrano chiles. Sprinkle the sliced jícama with salt, arrange on a platter, and top with the chopped jícama mixture. Garnish with radishes or radish roses and cilantro sprigs and serve.

PER PORTION

Calories	29	Protein	1 g
Fat	.10 g	Carbohydrate	7 g
Saturated Fat	0	Fiber	1 g
Cholesterol	0	Sodium	3 mg

SHRIMP WITH CREAMY CHIPOTLE DIP

Makes 15 to 20 appetizer servings, 8 first-course servings

When I was little, I adored shrimp dipped in Russian dressing, which in those days was simply mayonnaise with chili sauce mixed in. This is my grown-up Mexican version of the dish. Buy the shrimp already cooked (if they're not rubbery), and this will be an easy and impressive hors d'oeuvre or first course.

2   pounds medium shrimp, peeled, deveined, cooked, and chilled
1   recipe Creamy Chipotle Dip (page 78)

Arrange the shrimp on a platter with the dip in the middle and serve.

Advance Preparation: The sauce will hold for a day in the refrigerator, but the longer it keeps, the hotter and more garlicky it gets.

PER PORTION

Calories	179	Protein	23 g
Fat	8 g	Carbohydrate	5 g
Saturated Fat	1 g	Fiber	0
Cholesterol	146 mg	Sodium	448 mg

CRUDITÉS WITH CREAMY CHIPOTLE DIP

Makes 16 servings

A beautiful platter of vegetables with this smoky, picante pale pink dip is always a welcome appetizer. Choose vegetables in season—asparagus alone, accompanied by radishes or cherry tomatoes, can be enough; or you might want an assortment.

4   **pounds mixed vegetables, such as broccoli, cauliflower, asparagus, green beans, carrots, jícama, yellow squash, sweet red peppers, celery, fennel, radishes, cucumbers, cherry tomatoes**
1   **recipe Creamy Chipotle Dip (page 78)**

Break broccoli and cauliflower into florets. Steam broccoli for 5 minutes and refresh under cold water.

Trim asparagus and green beans. Steam for 5 minutes or blanch in salted boiling water for 1 minute and refresh under cold water.

Peel carrots and jícama and cut into 2-inch-long sticks or spears.

Cut yellow squash into rounds or 2-inch-long spears.

Slice red peppers lengthwise into 2-inch-long strips.

Cut celery and fennel into 2-inch-long strips.

Trim radishes and make radish roses by cutting slits just inside the red outer skin on 3 or 4 sides, cutting from the root end almost down to the stem. Put the radishes in a bowl of cold water and refrigerate. They will open up in a few hours.

Score cucumbers with a fork and slice about 1/4 inch thick or cut 2-inch-long spears.

Arrange the vegetables on a platter, with the dip in the middle or in a bowl close by, and serve.

Advance Preparation: All of the vegetables can be prepared a day ahead of time and refrigerated. Keep carrots, celery, fennel sticks, and jícama in a bowl of water for a day or two to help retain freshness. The other vegetables can be sealed in plastic bags. The dip can also be made a day ahead of time, but the garlic will be stronger and the chipotles hotter.

Calories	66	Protein	3 g
Fat	3 g	Carbohydrate	7 g
Saturated Fat	.40 g	Fiber	2 g
Cholesterol	3 mg	Sodium	182 mg

TOMATILLO GUACAMOLE

Makes about 1¹/₄ cups, serving 8 as a dip

I love this guacamole, whose single avocado makes a creamy, delectable puree. Tomatillos bring the acidity avocados need to retain their beautiful green color and to complement their creamy, luxurious flavor. Chiles and cilantro add flavor and spice. Onion is traditional, so use it if you like; I usually make the guacamole without it because I love the pure flavors of the tomatillos and avocado.

¹/₂   **pound (about 4 large) fresh tomatillos, husked and rinsed, or one 13-ounce can, drained**

1   **jalapeño or 2 to 3 serrano chiles, to taste, seeded and roughly chopped**

6   **fresh cilantro sprigs**
     salt to taste, about ¹/₂ teaspoon

¹/₂   **small white onion, chopped and rinsed, optional**

1   **small avocado**

If you're using fresh tomatillos, either roast under a broiler, following the directions on page 31, or simmer them in water to cover for 10 minutes, flipping them over halfway through, until just softened. Drain and transfer to a blender. If you're using canned tomatillos, simply place in the blender.

    Add the chile, cilantro, and salt to the blender and blend the mixture to a coarse puree. Stir in the onion.

    Cut the avocado in half, remove the pit but don't discard it, and scoop out the flesh. Mash in a bowl with a fork, bean masher, or a mortar and pestle until smooth. Add the tomatillo puree and mix. Taste and adjust salt. Transfer to a bowl and place the avocado pit in the middle. Let sit a few minutes before serving to develop the flavors. Serve with oven- or microwave-toasted tortilla chips or crudités or use for the tostadas (nachos) that follow.

Advance Preparation: This will keep for a day in the refrigerator, but the flavors will not be as vivid. It's best eaten within a few hours.

PER PORTION

Calories	28	Protein	1 g
Fat	2 g	Carbohydrate	2 g
Saturated Fat	.31 g	Fiber	0
Cholesterol	0	Sodium	138 mg

NACHOS (TOSTADAS) WITH TOMATILLO GUACAMOLE

Makes 48 nachos, serving 8

8   corn tortillas, cut into sixths and toasted*
1   recipe Tomatillo Guacamole (page 112)
⅓   cup plain nonfat yogurt
    fresh cilantro leaves for garnish

Top each chip with a slightly heaped teaspoon of the guacamole and dot with about ¼ teaspoon yogurt. Decorate with cilantro leaves, arrange on a platter, and serve.

Advance Preparation: The guacamole and chips can be made several hours before assembling the tostadas.

* *To toast tortilla chips:* To bake the chips, preheat the oven to 325 degrees. Place the tortilla pieces on a baking sheet and bake for 20 to 30 minutes, until light brown and crisp, shaking the baking sheet every 10 minutes. Allow to cool on a rack. To microwave the chips, place about 6 to 10 pieces at a time on a plate or on the plate in your microwave oven. Microwave on HIGH (100%) power for 1 minute. If the pieces are not crisp, turn them over and microwave for another 40 to 60 seconds. If they are still not crisp and are just beginning to brown, microwave for another 20 to 30 seconds until crisp. Cool on a rack or in a basket.

Calories	89	Protein	3 g
Fat	3 g	Carbohydrate	15 g
Saturated Fat	.40 g	Fiber	2 g
Cholesterol	0	Sodium	186 mg

SHRIMP AND LIME NACHOS (TOSTADAS)

Makes 4 to 6 servings

You need only a small spoonful of this zesty topping for each chip. It's a terrific appetizer or first course; the only time-consuming bit is preparing the shrimp.

1 pound medium shrimp, peeled and deveined
  zest of 1 lime, finely chopped
4 to 5 tablespoons fresh lime juice to taste
2 garlic cloves, toasted*
2 teaspoons cumin seeds
1/4 cup plain nonfat yogurt
2 serrano or 1 jalapeño chile or more to taste, seeded and chopped
1/4 cup chopped fresh cilantro
  salt and freshly ground pepper to taste
6 corn tortillas, cut into quarters or sixths and toasted*
  thin lime slices and fresh cilantro sprigs for garnish

* *To toast garlic:* Heat a heavy skillet or comal over medium-high heat and toast the garlic in its skin, turning or shaking the pan often, until it smells toasty and is blackened in several places, about 10 minutes.

* *To toast tortilla chips:* To bake the chips, preheat the oven to 325 degrees. Place the tortilla pieces on a baking sheet and bake for 20 to 30 minutes, until light brown and crisp, shaking the baking sheet every 10 minutes. Allow to cool on a rack. To microwave the chips, place about 6 to 10 pieces at a time on a plate or on the plate in your microwave oven. Microwave on HIGH (100%) power for 1 minute. If the pieces are not crisp, turn them over and microwave for another 40 to 60 seconds. If they are still not crisp and are just beginning to brown, microwave for another 20 to 30 seconds until crisp. Cool on a rack or in a basket.

Bring a large pot of water to a boil and add the shrimp and lime zest. Cook for 3 to 5 minutes, until the shrimp are pink and cooked through. Drain, chop the shrimp coarsely, and toss the shrimp and lime zest with the lime juice. Transfer to a medium bowl and set aside.

Toast the cumin seeds in the pan in which you toasted the garlic, shaking the pan, for another minute, until the seeds begin to pop and smell toasty. Remove from the heat.

Crush the cumin seeds in a mortar and pestle or in a spice mill. Peel the garlic and mash in a mortar and pestle or with a fork. Mix with the yogurt and toss with the shrimp, chiles, and cilantro. Add salt and pepper to taste.

Top the tortilla chips with the shrimp mixture, garnish with sliced lime and cilantro sprigs, and serve.

Advance Preparation: The filling will keep for several hours in the refrigerator. The chips will hold for a day.

Variation
QUICK VERSION: Buy cooked shrimp (make sure they aren't rubbery).

PER PORTION

Calories	201	Protein	22 g
Fat	3 g	Carbohydrate	22 g
Saturated Fat	.43 g	Fiber	2 g
Cholesterol	140 mg	Sodium	210 mg

CRABMEAT TOSTADAS OR TACOS

Makes 8 appetizer servings or 4 main-dish servings

Crabmeat makes a luxurious topping for tostadas and also for soft tacos. The meat of fresh crab should be so sweet and succulent that hardly any adornments are required. Of course this will go faster if you buy lump crabmeat, but then again the topping will be more expensive as well.

1	pound cooked crabmeat, from 2 large crabs
1	tablespoon olive or canola oil
½	small onion, finely chopped
3	serrano or 2 jalapeño chiles, chopped
½	pound (2 medium or 1 large) tomatoes, peeled, seeded, and finely chopped
¼	cup chopped fresh cilantro
	salt and freshly ground pepper to taste
2	tablespoons fresh lime juice or more to taste
8	corn tortillas, heated* or cut into quarters and toasted*
	fresh cilantro leaves for garnish for tostadas

Shred the crabmeat and set aside.

Heat the oil in a large nonstick skillet over medium heat and add the onion. Cook, stirring, until it begins to soften, about 3 minutes. Add the chiles and tomatoes and cook, stirring, for 5 minutes, until the tomatoes begin to cook down. Stir in the crabmeat and cilantro, add salt and pepper, and remove from the heat. Stir in the lime juice, taste, and adjust the seasoning.

* *To heat tortillas:* Wrap in aluminum foil and heat through in a 350-degree oven for 15 minutes; or heat 1 or 2 at a time in a dry nonstick skillet over medium-high heat until flexible; or wrap in a clean kitchen towel and steam for 1 minute, then let sit for 10 minutes; or wrap in wax paper or a damp towel and heat in a microwave on HIGH (100%) power for 1 minute.

* *To toast tortilla chips:* To bake the chips, preheat the oven to 325 degrees. Place the tortilla pieces on a baking sheet and bake for 20 to 30 minutes, until light brown and crisp, shaking the baking sheet every 10 minutes. Allow to cool on a rack. To microwave the chips, place about 6 to 10 pieces at a time on a plate or on the plate in your microwave oven. Microwave on HIGH (100%) power for 1 minute. If the pieces are not crisp, turn them over and microwave for another 40 to 60 seconds. If they are still not crisp and are just beginning to brown, microwave for another 20 to 30 seconds until crisp. Cool on a rack or in a basket.

For *tostadas,* top chips with the crabmeat, garnish with cilantro leaves, and serve on a platter or plates. For *soft tacos,* place 2 warm tortillas on a plate, top with the crab mixture, and serve.

Advance Preparation: The topping will keep for a day in the refrigerator, but the fresher it is, the better.

PER PORTION

Calories	277	Protein	27 g
Fat	7 g	Carbohydrate	28 g
Saturated Fat	.88 g	Fiber	4 g
Cholesterol	114 mg	Sodium	403 mg

BLACK BEAN NACHOS (TOSTADAS)

Makes 12 to 16 servings

This is one of my most popular dishes. The last time I made it, for a lunch for 15 people, I had a tray of nachos out when my guests arrived. They were scarfed up in a minute, so I continued to make them throughout the event.

Unlike typical Tex-Mex nachos, these are served as they would be in Mexico, with just a small sprinkling of Mexican crumbling cheese (or you can use feta).

You can have all the elements made well in advance, so all you need to do is assemble and serve when the time comes.

> 1   recipe black Refried Beans (page 193)
> 12   corn tortillas, cut into quarters or sixths and toasted*
> ¼   pound queso fresco or cotija, crumbled
> 1   heaped cup Salsa Fresca (page 61)

* *To toast tortilla chips:* To bake the chips, preheat the oven to 325 degrees. Place the tortilla pieces on a baking sheet and bake for 20 to 30 minutes, until light brown and crisp, shaking the baking sheet every 10 minutes. Allow to cool on a rack. To microwave the chips, place about 6 to 10 pieces at a time on a plate or on the plate in your microwave oven. Mi-

Heat the beans and thin out if necessary with some of their broth. Spread a spoonful on each tortilla wedge. Sprinkle on some cheese and dot with salsa fresca. Serve at once.

Advance Preparation: Refried beans will keep for 3 days in the refrigerator and for several months in the freezer. Keep the liquid you saved in a jar so that you can moisten the beans before reheating. The frijoles can be reheated in a nonstick pan or in a lightly oiled baking dish. Cover the dish with foil and reheat for 30 minutes in a 325-degree oven. However, if you are storing the beans in the refrigerator in a baking dish, cover first with plastic or wax paper before you cover with aluminum so that the beans don't react with the aluminum. *Remember to remove the plastic before reheating.*

PER PORTION

Calories	253	Protein	12 g
Fat	6 g	Carbohydrate	39 g
Saturated Fat	2 g	Fiber	7 g
Cholesterol	7 mg	Sodium	632 mg

Variation

QUICK VERSION USING CANNED BEANS: Use canned black beans and refry, with all of the liquid in the can, as directed. You will need four 15-ounce cans black beans (Progresso and S&W are good brands). Do not blend the beans. Fry the spices as instructed and add the beans with their liquid. Mash with a bean masher or the back of a large wooden spoon in the pan. You will need to thin out with water.

You can also use prepared salsa, but there's nothing like salsa fresca here, and it's quickly made.

---

crowave on HIGH (100%) power for 1 minute. If the pieces are not crisp, turn them over and microwave for another 40 to 60 seconds. If they are still not crisp and are just beginning to brown, microwave for another 20 to 30 seconds, until crisp. Cool on a rack or in a basket.

FILLED MASA CUPS

Makes about 2 dozen cups, serving 8

These little antojitos are called *picadas* in Veracruz, *sopes* in other parts of Mexico. In Veracruz they are usually fried quickly just before serving, but they are comal baked in other parts of Mexico, which is obviously the way I prefer them. The little ridged rounds of masa are slightly crisp on the outside and moist on the inside. In Veracruz they are a constant at the breakfast table, filled with red salsa, green salsa, or pureed black beans, then sprinkled with a bit of cheese and sometimes onion or chopped cilantro. These make marvelous hors d'oeuvres and can also be served as a first course.

To make the picadas, make a masa dough as you would for tortillas (except it's salted), then moisten the dough slightly and press out thick, small rounds that are cooked briefly on a greased skillet or comal. The main difficulty in making them is that it's essential to pinch the rim around the edge as soon as they come off the heat, or they won't be flexible enough. Even I, who have asbestos fingers, find this difficult, since they're very hot. I solve the problem by wearing plastic gloves, which insulate my fingertips just enough.

For the Dough:
- 2 cups masa harina
- 1/2 teaspoon salt
- 1 1/4 to 1 1/3 cups hot water as needed
- 2 to 4 tablespoons cold water as needed

For the Topping:
- 1 cup thick Salsa Ranchera (page 63), Salsa Verde Cruda (page 67), black Refried Beans (page 193), or some of each
- 1 to 2 ounces queso fresco, cotija, or feta, crumbled, or Parmesan, grated, 1/4 to 1/2 cup, to taste
- 1 small onion, finely chopped and rinsed, optional

Combine the masa harina, salt, and 1 1/4 cups hot water in a bowl and knead together until smooth. Add a little more hot water if the dough seems dry. You can do this in a mixer, using the paddle attachment, or in a food processor. Knead for a couple of minutes. Wrap in a plastic bag and let stand for 20 to 30 minutes. The dough should be fairly moist but should not stick to your hands.

Stir a little more water, 1 tablespoon at a time, into the dough to make it soft but not so sticky that it's hard to work with. Shape into small rounds, about 1 inch in diameter.

Heat a greased heavy griddle, skillet, or comal over medium heat. Keep the rounds of dough covered with plastic wrap or a damp kitchen towel while you press out and cook the picadas. Place a ball on a square of plastic wrap or a Ziploc bag. Cover with another piece of plastic or a bag. Press out gently, using a tortilla press or a rolling pin, to a thickness of slightly less than 1/4 inch and a diameter of about 3 inches. Lift up the bottom piece of plastic wrap with the dough on it and peel off the top piece of plastic. Place the top piece of plastic wrap on your free hand and flip the masa onto it, then gently peel off the other piece of plastic, which is now on top. Now reverse the masa round onto the hot cooking surface. Cook for 2 minutes, until the bottom just begins to brown and blister, flip over, and cook for 1 minute on the other side. The tortilla should not be cooked through. Remove from the heat and transfer to a plate or a board. Wear rubber gloves so you don't burn your fingertips, and immediately pinch the edges to form a lip, as for a mini-pizza. Return to the heat for another 2 minutes. Repeat with the remaining dough. I usually cook 3 or 4 at a time.

Top with the sauce of your choice, sprinkle with cheese and onion, and serve.

To reheat: Preheat the oven to 250 degrees. Heat the picadas for 10 minutes, whether filled or unfilled, and serve.

Advance Preparation: The picadas are best if served as they are made, since the masa tends to dry out. But they can be made a few hours before serving and reheated. The masa will keep for a day or two in the refrigerator. The salsas and beans will all keep for a few days in the refrigerator.

PER PORTION

Calories	143	Protein	4 g
Fat	3 g	Carbohydrate	26 g
Saturated Fat	1 g	Fiber	3 g
Cholesterol	4 mg	Sodium	250 mg

Bite-Size Cornmeal Pancakes with Tomato-Corn Salsa

Makes 15 appetizer servings

Topped with a spoonful of tomato-corn salsa, these grainy, earthy pancakes have a soulful southwestern taste. The pancakes freeze well, so you can make them well in advance of your party.

1	pound (4 medium or 2 large) tomatoes, finely chopped
1/2	small red onion, finely chopped
1	to 3 jalapeño or serrano chiles to taste, minced
1/4	cup chopped fresh cilantro or more to taste
1	tablespoon balsamic vinegar if tomatoes aren't sweet and in season
	salt to taste, about 1/2 teaspoon
1	ear corn, kernels removed
1	recipe Yeasted Cornmeal Pancakes (page 102), made 2 inches in diameter
1/2	cup plain nonfat yogurt
	fresh cilantro leaves and sprigs

Mix together the tomatoes, onion, chiles, cilantro, vinegar, and salt. Steam the corn kernels for about 5 minutes, until barely tender and quite juicy. Remove from the heat, refresh under cold water, and stir into the tomato mixture. Taste and adjust seasonings.

Warm the pancakes and transfer to a plate or platter. Top with a teaspoon of salsa, then a dot of yogurt. Garnish with leaves and sprigs of cilantro and serve.

Advance Preparation: The pancakes will keep in the refrigerator for 3 days and freeze well. Transfer directly from the freezer to a 350-degree oven and heat through for 30 minutes. The salsa will hold for several hours, in or out of the refrigerator.

PER PORTION

Calories	101	Protein	4 g
Fat	2 g	Carbohydrate	17 g
Saturated Fat	.49 g	Fiber	1 g
Cholesterol	30 mg	Sodium	241 mg

Variation

BITE-SIZE CORNMEAL PANCAKES WITH GREEN TOMATILLO MOLE: This is one of my favorite hors d'oeuvres. I serve it even when the rest of my meal isn't Mexican. It's worth keeping a batch of the little pancakes and the sauce in the freezer, just so you can throw this together. Make the pancakes as directed. Make half of the recipe (or a whole recipe and freeze half) of the green tomatillo mole. Warm the pancakes, transfer to a platter, and top with a teaspoonful of the mole on page 70. Place about ¹/₂ teaspoon yogurt on top of the mole and decorate the top with a leaf of fresh cilantro. Decorate the platter with cilantro sprigs and radishes and serve.

Advance Preparation: The pancakes will keep for a couple of days in the refrigerator, as will the sauce. Both the pancakes and the sauce freeze well, for several months. When you thaw the sauce, you will have to whisk it to recover its texture.

PER PORTION

Calories	112	Protein	4 g
Fat	3 g	Carbohydrate	17 g
Saturated Fat	.57 g	Fiber	1 g
Cholesterol	30 mg	Sodium	258 mg

MUSSELS ON THE HALF-SHELL WITH SALSA FRESCA

Makes 10 servings

These zesty mussels make a delightful, refreshing appetizer; tip them from the shell into your mouth and have a sip of margarita.

For the Mussels:
- 2 pounds mussels
- 2 tablespoons salt or vinegar
- 1 cup dry white wine
- 1 cup water
- 2 shallots or 1 onion, chopped
- 2 garlic cloves, crushed

For the Salsa:

1   pound (4 medium or 2 large) tomatoes, chopped

¼   small red onion, minced and rinsed

1   to 3 jalapeño or serrano chiles to taste, seeded for a milder salsa
      and minced

¼   cup chopped fresh cilantro or more to taste

1   tablespoon balsamic vinegar or fresh lime juice, optional
      salt to taste
      fresh cilantro sprigs for garnish

First clean the mussels. Scrub them with a small brush or toothbrush and pull out their beards. Discard any with cracked or open shells. Place in a bowl and rinse in several changes of cold water. Then cover with cold water and stir in the salt or vinegar. Let sit for 15 minutes. Drain, rinse, and soak again for 15 minutes. Drain and rinse.

Combine the wine, water, shallots, and garlic in a large pot and bring to a boil. Add the mussels, cover, and steam for 5 minutes, shaking the pot or stirring halfway through to redistribute the mussels. (You may have to do this in 2 batches; remove the first batch of mussels when the shells open, leaving the cooking liquid, and repeat with the second batch.) When you have cooked all the mussels, remove the pot from the heat, but do not drain.

Remove the mussels from their shells and set the shells aside. Discard any mussels that haven't opened. Rinse the mussels quickly to remove any lingering sand. Strain the cooking liquid through a cheesecloth-lined strainer and measure out ½ cup.

Toss together the salsa ingredients and stir in ½ cup of the reserved strained cooking liquid. Toss the mussels with this mixture, cover, and refrigerate for 1 hour or longer.

To serve, place mussels on half-shells and spoon on some sauce. Arrange on a platter and garnish with cilantro.

PER PORTION

Calories	48	Protein	4 g
Fat	.72 g	Carbohydrate	4 g
Saturated Fat	.13 g	Fiber	1 g
Cholesterol	7 mg	Sodium	81 mg

Variation
MUSSELS ON THE HALF-SHELL WITH CILANTRO PESTO

For the Pesto:
- 2   large garlic cloves, peeled
- 2   cups fresh cilantro leaves, tightly packed
- 1   cup fresh basil leaves, tightly packed
-     salt
- 2   tablespoons olive oil
- 1/2 cup strained cooking water from the mussels
- 2   tablespoons freshly grated Parmesan cheese
-     fresh cilantro sprigs and lemon or lime wedges for garnish

Prepare the mussels as directed.

Make the pesto. Turn on a food processor fitted with the steel blade and drop in the garlic cloves. When chopped (they will adhere to the sides of the bowl), stop the machine, stir down the sides, and add the cilantro, basil leaves, and about 1/4 teaspoon salt. Turn on the machine and chop the herbs. Stop the machine and stir down the sides of the bowl. With the machine running, add the olive oil and the cooking liquid from the mussels. Keep the machine running until you have a bright green puree. Add the cheese. Taste and adjust the salt.

In a large bowl, toss together the pesto with the mussels. If the pesto seems thick, thin it out with some more of the cooking broth from the mussels. Cover and refrigerate for 1 hour or longer.

To serve, place mussels on half-shells and spoon on some sauce. Arrange on a platter and garnish with cilantro and lemon or lime wedges.

Advance Preparation: The cooked mussels can be refrigerated in the marinade, both the salsa fresca and the cilantro pesto, for up to a day.

PER PORTION

Calories	72	Protein	4 g
Fat	4 g	Carbohydrate	3 g
Saturated Fat	.70 g	Fiber	0
Cholesterol	8 mg	Sodium	101 mg

STUFFED JALAPEÑO PEPPERS

*Makes 30 stuffed jalapeños, serving 8 to 10 as an appetizer or
first course, 6 as a main dish*

This version of chiles rellenos, with its marvelous sweet and savory filling,
comes from the state of Veracruz. The Spanish overtones in Veracruz cooking
are evident here, with the olives, olive oil, and almonds. The plantain reflects
the Caribbean influence. Boiling the jalapeños with sugar and coffee works to
extract their searing heat. But their nice flavor and just a bit of picante remains.
Don't prepare the chiles without wearing rubber gloves.

30	jalapeño chiles
1	quart water
1	tablespoon ground coffee
3	tablespoons sugar
¼	cup olive oil
2	medium onions, 1 chopped, 1 thinly sliced
2	large garlic cloves, minced or pressed
½	pound plum tomatoes, peeled, seeded, and chopped
	salt to taste
2	tablespoons chopped fresh parsley
2	tablespoons chopped almonds
1	ripe plantain, peeled and chopped
2	tablespoons chopped pitted green olives
1	small whole chicken breast, skinned, boned, cooked, and finely chopped,* or one 6-ounce can water-packed tuna, drained
2	tablespoons dry sherry
3	tablespoons cider vinegar
3	tablespoons water
2	large carrots, thinly sliced
4	bay leaves
10	peppercorns

* *To cook skinned and boned chicken breasts:* Place 1 quartered onion, 2 garlic cloves, and 5
cups of water in a saucepan and bring to a boil. Add 1 teaspoon salt and the chicken breasts
and bring back to a boil. Skim off any foam that rises, reduce the heat, cover partially, and
simmer for 12 to 15 minutes, until the meat is cooked through. Remove from the heat and
allow the chicken to cool in the broth if there is time.

Put on a pair of rubber gloves. Cut down the center of each chile, then across the top, so that you have cut a T that has a broad enough top stroke to allow you to open up the chile. Carefully open up the chiles and remove the seeds and veins.

Combine the water, coffee, and sugar and bring to a boil. Add the chiles and boil for 15 minutes. Remove from the heat, drain, and rinse the chiles. Cover again with water and leave in the water for 4 to 8 hours, changing the water several times if possible. Drain. Don't soak longer than 8 hours, or the chiles will become too water-logged. Pat the chiles dry and lightly salt the insides.

Heat 1 tablespoon of the oil in a heavy skillet over medium heat and add the onion. Cook, stirring, until just about tender, about 5 minutes. Add the garlic and cook, stirring, for another minute, until the garlic begins to color. Add the tomatoes, salt, parsley, almonds, plantain, and olives. Cook, stirring from time to time, for 10 minutes, until the mixture has cooked down and is fragrant. Stir in the chicken or tuna and sherry and remove from the heat. Taste and adjust the seasoning.

Fill the jalapeños with the chicken or tuna mixture and transfer to a platter.

Combine the remaining olive oil and the rest of the ingredients in a saucepan and bring to a simmer. Simmer over low heat for 10 minutes. Remove from the heat and allow to cool. Add salt to taste. Pour over the stuffed chiles. Cover and place in the refrigerator to chill. Serve the chiles cold. If serving as a main dish, accompany with rice and refried black beans.

Advance Preparation: The chiles need to be prepared at least 4 hours ahead of time. The filling will keep for a day in the refrigerator. The stuffed chiles will keep for a couple of days in the refrigerator.

PER PORTION

Calories	191	Protein	8 g
Fat	9 g	Carbohydrate	21 g
Saturated Fat	1 g	Fiber	3 g
Cholesterol	14 mg	Sodium	81 mg

Variation: Fill the jalapeños with the Shredded Shark or Mahimahi Salpicón from Veracruz on page 302.

STUFFED CHIPOTLE CHILES

Makes 36 stuffed chipotles, serving 12 to 18

This incendiary dish comes from the region of Xalapa in the state of Veracruz, where the chipotle chile, which is a smoke-dried jalapeño, reigns. Boiling the chipotles with sugar draws out some of their heat, but they remain fiery
hot, even with further soaking. They are not for the fainthearted, although the
filling itself is mild. The smoky flavor of the chile is marvelous against the
sweet and savory filling. Traditionally the chiles would be dipped in batter and
fried. To make a lower-fat dish, I spread a mixture of beaten egg whites and
yolks over the peppers and bake them so that they have a soufflélike topping
rather than a crisp batter coating. I like them this way. But the stuffed chiles
are also delicious with no batter at all. Do not attempt this recipe without
wearing rubber gloves when you prepare the chiles.

36	good-size (about $1/4$ pound) dried chipotle chiles
2	quarts water
3	tablespoons sugar
1	tablespoon olive oil
1	medium onion, chopped
2	large garlic cloves, minced or pressed
$1/2$	pound (3 medium) plum tomatoes, peeled, seeded, and chopped
	salt to taste
2	tablespoons chopped fresh parsley
1	ripe plantain, peeled and chopped
2	tablespoons chopped pitted green olives
$1/4$	cup raisins
1	teaspoon chopped fresh rosemary or $1/2$ teaspoon crumbled dried
$1/2$	teaspoon dried oregano, preferably Mexican
1	whole medium chicken breast, skinned, boned, cooked,* and finely chopped, or one 6-ounce can water-packed tuna, drained
2	tablespoons dry Spanish sherry
2	tablespoons all-purpose flour, sifted (omit if not using batter)
3	large eggs, separated, plus 1 egg white, optional

* *To cook skinned and boned chicken breasts:* Place 1 quartered onion, 2 garlic cloves, and
5 cups of water in a saucepan and bring to a boil. Add 1 teaspoon salt and the chicken
breasts and bring back to a boil. Skim off any foam that rises, reduce the heat, cover par-

Rinse the chiles and combine with the water and sugar in a large saucepan. Bring to a boil and boil for 15 minutes. Drain and rinse well. Cover with water and soak for 4 to 8 hours, changing the soaking water several times. Pour off the water and drain the chipotles on paper towels.

Put on a pair of rubber gloves. Make a slit down the middle of each chile and cut another slit across the top to form a T. Carefully remove the seeds. Set aside.

Heat the oil in a heavy skillet over medium heat and add the onion. Cook, stirring, until just about tender, about 5 minutes. Add the garlic and cook, stirring, for another minute, until the garlic begins to color. Add the tomatoes, salt, parsley, plantain, olives, raisins, rosemary, and oregano. Cook, stirring from time to time, for 10 minutes, until the mixture has cooked down and is fragrant. Stir in the chicken or tuna and sherry, cook together for a minute, and remove from the heat. Taste and adjust the seasoning.

Preheat the oven to 400 degrees. Oil a gratin dish or baking dish large enough to hold all the chiles so that they're not squeezed together too tightly.

Lightly salt the inside of the chiles. Place a heaped spoonful or two of the filling in the chiles and pull the sides together. They should be packed as full as you can get them. If you're using the batter, sprinkle the flour on a plate and gently roll the chiles in it so they're lightly coated. Place the chiles side by side in the baking dish.

If you're using the batter, beat the egg whites until they form stiff but not dry peaks. Beat the yolks and stir in about a quarter of the egg whites. Gently fold in the remaining whites. Carefully spread this mixture over the chiles.

Bake for 10 minutes without batter, 15 minutes with batter, until the top is browned. Serve right away if battered. Serve hot or at room temperature if unbattered.

Advance Preparation: The filling will keep for a day or two in the refrigerator. The chiles, filled but not topped with the egg mixture, will also keep for a day or two in the refrigerator.

PER PORTION (WITH BATTER)

Calories	102	Protein	7 g
Fat	3 g	Carbohydrate	12 g
Saturated Fat	.61 g	Fiber	1 g
Cholesterol	65 mg	Sodium	71 mg

tially, and simmer for 12 to 15 minutes, until the meat is cooked through. Remove from the heat and allow the chicken to cool in the broth if there is time.

PER PORTION (WITHOUT BATTER)

Calories	78	Protein	5 g
Fat	2 g	Carbohydrate	10 g
Saturated Fat	.23 g	Fiber	1 g
Cholesterol	11 mg	Sodium	51 mg

Variation: Fill the chipotles with the Shredded Shark or Mahimahi Salpicón from Veracruz on page 302.

Chapter
Five

Salads

Mixed Greens Salad with Sweet Potatoes and Crumbly Cheese
Nasturtium and Watercress Salad
Baby Lettuces with Lime and Balsamic Vinaigrette
Green Bean Salad
Cactus, Avocado, and Tomato Salad
Vinegared Oyster Mushrooms with Onions, Carrots, and Chiles
Chicken Salad with Chipotle Chiles
Pickled Vegetables
Crusty Hard Bread with Pickled Vegetables (Pedrazos)
Jícama and Orange Salad (Pico de Gallo)
Black Bean Salad
Corn and Potato Salad with Tomatillo Dressing
Rice Salad with Roasted Poblanos and Cumin Vinaigrette
Spinach Salad with Lime-Marinated Fish
Vinegar-Bathed Shrimp

When I lived in France, I was always amused by the salade mexicaine that was widespread in cafés and delis. It had canned corn in it; no Mexican flavors, but because of the corn it was deemed Mexican.

In Mexico I've never seen a salad with corn in it, though I've developed a delicious one for this book, a luscious mixture of corn and potatoes tossed with a tomatillo dressing. In fact, salad doesn't have a big place in the Mexican repertoire. The salads that I have seen are often made with cooked vegetables rather than raw. Since shredded lettuce or whole lettuce leaves, radishes, sliced carrots, raw onions, and uncooked tomato salsas are served with so many traditional Mexican dishes, perhaps there's no real need.

In any case, when I'm in Mexico I'm reluctant to eat the lettuce. So I crave a salad when I get back from my trips. There are wonderful ways to include a salad in a Mexican meal or make a meal out of a salad with Mexican flavors, however untraditional these ideas may be.

Although many of the recipes here are my own invention, some are authentic. The vinegared mushrooms and the vinegar-bathed shrimp are among the most delicious dishes I tasted in Veracruz. The cactus, avocado, and tomato salad is one I was served in a home in a Oaxaca village. The pickled vegetables are one of the most common table snacks in Mexico; I like to serve them as a gorgeous salad, piled onto a colorful platter. In Oaxaca, hard bread is sold to be topped with the pickled vegetables; called *pedrazos,* this is a luscious combination that reminds me of the bread salads of the Mediterranean or of the Provençal pan bagnat because of the way the bread is bathed with the vinegar.

The vinegars used in Mexico are much milder and sweeter than the wine vinegars we are used to. They are made from fruit, such as pineapple. When I drove through the state of Veracruz, I was intrigued by the bottles of vinegar hanging from the roadside pineapple stands, used in the mild fish and vegetable escabeches of the region. I've tried to achieve a similar flavor here using rice wine vinegar, which is also quite mild and a bit sweet.

Serve these recipes as starters or plan a light meal around them. Light salads like baby lettuces with lime and balsamic vinaigrette are meant to accompany more substantial dishes. But high-protein salads like the chicken salad with chipotle chiles, the black bean salad, or the vinegar-bathed shrimp make an excellent supper or lunch.

MIXED GREENS SALAD WITH
SWEET POTATOES AND CRUMBLY CHEESE

Makes 4 servings

I love the contrasts here—the sweet potatoes against salty, earthy cheese; the smooth potatoes and cheese against the fresh salad greens.

$3/4$ pound (2 small to medium) sweet potatoes, peeled and cut into $1/4$- to $1/2$-inch dice
1   tablespoon olive oil
1   tablespoon fresh lime juice
1   tablespoon balsamic vinegar
1   small garlic clove, minced or pressed
$1/2$ teaspoon Dijon mustard
      salt and freshly ground pepper to taste
$1/4$ cup low-fat (1%) buttermilk
6   ounces (5 cups) mixed baby salad greens
2   ounces queso fresco, cotija, or feta cheese, crumbled (about scant $1/2$ cup)

Steam the sweet potatoes for 5 minutes, until just tender. Remove from the heat and drain on a kitchen towel or on paper towels.

Heat 2 teaspoons of the olive oil in a medium nonstick skillet over medium heat. Add the sweet potatoes and cook, shaking the pan often, for 15 minutes, until the potatoes are browned. Remove from the heat and drain the potatoes on paper towels. Transfer to a bowl and toss with the lime juice.

Mix together the vinegar, garlic, mustard, salt, pepper, remaining olive oil, and buttermilk. Taste and adjust the seasoning.

Place the salad greens and cheese in a salad bowl and toss with the dressing. Top the salad with the sweet potatoes and serve.

Advance Preparation: The sweet potatoes can be prepared a day ahead of time, and the dressing will hold for a few hours, in or out of the refrigerator.

Calories	158	Protein	5 g
Fat	7 g	Carbohydrate	18 g
Saturated Fat	3 g	Fiber	3 g
Cholesterol	11 mg	Sodium	164 mg

NASTURTIUM AND WATERCRESS SALAD

Makes 4 servings

The idea for this salad comes from Mexico City restaurateur Carmen Ramírez Delgollado. It looks like a garden and tastes like one too.

1   cup (about 20) nasturtium flowers, quickly rinsed
1   large or 2 small bunches watercress, trimmed (4 cups leaves)
2   tablespoons slivered fresh mint leaves
1   tablespoon rice wine vinegar or champagne vinegar
¼   cup fresh orange juice
1   small garlic clove, minced or pressed
    salt and freshly ground pepper to taste
2   tablespoons canola or olive oil or 1 tablespoon oil and
        1 tablespoon plain nonfat yogurt

Combine the nasturtium flowers, watercress, and mint leaves in an attractive salad bowl.

Mix together the vinegar, orange juice, garlic, salt, pepper, and oil. Toss with the salad just before serving.

Advance Preparation: The watercress can be trimmed, washed, and dried hours before assembling the salad. Refrigerate in a plastic bag. The rest should be done quite close to serving time.

PER PORTION

Calories	75	Protein	1 g
Fat	7 g	Carbohydrate	3 g
Saturated Fat	.49 g	Fiber	1 g
Cholesterol	0	Sodium	15 mg

BABY LETTUCES WITH
LIME AND BALSAMIC VINAIGRETTE

Makes 6 servings

I like to serve a salad with most meals, and if they're full of complex flavors, as many of the dishes in this book are, the salad should be very clean and simple, like this one. You won't find pronounced Mexican flavors here, just a delightful salad that fits perfectly into a Mexican menu when a bit of salad is desired. The salad dressing looks like a small amount for so many greens, but baby salad greens are quite delicate and can easily be drowned by too much dressing.

¹/₂　pound (about 6 cups) tender young salad greens such as baby
　　　　spinach, oak leaf, arugula, dandelion greens, radicchio, Bibb
　　　　lettuce, and frisée
1　red or yellow bell pepper, cut into thin strips, optional

For the Dressing:
1　tablespoon fresh lime juice
1　tablespoon balsamic vinegar
1　small garlic clove, minced or pressed
　　salt and freshly ground pepper to taste
¹/₂　teaspoon Dijon mustard
¹/₄　cup olive oil

Toss together the lettuces and pepper strips.

Mix together the lime juice, vinegar, garlic, salt, pepper, and mustard. Whisk in the olive oil. Toss with the salad just before serving.

Advance Preparation: The dressing can be mixed, the lettuces washed, and the pepper sliced hours before serving. Wrap the lettuce in a clean kitchen towel, seal in a plastic bag, and refrigerate until ready to toss, which should be just before serving.

PER PORTION

Calories	89	Protein	1 g
Fat	9 g	Carbohydrate	2 g
Saturated Fat	1 g	Fiber	1 g
Cholesterol	0	Sodium	27 mg

GREEN BEAN SALAD

Makes 4 servings

This gorgeous salad has a perfect balance of tart and picante flavors. It's a salad for summer, when beautiful freshly harvested green beans hit the markets. Use a combination of green and yellow beans for even more color. Be careful not to overcook the beans; you want them to be crunchy.

1	pound green beans or a combination of green and yellow beans, trimmed and broken into 1-inch lengths (about 4 cups)
2	to 4 tablespoons finely chopped red or white onion to taste, rinsed if desired
1/2	pound (2 medium or 1 large) tomatoes, finely chopped
1/2	to 1 ripe red serrano chile to taste, seeded and sliced
1/4	cup chopped fresh cilantro
1/4	teaspoon dried oregano, preferably Mexican
3	tablespoons fresh lime juice
2	tablespoons olive oil
	salt to taste
2	large hard-cooked egg whites, finely chopped, for garnish

Steam the beans until crisp-tender, about 5 minutes. Remove from the heat and refresh under cold water. Toss with the remaining ingredients except the egg whites. Chill until ready to serve, or serve at room temperature. Sprinkle the egg whites over the top shortly before serving.

Advance Preparation: The salad will actually benefit from marinating for 15 to 30 minutes, but no longer than that or the color of the beans will fade. The beans can be prepared and steamed and the remaining vegetables, chiles, and herbs added to them, without tossing, hours before serving. Toss with the lime juice and olive oil and sprinkle on the egg whites up to 30 minutes before serving.

PER PORTION

Calories	118	Protein	4 g
Fat	7 g	Carbohydrate	12 g
Saturated Fat	1 g	Fiber	3 g
Cholesterol	0	Sodium	40 mg

CACTUS, AVOCADO, AND TOMATO SALAD

Makes 4 to 6 servings

I was served this gorgeous salad in the home of the Oaxacan painter Rudolfo Murales, one sunny morning in March. We were greeted in the Oaxacan fashion, with small copitas of mezcal, then invited to a beautiful table in the courtyard, where we were served a delicious almuerzo of black bean tamales, yellow mole quesadillas, and this salad. The beautiful red, white, and green salad is so rich-tasting that it's difficult to believe there isn't more of a dressing. The lime juice combines with the natural juices of the vegetables so that they speak for themselves, with the addition of heaps of cilantro for seasoning. Preparing the cactus paddles goes very quickly indeed, and they lose all their okralike slime when you cook them for 15 minutes in heavily salted boiling water to which you've added a bit of baking soda.

1	pound (3 large) cactus paddles
	salt to taste
1/4	teaspoon baking soda
1	medium Hass avocado
1	pound (4 medium or 2 large) tomatoes, chopped and rinsed
1	medium white or 1/2 torpedo onion, chopped and rinsed
1/2	cup chopped fresh cilantro, tightly packed
5	tablespoons fresh lime juice

Clean the cactus paddles. Carefully hold the end where the paddle has been cut from the plant, watching out for spines, and, using a sharp paring knife, trim off the outer edge of the paddle. Using a potato peeler or a sharp knife, scrape off all of the spiny nodes. Cut into 1/2-inch dice.

Bring a large pot of water to a rolling boil and add a tablespoon of salt and 1/4 teaspoon baking soda. Add the diced cactus and boil, uncovered, until tender, about 15 minutes. Drain.

Halve the avocado, pit, peel, and cut into 1/2-inch dice. Toss with the cactus, tomatoes, onion, and cilantro. Season generously with salt (about 1/2 teaspoon) and lime juice and serve.

Advance Preparation: This will hold for an hour or two in the refrigerator.

PER PORTION

Calories	139	Protein	5 g
Fat	5 g	Carbohydrate	22 g
Saturated Fat	.84 g	Fiber	7 g
Cholesterol	0	Sodium	301 mg

Variations

MORE AVOCADO: This is, obviously, higher in fat but more like the one we ate in Oaxaca. Add another avocado and proceed as directed.

CACTUS, AVOCADO, AND TOMATO SALSA: Chop the vegetables into ¼-inch or smaller dice. Add 2 to 3 serrano or jalapeño chiles, minced, and proceed as directed.

VINEGARED OYSTER MUSHROOMS WITH ONIONS, CARROTS, AND CHILES

Makes 6 to 8 servings

These picante mushrooms aren't quite pickled, but they are not what we think of as a vinaigrette either. They make a nice starter, alone or piled onto salad greens. They also make a delicious accompaniment to grilled chicken or fish.

     leaves from 2 fresh rosemary sprigs
     leaves from 2 fresh oregano or marjoram sprigs
½   teaspoon ground cumin
¼   teaspoon freshly ground black pepper
1   small or ½ large head of garlic, cloves separated and peeled
½   teaspoon salt or more to taste
5   tablespoons rice wine vinegar, apple cider vinegar, or champagne vinegar
2   tablespoons olive oil
2   medium onions, sliced and separated into rings
2   large carrots, thinly sliced
2   jalapeño chiles, seeded and sliced
2   pounds fresh oyster mushrooms
4   bay leaves
2   tablespoons chopped fresh parsley for garnish

Pound together the herbs, spices, and garlic with $1/4$ teaspoon salt in a mortar and pestle. (You can use a food processor for this, but the ingredients will be chopped rather than a paste, and the mixture won't be as pungent.) Add a tablespoon of the vinegar and combine well.

Heat the olive oil in a large heavy nonstick skillet over medium-low heat and add the onions and carrots. Cook, stirring, until tender, about 5 to 8 minutes. Add the garlic paste and chiles and cook, stirring, for another minute or two, until the garlic begins to color. Add the mushrooms and turn the heat to medium. Stir until the mushrooms begin to release their liquid. Add the remaining vinegar, remaining salt, and the bay leaves. Turn the heat to low and simmer, stirring from time to time, for 15 minutes, until the mushrooms have cooked down and the mixture is fragrant. Taste and adjust the salt. Remove from the heat.

Transfer to a serving bowl and allow to cool completely. Stir to redistribute the juices, sprinkle with parsley, and serve.

Advance Preparation: These will keep in the refrigerator for a week.

PER PORTION

Calories	135	Protein	6 g
Fat	5 g	Carbohydrate	20 g
Saturated Fat	.71 g	Fiber	4 g
Cholesterol	0	Sodium	205 mg

CHICKEN SALAD WITH CHIPOTLE CHILES

Makes 4 servings

This lively salad makes a terrific main dish. It's also delicious as a topping for warm tortillas or tostadas.

For the Chicken:

- 7 cups water
- 1 medium onion, $1/2$ quartered, $1/2$ chopped and rinsed if desired
- 4 garlic cloves, peeled and crushed
- 1 teaspoon salt
- 1 medium chicken, quartered and skinned

$^1/_2$ teaspoon dried thyme
$^1/_2$ teaspoon dried oregano, preferably Mexican
 2 bay leaves
 4 large radishes, chopped
$^1/_2$ cup chopped fresh cilantro
 1 serrano chile, minced, optional

For the Dressing:
 2 tablespoons fresh lime juice
 3 tablespoons cider vinegar
 1 garlic clove, minced or pressed
$^1/_2$ teaspoon ground cumin
$^1/_4$ teaspoon salt or more to taste
    freshly ground pepper to taste
$^1/_3$ cup chicken stock
$^1/_4$ cup plain nonfat yogurt
 2 tablespoons olive oil

For Garnish:
 8 romaine lettuce leaves, cut crosswise into wide strips
 4 large radishes, thinly sliced
 3 canned or pickled chipotle chiles, cut in half, seeded, then
        quartered
 2 or 3 tomatoes, cut into wedges

In a 4-quart pot, combine the water, quartered onion, and crushed garlic and bring to a boil. Add the salt and the dark meat quarters of the chicken. Skim off any foam that rises and add the herbs. Reduce the heat to medium, cover partially, and simmer for 10 minutes. Add the white meat quarters, skim off any foam that rises once the water comes back to a boil, cover partially, and simmer for 15 minutes or until all the meat is tender. Remove the pot from the heat, uncover, and let the chicken cool in the broth. Remove the meat from the bones and shred. Strain the broth through a cheesecloth-lined strainer, set aside $^1/_3$ cup, and reserve the rest for another use.

Combine the chicken, chopped onion, chopped radishes, cilantro, and serrano in a bowl. Salt lightly.

Mix together the lime juice, vinegar, garlic, cumin, salt, and pepper. Stir in the chicken stock, yogurt, and oil. Combine well, taste, and adjust the seasonings. Toss two thirds of the dressing with the chicken.

Toss the lettuce with 2 tablespoons of the dressing and make a layer on the bottom of a wide bowl or on a platter. Top with the chicken. Sprinkle on the sliced radishes. Surround or dot the chicken with the chipotle quarters and tomato wedges. Stir the remaining dressing, pour it on, and serve.

NOTE: For a higher-fat version, add 1 small avocado, thinly sliced or diced. Diced, it can be tossed with the chicken. Sliced, it should garnish the chicken, surrounding it or topping it, with the dressing poured over.

Advance Preparation: The shredded cooked chicken will keep for 3 days in the refrigerator. The completed salad is best served shortly after it is tossed with the dressing.

PER PORTION

Calories	339	Protein	38 g
Fat	17 g	Carbohydrate	10 g
Saturated Fat	4 g	Fiber	2 g
Cholesterol	108 mg	Sodium	573 mg

PICKLED VEGETABLES

Makes about 4 cups, serving 8 as an appetizer

In addition to pickled chiles, delicious pickled vegetables are common throughout Mexico. They adorn tables in cafeterias, they're sold in markets, and in Oaxaca they're used for a scrumptious combination called *pedrazos,* hard bread bathed with the pickled vegetables. They can just as easily serve as a snack, a condiment, or a salad. As in many other recipes, I use rice wine vinegar (second choice: mild champagne vinegar) to approximate the flavor of the fruit vinegars often used in Mexico.

- 4 **jalapeño or serrano chiles or a mixture**
- 2 **tablespoons olive oil**
- 10 **large garlic cloves, peeled and slightly crushed**
- 2 **medium onions, thinly sliced**
- 2 **large carrots, sliced ¼ inch thick**
- 2 **cups rice wine vinegar, champagne vinegar, or apple cider vinegar or more as needed**
- 1 **cup water**

salt to taste, about $\frac{1}{2}$ teaspoon

$\frac{1}{2}$ teaspoon freshly ground pepper

$\frac{1}{4}$ teaspoon ground cloves

5 bay leaves

1 fresh rosemary sprig

1 teaspoon dried oregano, preferably Mexican

1 cup cauliflower florets

1 cup broccoli florets

10 large radishes, quartered if large, halved if small

1 cup green beans or peas or $\frac{1}{2}$ cup each, trimmed and cut into 1–inch lengths

2 medium waxy potatoes, such as red-skinned new potatoes, cut into 1-inch pieces and steamed until crisp-tender, about 10 minutes

Using a toothpick, a skewer, or the tip of a sharp knife, pierce the chiles in a few places so that they absorb the marinade.

Heat the oil over medium heat in a heavy saucepan large enough to hold all the vegetables. Add the garlic, onions, and carrots and cook, stirring, until the onions are tender, about 5 minutes. Add the chiles and cook, stirring, for 5 minutes, until they soften slightly. Add the vinegar, water, salt, spices, and herbs and stir together. Add the cauliflower, broccoli, radishes, and green beans. If the vegetables are not submerged in liquid, add more vinegar or, for a milder bath, add 2 parts vinegar to 1 part water. Bring to a boil. Reduce the heat to low, cover, and simmer for 10 minutes, stirring from time to time, until the vegetables are crisp-tender and the chiles olive green. Remove from the heat, stir in the steamed potatoes, and allow to cool. Taste and adjust the salt. Remove the rosemary.

Transfer the chiles and vegetables with their marinade to a large bowl or glass jars. Top up with equal parts vinegar and water if they are not submerged in the marinade. Cover and refrigerate. Wait a day or more before using.

Advance Preparation: These will keep for several weeks in the refrigerator if submerged in the marinade.

PER PORTION

Calories	125	Protein	3 g
Fat	4 g	Carbohydrate	21 g
Saturated Fat	.47 g	Fiber	4 g
Cholesterol	0	Sodium	161 mg

CRUSTY HARD BREAD WITH
PICKLED VEGETABLES (PEDRAZOS)

Makes 8 servings

Bags of thick, rock-hard slices of bolillo-like bread hang from the rafters of stands in the Oaxacan market. You buy the bread, and you buy marinated vegetables, which are spooned into the bag with the bread so that the slices soften in the marinade. What a wonderful mixture you get! I offer a saladlike version here. Use good country bread and make sure it's hardened all the way through so it stays in one piece.

1   loaf of country bread, cut into 3-inch-wide slices 1 inch thick
1   recipe Pickled Vegetables (see previous recipe)

Leave the bread out at room temperature until hard or dry it on a baking sheet in a 250-degree oven for 1½ hours. It should be hard all the way through.

Place the slices of bread in a wide salad bowl or on a platter and top with the pickled vegetables and all of their marinade. Let sit for 30 minutes before eating.

Advance Preparation: This is a great dish to make with any pickled vegetables lingering in the refrigerator. They keep for weeks. The assembled dish will hold for several hours, though it's easy to assemble 30 minutes before serving.

PER PORTION

Calories	318	Protein	9 g
Fat	6 g	Carbohydrate	57 g
Saturated Fat	1 g	Fiber	6 g
Cholesterol	0	Sodium	575 mg

JÍCAMA AND ORANGE SALAD (PICO DE GALLO)

Makes 4 to 6 servings

This mixture is known all over Mexico as *pico de gallo* (rooster's beak), a salsa made with finely chopped jícama and orange, seasoned with chile piquín and lime juice. I've often heard the name used for fresh tomato salsas, especially in the Southwest. But this is the authentic dish. If you cannot get chile piquín, use another ground red chile, but not prepared chile powder. Diana Kennedy suggests hot paprika as a substitute. Rick Bayless prefers a dried red New Mexico chile, heightened with a bit of cayenne. I usually use ground hot New Mexico chile by itself. This dish can be served as a salad or in an assortment of antojitos; it can go alongside grilled chicken breasts or fish; or it can top a bed of salad greens—that's why it's in the salad chapter.

1	medium jícama, peeled and diced quite small (about 2 cups)
¼	cup fresh lime juice
	salt to taste
2	navel oranges, sectioned and diced
	pure ground chile powder to taste
2	tablespoons chopped fresh cilantro
1	head of leaf lettuce or 2 cups baby salad greens

Toss together the jícama, lime juice, and salt. Let sit at room temperature for 1 hour, tossing every so often. Add the remaining ingredients except the lettuce and toss together. Let sit for at least 15 minutes, preferably 2 hours.

Line a bowl or platter with lettuce, top with the jícama mixture, and serve.

Advance Preparation: The dish *must* be prepared about 2 hours before serving and will keep in the refrigerator for a day.

PER PORTION

Calories	66	Protein	2 g
Fat	.26 g	Carbohydrate	16 g
Saturated Fat	0	Fiber	3 g
Cholesterol	0	Sodium	7 mg

Black Bean Salad

Makes 4 main-dish servings, 8 starter servings

Black beans look shiny and jewellike in this pretty salad, which makes a terrific starter and a wonderful light lunch or supper. I love the contrast of the crunchy, juicy peppers against the soft beans. This recipe makes quite a big salad; it's so nutritious that I often eat it as a main dish.

For the Beans:

1   pound black beans, washed, picked over, soaked overnight or for
       at least 6 hours and drained if desired
1   medium onion, chopped
4   large garlic cloves or to taste, minced or pressed
2   quarts water
1   to 2 teaspoons salt to taste

For the Vinaigrette and Salad:

2   tablespoons fresh lime juice or more to taste
1/4 cup red wine vinegar
1   heaped teaspoon Dijon mustard
1   garlic clove, minced or pressed
1   teaspoon ground cumin
1/2 teaspoon ground New Mexico chile powder, optional
       salt and freshly ground pepper to taste
1   tablespoon olive oil
1   red bell pepper, diced
1   green bell pepper, diced
2   tablespoons chopped fresh chives
1/2 cup chopped fresh cilantro
6   ounces (5 cups) mixed salad greens or fresh spinach
2   ounces goat cheese, queso fresco, or feta, crumbled (about
       1/2 cup), optional
       fresh cilantro sprigs for garnish

COOK THE BEANS: Combine the beans, onion, half the garlic, and the water in a large heavy saucepan or Dutch oven and bring to a boil. Reduce the heat, cover, and simmer for 1 hour. Add the remaining garlic and the salt and test the beans for doneness. If they are soft all the way through, turn off the heat and let sit, covered, until cool. If they are the least bit crunchy, continue to simmer for 30 to 60 minutes, until the beans are tender but not mushy. Remove from the heat. Taste and adjust the seasoning.

Carefully strain off the cooking liquid into a bowl. Transfer the beans to a bowl, taking care not to crush them.

MAKE THE DRESSING: Mix together the lime juice, vinegar, mustard, garlic, cumin, chile powder (for a more picante dish), salt, and pepper. Whisk in the oil and 1 cup of liquid from the beans. Toss with the beans. Add the diced peppers and chives and toss again. Cover with plastic wrap and set aside, either in or out of the refrigerator, for 1 hour or longer.

Toss the beans with the cilantro. Taste and adjust the seasoning.

Line salad plates or a platter or bowl with the salad greens. Top with the beans. Sprinkle on the crumbled cheese, garnish with cilantro sprigs, and serve.

Advance Preparation: The beans can be cooked and marinated a day ahead of time and kept in the refrigerator. It's best to wait before you add the cilantro until an hour or less before serving so that the cilantro retains its bright color. Although they won't look quite as pretty after a day, the marinated beans, with the cilantro and peppers, will keep, because of the vinegar, for several days in the refrigerator, and they're nice to have on hand. Heat leftovers and serve over warm corn tortillas for a quick, hearty taco.

PER PORTION

Calories	467	Protein	27 g
Fat	5 g	Carbohydrate	81 g
Saturated Fat	1 g	Fiber	3 g
Cholesterol	0 mg	Sodium	624 mg

CORN AND POTATO SALAD WITH TOMATILLO DRESSING

Makes 4 servings

This is a great summer salad. I often make it with leftover corn on the cob—we usually cook more than we can eat. The potatoes make a nice contrast with the sweet, crunchy corn kernels, and the slightly picante pale green tomatillo dressing is perfect. It is slightly juicy, which is why you need a bed of lettuce to set the salad on. I love the addition of fava beans, but leave them out if difficult to come by.

Use leftovers as a topping for soft tacos or as a filling for quesadillas.

For the Dressing:

¼ pound (about 2 large) fresh tomatillos, husked and rinsed, or half of a 13-ounce can, drained
1 serrano chile, seeded for a milder dressing and coarsely chopped
1 tablespoon fresh lime juice
1 tablespoon chopped onion, rinsed
1 garlic clove, peeled
6 fresh cilantro sprigs or more to taste
1 tablespoon olive oil
salt to taste

For the Salad:

kernels from 2 ears corn
6 ounces (2 smallish) red-skinned new potatoes, scrubbed and cut into ½-inch dice
½ pound fresh fava beans, removed from their pods, optional
1 medium tomato, cut into ¼-inch dice
½ small red onion, chopped and rinsed, optional
¼ cup chopped fresh cilantro
salt and freshly ground pepper to taste
1 small head or ½ larger head of romaine lettuce

If you're using fresh tomatillos, either roast under the broiler, following the directions on page 31, or simmer in water to cover for 10 minutes, until soft. Drain. Place fresh or canned tomatillos in a blender with the remaining dressing ingredients and blend until smooth. Transfer to a bowl, taste, and adjust the salt. Set aside and allow the flavors to develop while you prepare the salad ingredients.

Steam the corn kernels above $1/2$ inch of boiling water for 5 to 7 minutes, until tender. Remove from the heat and refresh with cold water.

Steam the potatoes until crisp-tender, about 10 minutes. Remove from the heat and toss with the corn.

Bring a small pot of water to a boil and drop in the fava beans. Boil for 1 minute and immediately transfer to a bowl of cold water. Pop off the shells and toss with the corn, potatoes, and remaining salad ingredients, except lettuce, in a bowl.

If the dressing is quite thick, thin out with a couple of tablespoons of water. Toss with the salad. Allow to cool and chill if desired. Taste and adjust the seasonings.

Line individual plates or a bowl or platter with lettuce leaves. Top with the corn salad and serve.

Advance Preparation: This salad does not benefit from time, since the colors and flavors fade, but it will hold in the refrigerator for a few hours.

PER PORTION

Calories	139	Protein	5 g
Fat	4 g	Carbohydrate	22 g
Saturated Fat	.57 g	Fiber	5 g
Cholesterol	0	Sodium	23 mg

RICE SALAD WITH ROASTED POBLANOS AND CUMIN VINAIGRETTE

Makes 6 to 8 servings

I often make this beautiful salad for Mexican buffets. It also makes a great first course for a dinner party. The rice is tossed with bright vegetables, roasted poblano chiles, cilantro, and a yogurt vinaigrette, then piled onto salad greens.

For the Salad:

1³⁄₄ cups water
1 cup long-grain white rice
¹⁄₄ teaspoon salt
1 large poblano chile, roasted*
1 cup fresh or thawed frozen peas or 1 cup trimmed green beans
   kernels from 1 ear corn
1 small red bell pepper, cut into ¹⁄₄-inch dice
1 green bell pepper, cut into ¹⁄₄-inch dice
1 bunch of scallions, both white and green parts, sliced, or ¹⁄₄ cup
   chopped fresh chives, optional
¹⁄₃ long European or ¹⁄₂ regular cucumber, seeded and cut into
   ¹⁄₄-inch dice (1 cup)
¹⁄₄ cup chopped fresh cilantro

For the Dressing:

1 to 2 tablespoons rice wine vinegar or cider vinegar to taste
2 tablespoons fresh lemon or lime juice
1 garlic clove, minced or pressed
1 teaspoon Dijon mustard
1 teaspoon ground cumin
²⁄₃ cup plain nonfat yogurt
   salt and freshly ground pepper to taste
2 tablespoons olive oil

* *To roast peppers:* Roast the pepper(s) either directly over a gas flame or under a broiler, turning often until uniformly charred. When the pepper is blackened on all sides, transfer to a bowl or plastic bag, cover or seal, and cool. Remove the charred skin, rinse, and pat dry. Remove the seeds and veins (wear rubber gloves for hot chiles).

For the Plate:

1   **small head of leaf or Boston lettuce or 2 cups mixed baby salad**
     greens
     radishes or cherry tomatoes
     fresh cilantro sprigs

COOK THE RICE: Bring the water to a boil in a 2-quart saucepan and add the rice and salt. When the water comes back to a boil, stir once, cover, reduce the heat, and simmer for 15 minutes or until the water has evaporated. Remove from the heat and let sit, covered, for 10 minutes.

Cut the poblano chiles into $1/4$-inch dice.

Place the peas or beans and corn kernels, in a steamer set above $1/2$ inch of water and bring the water to a boil. Cover and steam the vegetables for 5 minutes. Remove from the heat and refresh the vegetables with cold water to stop the cooking.

Toss the rice with all the vegetables and herbs in a large bowl.

PREPARE THE DRESSING: Mix together the vinegar, lemon juice, garlic, mustard, cumin, yogurt, salt, and pepper. Stir in the olive oil and mix well. Toss with the rice mixture. Taste and adjust the seasonings.

Line a platter or salad bowl or individual plates with a bed of lettuce leaves. Top with the salad, garnish with radishes and cilantro sprigs, and serve.

Advance Preparation: The rice mixture can be prepared up to a day ahead of time. Don't toss with the dressing more than a few hours before serving, or the vegetables will lose their bright color.

PER PORTION

Calories	224	Protein	7 g
Fat	5 g	Carbohydrate	38 g
Saturated Fat	.72 g	Fiber	3 g
Cholesterol	1 mg	Sodium	139 mg

Variations: When you cook the rice, add $1/4$ teaspoon saffron threads to the water for a beautiful golden color. Or use brown rice, cooking it in 2 cups water for 40 minutes.

SPINACH SALAD WITH LIME-MARINATED FISH

Makes 4 servings

This refreshing salad topped with seviche can adapt to all sorts of menus. It's fantastic as a first course before a fish, meat, or vegetarian main dish. It can also stand alone for a light lunch or supper.

In summer, use fresh tomatoes, and in winter let bright red peppers stand in. Mackerel is a close relative of sierra, which is often used in Mexican seviches, but halibut is milder tasting and may be easier to find.

½	pound halibut or mackerel fillets
¾	cup fresh lime juice, from about 6 limes
1	small red onion, thinly sliced and rinsed
2	garlic cloves, minced or pressed
1	to 2 fresh or pickled jalapeño or serrano chiles to taste, seeded for a milder seviche
1	tablespoon drained capers, rinsed
½	teaspoon dried oregano, preferably Mexican salt, ¼ to ½ teaspoon, and freshly ground pepper to taste
2	tablespoons olive oil
1	large or 2 medium tomatoes, sliced, or 1 red bell pepper, thinly sliced
¼	cup chopped fresh cilantro
½	pound fresh spinach, stemmed, washed, and dried
2	large (about 2 ounces) mushrooms, thinly sliced

Cut the fish into strips about ¼ inch thick and 1 to 2 inches long. Toss with the lime juice in a noncorrosive bowl, cover, and refrigerate for about 5 to 6 hours. The fish should be "cooked" through. Give the fish a stir every once in a while to redistribute the lime juice.

Add the onion, garlic, chiles, capers, oregano, salt, pepper, and 1 tablespoon of the olive oil to the fish, toss together, and refrigerate for another 30 minutes to an hour. Remove from the refrigerator and stir in the tomatoes or sliced red pepper and cilantro.

Pour off the marinade from the fish. Mix with the remaining tablespoon of olive oil. Toss with the spinach and mushrooms. Place the spinach in a wide bowl or line a platter or individual serving plates. Top with the fish and serve.

Advance Preparation:　You can marinate the fish for up to a day, before serving this dish.

PER PORTION

Calories	155	Protein	15 g
Fat	7 g	Carbohydrate	10 g
Saturated Fat	.92 g	Fiber	3 g
Cholesterol	18 mg	Sodium	243 mg

VINEGAR-BATHED SHRIMP

Makes 6 to 8 servings

The shrimp are cooked and tossed in a mild vinegar marinade, which should be neither too vinegary nor too picante. The best vinegar to use for these camarones en escabeche is rice wine vinegar (in Veracruz they use pineapple vinegar). Serve the lively shrimp salad over leaves of romaine lettuce.

- **2 pounds medium shrimp**
- **3 cups water**
- **1 tablespoon olive oil**
- **2 medium onions, thinly sliced**
- **2 large carrots, thinly sliced**
- **6 large garlic cloves, minced or pressed**
- **2 to 4 serrano or jalapeño chiles, either fresh or pickled, to taste, finely chopped**
- **4 bay leaves**
- **¹/₃ cup rice wine, champagne, or cider vinegar or more to taste**
- **¹/₄ teaspoon freshly ground pepper**
- **1 teaspoon ground cloves**
- **1 teaspoon dried oregano, preferably Mexican salt to taste, about ¹/₂ teaspoon**
- **¹/₄ cup chopped fresh cilantro romaine lettuce leaves and sliced tomatoes for serving**

Peel and devein the shrimp, saving the shells. Bring the water to a boil in a saucepan and add the shells. Skim off any foam that rises, reduce the heat, and simmer for 30 minutes. Strain through a cheesecloth-lined strainer and set aside ½ cup of the stock (you can freeze the rest or use for another purpose, such as cooking rice if you are going to accompany this with rice).

Heat the oil in a large heavy nonstick skillet over medium heat and cook the onion and carrots, stirring, until tender, about 5 to 8 minutes. Add the garlic and the shrimp and cook, stirring, until the shrimp begins to turn pink, about 3 minutes.

Add half the chiles, the bay leaves, vinegar, pepper, cloves, oregano, salt, and reserved shrimp stock and bring to a simmer. Reduce the heat to low and simmer for 5 minutes, stirring from time to time. The shrimp should now be cooked through.

Remove from the heat and allow the mixture to cool. Chill if desired. Stir it occasionally to redistribute the marinade. Stir in the remaining chiles and the cilantro and adjust the seasonings.

Line a platter or salad bowl with lettuce leaves and top with the shrimp mixture. Garnish with tomato wedges and serve.

Advance Preparation: The cooked shrimp will keep for a couple of days in the refrigerator, without the cilantro. Stir from time to time. Add the cilantro just before serving.

PER PORTION

Calories	201	Protein	26 g
Fat	5 g	Carbohydrate	13 g
Saturated Fat	.76 g	Fiber	2 g
Cholesterol	186 mg	Sodium	381 mg

Chapter
Six

Soups

Soups were practically all I ate during my early stays in Mexico. Mexico is a country that loves its soups, and I was very lucky indeed to have such an introduction to its fantastic repertoire. Restaurants always offer at least one soup on their menu, usually a classic tortilla soup, or in the Yucatán a tortilla soup that is flavored with fresh lime juice or a garlic soup. These are simple light soups made with chicken or meat broth to which savory vegetables, herbs, sometimes a bit of shredded chicken, and/or chiles are added. In this collection I give you the choice of chicken broth, vegetable (or garlic) broth, or sometimes plain old water as a base.

What makes Mexican soups special, and decidedly Mexican, is the finishing touches, whether a splash of lime juice, a sprinkling of cilantro, or the addition of diced avocado or chipotle chiles. Mexican soup broths are fragrant with unexpected herbs, too, such as mint or the earthy epazote. The soups are served as a first course, in small bowls, and they are a wonderful way to begin a meal. In fact I think they make a great light meal in themselves, served with a salad and bread or tortillas, especially the heartier soups like black bean soup and the gorgeous minty fava bean soup. But I've placed the really hearty meal-in-a-bowl soups and stews, the ones that I would serve as the central dish of a dinner party, in other chapters. You'll find rich-tasting fish soups and stews in Chapter 10 and a lighter, smoky shrimp chilpachol from Veracruz here. Thick, luscious green and red pozoles with chicken or rabbit are in Chapter 11, and you'll find hearty vegetarian pozoles, chilis, and a Veracruzana "soup" that is really more of a stew made with black beans and greens in Chapter 12.

Not all of the soups here are traditional. I was so inspired by late-summer produce when I began working on this book that I couldn't keep myself from making things up. The roasted tomato soups are inspired by the technique that is used so often to achieve a particularly deep flavor in Mexican cooking. But the soups themselves are the result of the wonderful tomato harvest I look forward to every year. The same goes for the summer vegetable soup and the Mexican-style gazpacho. I've never seen these soups in Mexico, but each one of them makes me think of that country and its incredible cuisine.

$\mathscr{S}$TOCKS

CHICKEN OR TURKEY STOCK

Makes 2¹/₂ quarts

Many Mexican soups rely on excellent chicken stock, and happily recipes that call for stock often also call for poached chicken, so you can use the poaching liquid for the stock. I try to keep this stock on hand for other soups that need a good stock, freezing it in 1-quart containers. You can make stock with fresh or cooked carcasses or with a whole chicken, skinned and cut up. Make it a day before using it so that you can skim off the fat once the stock has cooled.

fresh carcass and giblets of 1 chicken or turkey or the carcass of a cooked chicken or turkey or 1 medium chicken, skinned and cut into pieces

3   medium carrots, sliced
2   medium onions, quartered
1   leek, white and tender green parts, rinsed well and sliced
5   or 6 garlic cloves to taste, peeled and crushed
      a bouquet garni made with a bay leaf, 2 fresh thyme sprigs, and 2 fresh parsley or cilantro sprigs
2   celery ribs, sliced
3   quarts water—enough to cover everything by an inch
1   teaspoon black peppercorns
      salt to taste, 1 teaspoon per quart of water

If you're using a fresh carcass, crack the bones slightly with a hammer. Combine all the ingredients in a soup pot. Bring to a boil and skim off any foam that rises. Reduce the heat, cover partially, and simmer over very low heat for 2 hours. Strain through a cheesecloth-lined strainer into a large bowl or pot. Remove the bones or the chicken pieces from the strainer and place in a bowl. Allow to cool until you can handle them, then pick off the meat from the bones and set aside for another purpose.

Cover the stock and refrigerate overnight. The next day, lift off all the fat that has accumulated on top. Taste and adjust the salt. Freeze in 1-quart containers if not using right away.

Advance Preparation: This will keep for 3 or 4 days in the refrigerator and freezes well.

PER PORTION (1 CUP)

Calories	38	Protein	0
Fat	2 g	Carbohydrate	5 g
Saturated Fat	0	Fiber	0
Cholesterol	0	Sodium	553 mg

VEGETABLE STOCKS

Makes about 7 cups

These are all easy to make and suitable for any of the soups in this chapter. The vegetable stock is a great all-purpose stock. The garlic stock is the one I'd recommend to replace chicken stock where that is called for. The corncob stock is sweet and fragrant, perfect for corn and summer vegetable soups.

Vegetable Stock

2 quarts water
2 large onions, quartered
4 to 6 garlic cloves to taste, peeled and slightly crushed
2 large carrots, sliced
2 large leeks, including some of the green, rinsed well and sliced
2 medium potatoes, scrubbed and quartered
1 teaspoon black peppercorns
a bouquet garni made with a bay leaf, a few fresh parsley or cilantro sprigs, and 1 or 2 fresh thyme sprigs
salt to taste, 1 to 2 teaspoons

Garlic Stock

- 2 heads of garlic, cloves separated and peeled
- 2 quarts water
- 1 tablespoon olive oil, optional
- 1 bay leaf
- 2 fresh thyme sprigs or $1/4$ teaspoon dried
- 4 fresh parsley sprigs
  pinch of dried leaf sage
- 2 teaspoons salt or to taste

Combine all the ingredients in a stockpot. Bring to a gentle boil, then cover and reduce the heat. Simmer for 1 to 2 hours. Strain.

Corncob Stock

- 6 corncobs, stripped of corn but uncooked, broken in half
- 1 medium onion, coarsely chopped
- 8 garlic cloves, peeled and slightly crushed
- 2 quarts water
  salt to taste, about 1 tablespoon

Combine all the ingredients and bring to a boil. Reduce the heat, cover, and simmer for 1 hour. Remove from the heat and allow to cool. Strain into a large bowl. Squeeze the corncobs to extract as much tasty juice from them as you can. Use in vegetable soups.

Advance Preparation: All 3 stocks will keep for about 3 days in the refrigerator and can be frozen. The corncob stock won't be quite as vivid as when freshly made.

PER PORTION (1 CUP; VEGETABLE)

Calories	14	Protein	0
Fat	.01 g	Carbohydrate	3 g
Saturated Fat	0	Fiber	0
Cholesterol	0	Sodium	474 mg

PER PORTION (1 CUP; GARLIC)

Calories	14	Protein	1 g
Fat	.05 g	Carbohydrate	3 g
Saturated Fat	0	Fiber	0
Cholesterol	0	Sodium	630 mg

PER PORTION (1 CUP; CORNCOB)

Calories	19	Protein	1 g
Fat	.16 g	Carbohydrate	4 g
Saturated Fat	.02 g	Fiber	0
Cholesterol	0	Sodium	473 mg

TORTILLA SOUP

Makes 4 to 6 servings

I usually make my tortilla soup with a garlic stock base, but chicken stock is more traditional. This light, warming soup is ubiquitous in Mexico; the stock is enriched with tomato, onion, and garlic, and the finishing touch is a bit of lime juice and a sprinkling of toasted pasilla chile (I've used guajillo, too, when I didn't have pasillas on hand; it's a bit hotter). All of this is ladled over a bowl of crisp tortilla strips, and the soup is topped with a bit of cheese, optional in this version.

1	tablespoon olive or canola oil
1/2	onion, minced
2	large garlic cloves, minced or pressed
1	pound (4 medium or 2 large) tomatoes, peeled
6	cups garlic or chicken stock (pages 158–160)
1	or 2 pasilla or guajillo chiles, toasted*
3	tablespoons chopped fresh cilantro, plus more for garnish
	salt to taste
2	tablespoons fresh lime juice
8	corn tortillas, cut into strips and toasted*
1/4	cup grated Gruyère or Parmesan cheese or crumbled queso fresco, optional
2	limes, cut into wedges

* *To toast chiles:* Wearing rubber gloves, open up the chiles and remove the seeds and veins. Heat a heavy skillet or comal over medium heat and toast the chiles on both sides, pressing them down with a metal spatula and turning them as soon as they sizzle and blister, in a matter of seconds. Remove from the heat at once, break into small pieces, and transfer to a bowl or plate.

* *To toast tortilla strips:* To bake the strips, preheat the oven to 325 degrees. Place the tortilla pieces on a baking sheet and bake for 20 to 30 minutes, until light brown and crisp, shaking the baking sheet every 10 minutes. Allow to cool on a rack. To microwave the strips, place about 6 to 10 pieces at a time on a plate or on the plate in your microwave oven. Microwave on HIGH (100%) power for 1 minute. If the pieces are not crisp, turn them over and microwave for another 40 to 60 seconds. If they are still not crisp and are just beginning to brown, microwave for another 20 to 30 seconds until crisp. Cool on a rack or in a basket.

Heat 1 teaspoon of the olive oil over medium-low heat in a nonstick pan and add the onion. Cook, stirring, until tender, about 5 minutes. Add the garlic and stir together for about 30 seconds, just until the garlic begins to color. Transfer to a blender, add the tomatoes, and puree until smooth. Strain through a medium-mesh strainer.

Heat the remaining oil in a soup pot or Dutch oven over medium-high heat and add the tomato puree. Cook, stirring, until the puree cooks down and thickens, about 8 to 10 minutes. Add the stock and stir well, then cover and simmer for 30 minutes over very low heat.

Shortly before serving, add the chiles to the soup and cook for 3 minutes, until soft. Add the cilantro and cook for 1 minute. Taste the broth and adjust salt and the seasonings. Stir in the lime juice.

Distribute the toasted tortilla strips among wide soup bowls. Ladle in the soup, top with a sprinkling of cheese, and serve at once with lime wedges.

Advance Preparation: The soup base (with the tomatoes but without the chiles or cilantro) will keep for 2 days in the refrigerator and can be frozen. The tortilla strips will keep for several hours.

PER PORTION

Calories	219	Protein	6 g
Fat	6 g	Carbohydrate	42 g
Saturated Fat	.78 g	Fiber	5 g
Cholesterol	0	Sodium	1,038 mg

Variation

ENRICHED TORTILLA SOUP: Add 2 eggs to the recipe. The soup should be just simmering. Just before serving, beat the eggs lightly and ladle in a bit of the hot broth. Stir the eggs back into the simmering soup. Remove from the heat and serve as directed.

Yucatecan Lime Soup

Makes 4 servings

This is not exactly the same soup as the one I ate almost daily at a beach hotel in the Yucatán. The limes there are different, with a taste somewhere between that of lime and Seville orange. In the Yucatán the tortillas would be fried as they are in tortilla soup. But everything I adore about this soup is here. The light chicken broth is simmered for a very short time with sautéed onion, pepper, and tomato, and the mixture is lifted to the most delicious level at the very end by a little lime juice and cilantro.

$^{1}/_{2}$	(about $^{1}/_{4}$ pound) chicken breast, skinned and boned
2	large garlic cloves, crushed
6	cups water
$^{1}/_{2}$	teaspoon dried oregano, preferably Mexican
	salt and freshly ground pepper to taste
1	tablespoon olive or canola oil
$^{1}/_{2}$	small white onion, chopped
1	small green bell pepper, chopped
$^{1}/_{2}$	pound (2 medium or 1 large) tomatoes, peeled, seeded, and finely chopped
	juice of 1 lime
$^{1}/_{4}$	cup chopped fresh cilantro
8	corn tortillas, cut into strips and toasted*
$^{1}/_{2}$	lime, thinly sliced
2	serrano chiles, chopped, for serving, optional

Combine the chicken breast, garlic, and water in a soup pot or a large saucepan and bring to a simmer. Skim off any foam that rises, add the oregano, cover partially, and simmer for 15 minutes, until the chicken breast is cooked

---

* *To toast tortilla strips:* To bake the strips, preheat the oven to 325 degrees. Place the tortilla pieces on a baking sheet and bake for 20 to 30 minutes, until light brown and crisp, shaking the baking sheet every 10 minutes. Allow to cool on a rack. To microwave the strips, place about 6 to 10 pieces at a time on a plate or on the plate in your microwave oven. Microwave on HIGH (100%) power for 1 minute. If the pieces are not crisp, turn them over and microwave for another 40 to 60 seconds. If they are still not crisp and are just beginning to brown, microwave for another 20 to 30 seconds, until crisp. Cool on a rack or in a basket.

through. Remove the chicken from the broth and season the broth with 1 teaspoon or more salt and pepper. When the chicken breast has cooled, shred it and set aside.

Heat the oil in a heavy nonstick skillet over medium heat and add the onion and green pepper. Cook, stirring, until the onion is tender, about 3 to 5 minutes. Add the tomatoes and a little salt and cook, stirring, for about 5 minutes, until the tomato has cooked down a bit and the mixture is aromatic. Stir the mixture into the chicken broth. Taste and adjust the salt and bring to a simmer. Add the shredded chicken and lime juice and simmer very gently for a couple of minutes.

Remove the soup from the heat and stir in the cilantro. Fill each bowl with toasted tortilla strips, ladle in the soup, and serve at once, floating a round of lime in each bowl and passing the chopped serranos.

NOTE: In the Yucatán the rounds of lime are simmered in the broth for a couple of minutes, but I find that they can cause the broth to become bitter if left too long, so I'd rather add the juice and float the rounds of lime as a garnish.

Advance Preparation: The soup is a last-minute affair, although the tortillas can be toasted several hours or even a day ahead of time.

PER PORTION

Calories	190	Protein	8 g
Fat	5 g	Carbohydrate	30 g
Saturated Fat	1 g	Fiber	4 g
Cholesterol	11 mg	Sodium	650 mg

CHICKEN AND POTATO SOUP WITH LIME

Makes 4 servings

Lime juice is one of the defining flavors of many Mexican soups. This one couldn't be simpler. The garlic, potatoes, and lime juice make this chicken soup particularly comforting.

6   cups chicken, turkey, or vegetable stock (pages 158–160)
2   large garlic cloves, minced or pressed
1   pound (4 medium) waxy potatoes, scrubbed and sliced
1   cup shredded cooked chicken, from the carcass used for the
       stock or from ¹/₂ whole large or 1 small skinless chicken
       breast*
     salt and freshly ground pepper to taste
¹/₄   cup fresh lime juice
¹/₄   cup chopped fresh cilantro
4   corn tortillas, cut into wedges and toasted*

Combine the stock, garlic, and potatoes in a soup pot and bring to a simmer. Cover partially and simmer for 15 to 20 minutes, until the potatoes are tender. Add the chicken, heat through, and adjust the salt and pepper. Stir in the lime juice and cilantro.

Distribute the tortilla chips among 4 soup bowls. Ladle in the soup and serve at once.

* *To cook skinned chicken breasts:* Place 1 quartered onion, 2 garlic cloves, and 5 cups of water in a saucepan and bring to a boil. Add 1 teaspoon salt and the chicken breasts and bring back to a boil. Skim off any foam that rises, reduce the heat, cover partially, and simmer for 12 to 15 minutes, until the meat is cooked through. Remove from the heat and allow the chicken to cool in the broth if there is time.

* *To toast tortilla chips:* To bake the chips, preheat the oven to 325 degrees. Place the tortilla pieces on a baking sheet and bake for 20 to 30 minutes, until light brown and crisp, shaking the baking sheet every 10 minutes. Allow to cool on a rack. To microwave the chips, place about 6 to 10 pieces at a time on a plate or on the plate in your microwave oven. Microwave on HIGH (100%) power for 1 minute. If the pieces are not crisp, turn them over and microwave for another 40 to 60 seconds. If they are still not crisp and are just beginning to brown, microwave for another 20 to 30 seconds, until crisp. Cool on a rack or in a basket.

Advance Preparation: You can make the soup through the cooking of the potatoes hours or even a day ahead of time. The chicken, lime, and cilantro, however, should be added just before serving.

PER PORTION

Calories	276	Protein	15 g
Fat	6 g	Carbohydrate	42 g
Saturated Fat	1 g	Fiber	1 g
Cholesterol	31 mg	Sodium	908 mg

Variation: For a delicious, colorful touch, add 1 pound fresh fava beans. Remove the beans from their pods and drop into a pot of boiling water for 1 minute. Drain, rinse with cold water, and pop off the shells. Add to the soup with the chicken.

GARLIC SOUP WITH TOASTED CHILES, CROUTONS, AND CILANTRO

Makes 4 servings

This simple version of sopa de ajo reminds me of its Provençal counterpart, but the cilantro and toasted chile garnish make this soup uniquely Mexican. I enjoy this soup without added heat, but for those who like things picante, guajillos are the chiles to use.

- 2 guajillo or pasilla chiles, toasted*
- 4 to 6 slices of French or country bread
- 7 large garlic cloves, 1 cut in half lengthwise, 6 minced or pressed
- 6 cups chicken stock (page 158) or water
- 2 to 3 teaspoons salt to taste (if using water)
- 1 fresh rosemary sprig
- 2 large eggs, lightly beaten
- 2 tablespoons chopped fresh cilantro

* *To toast chiles:* Wearing rubber gloves, open up the chiles and remove the seeds, veins, and stems. Heat a heavy skillet or comal over medium heat and toast the chiles on both sides, pressing them down with a metal spatula and turning them as soon as they sizzle and blister, in a matter of seconds. Remove from the heat at once.

Crumble the toasted chiles into small pieces and set aside in a bowl.

Toast the bread lightly (it should still be soft on the inside). Rub with the cut clove of garlic and set aside.

Bring the stock or water to a boil and add the salt, minced garlic, and rosemary. Reduce the heat to low, cover, and simmer for 15 minutes.

Just before serving, beat the eggs in a bowl. Ladle a bit of hot soup into the eggs, stir together, then stir the eggs back into the simmering soup. Stir in the cilantro and remove from the heat. Taste and adjust the salt.

Place a piece of garlic toast in each bowl, ladle on the soup, and sprinkle on a bit of toasted chile. Serve hot.

Advance Preparation: The garlic croutons and toasted chiles can be prepared hours ahead of serving, and the garlic can be simmered in the stock a few hours before adding the final egg enrichment. Once the egg is added, the soup should be served right away.

PER PORTION

Calories	276	Protein	15 g
Fat	6 g	Carbohydrate	42 g
Saturated Fat	.82 g	Fiber	3 g
Cholesterol	31 mg	Sodium	908 mg

CHICKPEA AND VEGETABLE SOUP WITH CHICKEN, LIME, AND CHIPOTLES

Makes 6 servings

There are many versions of this traditional Mexican soup called *sopa tlalpeño.* What runs through all of them is the presence of chicken, chickpeas, avocado, and hot, smoky chipotle peppers. For this low-fat version it's best to cook the chicken the day before so you can skim the fat from the stock. Since the avocado is a key ingredient here, I've reduced fat by simmering rather than frying the vegetables. The soup is light, heady, and delicious.

> 1   **large (about 1¼ pounds) whole chicken breast, skinned**
> 2   **quarts water**
> 2   **medium onions, 1 quartered, 1 diced**

4	large garlic cloves, 2 peeled and crushed slightly, 2 minced or pressed
½	teaspoon dried oregano, preferably Mexican
½	teaspoon dried thyme
3	fresh cilantro sprigs
1	bay leaf
2	cups cooked chickpeas (canned are fine)
1	large carrot, diced (about ¾ cup)
1	medium zucchini or 2 smaller zucchini or round summer squash, diced (about 1 cup)
2	tablespoons chopped fresh epazote or cilantro
	salt to taste
1	to 3 canned or pickled chipotle chiles to taste, rinsed, seeded, and cut into thin strips
1	small avocado, peeled, pitted, and diced
2	limes, cut into wedges, for serving

Combine the chicken, water, quartered onion, and crushed garlic in a large saucepan or Dutch oven and bring to a simmer over medium heat. Skim off any foam that rises, then add the dried herbs, cilantro sprigs, and bay leaf. Cover partially, reduce the heat to low, and simmer for 15 minutes or until the chicken is cooked through. Remove the chicken from the broth and, when cool enough to handle, bone and shred the meat. Set aside in a bowl. (If you have cooked the chicken the day before you wish to serve the soup, place the chicken in a bowl, salt lightly, cover, and refrigerate.)

Strain the stock through a cheesecloth-lined strainer and, if using right away, skim off any visible fat. If using the next day, refrigerate in a covered bowl, and the next day you can easily lift the fat off the top. Add enough water to measure 2 quarts stock.

Combine the chicken stock, chickpeas, diced onion, minced garlic, carrot, squash, and epazote (but not cilantro) and bring to a simmer. Add salt, cover, and simmer for 20 to 30 minutes, until the vegetables are tender. Taste and adjust the seasonings.

Just before serving, stir in the sliced chipotles, shredded chicken, and cilantro. Heat through, taste, and adjust the seasonings. Place a portion of diced avocado in each bowl. Ladle in the soup and serve with a lime wedge, which each diner should squeeze into his or her soup. Alternatively you can place a slice or two of chipotle in each bowl along with the avocado instead of stirring the chipotles into the soup. I recommend this if you plan to eat leftovers, since the soup will become too picante if the chiles sit in it overnight.

Advance Preparation: The soup will hold for a few days in the refrigerator. Do not stir in the chipotles until just before serving, or the broth will be too picante.

PER PORTION

Calories	264	Protein	23 g
Fat	6 g	Carbohydrate	33 g
Saturated Fat	1 g	Fiber	4 g
Cholesterol	36 mg	Sodium	311 mg

Variation

VEGETARIAN VERSION: Omit the chicken breast, quartered onion, crushed garlic cloves, oregano, and thyme. Double the quantity of carrots and squash. Substitute 2 quarts vegetable, garlic, or corncob stock (pages 159–160) for the chicken stock. Begin the recipe with simmering the vegetables in the stock.

SIMPLE CHICKEN CONSOMMÉ WITH TOMATO, MINT, CHILE, AND AVOCADO

Makes 6 servings

Soledad Diaz showed us how to make this delicious light soup in the kitchen of her delightful Restaurant El Topil in Oaxaca during a weeklong Oaxacan gastronomic and cultural odyssey led by Mexican cooking authority Rick Bayless. It's a simple soup, and its success depends on the quality of the stock you use. Chicken stock is traditional, but vegetarians should not deprive themselves; try the soup using garlic stock. The mint perfumes this soup in the most wonderful way, and the chopped, seeded jalapeño gives it a little spice but no burn.

2   **quarts chicken or garlic stock (pages 158–160)**
2   **fresh spearmint sprigs**
1   **medium white onion, finely chopped**
1   **jalapeño chile, seeded and finely chopped**

1   pound (4 medium or 2 large) tomatoes, peeled, seeded, and
      finely chopped
¹/₂   cup chopped fresh cilantro
1   small avocado, peeled, pitted, and finely chopped
2   limes, cut into wedges, for serving, optional

Combine the stock, spearmint, onion, and chile in a large saucepan and bring
to a boil. Boil for 5 minutes and add the tomatoes and cilantro. Turn the heat
to low, simmer for another 5 minutes, and remove from the heat. Taste and adjust the salt if necessary.

Place a spoonful of chopped avocado in each bowl, ladle in the soup, and
serve, with lime wedges to be squeezed into the soup if people wish.

Advance Preparation: This soup is a 10-minute operation, so nothing needs to be done ahead.

PER PORTION

Calories	106	Protein	2 g
Fat	5 g	Carbohydrate	14 g
Saturated Fat	.45 g	Fiber	2 g
Cholesterol	0	Sodium	749 mg

VERACRUZ-STYLE FAVA BEAN SOUP

Makes 6 servings

Fava beans are simmered with a large bunch of mint in this soup, and the resulting flavor is incredible. I learned it from a brilliant cook, Carmen Ramírez Delgollado, who comes from the state of Veracruz. I have always loved anything made with fava beans, but this soup, with its wonderful minty aroma, is the all-time favorite. The first time I tested the recipe, my husband and I ate the soup for dinner for three nights in a row and were sorry to see the end of it. In Mexico you can get skinned dried fava beans; in the U.S. you'll have to slip off the brown skins, as directed.

1   pound dried fava beans, washed, picked over, and soaked in
        water to cover for 6 hours or overnight
1   medium onion, chopped
4   large garlic cloves, minced or pressed
½   pound (2 medium or 1 large) tomatoes, peeled, seeded, and
        chopped
1   bunch (about 10 sprigs) fresh spearmint, tied together
2   quarts water, chicken stock, or garlic stock (pages 158–160)
        salt to taste, 2 teaspoons or more
2   guajillo chiles
1   tablespoon canola oil
1   tablespoon olive oil
        slivered fresh mint leaves for garnish

Bring a large pot of water to a boil. Drain the favas and drop into the water. Boil 1 minute, then drain and transfer to a bowl of cold water. Slip off the brown skins (this is tedious but necessary if you can't find hulled favas). Drain the favas and combine with the onion, half the garlic, the tomato, mint, and water in a large soup pot or Dutch oven. Bring to a boil, reduce the heat, cover, and simmer for 1 hour.

Add the remaining garlic and the salt and continue to simmer for another hour or until the beans begin to fall apart and thicken the soup. Using the back of a large spoon, mash some of the beans against the side of the pot. The soup should have the consistency of a semipuree, with some of the favas still intact but most broken down. Remove the bouquet of mint and any leaves that are floating in the soup. Taste and adjust the seasonings.

Using scissors, cut the tops off the guajillo chiles and shake out the seeds.

Cut into thin rings. Heat the canola oil in a heavy skillet and fry the rings until just crisp, being careful not to burn. This shouldn't take more than a minute, if that. Remove the chiles from the oil using a slotted spoon and drain on paper towels. Most of the oil should remain in the pan. Discard the oil.

Stir the olive oil into the simmering soup and serve, garnishing each bowl with a few rings of guajillo and a slivered leaf of fresh mint.

Advance Preparation: This will keep for 3 to 4 days in the refrigerator and can be frozen.

PER PORTION

Calories	322	Protein	21 g
Fat	6 g	Carbohydrate	47 g
Saturated Fat	.65 g	Fiber	12 g
Cholesterol	0	Sodium	748 mg

BLACK BEAN SOUP WITH TOMATOES AND CUMIN

Makes 4 servings

This soup comes from the highlands of the state of Veracruz, around the town of Xico. It's a simple, savory puree, enhanced with tomatoes and cumin. The Spanish influence on the cuisine of Veracruz is evident in the garlic croutons that float on the top, a special, somewhat surprising touch.

1	cup dried black beans, washed, picked over, and soaked for 6 hours or overnight
6	cups water
1	medium onion, chopped
4	large garlic cloves
	salt to taste
½	pound (2 medium or 1 large) tomatoes, peeled
1½	teaspoons ground cumin or more to taste
1	tablespoon canola oil
½	cup plain nonfat yogurt for garnish
12	½-inch-thick slices of Bolillo, baguette, or sourdough bread, toasted and rubbed with a cut clove of garlic

Drain the beans and combine with the water and half the onion in a soup pot.* Bring to a boil and skim off any foam that rises, then add 2 garlic cloves. Reduce the heat, cover, and simmer for 1 hour. Add salt and simmer for another 30 to 60 minutes, until tender.

Blend together the tomato, remaining onion, cumin, and remaining garlic.

Heat the oil in a heavy nonstick pan over medium-high heat and add a bit of the puree. If it sizzles, add the rest (wait a couple of minutes if it doesn't). Cook, stirring, for 5 to 10 minutes, until the mixture is thick and sticking to the pan. Stir in 1 cup of the liquid from the beans, turn the heat to medium-low, and simmer for 15 minutes, until the mixture is thick and fragrant. Stir into the beans.

Blend the beans in batches in a blender or food processor. The mixture should be somewhat coarse. Return to the pot, heat through, and adjust the seasonings, adding more salt or cumin as desired. Serve each bowl topped with a dollop of yogurt and 3 garlic croutons.

Advance Preparation: The soup will keep for 3 days in the refrigerator and freezes well.

PER PORTION

Calories	319	Protein	15 g
Fat	5 g	Carbohydrate	55 g
Saturated Fat	.53 g	Fiber	8 g
Cholesterol	1 mg	Sodium	124 mg

* Draining the beans is optional. If you don't drain them, measure the soaking water and add water to equal 6 cups.

Lentil Soup with
Chipotles and Plantain Garnish
Makes 4 to 6 servings

"Lentils need smoke," a friend recently said to me after I'd described this soup to her. That's why they are so often paired with sausage in European cuisines, I suppose. Here that flavor, as well as a bit of heat (but not too much), comes from chipotle peppers; they add a smoky, almost meaty depth to this savory lentil soup. The sweet fried plantain slices contrast beautifully.

1   cup dried brown lentils, washed and picked over
1   small onion, chopped
2   large garlic cloves, minced or pressed
1   bay leaf
1   teaspoon ground cumin
6   cups water
    salt to taste, 1 to 2 teaspoons
1   ripe plantain
    juice of ½ lemon
1   tablespoon canola oil
1½ to 2 canned chipotles en adobo to taste, rinsed, seeded, and
        sliced

Combine the lentils, onion, garlic, bay leaf, cumin, and water in a soup pot and bring to a boil. Reduce the heat, cover, and simmer for 40 minutes. Add the salt and simmer for another 15 minutes. Remove the bay leaf.

While the soup is simmering, slice the plantain about ⅓ inch thick and transfer to a bowl of water acidulated with the lemon juice. Heat the oil over medium heat in a large nonstick skillet in which the plantain slices will fit in one layer. Drain the plantains and pat dry on both sides with paper towels, then brown in the oil for 2 to 3 minutes on each side. Drain again on paper towels. Keep warm in a low oven or wrap in foil.

Coarsely puree the soup with a hand blender or puree half the soup in a blender and stir back in. Add the chipotles and heat through. Taste and adjust the seasonings.

Ladle the soup into soup bowls, float about 4 slices of plantain on each bowl, and serve at once.

Advance Preparation: The soup, without the chipotles or the plantains, will keep for 3 days in the refrigerator and can be frozen. If it stands too long with the chipotles, their heat will overpower the soup. Add the chipotles when you heat the soup and proceed with the recipe.

SHRIMP CHILPACHOL

Makes 6 generous servings

The chilpachol is one of the defining dishes of the state of Veracruz. It is a masa-thickened soup that is seasoned with chilpotles (chipotles), smoke-dried jalapeño peppers. The broth has wonderfully complex, smoky flavors—the smoked and toasted chiles, the toasted garlic and spices, the roasted tomatoes and onions, and the epazote that is added shortly before serving the soup. This chilpachol, which transports me right back to a small restaurant called La Choca in the historic river town of Boca del Rio, just south of Veracruz, contains shrimp, but you can use the same base for fish or crabmeat or even vegetables. Sometimes the shells are left on the shrimp, but shelling them first makes for a neater soup. I've made this soup several times, and each time the heat is different, depending on the size of the chipotles I use. How much you use is up to you; I prefer the soup less picante.

2 pounds (12 medium) plum tomatoes, roasted*
1 large onion, peeled, cut in half, roasted*
4 large garlic cloves, toasted*
1 fresh jalapeño chile, toasted*
4 small or 2 to 3 larger dried chipotle chiles, toasted*
1 strip of Mexican cinnamon or ½ teaspoon ground cinnamon, toasted*

* *To roast tomatoes and onions:* Preheat the broiler. Line a baking sheet with foil and place the tomatoes and halved onions on it. Place under the broiler, about 2 to 3 inches from the heat (at the highest rack setting). Turn the tomatoes after 2 or 3 minutes, when charred on

<table>
<tr><td>6</td><td>whole peppercorns, toasted*</td></tr>
<tr><td>2</td><td>corn tortillas, toasted* and ground in a spice mill (about ¼ cup),
or 2 ounces (about ¼ cup) masa, or ¼ cup masa harina
mixed with 3 tablespoons warm water</td></tr>
<tr><td>2</td><td>tablespoons olive oil</td></tr>
<tr><td>10</td><td>cups water</td></tr>
<tr><td></td><td>salt to taste, 2 to 3 teaspoons</td></tr>
<tr><td>1</td><td>large fresh epazote sprig, chopped (about 2 tablespoons), or
¼ cup chopped fresh cilantro</td></tr>
<tr><td>1</td><td>pound medium shrimp, peeled and deveined</td></tr>
<tr><td>2</td><td>or 3 corn tortillas, cut into wedges and toasted,* for serving,
optional</td></tr>
<tr><td></td><td>limes, cut into wedges, for serving</td></tr>
</table>

Peel the roasted tomatoes and transfer to the blender along with any juice that has accumulated in the bowl. Coarsely chop the roasted onion and transfer to the blender. Peel the toasted garlic, stem the jalapeño, and add the garlic, fresh and dried chiles, and ground toasted spices to the blender. If you're using ground toasted tortillas to thicken the soup, add to the blender (set aside masa

---

one side (this may take longer in an electric oven), and repeat on the other side. Remove from the heat and transfer to a bowl. The onions will take about 5 minutes longer than the tomatoes and should be turned several times, until browned on the edges and in spots and slightly softened.

* *To toast garlic and fresh chiles:* Heat a heavy skillet or comal over medium-high heat and toast the garlic in its skin and the chile, turning or shaking the pan often, until the garlic smells toasty and is blackened in several places and the chile is softened and brown in spots, about 10 minutes. Remove from the heat.

* *To toast dried chiles:* Wearing rubber gloves, open up the chiles and remove the seeds and veins. Heat a heavy skillet or comal over medium heat and toast the chiles on both sides, pressing them down with a metal spatula and turning them as soon as they sizzle and blister, in a matter of seconds. Remove from the heat at once.

* *To toast spices:* In a heavy skillet or comal over medium heat, toast whole spices for a few seconds, just until they darken slightly and begin to smell toasty. Remove from the heat and grind in a spice mill.

* *To toast tortilla chips:* To bake the chips, preheat the oven to 325 degrees. Place the tortilla pieces on a baking sheet and bake for 20 to 30 minutes, until light brown and crisp, shaking the baking sheet every 10 minutes. Allow to cool on a rack. To microwave the chips, place about 6 to 10 pieces at a time on a plate or on the plate in your microwave oven. Microwave on HIGH (100%) power for 1 minute. If the pieces are not crisp, turn them over and microwave for another 40 to 60 seconds. If they are still not crisp and are just beginning to brown, microwave for another 20 to 30 seconds, until crisp. Cool on a rack or in a basket.

or masa harina until later). Blend the ingredients together until smooth, and strain into a bowl.

Heat the oil in a large heavy soup pot or Dutch oven over medium-high heat. Drizzle in a small amount of the puree and, if it sizzles loudly, add the rest (wait a few minutes if it doesn't). Stir the mixture and turn the heat to medium. Cook, stirring often, for about 10 to 15 minutes, until the mixture is thick.

If you're using masa or reconstituted masa harina, add 1 cup of the water to the mixture and stir with a wooden spoon or a whisk to dissolve. Add the remaining water to the tomato mixture, stir well, and strain in the dissolved masa or masa harina. Stir while you bring to a simmer and add salt to taste. Simmer for 15 minutes, stirring occasionally, and remove from the heat. Taste and adjust the salt.

Ten minutes before serving, bring the broth to a boil and add the epazote (but not cilantro) and shrimp. Simmer for 10 minutes. If you're using cilantro, stir it in now. Taste and adjust the seasonings. Serve, distributing the shrimp evenly among the bowls and topping each serving with a few wedges of toasted tortilla if you wish. Pass cut limes for people to squeeze into their soup.

Advance Preparation: The broth can be prepared hours ahead of serving and will keep for a few days in the refrigerator. It can also be frozen.

PER PORTION

Calories	213	Protein	16 g
Fat	7 g	Carbohydrate	24 g
Saturated Fat	1 g	Fiber	4 g
Cholesterol	93 mg	Sodium	1,054 mg

Variation

VEGETARIAN VERSION: Omit the shrimp and substitute 1/2 pound red-skinned potatoes, cut into 1/2-inch dice, kernels from 2 ears of corn, 1 pound summer squash, cut into 1/4-inch dice, and one 15-ounce can of chickpeas, drained. Follow the recipe through simmering the stock with the masa. Add the vegetables and simmer for 15 minutes, or until tender. Proceed as directed.

PER PORTION

Calories	183	Protein	6 g
Fat	6 g	Carbohydrate	30 g
Saturated Fat	.72 g	Fiber	5 g
Cholesterol	0	Sodium	780 mg

LIGHT AND FRAGRANT CORN SOUP

Makes 4 servings

This is a gorgeous soup. The intensity of the sweet corn is incredible, provided you make it at the height of the corn season. The soup is rather thin, with a silky-creamy texture, which contrasts nicely with the tomato, corn, and cilantro salsa (though the soup would be just as good with no garnish at all). It's important to make the stock here, because you need its sweet flavor.

For the Stock:
1 onion, quartered
1 pound leeks (about 3), white part only, cleaned and sliced
1 pound carrots, sliced
2 garlic cloves, peeled and slightly crushed
2 ears corn, shucked and cut into 2-inch lengths, or cobs left from corn for soup (below)
2 quarts water
1 teaspoon salt

For the Soup:
1 tablespoon canola oil
1 white or Vidalia onion, chopped
 kernels from 5 ears corn
 salt to taste

For the Tomato Salsa:
2 medium tomatoes, peeled, seeded, and chopped
1 serrano chile, seeded and minced
2 to 3 tablespoons chopped fresh cilantro to taste
 kernels from 1/2 ear corn, steamed until tender
 salt to taste

Combine all the ingredients for the stock in a large saucepan or pasta pot, bring to a boil, reduce the heat, and simmer for 1 to 2 hours. Taste and adjust the seasonings. Strain and set aside.

Heat the oil in a heavy soup pot or Dutch oven over medium-low heat and add the onion. Cook, stirring, until the onion is tender, about 5 minutes.

Add the corn and a little salt and cook gently for about 3 minutes, stirring often. Add the stock, bring to a simmer, cover, and simmer over low heat for 30 minutes.

While the soup is cooking, mix together the ingredients for the tomato addition.

Blend the soup in a blender or food processor fitted with the steel blade, then press through a strainer. Make sure you get as much pulp through as you can, leaving behind the skins from the corn kernels. Return to the soup pot and heat through. Taste and adjust the seasonings.

Serve the soup in wide soup bowls, adding a spoonful of the tomato mixture to the middle of each bowl.

Advance Preparation: This will hold for a couple of hours on top of the stove and can be reheated gently. However, the flavor will deteriorate over time and certainly overnight in the refrigerator.

PER PORTION

Calories	209	Protein	6 g
Fat	5 g	Carbohydrate	40 g
Saturated Fat	.50 g	Fiber	7 g
Cholesterol	0	Sodium	597 mg

CORN, TOMATO, AND POBLANO SOUP

Makes 6 generous servings

These three utterly Mexican ingredients occur together often. This soup differs from the other corn soups because it isn't a puree but more of a pure vegetable soup. The corn is cooked al dente, which made a young friend comment that it's a "crunchy soup." You need a good, tasty stock here; it makes sense to use corncob stock, given all the corn kernels called for.

1   tablespoon canola or olive oil
1   medium onion, chopped
4   garlic cloves, minced or pressed
      kernels from 6 ears corn

$^1/_2$ **pound (2 medium or 1 large) tomatoes, peeled, seeded, and diced**

       salt and freshly ground pepper to taste

6   **cups corncob, chicken, vegetable, or garlic stock (pages 158–160)**

$^1/_2$ **teaspoon dried oregano, preferably Mexican**

3   **medium or 2 large poblano chiles, roasted,* and cut into $^1/_2$-inch dice**

$^1/_4$ **cup chopped fresh parsley or cilantro**

2   **limes, cut into wedges, for serving, optional**

Heat the oil in a heavy soup pot or Dutch oven over medium heat and add the onion. Cook, stirring, until the onion is tender, about 5 minutes. Add the garlic and cook together for about 30 seconds, until the garlic is fragrant. Add the corn and tomatoes and about $^1/_2$ teaspoon salt. Cook, stirring, for about 5 minutes, until the corn is slightly tender and the mixture smells fragrant. Stir in the stock and oregano and bring to a simmer. Cover and simmer for 10 minutes. Stir in the poblanos, taste, and adjust the salt. Stir in the parsley and serve at once, passing lime wedges for guests to squeeze into their soup if they wish.

Advance Preparation: This soup will hold at room temperature for several hours, but don't stir in the poblanos and parsley until just before you reheat and serve. If you stir in the peppers too soon, the soup will become too picante, and you'll lose the nice balance of flavors.

PER PORTION

Calories	155	Protein	5 g
Fat	4 g	Carbohydrate	30 g
Saturated Fat	.35 g	Fiber	5 g
Cholesterol	0	Sodium	495 mg

* *To roast chiles:* Roast the chiles either directly over a gas flame or under a broiler, turning often until uniformly charred. When the chile is blackened on all sides, transfer to a plastic bag or a bowl, seal or cover, and cool. Remove the charred skin, rinse, and pat dry. Remove the seeds and veins (wear rubber gloves for chiles).

CREAMY CORN AND POBLANO SOUP

Makes 4 generous servings

This soup is so thick and rich tasting that everyone thinks there's cream in it. It's just the corn—and there's a lot of it—that makes it so rich. The poblanos give it a slightly green hue and a picante hit.

1   tablespoon canola oil
1   medium white onion, chopped
2   garlic cloves, minced or pressed
     kernels from 6 ears corn (about 4 heaped cups), for soup, plus
         kernels from 1 ear for garnish
     salt to taste
1   quart chicken, vegetable, corncob, or garlic stock (pages 158–160)
2   medium to large poblano chiles, roasted*
¹/₄   cup chopped fresh cilantro for garnish

Heat the oil in a heavy soup pot or Dutch oven over medium heat and add the onion. Cook, stirring, until the onion is tender, about 5 minutes. Add the garlic and cook together for about 30 seconds, until the garlic is fragrant. Add the corn for the soup and about ¹/₂ teaspoon salt and cook, stirring often, for 5 minutes, until the corn is slightly tender. Add the stock, bring to a simmer, cover, and simmer for 15 minutes. Remove from the heat.

Steam the kernels for the garnish for 5 to 8 minutes, until tender.

Add the roasted chiles to the soup and puree the soup in batches in a blender (a hand blender or food processor won't give the same thick, creamy texture). Return to the heat and add salt to taste. Heat through and serve, topping each serving with a tablespoon or two of steamed corn kernels and a sprinkling of cilantro.

Advance Preparation: The roasted chiles will keep for a few days in the refrigerator. The soup is best served on the day it's made but can stand for several hours.

* *To roast chiles:* Roast the chiles either directly over a gas flame or under a broiler, turning often until uniformly charred. When the chile is blackened on all sides, transfer to a plastic bag, seal, and cool. Remove the charred skin, rinse, and pat dry. Remove the seeds and veins (wear rubber gloves for chiles).

Calories	224	Protein	7 g
Fat	7 g	Carbohydrate	40 g
Saturated Fat	.52 g	Fiber	6 g
Cholesterol	0	Sodium	854 mg

ROASTED YELLOW TOMATO SOUP

Makes 4 servings

This soup is just sensational. Every time I taste it I can't believe how incredibly intense and rich it tastes. Of course, the tomatoes have to be delicious to begin with—the best summer harvest you can find. You can serve it with a red salsa or chopped tomato garnish for flavor, color, and texture contrast, but it doesn't really *need* anything more.

4   pounds (16 medium or 8 large) yellow tomatoes, roasted*
1   cup water
1   tablespoon olive oil
2   large garlic cloves or more to taste, minced or pressed
    salt to taste, at least 1½ teaspoons
¼   teaspoon sugar

For Garnish (optional):
2   medium red tomatoes, finely chopped
1   tablespoon chopped fresh cilantro, cilantro sprigs, or 1 teaspoon chopped epazote
1   ounce crumbled or thinly sliced queso fresco, feta, or goat cheese

Puree the peeled tomatoes, along with any juice that has accumulated in the bowl, in a blender or a food processor fitted with the steel blade. Strain into a

---

* *To roast tomatoes:* Preheat the broiler. Line a baking sheet with foil and place the tomatoes on it (you may have to do this in two batches). Place under the broiler, about 2 to 3 inches from the heat (at the highest rack setting). Turn after 2 or 3 minutes, when the tomatoes have charred on one side (this may take longer in an electric oven), and repeat on the other side. Remove from the heat and transfer to a bowl. When the tomatoes are cool enough to handle, peel and core.

bowl through a medium-mesh strainer. Rinse out the blender or food processor with the water and strain into the bowl.

Heat the oil in a large heavy saucepan, soup pot, or Dutch oven over medium-low heat. Add the garlic and cook just until it begins to color, 30 to 60 seconds. Add the tomato puree, salt, and sugar, turn the heat to medium-high, and bring to a boil. Reduce the heat to medium-low. Simmer, stirring often (make sure you stir down the soup that adheres to the sides of the pot), for 20 minutes, until the mixture has thickened. The color will darken to a more orangey hue. Remove from the heat, taste, and adjust the salt and garlic.

Serve, garnishing if you wish with tomato, cilantro, and cheese.

Advance Preparation: The soup can be made up to a day ahead of time and reheated gently. It can also be served cold.

PER PORTION

Calories	121	Protein	4 g
Fat	5 g	Carbohydrate	20 g
Saturated Fat	.65 g	Fiber	5 g
Cholesterol	0	Sodium	861 mg

Variation
ROASTED RED TOMATO SOUP WITH CILANTRO PESTO: Substitute 3½ pounds red tomatoes for the yellow tomatoes (red tomatoes are juicier than yellow tomatoes, so you need less). Instead of the garnish called for, make cilantro pesto (see Mussels on the Half-Shell with Cilantro Pesto on page 124), substituting 1 medium tomato, peeled and seeded, for the ½ cup cooking liquid from the mussels. Top each serving with a spoonful of pesto.

PER PORTION

Calories	164	Protein	6 g
Fat	8 g	Carbohydrate	23 g
Saturated Fat	2 g	Fiber	6 g
Cholesterol	2 mg	Sodium	647 mg

LATE-SUMMER VEGETABLE SOUP

Makes 6 servings

This is a soup to make when all of those mid- to late-summer vegetables—fresh corn, green and yellow squash, and sweet, juicy tomatoes—are piled high in the markets. Thick with diced vegetables and corn kernels, it has great texture. The roasted poblano pepper added toward the end of the cooking gives it a slightly picante lift and a Mexican soul.

1	tablespoon canola oil
1	medium white onion, chopped
4	garlic cloves, minced or pressed
	kernels from 2 ears white or yellow corn
1	pound (4 medium) new potatoes, scrubbed and cut into ¼-inch dice
1	pound (3 medium) zucchini, scrubbed and cut into ¼-inch dice
1	pound (3 medium) yellow squash, scrubbed and cut into ¼-inch dice
1	pound (4 medium or 2 large) tomatoes, peeled and diced
2	sprigs epazote or parsley
6	cups chicken stock, vegetable stock (pages 158–160), or water
	salt, about 2 teaspoons, and freshly ground pepper to taste
2	medium or 1 large poblano chile, roasted and diced
2	ounces queso fresco or feta cheese, crumbled (about ½ cup), for garnish, optional
12	squash blossoms, if available, for garnish

Heat the oil in a heavy soup pot or Dutch oven over medium-low heat. Add the onion and cook, stirring, until the onion begins to soften, about 3 minutes. Add the garlic and corn kernels and continue to cook, stirring, for another few minutes, until the onion is tender but not beginning to color. Add the potatoes, squash, tomatoes, epazote, stock, and salt and pepper, and bring to a boil. Reduce the heat, cover, and simmer for 30 minutes, until the vegetables are fragrant and tender. Taste and adjust the salt.

Stir the diced chiles into the soup and simmer for 5 minutes.

Taste the soup and adjust the seasonings. Ladle into bowls and garnish each with a sprinkling of cheese and one or two squash blossoms (depending on size).

Advance Preparation: The soup keeps for 3 or 4 days in the refrigerator. However, it will continue to get spicier once the poblanos are added, so if you can, wait until you reheat the soup before adding the peppers.

PER PORTION

Calories	210	Protein	6g
Fat	5g	Carbohydrate	39 g
Saturated Fat	.29 g	Fiber	5 g
Cholesterol	0	Sodium	579 mg

MEXICAN-STYLE GAZPACHO

Makes 4 to 6 servings

The Spanish never would have had red gazpacho had it not been for the tomato, an import from the New World. So I'm bringing it back home here. If you can make this with yellow tomatoes, you'll have an incredibly beautiful set of contrasts. But the soup is equally ravishing with red tomatoes.

For the Soup Base:
- 4   thick slices (about 1 ounce) stale French bread, crusts removed
- 2   pounds (8 medium or 4 large) ripe yellow or red tomatoes, peeled and quartered
- 4   large garlic cloves or more to taste, peeled
- 2   jalapeño or 4 serrano chiles, seeded, for a milder soup
- 2   tablespoons red wine vinegar or more to taste
-    salt, about 1 teaspoon, and freshly ground pepper to taste
- 2   cups ice-cold water
- ¼   cup chopped red or white onion, rinsed
- 1   teaspoon crushed cumin seeds

For the Garnish and Texture:
- 1   small cucumber, peeled, seeded, and minced
- 1   red or green bell pepper, minced
- 1   to 3 serrano or jalapeño chiles to taste
- ¾   pound (about 3 medium) tomatoes, diced
- ¼   cup chopped fresh cilantro

Soak the bread in water to cover until soft, about 5 to 10 minutes. Squeeze out the water.

Blend together the bread with the remaining soup base ingredients in a blender until smooth. Taste and adjust seasonings. Chill for several hours.

Toss together the garnish ingredients except cilantro or pass in separate bowls. Ladle soup into each bowl, then top with the garnishes. Decorate with cilantro and serve.

Advance Preparation: This will hold for a day in the refrigerator.

PER PORTION

Calories	168	Protein	6 g
Fat	2 g	Carbohydrate	35 g
Saturated Fat	.33 g	Fiber	6 g
Cholesterol	0	Sodium	754 mg

Chapter
Seven

Beans and Rice

A Great Pot of Beans: Black Beans with Epazote
Refried Beans
Refried Black Beans with Plantain Pancakes
Veracruz-Style Beans and Rice
Green Rice with Cilantro and Spinach or Parsley (Arroz Verde)
White Rice with Herbs
Brown Rice with Corn and Zucchini
Red Rice with Peas and Carrots

I've put beans and rice together in this short chapter because the two, although seldom served together ("combination plates" notwithstanding) are a staple in Mexican cooking, to be served again and again with other Mexican dishes.

Beans are especially important in Mexican cooking. Beans and corn tortillas, an excellent complete protein source, constitute the bulk of the diet for many rural Mexicans, which explains why they have developed such delicious ways to cook beans. They are simmered in the pot, the olla, with onion, garlic, and herbs, resulting in a soupy, fragrant broth that is eaten along with the beans. Cooked beans in their broth are fried—*refried,* as the Spanish word describes it—in lard in Mexico (but not in these recipes), to a scrumptious paste that is eaten on its own with tortillas, spread onto tostadas, thrown into eggs, and so on. Refried beans are often called *frijoles,* which is also the Spanish word for "beans."

Black beans may be the staple in southern Mexico, but they're far from the only beans you'll see in the markets there and throughout the country. On my last trip to Oaxaca, in one stall I counted three different types of white beans (they're used in the green herb mole), black-eyed peas, hulled dried fava beans that were the most beautiful yellow color (they are in the fava bean soup), gorgeous scarlet runner beans, little green flageolets, and chickpeas. In New Mexico there are other beans, beautiful pale speckled beans that become pink when cooked and red beans. Although I've stuck to a few basic recipes in this chapter, you'll find the other beans in soups and stews and salads throughout the book. And you can always substitute pinto or pink beans for the black beans in the recipes here.

SOAKING THE BEANS AND DISCARDING THE SOAKING WATER. In this country we usually soak our beans to speed up the cooking and throw out the soaking water because doing so is believed by some to make beans more digestible. Mexicans do not normally soak beans, and when they do they do not discard the soaking water. Beans are simmered for a very long time, and they soften beautifully. Whether discarding the soaking water improves digestibility is debatable, and when you throw out that water you lose some of the color and flavor of the beans, particularly black beans. So in my recipes using fresh water to cook the beans is an option. You might try making the beans both ways and see if you detect a difference.

Rice was brought to Mexico by the Spanish. It is almost always first cooked in oil, then simmered, and served alongside fish or meat, stews, or tortilla-based dishes. My favorite Mexican rice dishes are the colored rices, like green rice, which is cooked with herbs and/or spinach, and red rice, cooked with tomato and other vegetables.

The cuisine of Veracruz has many Spanish overtones, but it also has Caribbean influences. The Veracruz-style beans and rice will remind you of similar Creole and Caribbean dishes, except here you'll find jalapeño chiles, a sure sign that it's a Mexican dish.

A GREAT POT OF BEANS: BLACK BEANS WITH EPAZOTE

Makes 4 servings as a main course, 6 as a side dish

Epazote has an amazing effect on beans. Rather than stand out the way this earthy herb can when it's cooked with vegetables, epazote gives itself wholly over to the beans. The epazote seems to complete the dish without adding an extra flavor. With garlic, onion, salt, and epazote, black beans are intensely satisfying; they need nothing else.

1	pound dried black beans, washed and picked over
14	cups water if discarding the soaking water; 2 quarts if not
1	tablespoon canola oil
1	medium onion, chopped
4	garlic cloves, minced or pressed
2	epazote sprigs
	salt to taste, 1 to 2 teaspoons

Soak the beans in 6 cups water for at least 6 hours. Drain if desired.

Heat the oil in a large heavy bean pot or Dutch oven over medium heat. Add the onion and cook, stirring, until the onion is just about tender, 3 to 5 minutes. Add 1 garlic clove, stir together for about 30 seconds, and add the beans, another garlic clove, and 2 quarts water, or enough to cover the beans by 1 inch. Bring to a boil, add the epazote, reduce the heat, cover, and simmer for 1 hour.

Add the salt and remaining garlic. Continue to simmer for another hour, until the beans are tender and the broth is thick and fragrant. Let sit overnight for the best flavor.

NOTE: Use this recipe for pinto beans and pink beans as well as black beans.

Advance Preparation: The beans will keep in the refrigerator for about 4 days. They get better overnight. They also freeze well.

Calories	438	Protein	25 g
Fat	5 g	Carbohydrate	75 g
Saturated Fat	.65 g	Fiber	16 g
Cholesterol	0	Sodium	831 mg

Variation

BEANS COOKED WITH ONION, GARLIC, AND CILANTRO: For black beans, pinto beans, and pink beans, substitute 2 tablespoons cilantro for the epazote. Add the cilantro with the salt and remaining garlic.

REFRIED BEANS

Makes 6 servings as a side dish

Most people are skeptical when I tell them I make my frijoles without lard—until they taste the beans. My feeling is that as long as the frijoles have a "big taste," they will please; and although it isn't authentic, that taste needn't be the flavor of lard. I season my cooked beans with lots of garlic, onion, and cilantro or epazote and my refried beans with cumin and ground chile. If the pot of beans is incredibly savory to begin with, the refried beans will taste even better, since all of the flavors intensify as the bean broth is reduced. That's what this recipe is: beans that are mashed and cooked in a reduction of their broth. Black beans are best, but the recipe works for pintos as well.

1	pound dried black beans or pintos, washed and picked over
14	cups water if discarding the soaking water; 2 quarts if not
2	tablespoons canola oil
1	onion, chopped
4	large garlic cloves, or more to taste, minced or pressed
2	to 3 teaspoons salt or more to taste
2	large fresh epazote sprigs or 2 heaped tablespoons fresh cilantro leaves
1	tablespoon ground cumin
2	teaspoons pure ground mild or medium-hot chile powder (page 81)

Soak the beans in 6 cups water overnight or for at least 6 hours. Drain if desired.

Heat 2 teaspoons of the oil in a heavy bean pot over medium-low heat and add the onion. Cook, stirring, until the onion softens, and add 2 garlic cloves. Cook, stirring, for about 1 minute. Add the beans and 2 quarts water, or enough to cover the beans by an inch, and bring to a boil. Reduce the heat, cover, and simmer for 1 hour. Add the remaining garlic, the salt, and the epazote, cover, and simmer for another hour, until the beans are soft and their liquid is thick and soupy. Taste and adjust the salt. Remove from the heat.

Drain off about 1 cup of liquid from the beans, reserving it in a separate bowl to use later for moistening the beans should they dry out. Mash half the beans coarsely in a food processor or with a bean or potato masher. Don't puree them, however. You want texture. Stir the mashed beans back into the pot.

Heat the remaining oil in a large heavy nonstick frying pan over medium heat and add the cumin and ground chile. Cook, stirring over medium heat, for about a minute, until the spices begin to sizzle and cook; turn the heat to medium-high and add the beans (this can be done in batches, in which case cook the spices in batches as well). Fry the beans, until they thicken and begin to get crusty on the bottom and aromatic. Stir up the crust each time it forms and mix into the beans. Cook for about 20 minutes, stirring often and mashing the beans with the back of your spoon or a bean masher. The beans should be thick but not dry. Add some of the liquid you saved from the beans if they seem too dry, but save some of the liquid for moistening the beans before you reheat them if you're serving them later. Taste the refried beans and adjust the salt. Set aside in the pan if you're serving within a few hours. They will continue to dry out. Otherwise transfer the beans to a lightly oiled baking dish and cover with foil.

Advance Preparation: Refried beans will keep for 3 days in the refrigerator and for several months in the freezer. Keep the reserved liquid in a jar so that you can moisten the beans before reheating. The frijoles can be reheated in a nonstick pan or in a lightly oiled baking dish. Cover the dish with foil and reheat for 30 minutes in a 325-degree oven. However, if you are storing the beans in the refrigerator in a baking dish, cover first with plastic or wax paper before you cover with aluminum, so that the beans don't react with the aluminum. *Remember to remove the plastic before reheating.*

PER PORTION

Calories	319	Protein	17 g
Fat	6 g	Carbohydrate	51 g
Saturated Fat	.59 g	Fiber	11 g
Cholesterol	0	Sodium	931 mg

QUICK VERSION: Although canned beans never taste as good as beans you cook with lots of onion, garlic, and herbs, they are suitable for making refried beans in a hurry, and why deprive yourself of refried beans if time is short? For 2 cups refried beans you will need two 15-ounce cans of beans (4 cans yield the same amount as this recipe). Do not drain off the liquid or even puree the beans. Heat the oil and fry the spices as directed. Pour in the beans with their liquid and mash with a bean masher or the back of a large wooden spoon right in the pan. Cook, stirring, exactly as instructed for the refried beans. There is less liquid in a can of beans than you get when you cook them, so you will have to add water; the refried canned beans will dry out considerably.

REFRIED BLACK BEANS WITH PLANTAIN PANCAKES

Makes 6 servings

This marvelous combination is a specialty of Veracruz, where they also make plantain empanadas filled with black beans. But I always have trouble with plantain empanada dough, so I make the pancakes instead and get the same fantastic marriage of flavors.

Make the preceding recipe, using black beans. Make the recipe for Plantain Pancakes (page 358), using 2 plantains. Serve the black beans with the pancakes on the side or set on top of the beans.

Advance Preparation: See previous recipe for the beans. The plantain pancakes will keep for several days in the refrigerator, wrapped in plastic.

PER PORTION

Calories	451	Protein	18 g
Fat	11 g	Carbohydrate	75 g
Saturated Fat	1 g	Fiber	5 g
Cholesterol	0	Sodium	934 mg

VERACRUZ-STYLE BEANS AND RICE

Makes 4 servings as a main dish, 6 as a side dish

This is as close to New Orleans dirty rice as you can get in Mexico. The mixture of black beans and rice is perked up with chiles, either serranos or jalapeños, while sliced onion adds texture. I could eat this any day, for a meal or a side dish. In Veracruz the dish would be served with crisp deep-fried green plantains (tostones) or twice-fried ripe plantains (platanos machucos). I serve it with thin plantain pancakes.

1	tablespoon canola oil
$\frac{1}{2}$	medium onion, thinly sliced
2	to 3 serrano or jalapeño chiles, seeded for a milder dish and thinly sliced
1	garlic clove, minced or pressed
2	cups cooked medium- or long-grain white rice
$1\frac{1}{2}$	cups cooked black beans (page 192) with a little of their cooking liquid
$\frac{1}{2}$	cup additional liquid from the beans
	salt to taste
	Plantain Pancakes (page 358) for serving, optional

Heat the oil in a large heavy saucepan or nonstick skillet over medium heat. Add the onion and chiles and cook, stirring, until the onion is tender, about 5 minutes. Add the garlic and cook, stirring, for another minute, just until the garlic begins to smell fragrant. Stir in the rice, beans, and about $\frac{1}{2}$ cup broth from the beans. Stir gently for about 5 minutes, until the mixture is heated through. It should be quite moist, like a thick stew; add the additional $\frac{1}{2}$ cup cooking liquid from the beans if it seems dry. Serve at once, with plantain pancakes, if desired.

Advance Preparation: Although the finished dish—which takes only minutes—should be served right away, before the rice absorbs too much broth from the beans, you can hold the dish for a few hours if you have more of the broth on hand. The rice will be softer, but the mixture will still taste wonderful.

PER PORTION

Calories	242	Protein	7 g
Fat	4 g	Carbohydrate	43 g
Saturated Fat	.41 g	Fiber	3 g
Cholesterol	0	Sodium	134 mg

Variation

QUICK VERSION: Use one 15-ounce can black beans with the liquid. You will have to add about $\frac{1}{2}$ to 1 cup water, chicken stock, or vegetable stock.

PER PORTION

Calories	255	Protein	9 g
Fat	5 g	Carbohydrate	45 g
Saturated Fat	.31 g	Fiber	6 g
Cholesterol	0	Sodium	330 mg

GREEN RICE WITH CILANTRO AND SPINACH OR PARSLEY (ARROZ VERDE)

Makes 4 to 6 servings as a side dish

This lovely green rice has a fresh, herbal taste. Serve it as a side dish with fish, chicken, or any of the tacos, enchiladas, or quesadillas in this collection.

2¼ cups chicken, vegetable, or garlic stock (pages 158–160) or water
1 cup fresh parsley or spinach leaves
½ cup fresh cilantro leaves
1 tablespoon canola oil
½ medium onion, chopped
1 large garlic clove, minced or pressed
1 poblano chile, finely chopped, optional
1 cup long-grain rice
salt, about ½ teaspoon if not using stock

Combine half the stock with the parsley and cilantro in a blender and blend at high speed until smooth. Have the remaining stock at a bare simmer in a saucepan.

Heat the oil in a heavy saucepan over medium heat and add the onion. Cook, stirring, until just tender, about 3 minutes. Add the garlic, poblano, and rice. Cook, stirring, for 3 to 5 minutes, until the rice sticks to the bottom of the pot and the onion is just beginning to color. Add the simmering stock and bring to a boil. Reduce the heat, cover, and simmer for 5 minutes. The liquid will be just about gone.

Add the remaining stock with the blended herbs to the rice, stir the mixture, and raise the heat to bring back to a boil. Reduce the heat again, cover, and continue to simmer until the liquid is absorbed and the rice tender, about 15 minutes. Remove from the heat and let sit, covered, for 10 minutes. Fluff the rice with a fork, taste, and adjust the salt. Serve.

Advance Preparation: The rice is best when it's served right after it's cooked, but you can prepare this a few hours ahead and reheat it in a non-stick pan or in a lightly oiled covered gratin dish in a 350-degree oven for 20 minutes, or in a microwave for a couple of minutes. If you do prepare the rice ahead of time, remove it from the heat and immediately transfer it from the saucepan to a lightly oiled 2-quart gratin dish. Spread the rice out evenly in the dish and allow to cool, then cover with foil.

Calories	235	Protein	4 g
Fat	5 g	Carbohydrate	43 g
Saturated Fat	.31 g	Fiber	2 g
Cholesterol	0	Sodium	321 mg

WHITE RICE WITH HERBS

Makes 4 to 6 servings as a side dish

In Oaxaca this herby rice would be made with a small-leafed, mild-tasting herb called *chipil*. I've never seen chipil in the United States, but that doesn't stop me from making this rendition, which can be made with cilantro or other chopped herbs, such as parsley and tarragon. The important thing is to use a large quantity of the chopped herbs, half of which are added during the cooking, the other half at the end of cooking for vivid color and flavor.

2   cups vegetable, garlic, or chicken stock (pages 158–160)
     salt to taste, 1/4 to 1/2 teaspoon
1   tablespoon canola oil
1   cup medium- or long-grain rice
1/2   medium or 1 small onion, finely chopped
2   garlic cloves, minced or pressed
1 1/2   cups coarsely chopped cilantro, parsley leaves, or a combination
     of parsley, cilantro, and tarragon leaves, loosely packed

Bring the stock to a bare simmer in a saucepan and add the salt.

Heat the oil in a heavy 2-quart saucepan over medium heat and add the rice and onion. Cook, stirring, until the onion is tender but not browned and the grains of rice are separate, about 3 to 5 minutes. Add the garlic and cook for about 30 seconds, just until the garlic begins to smell fragrant.

Stir in the simmering stock and half the herbs, bring the mixture to a boil, stir down the sides of the pan, reduce the heat, cover, and simmer over low heat for 15 minutes, until the water is absorbed. Remove from the heat and let sit, covered, for 5 to 10 minutes. The grains should be tender. Stir in the remaining herbs and serve.

Advance Preparation: You can make this several hours ahead, but if you do, instead of allowing the rice to sit after you remove it from the heat, transfer it at once to a lightly oiled 2-quart baking dish and let cool, uncovered, without stirring in the second half of the herbs. Cover with foil and reheat for 15 minutes in a 325-degree oven. Stir in the herbs and serve.

PER PORTION

Calories	218	Protein	4 g
Fat	4 g	Carbohydrate	41 g
Saturated Fat	.31 g	Fiber	1 g
Cholesterol	0	Sodium	450 mg

BROWN RICE WITH CORN AND ZUCCHINI

Makes 4 to 6 servings as a side dish

I'd never call this authentic Mexican, but I love the way it goes with Mexican food. Brown rice has a marvelous chewy texture, which pairs beautifully with the crunchy-juicy corn and zucchini. This is easy to throw together and goes with just about anything.

2¹/₃ **cups water, chicken stock, or vegetable stock (pages 158–160)**
2 **teaspoons canola oil**
2 **tablespoons chopped onion**
1 **cup long-grain brown rice**
¹/₂ **teaspoon salt or more to taste if using water**
kernels from 1 ear corn
1 **medium zucchini, cut into ¹/₄-inch dice**
freshly ground pepper to taste

Bring the water to a simmer in a saucepan.

Heat the oil in a heavy saucepan over medium heat and add the onion and rice. Cook, stirring, for about 4 to 5 minutes or until the rice is beginning to pop and smell toasty.

Add the simmering water and salt. Bring back to a boil, then reduce the heat to low, cover, and simmer for 30 minutes. Stir in the corn and zucchini, cover, and continue to simmer for 10 minutes or until the liquid has evaporated. Remove from the heat, grind on some pepper, and serve.

Advance Preparation: Although rice is always best when it's served right after it's cooked, you could prepare this a few hours ahead and reheat it in a nonstick pan or in a lightly oiled covered gratin dish in a 350-degree oven for 20 minutes or for a couple of minutes in the microwave. Transfer the cooked rice at once to a lightly oiled 2-quart baking dish and let cool uncovered, then cover with foil.

PER PORTION

Calories	218	Protein	5 g
Fat	4 g	Carbohydrate	42 g
Saturated Fat	.46 g	Fiber	3 g
Cholesterol	0	Sodium	282 mg

RED RICE WITH PEAS AND CARROTS

Makes 4 servings as a side dish

This is a classic. I have a few different ways of cooking my red rice, but this one is the most traditional, though I use less oil than a Mexican cook would—and I give you the option of using olive oil. Olive oil may not seem Mexican at all, but it's used in Veracruz and in the Yucatán.

- 2 cups chicken stock, vegetable stock, or water (pages 158–160)
- 1 tablespoon canola or olive oil
- 1 small onion, finely chopped
- 1 small carrot, cut into small dice
- 1 cup medium- or long-grain rice
- 2 large garlic cloves, minced or pressed
- 1 medium tomato, peeled, seeded, and pureed, or half of a 15-ounce can, drained, seeded, and pureed (³/₄ cup)
- ¹/₂ to 2 teaspoons salt, or more to taste
- 1 cup fresh or thawed frozen peas
- 2 tablespoons chopped fresh cilantro or parsley for garnish

Bring the stock to a bare simmer in a saucepan.

Heat the oil in a heavy saucepan over medium heat and add the onion, carrot, and rice. Cook, stirring, until the rice and onion begin to brown slightly and stick to the pan, about 5 minutes. Add the garlic and stir for another half-minute, until it begins to color.

Stir in the pureed tomato and cook, stirring, for 1 minute. Stir in the simmering stock and the salt and return to a simmer. Give the rice a stir, scraping the sides of the pan, cover, and reduce the heat to low. Simmer for 15 minutes or until the rice is tender and the liquid has been absorbed.

Meanwhile steam fresh peas for 5 minutes or heat thawed frozen peas in boiling water for 1 minute.

When the rice is tender, remove from the heat, taste, and adjust the seasonings. Add the peas and fluff the rice with a fork or spoon while stirring in the peas. Sprinkle with chopped cilantro and serve.

Advance Preparation: You can make this several hours ahead of serving, but if you do, instead of allowing the rice to sit after you remove it from the heat, transfer it at once to a lightly oiled 2-quart baking dish and let cool, uncovered. Cover with foil and reheat for 15 minutes in a 325-degree oven or for a couple of minutes in a microwave.

PER PORTION

Calories	281	Protein	6 g
Fat	5 g	Carbohydrate	52 g
Saturated Fat	.34 g	Fiber	4 g
Cholesterol	0	Sodium	700 mg

Chapter
Eight

Tortilla Dishes:

Tacos, Tostadas, Enchiladas, Quesadillas, Chilaquiles

SOFT TACOS

Soft Tacos or Tostadas with Chicken and Tomatillo Salsa

Soft Tacos or Tostadas with Chicken, Corn, and Avocado

Soft Tacos with Oyster Mushrooms and Tomatoes

Soft Tacos with Summer Squash, Corn, Tomatoes, and Onions

Soft Tacos with Squash and Potatoes

Shredded Fish Tacos

Soft Tacos with Fish and Potatoes

Soft Tacos with Turkey Picadillo

TOSTADAS

Main-Dish Black Bean Tostadas (aka Chalupas)

Vegetable Tostadas with Red Chile Sauce

ENCHILADAS

Green Enchiladas with Chicken Filling

Green Enchiladas with Spinach and Corn Filling

Picante Shrimp Enchiladas with Chipotle Sauce

Mushroom and Garlic Enchiladas with Chipotle Tomato Sauce

Enfrijoladas

QUESADILLAS

Basic Cheese Quesadillas Several Ways

Baked Quartered Quesadillas

Quesadillas with Potatoes and Sorrel

Quesadillas with Broccoli and Garlic

Chicken and Tomatillo Quesadillas

Quesadillas with Oyster Mushrooms and Chipotles

Garlicky Zucchini Quesadillas

Swiss Chard Quesadillas

Quesadillas with Goat Cheese, Roasted Peppers, and Black Beans

Scrambled Egg and Green Chile Quesadillas (or Soft Tacos)

Potato Peel Quesadillas

Squash Blossom Quesadillas

CHILAQUILES

Green Chilaquiles

Red Chilaquiles

Green Chilaquiles with Chicken, Corn, and Squash

Black Bean Chilaquiles

I have a feeling that this is the chapter you've been waiting for. This, to most Americans, is Mexican food: it comes in or on a tortilla.

Of course this isn't true. In Mexico these masa-based foods are categorized as *antojitos,* snacks to be eaten before the main dish or as a light meal. The more serious, complex Mexican dishes are stews and moles, fish dishes, and barbecues. But even they can fill or top a tortilla.

As far as I'm concerned, tortilla-based dishes make a splendid meal. What's more, most of the tacos and quesadillas here are so simple they can be made after work. They're fun for kids and full of exciting flavors for adults.

Coming up with low-fat tacos, quesadillas, and other tortilla dishes isn't difficult once you understand that in Mexico these foods are often cooked on a griddle, not fried in oil. It varies from region to region. Even in the Mission district of San Francisco, you are as likely to get a taco on a dry, griddle- or steam-heated soft tortilla as on a fried one. The dishes called *tostadas,* misnamed *chalupas* in most of our border-Mex restaurants (actual chalupas are fried boat-shaped masa containers), are called *tostadas* because the tortillas are toasted before being topped.

The possibilities become endless, and I let my imagination go with seasonal vegetable, fish, and chicken combinations. The tortillas are first heated—either by steam, on the griddle, in the oven, or in the microwave—then topped or filled.

The nomenclature for these tortilla-based foods varies throughout Mexico. What we think of as a taco may be called an empanada in one place and a quesadilla in another (and the quesadilla may not even contain queso!). I was served delicious shrimp enchiladas at the Parador Real, near Xico, that were called *tacos de camarones* on the menu. Even in these pages the tacos and some of the quesadillas are very closely related, differing only in the way the filled tortilla is heated before being served.

I could have filled a book with these foods, which have become a part of my regular diet. As it is, I've left out entire categories of masa snacks (sopes or gorditas, real chalupas), the ones that really do depend on frying. I know you will find many recipes here for everyday dining and some special dishes for entertaining. I hope you will begin to think of tortillas as potential wrappers or beds for all sorts of vegetable, fish, and meat dishes. With a little salsa on the table, dinner can be light Mexican food in no time.

Soft Tacos

It used to be that pasta was our most frequent dinner. Now it's soft tacos. I think they're more suited to a low-calorie diet, because two tacos is usually a sufficient serving for a light supper main dish, and the tortillas contain only two thirds of the calories in 3 ounces of pasta, my usual serving size.

I find myself wrapping food in warm corn tortillas all the time now. For a quick lunch I might heat a couple of tortillas, either directly above a gas flame or in a dry skillet, and fill them with chopped tomatoes, queso fresco or nonfat cottage cheese, perhaps a bit of avocado doused with lime juice, and cilantro. This utterly satisfying, low-fat lunch takes me about 10 minutes to prepare and eat.

The tacos here can be folded, or the toppings can merely sit on the tortilla. If you're eating them with your hands, you'll want to fold the tortilla over. Some of the toppings here include salsas; others are meant to be served with a salsa of your choice, either homemade or commercial.

SOFT TACOS OR TOSTADAS WITH CHICKEN AND TOMATILLO SALSA

Makes 8 tacos, serving 4, or 48 tostadas, serving 8 as an appetizer

This moist shredded chicken tossed with zesty green tomatillo salsa makes a fine topping for either soft tacos or tostadas (nachos). They're completed with a little yogurt and lime-dressed cucumber for a low-low-fat version, avocado for a less-low-fat version (but one avocado goes a long way here).

1   large (about 1 to 1¹/₄ pounds) whole chicken breast, halved and skinned, cooked and shredded*
    salt and freshly ground pepper to taste

---

* *To cook chicken breasts:* Place 1 quartered onion, 2 garlic cloves, and 6 cups of water in a saucepan and bring to a boil. Add 1 teaspoon salt and the chicken breasts and bring back to a boil. Skim off any foam that rises, then add ¹/₂ teaspoon dried thyme, ¹/₂ teaspoon dried oregano or marjoram, and 1 bay leaf. Reduce the heat, cover partially, and simmer for 13 to 15 minutes, until the meat is cooked through. Remove from the heat and allow the chicken to cool in the broth if there is time. Remove the chicken from the broth. Bone and shred the meat (you should have about 1¹/₂ to 1³/₄ cups). Strain the stock through a cheesecloth-lined strainer and set aside for another purpose.

1   cup Salsa Verde Cruda (page 67) or a commercial brand, plus
    additional for serving
¼   cup chopped fresh cilantro leaves, plus more for garnish
1   small avocado, diced, or 1 cup finely minced, peeled, seeded
    cucumber
    juice of 1 large lime
8   corn tortillas, heated,* or 48 toasted tortilla chips*
¾   cup plain nonfat yogurt

FOR TACOS: Toss the shredded chicken breasts with salt, pepper, salsa, cilantro, avocado or cucumber, and lime juice.

Top each heated tortilla with about 3 heaped tablespoons of the filling and a small spoonful of yogurt, garnish with cilantro, and serve, with additional salsa on the side.

FOR TOSTADAS (NACHOS):   Toss the shredded chicken breasts with salt, pepper, salsa, and cilantro. Place a spoonful of the mixture on each tortilla chip. Top with a small dollop of yogurt. Toss together the diced avocado or cucumber and lime juice and add salt to taste. Place a small spoonful on top of each tostada, decorate with cilantro, arrange on a platter or plates, and serve.

Advance Preparation: The chicken and salsa can be prepared a day or two ahead of time and kept in the refrigerator.

PER PORTION

Calories	403	Protein	46 g
Fat	8 g	Carbohydrate	37 g
Saturated Fat	1 g	Fiber	4 g
Cholesterol	96 mg	Sodium	886 mg

To heat tortillas: Wrap in aluminum foil and heat through in a 350-degree oven for 15 minutes; or heat 1 or 2 at a time in a dry nonstick skillet over medium-high heat until flexible; or wrap in a clean kitchen towel and steam for 1 minute, then let sit for 10 minutes; or wrap in wax paper or a damp towel and heat in a microwave on HIGH (100%) power for 1 minute.

To toast tortilla chips: To bake the chips, preheat the oven to 325 degrees. Place the tortilla pieces on a baking sheet and bake for 20 to 30 minutes, until light brown and crisp, shaking the baking sheet every 10 minutes. Allow to cool on a rack. To microwave the chips, place about 6 to 10 pieces at a time on a plate or on the plate in your microwave oven. Microwave on HIGH (100%) power for 1 minute. If the pieces are not crisp, turn them over and microwave for another 40 to 60 seconds. If they are still not crisp and are just beginning to brown, microwave for another 20 to 30 seconds. Cool on a rack or in a basket.

Soft Tacos or Tostadas with Chicken, Corn, and Avocado

Makes 4 main-dish servings, 8 appetizer servings

I love all the different textures and fresh flavors in this dish. The topping is almost like a salad. Use leftover chicken or poach a whole skinned chicken breast. Ideal in late summer and early fall, when tomatoes and corn are at their sweetest, it makes a wonderful supper. Or you can make tostadas (nachos) and serve it as an appetizer or first course.

2	ears corn
1	large whole chicken breast (about 1¼ pounds), skinned, halved, cooked, and shredded,* or about 1½ to 1¾ cups shredded cooked chicken breast
½	small avocado, peeled, pitted, and finely diced
5	to 6 tablespoons fresh lime juice to taste
1	large (about ½ pound) tomato, finely chopped
3	fresh serrano or 1 to 2 jalapeño chiles, seeded for a milder dish and minced
6	tablespoons chopped fresh cilantro
8	corn tortillas, heated,* or 48 toasted tortilla chips* salsa for serving, optional

* *To cook chicken breasts:* Place 1 quartered onion, 2 garlic cloves, and 6 cups of water in a saucepan and bring to a boil. Add 1 teaspoon salt and the chicken breasts and bring back to a boil. Skim off any foam that rises, then add ½ teaspoon dried thyme, ½ teaspoon dried oregano or marjoram, and 1 bay leaf. Reduce the heat, cover partially, and simmer for 13 to 15 minutes, until the meat is cooked through. Remove from the heat and allow the chicken to cool in the broth if there is time. Remove the chicken from the broth. Bone and shred the meat (you should have about 1½–1¾ cups). Strain the stock through a cheesecloth-lined strainer and set aside for another purpose.

* *To heat tortillas:* Wrap in aluminum foil and heat through in a 350-degree oven for 15 minutes; or heat 1 or 2 at a time in a dry nonstick skillet over medium-high heat until flexible; or wrap in a clean kitchen towel and steam for 1 minute, then let sit for 10 minutes; or wrap in wax paper or a damp towel and heat in a microwave on HIGH (100%) power for 1 minute.

* *To toast tortilla chips:* To bake the chips, preheat the oven to 325 degrees. Place the tortilla pieces on a baking sheet and bake for 20 to 30 minutes, until light brown and crisp, shaking the baking sheet every 10 minutes. Allow to cool on a rack. To microwave the chips,

Steam or boil the corn for 5 minutes. Rinse with cold water, then remove the kernels from the cob.

Toss together the chicken, corn, and remaining ingredients except tortillas and salsa. Taste and adjust the seasonings.

For Soft Tacos: Place 2 heated tortillas on each plate, top with the chicken mixture, and serve.

For Tostadas (Nachos).   Top toasted tortilla chips with the mixture and serve.

Advance Preparation: The chicken will keep for a couple of days in the refrigerator. The topping can be made several hours ahead of serving.

PER PORTION

Calories	337	Protein	28 g
Fat	9 g	Carbohydrate	39 g
Saturated Fat	2 g	Fiber	5 g
Cholesterol	60 mg	Sodium	149 mg

place about 6 to 10 pieces at a time on a plate or on the plate in your microwave oven. Microwave on HIGH (100%) power for 1 minute. If the pieces are not crisp, turn them over and microwave for another 40 to 60 seconds. If they are still not crisp and are just beginning to brown, microwave for another 20 to 30 seconds until crisp. Cool on a rack or in a basket.

SOFT TACOS WITH
OYSTER MUSHROOMS AND TOMATOES

Makes 4 servings

One bright, sunny morning I went to one of the many farmers' markets in San Francisco and bought, among other things, lots of oyster mushrooms. Then I went to the Mission district and bought still-warm tortillas and lots of cilantro. We lunched in a funky taqueria, where I ate a "vegetarian taco," a warm, un-fried tortilla piled high with Mexican-style rice and beans, lettuce, and gua-camole. It was at that point that I realized that a taco need not require a fried tortilla at all, and that many of the vegetables I had bought at the market would make terrific toppings. Here is what Bill and I had for dinner that night.

2	pounds (8 medium or 4 large) tomatoes, peeled and quartered
4	to 6 large garlic cloves, to taste, 2 minced or pressed, the others peeled and halved, green shoots removed
1	serrano chile, seeded and coarsely chopped
2	teaspoons olive oil
1	medium onion, chopped
2	pounds oyster mushrooms or large regular mushrooms if oyster mushrooms are unavailable, cleaned and sliced about ½ inch thick
	salt to taste
2	tablespoons either dry red or white wine, such as a merlot or Côtes-du-Rhône, or a sauvignon blanc
	freshly ground pepper to taste
2	tablespoons chopped fresh parsley
¼	cup chopped cilantro
8	corn tortillas, heated*
1	ounce (¼ cup) crumbled queso fresco, freshly grated Parmesan, or feta

Combine the tomatoes, all but the 2 minced garlic cloves, and the serrano chile in a blender and puree until smooth. Set aside.

* *To heat tortillas:* Wrap in aluminum foil and heat through in a 350-degree oven for 15 min-utes; or heat 1 or 2 at a time in a dry nonstick skillet over medium-high heat until flexible; or wrap in a clean kitchen towel and steam for 1 minute, then let sit for 10 minutes; or wrap in wax paper or a damp towel and heat in a microwave on HIGH (100%) power for 1 minute.

Heat the oil in a large nonstick skillet over medium-low heat and add the onion. Cook, stirring, until tender, about 5 minutes. Add the mushrooms and about ½ teaspoon salt, and turn the heat to medium-high. Cook, stirring often, until the mushrooms soften and most of the water they have released has evaporated, about 10 minutes. Add the wine, pepper, and minced garlic, turn the heat to medium, and continue to cook another few minutes, until the garlic is fragrant and the liquid from the mushrooms has just about evaporated. Add the tomato puree, stir together, and cook for another 10 to 15 minutes, until the tomatoes have cooked down and thickened. Stir in the parsley and cilantro, add salt to taste, and remove from the heat.

Stir the mushroom filling over medium heat until the mixture begins to simmer. Place 2 hot tortillas on each plate. Top with the mushroom and tomato filling. Sprinkle on some cheese. Fold the tortillas over the filling, or leave flat on the plate, and serve at once.

Advance Preparation: The filling can be made hours ahead of assembling the tacos and reheated gently just before serving.

PER PORTION

Calories	284	Protein	11 g
Fat	7 g	Carbohydrate	49 g
Saturated Fat	2 g	Fiber	9 g
Cholesterol	5 mg	Sodium	435 mg

SOFT TACOS WITH SUMMER SQUASH, CORN, TOMATOES, AND ONIONS

Makes 6 servings

The filling for these lively tacos is a sort of succotash, a colorful mixture of squash, corn, tomatoes, onions, and chiles. I like to call them "New World tacos" because so many of the ingredients are indigenous to the Americas. Use the sweetest corn you can find. Each mouthful will then be the most surprising, pleasing mixture of sweet, juicy, and picante textures. I add blended cottage cheese because I think the filling needs something creamy or cheesy, but a stronger cheese would interfere too much with the sweet flavors of the vegetables, chiles, and cilantro. You can add a can of beans—pinto or black—if you want more protein and body in these tacos.

1	tablespoon olive oil
1	medium Bermuda onion or $1/2$ torpedo onion, chopped
	salt to taste, $1/2$ to 1 teaspoon
4	fairly small yellow pattypan squash or 2 yellow zucchini-shaped squash, diced into $1/4$-inch pieces (about $2^1/2$ cups)
4	fairly small green pattypan squash or 2 medium zucchini, cut into $1/4$-inch dice (about $2^1/2$ cups)
3	large garlic cloves, minced or pressed
6	medium tomatoes, peeled, seeded, and chopped
1	green Anaheim chile, seeded and finely chopped
1	jalapeño chile, seeded and finely chopped
	kernels from 2 ears corn, preferably white
$1/2$	cup chopped fresh cilantro
1	cup cooked pinto or black beans, optional
	freshly ground pepper to taste
12	corn tortillas, heated*
$1/2$	cup nonfat cottage cheese blended until smooth with 2 tablespoons nonfat yogurt

Heat the oil in a large nonstick skillet over medium heat and add the onion. Cook, stirring, until tender, about 5 minutes. Add a couple of pinches of salt and the squash. Stir together and continue to cook for about 5 minutes, until the squash is beginning to soften. Add a couple of tablespoons of water if the vegetables begin to stick to the pan. Add the garlic and stir together for about 1 minute, until the garlic begins to smell fragrant. Add 4 of the tomatoes and the chiles. Turn the heat to medium-low and cook, stirring often, for about 10 minutes, until the vegetables are tender and aromatic. Add the corn and cook for about 5 minutes, until the kernels are crisp-tender. Add all but 2 tablespoons of the cilantro, the remaining tomatoes, and the beans. Stir together, taste, adjust the salt, and add the pepper. Remove from the heat.

Top the hot tortillas with the vegetables and place a tablespoon of the cottage cheese mixture on top. Garnish with the remaining cilantro and serve.

* *To heat tortillas:* Wrap in aluminum foil and heat through in a 350-degree oven for 15 minutes; or heat 1 or 2 at a time in a dry nonstick skillet over medium-high heat until flexible; or wrap in a clean kitchen towel and steam for 1 minute, then let sit for 10 minutes; or wrap in wax paper or a damp towel and heat in a microwave on HIGH (100%) power for 1 minute.

Advance Preparation: The filling can be made hours ahead of serving and reheated in the pan.

PER PORTION

Calories	231	Protein	9 g
Fat	4 g	Carbohydrate	43 g
Saturated Fat	.59 g	Fiber	2 g
Cholesterol	2 mg	Sodium	447 mg

SOFT TACOS WITH SQUASH AND POTATOES

Makes 6 servings

These tacos topped with New World ingredients are prettiest when you use a combination of yellow and green squash and red-skinned potatoes.

- **2 pounds (8 medium or 4 large) tomatoes, roasted**
- **4 large garlic cloves, toasted**
- **4 to 6 serrano or 2 to 4 jalapeño chiles to taste, toasted**
- **1 pound (4 medium) red-skinned new potatoes, cut into ¹/₂-inch dice**
- **1¹/₂ pounds summer squash, preferably a mixture of green and yellow, cut into ¹/₂-inch dice (5 cups)**
- **1 tablespoon canola oil**
- **¹/₂ torpedo onion or 1 medium red onion, chopped**
- **¹/₂ teaspoon dried oregano, preferably Mexican salt to taste, ¹/₂ teaspoon or more**
- **2 to 4 tablespoons chopped fresh cilantro to taste**
- **12 corn tortillas, heated***
- **2 ounces queso fresco, cotija, or not-too-salty feta, crumbled (¹/₂ cup)**

* To heat tortillas: Wrap in aluminum foil and heat through in a 350-degree oven for 15 minutes; or heat 1 or 2 at a time in a dry nonstick skillet over medium-high heat until flexible; or wrap in a clean kitchen towel and steam for 1 minute, then let sit for 10 minutes; or wrap in wax paper or a damp towel and heat in a microwave on HIGH (100%) power for 1 minute.

Transfer the tomatoes to a blender along with any juice in the bowl. Peel the garlic, and stem and coarsely chop the chiles. Add to the blender and puree until fairly smooth. Set aside.

Steam the potatoes for 15 minutes or until tender. Steam the squash for 8 to 10 minutes, until tender but still bright. Remove from the heat.

Heat the oil in a large heavy nonstick skillet over medium heat and add the onion. Cook, stirring, until tender, about 5 minutes. Add the tomato puree and the oregano. Cook, stirring, for 5 minutes, until the sauce thickens and begins to stick to the pan. Stir in the potatoes and squash and salt lightly. Stir together for about 5 to 10 minutes, until the tomatoes have cooked down and the squash is tender but still bright. Stir in the cilantro. Taste and adjust the seasonings.

Top the heated tortillas with the vegetable mixture, add a sprinkling of cheese, fold over if you wish, and serve.

Advance Preparation: The topping can be made a day ahead of time and reheated. The tomato puree will hold for a couple of days in the refrigerator.

PER PORTION

Calories	288	Protein	9 g
Fat	7 g	Carbohydrate	51 g
Saturated Fat	2 g	Fiber	7 g
Cholesterol	7 mg	Sodium	355 mg

SHREDDED FISH TACOS

Makes 4 servings

This marvelous fish topping is spiced not only with fresh chiles but also with pepper, coriander seeds, and cinnamon. The flavors have an almost Indian feeling. Use a saltwater white-fleshed fish.

1	pound fish fillets, such as shark, snapper, or mahimahi
1/2	pound (2 medium or 1 large) tomatoes, peeled and seeded
2	fresh green serrano or jalapeño chiles, coarsely chopped
12	peppercorns
1/2	teaspoon coriander seeds or 1/4 teaspoon ground coriander
1/4	teaspoon ground cinnamon or a 1/2-inch cinnamon stick
2	garlic cloves, peeled
1/2	teaspoon salt or more to taste
1/4	cup water
1	tablespoon canola oil
1/2	small onion, chopped (about 1/4 cup)
2	tablespoons fresh lime juice, optional
8	corn tortillas, heated*
	fresh cilantro sprigs for garnish

Place the fish fillets on a steamer set above 1/2 inch water in a saucepan. Bring the water to a boil, cover, and steam for 5 to 8 minutes, depending on thickness, until they fall apart easily when poked with a fork. Remove from the heat and set aside until cool enough to handle. Remove any lingering bones and shred the fish, using your fingers or a fork.

Place the tomatoes in a blender with the chiles and blend until smooth. Set aside.

Grind the spices together. Pound the garlic in a mortar and pestle and add the salt and spices. Grind together to a paste and work in the water. The mixture should be smooth. Stir into the tomato mixture.

* To heat tortillas: Wrap in aluminum foil and heat through in a 350-degree oven for 15 minutes; or heat 1 or 2 at a time in a dry nonstick skillet over medium-high heat until flexible; or wrap in a clean kitchen towel and steam for 1 minute, then let sit for 10 minutes; or wrap in wax paper or a damp towel and heat in a microwave on HIGH (100%) power for 1 minute.

Heat the oil over medium heat in a heavy nonstick skillet and add the onion. Cook, stirring, for about 3 to 5 minutes, until tender. Add the tomato puree and cook, stirring, until the tomato mixture cooks down and thickens, about 5 minutes. Stir in the fish and continue to cook together until the mixture is well blended. Remove from the heat, taste, and adjust the salt. Add the lime juice if desired.

Place 2 heated tortillas on each plate, top with the fish, garnish with cilantro sprigs, and serve.

Advance Preparation: The fish topping will keep for several hours in or out of the refrigerator and can be reheated gently before topping the tortillas.

PER PORTION

Calories	308	Protein	27 g
Fat	10 g	Carbohydrate	28 g
Saturated Fat	1 g	Fiber	4 g
Cholesterol	58 mg	Sodium	449 mg

SOFT TACOS WITH FISH AND POTATOES

Makes 4 servings

I first made this dish with leftover grilled fish from a dinner party and liked it so much that now I don't wait around for that leftover fish; I go right to the fishmonger and buy fresh swordfish, snapper, or halibut. The topping is quickly made, and I serve it at room temperature over hot tortillas. It's incredibly fresh tasting and light, yet substantial enough for a main dish—a perfect summer meal.

1/2 pound (2 medium) waxy potatoes, scrubbed and quartered
3/4 pound fish fillet or steak, such as swordfish, halibut, or snapper
3 to 4 serrano or 2 to 3 jalapeño chiles, to taste, seeded for a milder dish and minced
1 small red onion, finely chopped (about 1/2 cup) and rinsed
1 pound tomatoes such as cherry tomatoes, cut into eighths if cherry tomatoes or into 1/4-inch dice if regular tomatoes

¼ cup fresh lime juice, from 2 medium limes
¼ cup chopped fresh cilantro
    salt and freshly ground pepper to taste
8 corn tortillas, heated*
    additional cooked or uncooked salsa for serving, optional

Steam the potatoes until tender, about 10 minutes. Remove from the heat, cut into ½-inch dice, and set aside.

If you're using fish fillets, steam for 5 minutes or until the fish falls apart easily when poked with a fork. Remove from the heat and transfer to a plate. If you're using a steak, grill in a grill pan for about 3 minutes on each side or until the fish falls apart easily when poked with a fork. Transfer to a plate. When the fish is cool enough to handle, either cut into ½-inch pieces or flake into approximately ½-inch pieces by pulling apart at the natural grooves of the flesh, then cutting into smaller pieces.

In a large bowl, toss together the potatoes, fish, chiles, onion, tomatoes, lime juice, and cilantro. Add salt and pepper to taste.

Place 2 hot tortillas on each plate and top with the potato and fish mixture. Fold the tortillas over the mixture if desired and serve with additional salsa if you wish.

Advance Preparation: The topping will hold for several hours, in or out of the refrigerator.

PER PORTION

Calories	299	Protein	22 g
Fat	5 g	Carbohydrate	43 g
Saturated Fat	1 g	Fiber	5 g
Cholesterol	33 mg	Sodium	175 mg

* *To heat tortillas:* Wrap in aluminum foil and heat through in a 350-degree oven for 15 minutes; or heat 1 or 2 at a time in a dry nonstick skillet over medium-high heat until flexible; or wrap in a clean kitchen towel and steam for 1 minute, then let sit for 10 minutes; or wrap in wax paper or a damp towel and heat in a microwave on HIGH (100%) power for 1 minute.

SOFT TACOS WITH TURKEY PICADILLO

Makes 6 to 8 servings

This complex picadillo of sweet, savory, and picante flavors is absolutely marvelous. In addition to these tacos, try it as a filling for chiles rellenos or for enchiladas with a tomato sauce.

1½	pounds (6 medium or 3 large) tomatoes, roasted,* or one 28-ounce can
⅓	cup water (if using fresh tomatoes)
1	tablespoon canola oil
1	medium onion, finely chopped
2	large garlic cloves, minced or pressed
1½	pounds ground turkey
¼	teaspoon freshly ground black pepper
1	teaspoon ground cinnamon
¼	teaspoon ground cloves
¼	cup raisins
4	teaspoons rice wine vinegar or cider vinegar
	salt to taste, ½ to 1 teaspoon
1	tart apple, peeled, cored, and finely chopped
12	to 16 corn tortillas, heated*
1	cup tomato-based salsa such as Salsa Ranchera, Roasted Tomato and Chile Guajillo Salsa, or a commercial salsa

Transfer the roasted tomatoes to a blender along with any juice that has accumulated in the bowl, plus ⅓ cup water. If you're using canned tomatoes, simply transfer to the blender with their juice. Puree the tomatoes until smooth.

---

* *To roast tomatoes:* Preheat the broiler. Line a baking sheet with foil and place the tomatoes on it. Place under the broiler, about 2 to 3 inches from the heat (at the highest rack setting). Turn after 2 or 3 minutes, when the tomatoes have charred on one side (this may take longer in an electric oven), and repeat on the other side. Remove from the heat and transfer to a bowl. When the tomatoes are cool enough to handle, peel and core.

* *To heat tortillas:* Wrap in aluminum foil and heat through in a 350-degree oven for 15 minutes; or heat 1 or 2 at a time in a dry nonstick skillet over medium-high heat until flexible; or wrap in a clean kitchen towel and steam for 1 minute, then let sit for 10 minutes; or wrap in wax paper or a damp towel and heat in a microwave on HIGH (100%) power for 1 minute.

Heat the oil in a large heavy nonstick skillet over medium heat and add the onion. Cook, stirring, until tender, about 5 minutes. Add the garlic and cook, stirring, for about a minute, until it just begins to color. Add the ground turkey. Stir and cook until lightly browned, about 5 to 8 minutes. Pour off any liquid from the pan.

Add the tomato puree, ground spices, raisins, vinegar, and salt and bring to a simmer. Simmer for 20 minutes, stirring often, then stir in the apple. Continue to simmer for 10 minutes or until the tomatoes have cooked down and the mixture is thick and somewhat homogenous. Taste and adjust the seasonings. Remove from the heat.

Place 2 heated tortillas on each plate, top with the turkey picadillo, fold over if you wish, and serve with the salsa of your choice.

Advance Preparation: The filling will keep for 3 or 4 days in the refrigerator.

PER PORTION

Calories	405	Protein	25 g
Fat	14 g	Carbohydrate	47 g
Saturated Fat	3 g	Fiber	7 g
Cholesterol	83 mg	Sodium	585 mg

Tostadas

In Mexico tostadas are either whole tortillas or tortilla wedges toasted on a co-mal until crisp and topped. In this country the tortillas are usually deep-fried, and the wedges often go by the name *nachos*. The whole tortillas are sometimes misnamed *chalupas,* although I'm seeing them correctly called *tostadas* more often now. Whatever you call them, the main thing is that you make the dish. They are among the most popular dishes in my repertoire.

MAIN-DISH BLACK BEAN TOSTADAS (AKA CHALUPAS)

Makes 6 servings

These main-dish tostadas are similar to the black bean nachos on page 117, but bigger, with more dimensions. What I love about them is the flavor of the refried black beans against the crisp tortillas, contrasted with the crunchy, fresh-tasting lettuce, the picante salsa fresca, and the rich, nutty almonds. I've kept the almonds in, even though they're rich, because you need very few, and they really make this dish special. After years and years of serving these at parties, I've found that it's best to cut half of the tortillas in two, because although the recipe makes enough for 12 tostadas, many guests can't eat more than one and a half. So I make half-tostadas for the second round.

1	cup low-fat ricotta or nonfat cottage cheese
1/3	cup plain nonfat yogurt
1 1/2	cups Salsa Fresca (page 61)
2	cups shredded lettuce
12	corn tortillas, 6 cut in half, toasted*
	scant 1/2 cup (2 1/2 ounces) almonds, roasted* and coarsely chopped
1	recipe black Refried Beans (page 193)

Blend the ricotta cheese in a food processor fitted with the steel blade until smooth. Add the yogurt and continue to blend until completely smooth. Set aside.

Have all the ingredients in separate bowls within easy reach.

Reheat the beans in the pan, adding liquid saved from the bean pot if they seem dry. Or heat the beans for 30 minutes in a covered baking dish in a 325-degree oven (spoon some bean broth over the top if they seem dry). Spread a generous spoonful of black beans over each crisped tortilla. Top this with a layer of the yogurt-ricotta mixture, then a generous handful of lettuce. Next spoon on some salsa, sprinkle on some chopped toasted almonds, and serve.

Advance Preparation: The refried beans will hold for 3 days in the refrigerator and can be frozen. The tostada crisps will hold for several hours. The ricotta or cottage cheese can be blended and mixed with the yogurt 2 or 3 days ahead of time. Stir before using. And the toasted almonds will keep for weeks in the refrigerator. If you're storing the refried beans, cover with plastic wrap or wax paper before covering with foil so that the beans don't react with the aluminum. Remember to remove the plastic wrap before reheating!

PER PORTION

Calories	568	Protein	27 g
Fat	15 g	Carbohydrate	85 g
Saturated Fat	2 g	Fiber	16 g
Cholesterol	10 mg	Sodium	1,204 mg

Variation

QUICK VERSION: Use canned black beans and refry, with all of the liquid in the can, as directed. You will need four 15-ounce cans black beans

---

* *To toast tortillas:* To bake the tortillas, preheat the oven to 325 degrees. Place the tortillas on a baking sheet and bake for 20 to 30 minutes, until light brown and crisp, shaking the baking sheet every 10 minutes. Allow to cool on a rack. To microwave the tortillas, place 1 or 2 whole tortillas or 2 or 3 halves at a time on a plate or on the plate in your microwave oven. Microwave on HIGH (100%) power for 1 minute. If the tortillas are not crisp, turn them over and microwave for another 40 to 60 seconds. If they are still not crisp and are just beginning to brown, microwave for another 30 seconds to a minute, until crisp. Cool on a rack or in a basket.

Note: Once you've tried this set of directions for microwaving you might want to experiment. The time on mine varies, depending on how moist the tortillas were to begin with. But it always works well, whether it takes 1, 2, or 3 minutes.

* *To roast almonds:* Preheat the oven to 375 degrees. Place the almonds on a baking sheet and roast for 10 minutes, until they smell toasty and are beginning to brown.

(Progresso and S&W are good brands). Do not blend the beans. Fry the spices as instructed and add the beans with their liquid. Mash with a bean masher or the back of a large wooden spoon in the pan. You will need to thin out with water.

You can use commercial salsa, but there's nothing like salsa fresca here, and it's quickly made.

PER PORTION

Calories	528	Protein	26 g
Fat	16 g	Carbohydrate	74 g
Saturated Fat	2 g	Fiber	21 g
Cholesterol	10 mg	Sodium	2,073 mg

VEGETABLE TOSTADAS WITH RED CHILE SAUCE

Makes 6 servings

This is based on a dish I learned from Rick Bayless. They are called *tostadas de chileajo* in Mexico, *chileajo* meaning just what it sounds like in Spanish—chile and garlic. Here diced vegetables are cooked until crisp-tender, marinated in the sauce, then spooned onto crisp tortillas and sprinkled with a bit of cheese and onion. I usually cut my tortillas in half, so they're easier to handle. This is a very useful dish; it's served at room temperature and everything is done hours ahead of serving.

For the Sauce:
4   medium (about 1 ounce) guajillo chiles, stemmed, seeded, and deveined
1   ancho chile, stemmed, seeded, and deveined
6   large garlic cloves, toasted*
1/8 teaspoon ground cloves
1/8 teaspoon freshly ground black pepper
1/2 teaspoon dried oregano, preferably Mexican
1   cup water
1   tablespoon canola oil
1   tablespoon cider vinegar or rice wine vinegar

1 teaspoon sugar
   salt to taste, $1/2$ teaspoon or more

For the Vegetables and Tostadas:
2   small (about 6 ounces) waxy potatoes, cut into $1/2$-inch dice
2   small or 1 large (about $1/4$ pound) carrot, cut into $1/2$-inch dice
$1/4$ pound (about 1 cup) green beans, trimmed and cut into $1/2$-inch
        lengths
$2/3$ cup peas, fresh or thawed frozen
1   medium yellow squash, cut into $1/2$-inch dice, or 2 ears corn in
    season, kernels removed
12 corn tortillas, cut in half and toasted*
1   ounce queso cotija, feta, or Parmesan, crumbled (about $1/4$ cup)
$1/2$ small white or red onion, thinly sliced and rinsed

First make the sauce. Place the chiles in a bowl and cover with boiling water. Weight with a plate so that they are submerged and soak for 30 minutes.

Drain the chiles and transfer to a blender or food processor fitted with the steel blade along with the garlic, ground spices, oregano, and $1/2$ cup water. Blend until smooth and strain through a medium-mesh strainer into a bowl.

Heat the oil in a medium nonstick skillet over medium-high heat. Add a bit of the chile mixture and, if it sizzles loudly, add the rest (wait a couple of minutes if it doesn't). Stir constantly until the puree is thick, dark, and beginning to stick to the pan, about 2 to 3 minutes. Reduce the heat to medium-low and add the vinegar, sugar, salt, and enough of the remaining water to give the sauce the consistency of ketchup. Simmer, stirring, for a minute, just long enough to blend the flavors. Remove from the heat, taste, and adjust the salt. Allow to cool while you prepare the vegetables.

* *To toast garlic:* Heat a heavy skillet or comal over medium-high heat and toast the garlic in its skin, turning or shaking the pan often, until it smells toasty and is blackened in several places, about 10 minutes. Remove from the heat and peel.

* *To toast tortilla chips:* To bake the chips, preheat the oven to 325 degrees. Place the tortilla pieces on a baking sheet and bake for 20 to 30 minutes, until light brown and crisp, shaking the baking sheet every 10 minutes. Allow to cool on a rack. To microwave the chips, place about 2 to 3 halves at a time on a plate or on the plate in your microwave oven. Microwave on HIGH (100%) power for 1 minute. If the pieces are not crisp, turn them over and microwave for another 40 to 60 seconds. If they are still not crisp and are just beginning to brown, microwave for another 20 to 30 seconds until crisp. Cool on a rack or in a basket.

Steam the vegetables or boil them in salted water until just tender. The potatoes and carrots will take 5 to 8 minutes, the green beans, peas, and zucchini about 5 minutes. Refresh the vegetables under cold water as they are cooked and transfer to a bowl. Salt the vegetables lightly and toss with the sauce. Cover and marinate the vegetables for a couple of hours before serving if time allows.

Top each crisp tortilla with 2 heaped tablespoons of the vegetables, sprinkle with cheese and onion, and serve.

NOTE: You can make nacho-size tostadas with the same ingredients. Cut tortillas into quarters and crisp in the microwave or the oven. Chop the onion rather than slicing it and proceed as directed.

Advance Preparation: The sauce will keep for several days in the refrigerator, and the vegetables can be cooked and marinated a day ahead.

PER PORTION

Calories	197	Protein	7 g
Fat	3 g	Carbohydrate	39 g
Saturated Fat	.17 g	Fiber	5 g
Cholesterol	4 mg	Sodium	358 mg

Enchiladas

Enchiladas are simply tortillas that have been dipped in a chile sauce before being filled and rolled. In this country they have come to mean any rolled tortilla dish, whatever the sauce. But in Mexico the name of the dish varies with the sauces: if it is a chile sauce, it's an enchilada; if it's a tomato sauce, it's an entomatada; when the tortillas are dipped in mole, the dish is enmoladas, and when black beans are the basis for the dish, it is enfrijoladas.

I was a bit more challenged when it came to making low-fat versions of these dishes, because traditionally the tortillas are softened in oil before being dipped into the sauce, filled, and rolled. Frying makes them pliable and less fragile once they're sauced. The sauce also adheres well to fried tortillas.

But when I learned to make enfrijoladas from Rick Bayless, he steam-heated the tortillas, and the resulting dish was delicious, so I began making all of my enchiladas using that method. This worked well much of the time, though I was sometimes dismayed because the tortillas became fragile and fell apart. So I tried the microwave, which worked better if I wrapped the tortillas, only 4 at a time, in a dampened dish towel. This method works very well. The main difference you will find between traditionally prepared enchiladas and these is that they won't be caked with sauce; the tortilla will be more recognizable as a tortilla, but you'll still have the flavor of the sauce.

Sauces are what make enchiladas so special. The fillings can vary, and I urge you to substitute one thing for another if you wish. For instance, you may not eat meat, but that doesn't mean you can't enjoy the green enchiladas. I've also given you vegetarian filling suggestions where meat is called for.

In Mexico enchiladas are served as they're assembled. Here, however, I'm giving you instructions for reheating them in the oven before serving. The tortillas may become a little more fragile, but you will be more relaxed.

GREEN ENCHILADAS WITH CHICKEN FILLING

Makes 4 servings

This is a low-fat version of the simple classic enchilada verde served all over Mexico. Instead of quick-frying the tortilla in oil to soften it before dipping in the sauce, I heat the tortillas in a microwave, or I steam them. The resulting enchiladas are more fragile than those fried first in oil, so they should be served quickly. The key to a delicious green enchilada is a delicious green sauce.

5	cups water
1	onion, quartered
2	garlic cloves, peeled and crushed
1	large whole chicken breast, skinned and split
1/2	teaspoon dried thyme or oregano or a combination
	salt to taste
1	recipe Cooked Green Tomatillo Salsa (page 68) made with stock reserved from cooking chicken
12	corn tortillas, heated*
1	ounce queso cotija or feta, crumbled (1/4 cup)
2	onion slices, separated into rings and rinsed
	sliced radishes or radish roses for garnish

COOK THE CHICKEN: Combine the water, quartered onion, and crushed garlic in a large saucepan or Dutch oven and bring to a boil over medium heat. Add the chicken breast. Skim off any foam that rises, then add the dried herbs. Cover partially, reduce the heat to low, and simmer for 13 to 15 minutes, until the chicken is cooked through. Add salt. Allow the chicken to cool in the broth if there is time. When cool enough to handle, remove the chicken from the broth, bone, and shred. Strain the stock through a cheesecloth-lined strainer into a bowl. Set aside 2 cups for the green sauce. Make the green sauce as instructed in the recipe on page 68.

ASSEMBLE THE ENCHILADAS: This should be done shortly before serving. Preheat the oven to 350 degrees, lightly oil a baking dish that will hold 12 rolled enchiladas, and heat the green sauce to a bare simmer.

---

* *To heat tortillas for enchiladas:* Wrap 4 tortillas at a time in a clean kitchen towel and steam for 1 minute, then let sit for 5 minutes, or wrap 4 at a time in wax paper or a damp towel and heat in a microwave on HIGH (100%) power for 30 seconds or on LOW for 1 minute. In this case the tortillas should be very flexible but shouldn't fall apart.

Toss the chicken with $^1\!/_2$ cup of the green sauce and keep warm in a saucepan. Spoon a cup of the sauce into a wide soup bowl. Dip a heated tortilla into the sauce, flip it over in the sauce, and place a scant 2 tablespoons of the chicken across the center. Roll up the tortilla and place in the baking dish. Fill all of the tortillas in this way. Pour the remaining sauce over the enchiladas, spread it around so that it covers the ends, and cover the dish tightly with foil.

Warm the enchiladas in the oven for 10 minutes (no longer, or they will fall apart), uncover, sprinkle with the cheese, onion, and radishes; and serve at once.

NOTE: You can also serve these as they are assembled, without heating through in the oven. Assemble, sprinkle with cheese, onion, radishes; and serve.

Advance Preparation: The shredded chicken and the salsa can be made up to 3 days ahead, but the assembly and baking should be done just before serving.

PER PORTION

Calories	325	Protein	22 g
Fat	7 g	Carbohydrate	45 g
Saturated Fat	.59 g	Fiber	5 g
Cholesterol	40 mg	Sodium	698 mg

In addition to chicken these can be filled with a number of other fillings, such as Veracruz-style chicken picadillo (page 314), turkey picadillo (page 316), a vegetarian filling, such as the vegetable mixture in the recipe for vegetable tostadas with red chile sauce (page 222), or red rice with peas and carrots (page 201).

Variations

CHICKEN ENTOMATADAS: Entomatadas are enchiladas sauced with a cooked tomato salsa. Substitute salsa ranchera (page 63) for the cooked green tomatillo salsa. Cook the chicken and make the enchiladas as directed, using the stock from the chicken to thin out the sauce as needed. Omit the radishes in the garnish and substitute $^1\!/_4$ cup chopped cilantro.

PER PORTION

Calories	354	Protein	22 g
Fat	9 g	Carbohydrate	50 g
Saturated Fat	.77 g	Fiber	7 g
Cholesterol	40 mg	Sodium	680 mg

GREEN ENCHILADAS WITH
SPINACH AND CORN FILLING

Makes 16 enchiladas, serving 5 to 6

Although chicken fills green enchiladas all over Mexico, the enchiladas have many vegetarian possibilities. These are bursting with texture and good flavors. The spinach and corn are marvelous together, moistened with the pungent green sauce. They make a light, fresh-tasting summer dish.

3 **pounds fresh spinach**
kernels from 4 ears corn
1 **jalapeño chile, seeded for a milder dish and finely chopped**
$1/4$ **cup water**
$1/2$ **cup chopped fresh cilantro**
salt and freshly ground pepper to taste
1 **recipe Cooked Green Tomatillo Salsa (page 68)**
16 **corn tortillas, heated***
$1/2$ **cup plain nonfat yogurt**
fresh cilantro sprigs for garnish

Rinse the spinach thoroughly in several changes of water. Heat a large nonstick skillet over high heat and add the spinach. Stir with a wooden spoon and wilt in the water left on the leaves. This should take a couple of minutes once the water begins to boil. When all the spinach has wilted, remove from the heat and rinse quickly with cold water. Place the spinach in a towel and squeeze out excess water, then chop. Rinse out the pan and wipe dry.

Combine the corn, jalapeño, and water in the skillet and bring the water to a boil over medium-high heat. Cook, stirring, for 5 minutes. Pour off any water remaining in the pan and remove from the heat.

Toss together the spinach, corn, jalapeño, and cilantro. Add salt and pepper. Stir in 1 cup of the green sauce. Keep warm in a saucepan if serving right away.

Assemble the enchiladas shortly before serving. Preheat the oven to 350

---

* *To heat tortillas for enchiladas:* Wrap 4 tortillas at a time in a clean kitchen towel and steam for 1 minute, then let sit for 5 minutes, or wrap 4 at a time in wax paper or a damp towel and heat in a microwave on HIGH (100%) power for 30 seconds or on LOW for 1 minute. In this case the tortillas should be very flexible but shouldn't fall apart.

degrees if you're not serving the enchiladas as you make them, lightly oil a baking dish that will hold 16 rolled enchiladas, and heat the remaining green sauce to a bare simmer.

Dip a heated tortilla in the sauce. Flip over so that the tortilla is thoroughly coated. Transfer to a plate or platter or the prepared baking dish and top with 2 heaped tablespoons of the spinach and corn mixture. Roll up the tortilla. Repeat with the remaining tortillas. Put 2 to 3 on each plate and, if serving right away, spoon sauce over the top and finish with yogurt and cilantro. If you wish to heat the enchiladas in the baking dish, pour the remaining sauce over the top. Cover the baking dish tightly with foil and bake for 10 minutes. Spoon on the yogurt. Garnish with cilantro sprigs and serve.

Advance Preparation: The salsa will hold for 4 days in the refrigerator and can be frozen. The spinach can be cleaned and cooked a day ahead of time and kept in the refrigerator.

PER PORTION

Calories	109	Protein	5 g
Fat	2 g	Carbohydrate	21 g
Saturated Fat	.20 g	Fiber	1 g
Cholesterol	0 mg	Sodium	260 mg

Variation
SPINACH AND CORN ENCHILADAS WITH GREEN TOMATILLO MOLE: This version is richer and absolutely luxurious. Substitute 2½ cups of green tomatillo mole (page 70) for the sauce in this recipe. Assemble the enchiladas as directed.

PICANTE SHRIMP ENCHILADAS WITH CHIPOTLE SAUCE

Makes 4 to 6 servings

I was introduced to these enchiladas at the Restaurant El Parador, outside the town of Xico in the highlands of Veracruz. The restaurant called them *tacos de camarones MMM picositas* because they were so picante and delicious. The enchiladas came to the table wrapped in banana leaves. Inside were tortillas filled with sweet, juicy, small Gulf shrimp, a mild contrast to the mouth-burning sauce. I have made the enchiladas using small bay shrimp with excellent results. And I've toned down the original sauce, but it's still searingly hot.

1	pound (4 medium or 2 large) tomatoes, roasted (page 31)
½	small can (about 6) chipotles en adobo with their sauce (use less if desired)
1	small head or ½ large head of garlic, peeled
2	quarts water
	salt to taste
14	ounces bay shrimp or small shrimp, peeled and deveined
1	tablespoon canola or sunflower oil
1	teaspoon sugar
2	cups shrimp-cooking water or chicken, vegetable, or garlic stock (pages 158–160)
12	corn tortillas, heated
½	small white onion, sliced into thin rings and rinsed
2	ounces queso fresco, crumbled (about ⅓ cup)
	lime wedges for serving

Transfer peeled tomatoes to a blender along with any liquid that has accumulated in the bowl. Add the chipotles and blend until smooth. Strain into a bowl through a medium-mesh strainer.

Pound the garlic to a paste in a mortar and pestle. You should have about 2 tablespoons puree.

Bring the water to a boil in a large saucepan and add 1 teaspoon salt and the shrimp. Cook for 3 to 5 minutes, until they turn pink. Remove from the water with a slotted spoon and set aside, reserving the water. If you're using cooked bay shrimp, bring the water to a boil, drop in, and immediately remove the shrimp.

Heat the oil in a heavy saucepan or nonstick skillet over medium heat and add the garlic paste. Cook, stirring, for about 3 to 5 minutes, until the garlic paste colors and smells fragrant. Add the tomato-chipotle mixture, sugar, and about $1/2$ teaspoon salt and cook, stirring, for 5 to 10 minutes, until it thickens and begins to stick to the bottom of the pan. Add $1^{1}/_{2}$ cups of the reserved cooking water from the shrimp and bring to a simmer. Simmer for about 10 minutes, stirring from time to time, until the sauce thickens and coats the front and back of a spoon. Taste and add salt and sugar as desired.

Assemble the enchiladas shortly before serving. If you're not serving the enchiladas as you make them, preheat the oven to 350 degrees and lightly oil a baking dish that will hold 12 rolled enchiladas.

Toss the shrimp with $1/2$ cup of the sauce and keep warm in a saucepan if you're serving the enchiladas as you make them. Dip a heated tortilla in the sauce, turning it over once to coat it with the sauce on both sides. Top with about 2 tablespoons of shrimp. Roll up the tortilla and transfer to the baking dish or a warm platter. Repeat with the remaining tortillas (heat 4 at a time in the microwave and keep the tortillas you aren't working with wrapped so they remain flexible).

Thin out the remaining sauce with the additional $1/2$ cup stock and spoon over the enchiladas. Cover tightly with foil and heat through, if you wish, for 10 minutes in the oven. Sprinkle on the onion and cheese and serve with lime wedges.

NOTE: The chipotle sauce makes a wonderful enchilada sauce for other fillings. Try shredded chicken, Veracruz-style chicken picadillo, or any vegetarian filling.

Advance Preparation: The sauce will keep for a few days in the refrigerator, but it becomes hotter, so be prepared. It's really best when freshly made. I have held these enchiladas successfully in a baking dish in the refrigerator for half a day, saucing and reheating them just before serving.

PER PORTION

Calories	440	Protein	29 g
Fat	12 g	Carbohydrate	54 g
Saturated Fat	3 g	Fiber	6 g
Cholesterol	161 mg	Sodium	836 mg

MUSHROOM AND GARLIC ENCHILADAS WITH CHIPOTLE TOMATO SAUCE

Makes 16 enchiladas, serving 5 to 6

This is a wonderful vegetarian enchilada. Everything goes together beautifully. The savory mushroom and garlic filling is nicely complemented by the smoky, moderately hot sauce.

For the Mushroom Filling:

1   tablespoon olive or canola oil

1   medium onion, chopped

2   pounds mushrooms, trimmed, cleaned, and sliced about 1/4 inch
       thick

4   large garlic cloves, thinly sliced
       salt and freshly ground pepper to taste

2   tablespoons dry white wine

2   tablespoons chopped fresh epazote or parsley

For the Sauce:

2   pounds (8 medium or 4 large) tomatoes, roasted*

2   serrano or 1 jalapeño chile, seeded for a milder sauce and
       coarsely chopped

2   large or 4 small canned chipotles en adobo, rinsed and seeded
       (wear rubber gloves)

1/4 to 1/2 small onion, coarsely chopped (about 2 to 4 tablespoons)
       to taste

2   garlic cloves, minced or pressed

1   tablespoon canola oil

1   to 2 cups vegetable or garlic stock (pages 159–160) or water, plus
       more as needed
       salt to taste, about 1/2 teaspoon or more

* *To roast tomatoes:* Preheat the broiler. Line a baking sheet with foil and place the tomatoes on it. Place under the broiler, about 2 to 3 inches from the heat (at the highest rack setting). Turn after 2 or 3 minutes, when the tomatoes have charred on one side (this may take longer in an electric oven), and repeat on the other side. Remove from the heat and transfer to a bowl. When the tomatoes are cool enough to handle, peel and core.

For the Enchiladas:

16 corn tortillas, heated*

1 to 2 ounces dry Mexican crumbling cheese such as cotija or feta, crumbled ($^1/_4$ to $^1/_2$ cup)

2 slices of onion, separated into rings and rinsed

$^1/_4$ cup chopped fresh cilantro for garnish

MAKE THE MUSHROOM FILLING: Heat the oil in a large heavy nonstick skillet over medium heat and add the chopped onion. Cook, stirring, until the onion is tender, about 5 minutes. Add the mushrooms and garlic and a bit of salt and pepper. Cook, stirring, until the mushrooms begin to release water, about 3 minutes. Add the wine and continue to cook, stirring, until the mushrooms are tender and the liquid in the pan just about evaporated, about 10 minutes. Stir in the epazote or parsley, cook for another minute or so and remove from the heat. Taste and adjust the seasonings.

MAKE THE SAUCE: Transfer the peeled tomatoes to a blender with the chiles, onion, and garlic. Puree, retaining a bit of texture. Heat the oil in a large heavy nonstick skillet over medium heat. Drop a bit of puree into the sauce and, if it sizzles, add the rest (if not, wait a minute). Cook, stirring, for about 10 minutes, until the sauce darkens, thickens, and begins to stick to the pan. Add 1 to 2 cups of stock or water and simmer for another 10 minutes, until the sauce is a medium consistency (if you are using plum tomatoes, you will need all of the stock because they are quite pulpy; other tomatoes are more watery). Add salt and remove from the heat.

ASSEMBLE THE ENCHILADAS: This should be done shortly before serving. Preheat the oven to 350 degrees, lightly oil a baking dish that will hold 16 rolled enchiladas, and heat the sauce to a bare simmer.

Toss the mushrooms with $^1/_2$ cup of the sauce and keep warm in a saucepan. Spoon a cup of the sauce into a wide soup bowl. One by one, keeping the remaining tortillas wrapped in the towel, dip a tortilla into the sauce and flip it over in the sauce so that both sides are covered. Place 2 tablespoons of the mushrooms across the center. Roll up the tortilla and place in the baking dish. Fill all of the tortillas in this way. If the sauce seems thick, thin it out with more stock (or water). Pour the remaining sauce over the enchiladas, spread it around so that it covers the ends, and cover the dish tightly with foil.

* *To heat tortillas for enchiladas:* Wrap 4 tortillas at a time in a clean kitchen towel and steam for 1 minute, then let sit for 5 minutes, or wrap 4 at a time in wax paper or a damp towel and heat in a microwave on HIGH (100%) power for 30 seconds or on LOW for 1 minute. In this case the tortillas should be very flexible but shouldn't fall apart.

Warm the enchiladas in the oven for 10 minutes (no longer, or they will fall apart), uncover, sprinkle with the cheese, onion, and cilantro, and serve at once.

Advance Preparation: The filling and the sauce can be made up to 3 days ahead, though the sauce will get hotter. The assembly and baking should be done just before serving.

PER PORTION

Calories	377	Protein	13 g
Fat	11 g	Carbohydrate	62 g
Saturated Fat	1 g	Fiber	10 g
Cholesterol	7 mg	Sodium	730 mg

ENFRIJOLADAS

Makes 4 to 6 servings

This enchilada in luscious black bean sauce makes a marvelous starter or main dish. It's best to do the final assembly at the last minute, although you can hold the enfrijoladas in the oven for a short while.

- ½ **pound dried black beans, washed and picked over**
- 7 **cups water (if draining the beans; 1 quart if not)**
- 1 **medium onion, chopped**
- 3 **large garlic cloves or more to taste, minced or pressed**
- 1 **to 2 teaspoons salt to taste**
- 2 **large fresh epazote sprigs or 2 heaped tablespoons fresh cilantro leaves**
- 1½ **teaspoons ground cumin**
- 12 **corn tortillas, heated***
- 2 **ounces queso fresco, feta, or goat cheese, crumbled (about ½ cup)**
- ½ **small white onion, thinly sliced and rinsed**
- 3 **tablespoons chopped fresh cilantro**

Soak the beans in 4 cups water for at least 6 hours or overnight. Drain if desired. (For a darker, richer broth, do not drain the beans. Remember that some people have a harder time digesting beans that are cooked in their soaking water.)

Combine the beans, chopped onion, and half the garlic in a bean pot and add 1 quart water or enough to cover the beans by an inch. Bring to a boil, reduce the heat, cover, and simmer for 1 hour. Add the remaining garlic, salt, and epazote, cover, and simmer for another hour, until the beans are soft and their liquid is thick and soupy. Taste and adjust the salt. Remove from the heat.

Puree the beans coarsely in a blender or food processor fitted with the steel blade. They should retain some texture. Return to the pan, stir in the cumin, and heat through. Thin out to a medium consistency, about the consistency of cream, taste, and adjust the salt. Reduce the heat to very low, cover, and keep at a very slow simmer.

Shortly before serving time, assemble the enfrijoladas.

Uncover the beans and give them a stir. If they have thickened, thin out again. Spread ¹/₂ cup of the beans over the bottom of a large baking dish or serving platter. Dip a softened tortilla into the beans in the pot, flip the tortilla over to coat on both sides, then remove from the beans and transfer to the platter or baking dish. The easiest way to do this, unless you have asbestos fingers (as many cooks do), is to use 2 large spoons. Fold the tortilla into quarters (in half, then in half again) and continue with the remaining tortillas. Arrange the quartered tortillas in overlapping rows on the platter or baking dish.

Spoon the remaining pureed beans over the sauced tortillas. Sprinkle with the cheese, sliced onion, and cilantro and serve at once.

Advance Preparation: The black beans will hold for 3 or 4 days in the refrigerator and can be frozen. You may need to thin them out a bit. You can hold the enfrijoladas in a 350-degree oven for about 10 minutes, but you should thin out the bean sauce a bit with water if you do, since it tends to thicken.

PER PORTION

Calories	434	Protein	20 g
Fat	6 g	Carbohydrate	77g
Saturated Fat	3 g	Fiber	12 g
Cholesterol	10 mg	Sodium	1,055 mg

* *To heat tortillas for enchiladas:* Wrap 4 tortillas at a time in a clean kitchen towel and steam for 1 minute, then let sit for 5 minutes; or wrap 4 at a time in wax paper or a damp towel and heat in a microwave on HIGH (100%) power for 30 seconds or on LOW for 1 minute. In this case the tortillas should be very flexible but shouldn't fall apart.

Quesadillas

Quesadillas don't necessarily contain queso! Nonetheless, many Americans expect them to and enjoy the ease and convenience of a quick cheese quesadilla dinner. With that in mind, I've developed a number of low-fat cheese quesadillas with wonderful fillings.

I blend together nonfat cottage cheese with a little bit of Parmesan, Monterey Jack, or Cheddar, then spread it on the warmed tortillas and heat them through until the cheese melts. All of the cheeses work; it really depends on which flavor you prefer. Parmesan and Cheddar contribute the most flavor, Parmesan being my favorite, and Monterey Jack is a great melter; I often combine Monterey Jack and Parmesan. The higher-fat cheese provides the rich taste and stringy melted cheese quality that you expect with quesadillas. From here there are many ways you can go with additional fillings.

ABOUT SERVING SIZES: Most of the recipes here make eight quesadillas, which will serve four for a light supper, accompanied by rice or beans and a salad. As part of a more elaborate menu you can plan on one per person if you are serving several other dishes, two per person if it is a single first-course dish.

BASIC CHEESE QUESADILLAS SEVERAL WAYS

Makes 4 servings as a light supper

These quesadillas are quick to prepare, and the cheese can be enhanced by any number of additional fillings. My favorite mixture for the grated cheese is two parts Monterey Jack and one part Parmesan. As for the heating method, the microwave is the quickest, but the texture of the tortillas and cheese is best and the quesadillas stay hotter longer if you use a dry skillet or the oven, the dry skillet being my number one choice. The microwave works only if you are eating the quesadillas right away, because the tortillas will become rubbery if they sit. With a microwave you can heat the tortillas, assemble the quesadillas and plate them, then heat each plate and send it out. Or you can heat several on one plate and transfer them afterwards. All of the methods can be used with each recipe.

1   **cup nonfat cottage cheese**
1¹⁄₂   **ounces Monterey Jack, mild or sharp white Cheddar, or**
   Parmesan or a combination, grated (¹⁄₃ cup)

8 corn tortillas
any green or red salsa for serving

Blend together the cottage cheese and grated cheese in a food processor until completely smooth.

USING THE OVEN: Preheat the oven to 400 degrees. Heat the tortillas one at a time, turning in a dry skillet over medium-high heat until flexible; or wrap in wax paper or a damp towel and heat for 30 seconds to a minute in the microwave, until flexible. Spread 2 tablespoons of the cheese mixture over each tortilla, leaving a ½-inch border around the edge, and fold the tortilla over. Place on an unoiled baking sheet. Heat, fill, and fold all the tortillas in this way. Heat through in the hot oven for 10 minutes, until the cheese melts and the tortillas just begin to crisp and curl up slightly on top. Transfer to plates and serve hot, passing salsa to spoon over the top.

USING A DRY SKILLET: Heat the tortillas, 2 or 3 at a time, in a dry skillet over medium-high heat until flexible. Spread 2 tablespoons of the cheese mixture over each tortilla, leaving a ½-inch border around the edge, and fold the tortilla over. Heat through, turning the folded tortilla over from time to time, until the cheese melts, about 5 to 8 minutes. Don't worry if some of the cheese runs out onto the pan (it probably will). Transfer to plates and serve hot, passing salsa to spoon over the top.

USING A MICROWAVE: Wrap 4 tortillas in microwave-safe plastic wrap, a dampened towel, or wax paper and heat for 30 seconds to 1 minute in the microwave, until flexible. Spread 2 tablespoons of the cheese mixture over each tortilla, leaving a ½-inch border around the edge, and fold the tortilla over. Place on a plate or plates and cover with plastic, paper towel, or wax paper. Repeat with the next 4 tortillas. Heat through in the microwave for 1 to 2 minutes, until hot and the cheese has melted, uncover, and serve hot, passing salsa to spoon over the top.

Advance Preparation: You can assemble the quesadillas up to a day before the final heating, when the cheese is melted. Keep them on a plate, cover *tightly* with plastic wrap, and refrigerate.

PER PORTION

Calories	196	Protein	12 g
Fat	4 g	Carbohydrate	27 g
Saturated Fat	2 g	Fiber	3 g
Cholesterol	16 mg	Sodium	338 mg

BAKED QUARTERED QUESADILLAS

Makes 4 servings

The technique here is based on the one Bobby Flay uses for the terrific quesadillas he serves at Mesa Grill, one of my favorite New York restaurants. Bobby uses flour tortillas. But I can't find a low-fat flour tortilla that I like; since they turn to cardboard in the oven, I use corn tortillas, which have more flavor anyway. They become slightly crunchy here, since they're baked at high heat.

THE INGREDIENTS ARE THE SAME AS IN THE PRECEDING RECIPE.

Preheat the oven to 450 degrees. Blend together the cottage cheese and grated cheese in a food processor until smooth.

Place 4 tortillas on a cutting board. Spread 2 tablespoons of the cottage cheese mixture on each tortilla. Top with another tortilla. Cut into quarters using a sharp knife or a serrated bread knife.

Transfer the quartered quesadillas to an ungreased baking sheet. Bake 10 to 12 minutes in the hot oven, until the tortillas are beginning to brown on the edges and the top tortilla begins to curl. Remove from the heat. With a spatula, transfer to plates and serve with salsa on the side.

Advance Preparation: The quesadillas may be assembled hours or even a day before baking. Cover *tightly* with plastic wrap and refrigerate overnight.

PER PORTION

Calories	196	Protein	12 g
Fat	4 g	Carbohydrate	27 g
Saturated Fat	2 g	Fiber	3 g
Cholesterol	16 mg	Sodium	338 mg

QUESADILLAS WITH POTATOES AND SORREL

Makes 4 servings

I love the combination of comforting steamed potatoes against sharp, tangy sorrel. The filling doesn't ask for anything picante for enhancement. You may want to serve the quesadillas with salsa—either green or red; I like them with or without. If you can't find sorrel, make these quesadillas with beet greens or spinach.

1	pound new or waxy potatoes, cut into $1/2$-inch dice
$1/4$	pound sorrel, stemmed and washed but not dried
	salt to taste
2	teaspoons olive oil
2	large garlic cloves, minced or pressed
1	cup nonfat cottage cheese
$1^{1}/_{2}$	ounces Parmesan cheese, grated ($1/3$ cup)
8	corn tortillas
	any green or red salsa for serving

Steam the potatoes until tender, about 10–15 minutes.

Heat a large heavy nonstick skillet over medium-high heat and wilt the sorrel in the liquid left on the leaves after washing. Remove from the heat as soon as the sorrel changes color, to olive green. This should take only about 1 to 2 minutes once the water boils. Refresh with cold water, gently press out liquid, and coarsely chop. Toss with the potatoes and add salt. Add the olive oil and toss together.

Turn on a food processor fitted with the steel blade and drop in the garlic. When it's chopped, turn off the machine and add the cottage cheese and Parmesan. Blend until smooth.

Heat the tortillas 1 or 2 at a time in a dry skillet or microwave, following the instructions for basic quesadillas. Spread 2 tablespoons of the cheese mixture over each tortilla, leaving a $1/2$-inch border around the edge, top with a spoonful of the potatoes and sorrel, and fold the tortilla over. Heat through in a dry skillet, oven, or microwave, following the instructions for basic quesadillas. Serve hot, passing salsa to serve on the side.

Advance Preparation: The potatoes and sorrel can be prepared a day ahead of time and held in the refrigerator. The quesadillas can be assembled and held in the refrigerator, covered with plastic wrap, for a day.

Calories	310	Protein	16 g
Fat	6 g	Carbohydrate	49 g
Saturated Fat	2 g	Fiber	5 g
Cholesterol	11 mg	Sodium	433 mg

QUESADILLAS WITH BROCCOLI AND GARLIC

Makes 4 servings as a light supper

This is one of those dishes you can throw together in no time. Although the word *broccoli* doesn't exactly conjure up Mexican food, this dish has all the right flavors.

2	large garlic cloves, minced or pressed
1	cup nonfat cottage cheese
1½	ounces sharp white Cheddar, Monterey Jack, or Parmesan cheese, grated (⅓ cup)
½	pound broccoli, cut into florets (approximately 3 cups)
8	corn tortillas
1	cup any red or green salsa

Blend together the garlic, cottage cheese, and grated cheese in a food processor until smooth.

Steam the broccoli until just tender, about 5 minutes. Drain, rinse with cold water, and slice the florets about ¼ inch thick.

Heat the tortillas, 1 or 2 at a time, in a dry skillet or microwave following the instructions for basic quesadillas. Spread each tortilla with 2 tablespoons of the cheese mixture, leaving a ½-inch border around the edge. Top with a layer of broccoli and fold the tortilla over. Heat the quesadillas in the oven, a dry skillet, or a microwave, as for basic quesadillas and serve salsa on the side.

NOTE: The baked quartered quesadilla method on page 238 works well with this filling.

Advance Preparation: The quesadillas may be assembled hours before baking.

Calories	260	Protein	15 g
Fat	7 g	Carbohydrate	37 g
Saturated Fat	3 g	Fiber	6 g
Cholesterol	16 mg	Sodium	510 mg

CHICKEN AND TOMATILLO QUESADILLAS

Makes 4 servings

Y ou can use leftover chicken from another dish or cook the chicken breast, which takes very little time. Chicken and green tomatillo salsa are always a popular combination at my house, and in this quesadilla the duo tastes very rich indeed, especially when the salsa is freshly made.

1/2	pound (4 large) tomatillos, husked and rinsed, or one 13-ounce can, drained
2	to 3 jalapeño or serrano chiles to taste, seeded for a milder salsa
1/2	medium onion, roughly chopped and rinsed
2	large garlic cloves, roughly chopped, optional salt to taste, about 1/2 teaspoon
6	to 8 fresh cilantro sprigs or more to taste
1/4	cup water as needed
1	cup nonfat cottage cheese
1 1/2	ounces sharp white Cheddar, Monterey Jack, or Parmesan cheese, grated (1/3 cup)
8	corn tortillas
1	large (about 1 to 1 1/4 pounds) whole chicken breast, halved, skinned, poached, and shredded* (about 1 1/2 cups)

* *To cook chicken breast:* Combine 6 cups water, a chopped onion, and 2 garlic cloves in a large heavy saucepan and bring to a boil. Add the chicken. Skim off any foam that rises, then add 1/2 teaspoon each dried thyme and marjoram or oregano and a bay leaf. Reduce the heat, cover partially, and simmer for 13 to 15 minutes, until cooked through. Remove

Make the tomatillo sauce so that its flavors can ripen while you cook the chicken. If you're using fresh tomatillos, roast under the broiler following directions on page 31, or simmer in water to cover for 10 minutes. Drain and place in a blender or a food processor fitted with the steel blade. If you're using canned tomatillos, place in the blender or food processor. Add the chiles, onion, garlic, salt, and cilantro. Blend to a coarse puree. Transfer to a bowl and thin out as desired with water. Taste and adjust the seasoning. Set aside.

Blend together the cottage cheese and grated cheese in a food processor until smooth.

Heat the tortillas, 1 or 2 at a time, in a dry skillet or microwave as directed in the basic quesadilla recipe. Spread 2 tablespoons of the cheese mixture over each tortilla, leaving a ¹/₂-inch border around the edge. Top with shredded chicken and a tablespoon of the green sauce and fold the tortilla over. Heat through in a dry skillet, microwave, or oven, following the directions for basic quesadillas. Serve hot, passing the remaining salsa to spoon over the top.

Advance Preparation: Both the salsa and the shredded cooked chicken will keep for a day or two in the refrigerator. The assembled quesadillas will also hold for a day in the refrigerator, covered tightly with plastic wrap.

PER PORTION

Calories	271	Protein	27 g
Fat	5 g	Carbohydrate	30 g
Saturated Fat	2 g	Fiber	1 g
Cholesterol	51 mg	Sodium	983 mg

from the heat and add about 1 teaspoon salt. Allow the chicken to cool in the broth if there is time. Remove the chicken breast from the broth. Bone and shred the meat (you should have about 1¹/₂–1³/₄ cups). Strain the stock through a cheesecloth-lined strainer and set aside for another purpose.

Quesadillas with Oyster Mushrooms and Chipotles

Makes 4 servings

I think these quesadillas have such rich flavor that they require no additional salsa. The combination of earthy, meaty oyster mushrooms and smoky, picante chipotle chiles is what makes them unforgettable. Two parts Monterey Jack and one part Parmesan makes a good flavor and texture combination.

1	tablespoon olive oil
1	medium onion, chopped
1	pound oyster mushrooms, cleaned, trimmed, and quartered or thickly sliced
	salt to taste
¼	cup dry, fruity red wine, such as a Beaujolais or Côtes-du-Rhône
2	canned chipotles en adobo, drained, seeded, and chopped
¼	cup chopped sun-dried tomatoes
1	teaspoon dried oregano, preferably Mexican
4	large garlic cloves to taste, minced or pressed
1	pound (4 medium or 2 large) tomatoes, peeled and chopped, or one 15-ounce can chopped tomatoes
2	tablespoons chopped fresh epazote or cilantro
1	cup nonfat cottage cheese
1½	ounces Monterey Jack and/or Parmesan cheese, grated (⅓ cup)
8	corn tortillas
	red salsa if desired

Heat the olive oil in a large heavy nonstick skillet over medium heat and add the onion. Cook, stirring, until the onion is tender, about 5 minutes. Add the mushrooms. Sprinkle with salt and heat over medium-high heat until they begin to release liquid. Cook, stirring, until the mushrooms are beginning to stick to the pan, about 5 to 10 minutes. Add the wine, chipotles, sun-dried tomatoes, and oregano. Turn the heat down to medium and cook, stirring, until the wine is just about gone, about 5 minutes. Add the garlic and stir together for a minute, until the garlic begins to color. Add the tomatoes and epazote and bring to a simmer. Simmer for 15 minutes, stirring often. The tomatoes should cook down, and the mixture should be thick. Remove from the heat, stir in the cilantro if using, taste, and adjust the seasonings.

Blend together the cottage cheese and grated cheese in a food processor until smooth.

Heat the tortillas, 1 or 2 at a time, in a dry skillet or a microwave, following the directions for basic quesadillas. Spread 2 tablespoons of the cheese mixture over each tortilla, leaving a ½-inch border around the edge. Top with a spoonful of mushrooms and fold the tortilla over. Heat through in a dry skillet, microwave, or the oven, following the directions for basic quesadillas. Serve hot, with salsa if desired.

Advance Preparation: You can assemble the quesadillas up to a day before the final heating, when the cheese is melted. Keep them on a plate, cover tightly with plastic wrap, and refrigerate.

PER PORTION

Calories	342	Protein	18 g
Fat	9 g	Carbohydrate	47 g
Saturated Fat	3 g	Fiber	7 g
Cholesterol	16 mg	Sodium	420 mg

GARLICKY ZUCCHINI QUESADILLAS

Makes 4 main-dish servings or 8 appetizer servings

I love the way the garlicky shredded zucchini and cheese melt together in these rich-tasting quesadillas. The flavors are delicate, the textures soft and lovely. I like to combine Monterey Jack with a bit of Parmesan for flavor here—say, ¼ cup Monterey Jack and 2 tablespoons Parmesan.

> 2 pounds zucchini, grated (8 cups, tightly packed)
> salt
> 1 tablespoon olive oil
> 4 large garlic cloves, minced or pressed
> salt to taste
> 1 cup nonfat cottage cheese
> 1½ ounces Monterey Jack, mild or sharp white Cheddar, and/or Parmesan cheese, grated (⅓ cup)

8   corn tortillas
any green or red salsa for serving

Sprinkle the zucchini shreds with salt and let them sweat in a colander for 20 to 30 minutes. Rinse and squeeze dry.

Heat the oil in a large heavy nonstick skillet over medium heat and add the zucchini and a bit of salt. Cook, stirring, until just about tender, about 5 to 10 minutes. Add the garlic and continue to cook for another 2 to 3 minutes, until fragrant and tender. Taste and adjust the salt.

Blend together the cottage cheese and grated cheese in a food processor until smooth.

Heat the tortillas, 1 or 2 at a time, in a dry skillet or microwave, following the instructions for basic quesadillas. Spread a heaped tablespoon of the cheese mixture over each tortilla, leaving a ½-inch border around the edge, top with zucchini, and fold the tortilla over. Heat through in a dry skillet, microwave, or the oven, following the instructions for basic quesadillas. Serve hot, passing salsa to spoon over the top.

Advance Preparation: You can assemble the quesadillas up to a day before the final heating, when the cheese is melted. Keep them on a plate, cover tightly with plastic wrap, and refrigerate.

PER PORTION

Calories	263	Protein	15 g
Fat	8 g	Carbohydrate	35 g
Saturated Fat	3 g	Fiber	4 g
Cholesterol	16 mg	Sodium	392 mg

SWISS CHARD QUESADILLAS

Makes 4 servings

This filling is as simple as can be and tastes like health itself. When I was developing the recipe, I thought it might be nice to add a hit of chile to the chard. But the chard tastes so wonderful seasoned just with garlic, salt, and pepper that I decided to leave it alone. You can add salsa fresca to the quesadillas if you wish. I think it's best to heat these quesadillas in a dry frying pan or in the microwave. The chard loses some of its vibrant quality after 10 minutes in the oven.

2	pounds Swiss chard leaves, from about 3 pounds with stems
2	teaspoons olive oil
2	large garlic cloves or more to taste, minced or pressed
	salt, about $\frac{1}{2}$ teaspoon, and freshly ground pepper to taste
1	cup nonfat cottage cheese
$1\frac{1}{2}$	ounces Parmesan cheese, grated (about $\frac{1}{3}$ cup)
8	corn tortillas
	Salsa Fresca (page 61) for serving

Remove the chard leaves from the stems. Wash thoroughly, but don't dry.

Heat the oil in a large nonstick skillet over medium heat and add the garlic. Cook, stirring, until the garlic begins to color and smell fragrant. Add the chard leaves, salt, and pepper. Cook, stirring, in the water left on the leaves until the chard has wilted and is tender, about 5 to 8 minutes. Remove from the heat and transfer to a bowl or cutting board. Chop coarsely (I do this in the bowl, with scissors). You should have about 3 cups.

Blend together the cottage cheese and Parmesan in a food processor until smooth.

Heat the tortillas, 1 or 2 at a time, following the instructions for basic quesadillas. Spread 2 tablespoons of the cheese mixture over each tortilla, leaving a $\frac{1}{2}$-inch border around the edge, top with 3 heaped tablespoons of chard, and fold the tortilla over. Heat through in a dry skillet or microwave, following the instructions for basic quesadillas. Serve hot, passing salsa to spoon over the top.

Advance Preparation: You can assemble the quesadillas up to a day before the final heating, when the cheese is melted. Keep them on a plate, cover tightly with plastic wrap, and refrigerate.

QUESADILLAS WITH GOAT CHEESE, ROASTED PEPPERS, AND BLACK BEANS

Makes 4 servings

Three distinct savory flavors merge here into a luscious, filling quesadilla. These taste so rich that they should please even the most skeptical of the low-fat skeptics.

> 2   large garlic cloves, minced or pressed
> 2   medium red bell peppers, roasted and peeled*
> 2   ounces goat cheese, crumbled (about ½ cup)
> ¾   cup nonfat cottage cheese
>   salt and freshly ground pepper to taste
> 2   cups cooked black beans in their cooking liquid (page 192) or
>   two 15-ounce cans
> 8   corn tortillas
> 1   cup Salsa Fresca (page 61) or commercial tomato salsa

Turn on a food processor fitted with the steel blade and drop in the garlic cloves to chop. Add the roasted peppers and process to a coarse puree. Add

---

* *To roast peppers:* Roast the peppers either directly over a gas flame or under a broiler, turning often until uniformly charred. When the pepper is blackened on all sides, transfer to a plastic bag, seal, and cool. Remove the charred skin, rinse, and pat dry. Remove the seeds and veins (wear rubber gloves for hot chiles).

the goat cheese and cottage cheese and blend until smooth. Season with salt and pepper.

Heat the beans in a saucepan over medium heat until simmering.

Heat the tortillas, 1 or 2 at a time, in a dry skillet or a microwave, following the instructions for basic quesadillas. Spread 2 tablespoons of the cheese mixture over each tortilla, leaving a $\frac{1}{2}$-inch border around the edge. Top the cheese with beans and a tablespoon or so of salsa and fold the tortilla over. Heat through in a dry skillet, oven, or the microwave, following the instructions for basic quesadillas. Transfer to plates and serve hot, passing additional salsa to spoon over the top.

Advance Preparation: The quesadillas can be assembled and held at room temperature, covered with plastic wrap, for several hours. The peppers can be roasted and the beans cooked several days ahead of time and kept in the refrigerator. The blended pepper and cheese mixture will keep for a day in the refrigerator.

PER PORTION

Calories	340	Protein	20 g
Fat	6 g	Carbohydrate	54 g
Saturated Fat	3 g	Fiber	6 g
Cholesterol	15 mg	Sodium	450 mg

SCRAMBLED EGG AND GREEN CHILE QUESADILLAS (OR SOFT TACOS)

Makes 8 quesadillas, serving 4 as a light main dish

I love the contrast of the hot chile—and there is plenty of it—against the smooth, comforting scrambled egg here. This filling or topping is easily thrown together. You can use it as a topping for soft tacos as well as for quesadillas.

2	teaspoons canola oil
1/3	cup finely chopped onion
6	large eggs, or 3 whole eggs and 5 egg whites, beaten
	salt to taste
4	medium poblano chiles, roasted* and cut into thin slices about 1 inch long
8	corn tortillas
	any green or red salsa for serving

Heat the oil in a heavy nonstick skillet over medium heat and add the onion. Cook, stirring, until tender, 3 to 5 minutes. Beat together the eggs and salt. Stir in the beaten eggs and the sliced chiles. Cook, stirring constantly, until just about set. Taste and adjust salt and continue to scramble until firm. Remove from the heat and allow to cool slightly.

FOR QUESADILLAS: Heat the tortillas one at a time, turning in a dry skillet over medium-high heat until flexible. Top with 2 tablespoons of the filling and fold over. Fill all of the tortillas in this way, then heat through in a skillet or microwave. If using the skillet, heat, turning the tortilla several times, for 3 to 5 minutes, until the tortilla begins to brown in spots. If using the microwave, wrap 4 tortillas in microwave-safe plastic wrap, a dampened towel, or wax paper and heat for 30 seconds to 1 minute in the microwave, until flexible. Spread 2 tablespoons of the filling over each tortilla, leaving a 1/2-inch border around the edge, and fold the tortilla over. Place on a plate or plates and cover with plastic or wax paper. Repeat with the next 4 tortillas. Heat through

---

* *To roast chiles:* Roast the chile either directly over a gas flame or under a broiler, turning often until uniformly charred. When the chile is blackened on all sides, transfer to a plastic bag or bowl, seal or cover, and cool. Remove the charred skin, rinse, and pat dry. Remove the seeds and veins (wear rubber gloves for hot chiles).

in the microwave for 1 minute, uncover, and serve hot, passing salsa to spoon over the top.

FOR SOFT TACOS: Top hot corn tortillas with the egg mixture, fold over, and serve with salsa.

Advance Preparation: The filling will hold for several hours, in or out of the refrigerator. The roasted peppers will keep for several days in the refrigerator.

PER PORTION (WHOLE EGGS)

Calories	272	Protein	14 g
Fat	11 g	Carbohydrate	31 g
Saturated Fat	3 g	Fiber	2 g
Cholesterol	319 mg	Sodium	180 mg

PER PORTION (EGGS AND EGG WHITES)

Calories	237	Protein	13 g
Fat	7 g	Carbohydrate	31 g
Saturated Fat	1 g	Fiber	2 g
Cholesterol	159 mg	Sodium	201 mg

POTATO PEEL QUESADILLAS

Makes 4 servings

This is a great idea, especially if you need peeled potatoes for another dish. There are a lot of textures and flavors at play here—the soft potato skins against the onions, the heat of the chile, and the earthy epazote. When my friend, restaurateur Carmen Ramírez Delgollado makes this dish, she fries the potato peels, but I steam them to cut down on fat. The texture is different, but the flavors are wonderful. Combine two parts Monterey Jack with one part Parmesan for a good flavor and texture mix.

	scrubbed peels from 4 pounds Yukon Gold or White Rose potatoes
1	tablespoon canola oil
2	medium onions, thinly sliced
4	to 6 garlic cloves to taste, minced or pressed
2	jalapeño chiles, seeded for a milder dish and minced
2	to 4 tablespoons chopped fresh epazote or 1 teaspoon dried oregano, preferably Mexican
	salt and freshly ground pepper to taste
1	cup nonfat cottage cheese
1½	ounces Monterey Jack, mild or sharp white Cheddar, and/or Parmesan cheese, grated (⅓ cup)
8	corn tortillas
	any green or red salsa for serving

Steam the potato peels until tender, about 5 to 10 minutes. Remove from the heat.

Heat the oil in a heavy nonstick skillet over medium heat and add the onions. Cook, stirring, until the onions are tender, about 5 minutes. Add the garlic, chiles, epazote, and steamed potato peels. Cook, stirring, for 10 minutes (turn the heat to medium-low if it begins to stick to the pan), until the mixture is tender and fragrant. Season with salt and pepper.

Blend together the cottage cheese and grated cheese in a food processor until smooth.

Heat the tortillas, 1 or 2 at a time, in a dry skillet or a microwave, following the directions for basic quesadillas. Spread 2 tablespoons of the cheese mixture over each tortilla, leaving a ½-inch border around the edge, top with the potato peel mixture, and fold the tortilla over. Heat through in a dry skillet, oven, or microwave, following the instructions for basic quesadillas. Serve hot, passing salsa to spoon over the top.

Advance Preparation: You can make the potato peel filling a day ahead of serving.

PER PORTION

Calories	360	Protein	17 g
Fat	8 g	Carbohydrate	56 g
Saturated Fat	2 g	Fiber	5 g
Cholesterol	16 mg	Sodium	374 mg

SQUASH BLOSSOM QUESADILLAS

Makes 4 servings

This pretty, savory filling has contrasting textures and subtle flavors. Squash blossoms are commonly used as a quesadilla filling throughout Mexico. This one includes squash as well as the blossoms, which is convenient if you buy your blossoms attached to the baby squash (usually zucchini). If you don't, the squash will still be in season, crunchy and sweet. In this filling the blossoms and squash are stewed with onion, tomato, garlic, and chile. I recommend seeding the chile so that the subtlety of the squash blossoms is not overpowered.

> about 6 ounces (30 large) squash flowers
> 1 tablespoon canola or olive oil
> 1 small onion, chopped
> 2 large garlic cloves, minced or pressed
> ¹/₂ to 1 jalapeño or 1 to 2 serrano chiles, seeded and finely chopped
> ¹/₂ pound (2 medium or 1 large) tomatoes, peeled and chopped
> ¹/₂ pound zucchini or summer squash, finely minced
> 2 tablespoons chopped fresh epazote or parsley
> salt to taste, ¹/₂ teaspoon or more
> 1 ounce queso fresco, cotija, feta, or Parmesan, crumbled (¹/₄ cup)
> 8 corn tortillas
> any red or green salsa for serving, optional

PREPARE THE SQUASH BLOSSOMS: Cut down the middle of each flower petal and remove the stamen from inside the blossom. Trim off the green base (calyx). If the squash blossoms are attached to baby zucchini, simply cut the zucchini off at the base of the blossom, then reach in and remove the stamens. Rinse the flowers gently and cut crosswise about ½ inch thick. You should have about 3 cups sliced flowers.

Heat the oil in a large heavy nonstick skillet over medium heat and add the onion. Cook, stirring, until the onion is tender, about 3 to 5 minutes. Add the garlic and chiles and cook, stirring, until the garlic begins to smell fragrant, about 30 to 60 seconds. Add the tomatoes, squash flowers, minced squash, epazote, and about ½ teaspoon salt. Stir together and, when the mixture begins to simmer, cover partially and turn the heat to medium-low. Cook, stirring from time to time, for 8 to 10 minutes, until the squash blossoms have cooked down and the mixture is fragrant. Remove from the heat, stir in the cheese, taste, and correct the salt.

To make the quesadillas, heat the tortillas one at a time, turning in a dry skillet over medium-high heat until flexible. Top with 2 tablespoons of the filling and fold over. Fill all of the tortillas in this way.

Heat the quesadillas, preferably in a skillet, though you can also use an oven or microwave. If you're using the skillet, heat, turning the tortilla several times, for 3 to 5 minutes, until the tortilla begins to brown and crisp in spots. If you're using the oven, preheat the oven to 400 degrees. Place the quesadillas on an ungreased baking sheet and heat through in the hot oven for 10 minutes, until the tortillas just begin to crisp. If you're using the microwave, place 2 or 3 filled tortillas on a plate or plates and cover with paper towels or wax paper. Heat through in the microwave for 1 minute. Serve hot, passing salsa to spoon over the top.

Advance Preparation: The filling will hold for several hours, in or out of the refrigerator. The quesadillas can be assembled several hours before heating through and wrapped in foil or plastic or kept on a plate and covered tightly with foil or plastic.

PER PORTION

Calories	204	Protein	6 g
Fat	7 g	Carbohydrate	32 g
Saturated Fat	2 g	Fiber	4 g
Cholesterol	5 mg	Sodium	414 mg

Chilaquiles

Throughout Mexico you find many different versions of chilaquiles, a sort of tortilla casserole. It's a favorite breakfast dish in Mexico; I think it makes a wonderful supper as well. In its simplest form chilaquiles is a satisfying dish consisting of nothing more than fried tortillas added to a salsa. The salsa can be red, green, or even pureed black beans. In many, perhaps most, versions the chilaquiles are topped with cream. My friend Carmen Ramírez Delgollado, owner of Restaurant El Bajio in Mexico City, merely sprinkles hers with crumbled white cheese and sliced onions. That's the way I present them here. And rather than fry the tortillas I toast them. This makes a less authentic chilaquiles, but it's delicious nonetheless. The most important thing is to serve the chilaquiles before the tortillas get soggy.

GREEN CHILAQUILES

Makes 4 main-dish servings

I think my favorite chilaquiles of all are these green ones. The tart salsa contrasts so nicely with the earthy tortillas. It's worth making the green salsa just to have the chilaquiles. This is a nice brunch dish; have the sauce and toasted tortillas ready and stir in the tortillas at the last minute. Toasted tortillas get soggy more quickly than fried tortillas.

1	pound (about 8 large) tomatillos, husked and rinsed, or two 13-ounce cans, drained
2	to 3 jalapeño or serrano chiles to taste, stemmed and seeded for a milder salsa
½	small white onion, roughly chopped (about ¼ cup)
1	large garlic clove, roughly chopped
	salt to taste, ½ to 1 teaspoon
8	fresh cilantro sprigs or more to taste
2	teaspoons canola or sunflower oil
2	cups vegetable, garlic, or chicken stock (pages 158–160)
8	corn tortillas, cut into 1-inch squares or eighths and toasted*
1	ounce queso cotija or fresco, crumbled (¼ cup)
1	small white or red onion, thinly sliced and rinsed
2	tablespoons chopped fresh cilantro for garnish

If you're using fresh tomatillos, simmer in water to cover for 10 minutes. Drain and place in a blender or a food processor fitted with the steel blade. If you're using canned tomatillos, place in the blender or food processor. Add the chiles, chopped onion, garlic, salt, and cilantro. Puree the mixture.

Heat the oil in a heavy saucepan or a nonstick skillet over medium heat. Drizzle a bit of the tomatillo mixture into the pan and, if it sizzles loudly, add the rest (wait a bit if it doesn't). Cook the tomatillo puree, stirring, until it thickens and begins to stick to the pan, about 5 minutes. Add the stock, stir together, and bring to a simmer. Simmer for 15 to 20 minutes, stirring occasionally, until the mixture is thick enough to coat the front and back of a spoon. Taste and adjust the salt. You should have 2½ cups.

Stir the crisp tortilla pieces into the simmering salsa and stir together for 30 seconds. The tortillas should remain crisp. Remove from the heat and serve, sprinkling each portion with cheese, onion, and cilantro.

Advance Preparation: The sauce will hold for 4 days in the refrigerator and can be reheated just before adding the tortilla pieces. The tortilla chips can be made a day ahead.

LEFTOVERS: Store leftovers in an ovenproof baking dish. Sprinkle on another ½ or 1 ounce of cheese. Preheat the oven to 350 degrees and heat through for 20 to 30 minutes, until the cheese has melted. This makes a sort of enchilada pie, or as I like to call it, "tortilla lasagne." It's comforting and delicious. You could layer vegetables or chicken with the leftover chilaquiles for a more substantial dish.

QUICK CHILAQUILES: You can use any leftover cooked green salsa for this dish. The proportions are 2½ cups salsa for 8 tortillas.

PER PORTION

Calories	210	Protein	7 g
Fat	6 g	Carbohydrate	34 g
Saturated Fat	.32 g	Fiber	4 g
Cholesterol	6 mg	Sodium	858 mg

* *To toast tortilla chips:* To bake the chips, preheat the oven to 325 degrees. Place the tortilla pieces on a baking sheet and bake for 20 to 30 minutes, until light brown and crisp, shaking the baking sheet every 10 minutes. Allow to cool on a rack. To microwave the chips, place about 6 to 10 pieces at a time on a plate or on the plate in your microwave oven. Microwave on HIGH (100%) power for 1 minute. If the pieces are not crisp, turn them over and microwave for another 40 to 60 seconds. If they are still not crisp and are just beginning to brown, microwave for another 20 to 30 seconds, until crisp. Cool on a rack or in a basket.

Variations

GREEN CHILAQUILES WITH EGGS: Reduce the stock to 1 cup. Make the salsa, then beat 4 large eggs or 2 large eggs and 5 egg whites together in a bowl and stir into the salsa. Turn the heat to low and cook, stirring, until the eggs have set. The mixture will be creamy. Stir in the tortilla pieces, stir together for 30 seconds, and remove from the heat. Sprinkle cheese and onion over the top or, alternatively, spoon on $1/2$ cup plain nonfat yogurt, sprinkle with onion, and serve.

RED CHILAQUILES

Makes 4 main-dish servings

Chilaquiles can be made with any number of salsas. I like them all equally, and they're all easily thrown together. Roma (plum) tomatoes have a low water content, so the sauce will require stock or water to achieve the right consistency for chilaquiles. Very juicy tomatoes might result in a sauce that has to be cooked down a bit.

2   pounds (8 medium, 4 large, or 10 to 12 plum) tomatoes, roasted
2   to 3 serrano or 1 to 2 jalapeño chiles or more to taste, seeded for
     a milder sauce and chopped
$1/4$ to $1/2$ small onion, chopped (2 to 4 tablespoons), to taste
2   garlic cloves, minced or pressed
2   teaspoons canola oil
$1/2$ to 1 cup water or chicken, vegetable, or garlic stock (pages
     158–160) as needed
     salt to taste, about $1/2$ teaspoon
8   corn tortillas, cut into 1-inch squares or 8 wedges and toasted*

* *To toast tortilla chips:* To bake the chips, preheat the oven to 325 degrees. Place the tortilla pieces on a baking sheet and bake for 20 to 30 minutes, until light brown and crisp, shaking the baking sheet every 10 minutes. Allow to cool on a rack. To microwave the chips, place about 6 to 10 pieces at a time on a plate or on the plate in your microwave oven. Microwave on HIGH (100%) power for 1 minute. If the pieces are not crisp, turn them over and microwave for another 40 to 60 seconds. If they are still not crisp and are just beginning to brown, microwave for another 20 to 30 seconds, until crisp. Cool on a rack or in a basket.

1 ounce queso cotija or fresco, crumbled (about ¼ cup)
1 small white or red onion, cut into thin rings and rinsed
2 tablespoons chopped fresh cilantro for garnish

Place the peeled tomatoes with their juices, chiles, chopped onion, and garlic in a blender and puree, retaining a bit of texture.

Heat the oil in a large heavy nonstick skillet over medium heat. Drop a bit of puree into the pan and, if it sizzles loudly, add the rest (wait a minute or two if it doesn't). Cook, stirring, for about 5 to 10 minutes, until the sauce darkens, thickens, and begins to stick to the pan. Add the water if the mixture seems dry and bring to a simmer. Simmer, stirring often, for about 15 minutes, until the sauce coats the front and back of a spoon. Add salt to taste. Stir in the tortilla pieces, stir together for about 30 seconds and serve, topping each helping with a sprinkling of cheese, sliced onion, and cilantro.

Advance Preparation: The sauce will keep for a few days in the refrigerator and can be reheated before stirring in the chips. The chips can be made a day ahead of time.

LEFTOVERS: Store leftovers in an ovenproof baking dish. Sprinkle on another ½ or 1 ounce of cheese. Preheat the oven to 350 degrees and heat through for 20 to 30 minutes, until the cheese has melted. You could layer vegetables or chicken with the leftover chilaquiles for a more substantial dish.

PER PORTION

Calories	217	Protein	7 g
Fat	6 g	Carbohydrate	37 g
Saturated Fat	.42 g	Fiber	6 g
Cholesterol	6 mg	Sodium	500 mg

GREEN CHILAQUILES WITH CHICKEN, CORN, AND SQUASH

Makes 4 main-dish servings

Once you get going with chilaquiles, there are all kinds of possibilities. The best comparison I can make is free-form lasagne. You can make a vegetarian version of this simply by omitting the chicken breast.

1	medium (about 4 to 5 ounces) boneless, skinless chicken breast
1	pound (about 8 large) fresh tomatillos, husked and rinsed, or two 13-ounce cans, drained
2	to 3 jalapeño or serrano chiles to taste, stemmed and seeded for a milder salsa
1	small white onion, half roughly chopped (about $^1/_4$ cup), half sliced, rinsed, and broken into rings
2	large garlic cloves, roughly chopped
	salt to taste, $^1/_2$ to 1 teaspoon
8	fresh cilantro sprigs or more to taste
2	teaspoons canola or sunflower oil
$2^1/_2$	cups vegetable, garlic, or chicken stock (pages 158–160)
$^1/_2$	pound zucchini or other summer squash, cut into $^1/_4$-inch dice (2 cups)
1	cup corn kernels, from 1 large ear
8	corn tortillas, cut into 1-inch squares or eighths and toasted*
$^1/_2$	cup plain nonfat yogurt or 1 ounce crumbled queso fresco, cotija, or feta
2	tablespoons chopped fresh cilantro for garnish

Poach the chicken breast in water to cover for about 15 minutes, until cooked through. Remove from the heat, allow to cool, and shred or cut into small dice. Set aside.

* *To toast tortilla chips:* To bake the chips, preheat the oven to 325 degrees. Place the tortilla pieces on a baking sheet and bake for 20 to 30 minutes, until light brown and crisp, shaking the baking sheet every 10 minutes. Allow to cool on a rack. To microwave the chips, place about 6 to 10 pieces at a time on a plate or on the plate in your microwave oven. Microwave on HIGH (100%) power for 1 minute. If the pieces are not crisp, turn them over and microwave for another 40 to 60 seconds. If they are still not crisp and are just beginning to brown, microwave for another 20 to 30 seconds, until crisp. Cool on a rack or in a basket.

If you're using fresh tomatillos, simmer in water to cover for 10 minutes. Drain and place in a blender or a food processor fitted with the steel blade. If you're using canned tomatillos, place in the blender or food processor. Add the chiles, chopped onion, garlic, salt, and cilantro. Puree the mixture.

Heat the oil in a heavy saucepan or a nonstick skillet over medium heat. Drizzle a bit of the tomatillo mixture into the pan and, if it sizzles loudly, add the rest (wait a bit if it doesn't). Cook the tomatillo puree, stirring, until it thickens and begins to stick to the pan, about 5 minutes. Add the stock, stir together, and bring to a simmer. Simmer for 10 minutes, stirring occasionally. Stir in the zucchini and corn and continue to simmer for 10 minutes, until the sauce is thick enough to coat the front and back of the spoon and the vegetables are tender. Stir in the shredded chicken. Taste and adjust salt.

Stir the crisp tortilla pieces into the simmering salsa and stir together for 30 seconds. The tortillas should remain crisp. Remove from the heat and serve, spooning yogurt or sprinkling cheese over each portion and topping with the onion slices and cilantro.

Advance Preparation: The sauce will hold for 4 days in the refrigerator and can be reheated just before adding the tortilla pieces. The tortilla chips can be made a day ahead of time.

PER PORTION (WITH CHICKEN)

Calories	277	Protein	16 g
Fat	5 g	Carbohydrate	45 g
Saturated Fat	.53 g	Fiber	5 g
Cholesterol	19 mg	Sodium	843 mg

PER PORTION (WITHOUT CHICKEN)

Calories	242	Protein	9 g
Fat	5 g	Carbohydrate	45 g
Saturated Fat	.43 g	Fiber	5 g
Cholesterol	1 mg	Sodium	823 mg

BLACK BEAN CHILAQUILES

Makes 4 generous servings

Chilaquiles made with a pureed black bean sauce—what a great idea! The black beans are blended to a thick puree, which is then seasoned with cumin and chile to make a delicious sauce for the corn tortillas.

1   cup dried black beans, washed and picked over
1   onion, chopped
3   large garlic cloves or more to taste, minced or pressed
7   cups water, if draining; 4, if not
1   to 2 teaspoons salt to taste
2   large fresh epazote sprigs or 2 heaped tablespoons cilantro leaves
1   tablespoon canola oil
1   to 2 serrano or jalapeño chiles to taste
1   teaspoon ground cumin
8   corn tortillas, cut into $^1/_2$-inch pieces or eighths and toasted*
1   ounce queso fresco, crumbled (about $^1/_4$ cup), or $^1/_2$ cup plain
      low-fat yogurt
$^1/_2$ small white or red onion, thinly sliced and rinsed
2   tablespoons chopped fresh cilantro for garnish

Soak the beans in cold water to cover for 6 hours or overnight and drain. (For a darker, richer broth, do not drain the beans. Remember that some people have a harder time digesting beans that are cooked in their soaking water.)

Combine the beans, onion, and half the garlic in a bean pot and add 1 quart water or enough to cover the beans by an inch. Bring to a boil, reduce the heat, cover, and simmer for 1 hour. Add the remaining garlic, salt, and epazote, cover, and simmer for another hour, until the beans are soft and their liquid is thick and soupy. Taste and adjust the salt. Remove from the heat.

* *To toast tortilla chips:* To bake the chips, preheat the oven to 325 degrees. Place the tortilla pieces on a baking sheet and bake for 20 to 30 minutes, until light brown and crisp, shaking the baking sheet every 10 minutes. Allow to cool on a rack. To microwave the chips, place about 6 to 10 pieces at a time on a plate or on the plate in your microwave oven. Microwave on HIGH (100%) power for 1 minute. If the pieces are not crisp, turn them over and microwave for another 40 to 60 seconds. If they are still not crisp and are just beginning to brown, microwave for another 20 to 30 seconds, until crisp. Cool on a rack or in a basket.

Puree the beans coarsely in a blender or food processor fitted with the steel blade. They should retain some texture.

Heat the oil in a large, heavy saucepan or a nonstick skillet over medium heat and add the chile. Cook, stirring, for a minute or two, until it softens a bit. Add the cumin and cook, stirring, for about 1 minute, until it begins to smell fragrant and toasty. Turn the heat to medium-high and add the pureed beans. They should sizzle. Cook, stirring often, for 10 to 15 minutes, until the mixture is a bit thicker than cream and fragrant. Stir in the chips. Stir for about 30 seconds—the chips should remain crisp—and serve, topping each helping with a sprinkling of cheese, a few slices of onion, and cilantro.

Advance Preparation: The beans will keep for 3 or 4 days in the refrigerator and can be reheated just before serving. They freeze well. The chips can be made a day ahead of time.

PER PORTION

Calories	361	Protein	16 g
Fat	7 g	Carbohydrate	61 g
Saturated Fat	2 g	Fiber	10 g
Cholesterol	5 mg	Sodium	962 mg

Chapter
Nine

Eggs

Fried Eggs with Spicy Cooked Tomato Sauce (Huevos Rancheros)
Scrambled Eggs with Onion, Chile, and Tomato
Veracruz-Style Scrambled Eggs with Refried Black Beans
Fried Eggs with Black Beans, Tortillas, and Salsa
Red Chilaquiles with Zucchini, Tomato, and Egg
Scrambled Eggs with Vegetables and Crisp Tortillas

Breakfast is a substantial meal in Mexico, and eggs are often the focal point. Eggs are cooked up with onions, tomatoes, and chiles, slathered with salsas, mixed with beans, potatoes, or crisp tortillas, and transformed into some of the most delicious dishes in the Mexican repertoire. Many of these dishes, like huevos rancheros and Mexican scrambled eggs, are familiar to us from Tex-Mex cooking.

As in all of my low-fat cookbooks, eggs do have a place. They are a perfect low-calorie protein. You can always replace some of the whole eggs with egg whites in the scrambled egg dishes here. For fried egg dishes, the eggs are fried with little if any oil in a nonstick pan, and I recommend just one egg per person rather than the usual two.

These dishes are equally wonderful for dinner. You can also fill tacos or quesadillas with the scrambled egg dishes. Dishes like scrambled eggs with onion, chile, and tomato and Veracruz-style scrambled eggs with refried black beans make fantastic fillings. If you're going to use the eggs for a taco or quesadilla filling, scramble them at medium-high heat to produce large curds (otherwise use medium-*low* heat, for creamy curds).

FRIED EGGS WITH SPICY COOKED TOMATO SAUCE (HUEVOS RANCHEROS)

Makes 4 servings

This dish is a classic. Even if my methods are far from authentic, all the flavors are there, enough to remind me of countless Mexican breakfasts I ate when I lived in Austin and in the Rio Grande Valley in the seventies. But after those meals I'd be uncomfortably full all day. This lightened version also makes a delightful supper as well as brunch or breakfast.

For the Sauce:
- 2 pounds (8 medium or 4 large) tomatoes, peeled and coarsely chopped
- 2 to 3 serrano or 1 to 2 jalapeño chiles or more to taste, seeded for a milder sauce and chopped
- 2 garlic cloves, minced or pressed
- 1/2 small onion, chopped
- 2 teaspoons canola oil

  salt to taste, about 1/2 teaspoon

For the Tortillas and Eggs:

8   corn tortillas, plus more to pass at the table, heated*
1   teaspoon canola oil
4   large eggs
    salt and freshly ground pepper to taste
1   tablespoon chopped fresh cilantro

Place the tomatoes, chiles, garlic, and onion in a blender and puree, retaining a bit of texture.

Heat the 2 teaspoons oil in a large heavy nonstick skillet over medium heat. Drop a bit of puree into the pan and, if it sizzles, add the rest (wait a bit if not). Cook, stirring, for about 5 to 10 minutes, until the sauce thickens and begins to stick to the pan. Keep warm while you heat the tortillas and fry the eggs. (If you have sauce already made, bring to a simmer in a saucepan.)

Have 4 plates ready. Heat 1 teaspoon oil in a nonstick skillet over medium heat and carefully break in the eggs. Cook sunny side up, until the whites are cooked through but the yolks still runny. Sprinkle with salt and pepper and turn off the heat.

Place 2 warm tortillas, overlapping, on each plate. Top with a fried egg. Spoon the hot sauce over the whites of the eggs and the tortillas, leaving the yolks exposed. Sprinkle with the cilantro and serve at once, passing additional tortillas at the table.

Advance Preparation: The sauce can be made a day or two ahead of time. The rest is a last-minute operation.

PER PORTION

Calories	268	Protein	11 g
Fat	10 g	Carbohydrate	36 g
Saturated Fat	2 g	Fiber	6 g
Cholesterol	213 mg	Sodium	437 mg

* *To heat tortillas:* Wrap in aluminum foil and heat through in a 350-degree oven for 15 minutes; or heat 1 or 2 at a time in a dry nonstick skillet over medium-high heat until flexible; or wrap in a clean kitchen towel and steam for 1 minute, then let sit for 10 minutes; or wrap in wax paper or a damp towel and heat in a microwave on HIGH (100%) power for 1 minute.

SCRAMBLED EGGS WITH ONION, CHILE, AND TOMATO

Makes 4 servings

This is one of the most classic Mexican egg dishes, huevos a la Mexicana. The dish is quickly thrown together, for a delicious breakfast, brunch, supper, or taco filling. My lightened version offers the option of substituting egg whites for some of the yolks. Have plenty of hot corn tortillas on hand to serve with the eggs.

1   tablespoon canola oil
2   to 3 serrano or 1 jalapeño chile to taste, seeded for a milder
     version and finely chopped
1   small onion, chopped
1   large or 2 medium tomatoes, seeded and diced
8   large eggs or 4 eggs plus 6 egg whites
2   tablespoons low-fat milk (if using the 4 eggs and 6 egg whites)
     salt to taste, $^1/_2$ teaspoon or more

For Garnishes (optional):
2   tablespoons chopped fresh parsley or cilantro
2   tablespoons crumbled queso fresco, cotija, or feta
2   slices of onion, broken into rings and rinsed

Heat the oil in a medium-sized heavy nonstick skillet over medium heat. Add the chiles and onion and cook, stirring, until the onion is tender, about 5 minutes. Add the tomato and cook for another 3 minutes. The mixture should not be juicy. Turn the heat to medium-low.

Beat the eggs together with the milk and salt, just enough to combine the whites and yolks. Add to the pan and cook, stirring all the while, until they are scrambled. Taste, adjust the salt, and serve with hot corn tortillas and any of the garnishes.

NOTE: If tomato juices accumulate in the pan, proceed with the recipe and pour off the juices from the pan before you serve the eggs so that your resulting dish won't be watery.

Advance Preparation: The vegetables can be ready to cook hours before serving, but the dish should be cooked just before you are ready to eat.

Calories	205	Protein	13 g
Fat	14 g	Carbohydrate	7 g
Saturated Fat	3 g	Fiber	1 g
Cholesterol	425 mg	Sodium	406 mg

PER PORTION (EGGS AND EGG WHITES)

Calories	158	Protein	13 g
Fat	9 g	Carbohydrate	7 g
Saturated Fat	2 g	Fiber	1 g
Cholesterol	213 mg	Sodium	429 mg

VERACRUZ-STYLE SCRAMBLED EGGS WITH REFRIED BLACK BEANS

Makes 4 servings

This is a wonderful Veracruzana breakfast dish called *huevos tirados.* *Tirar* means to throw, and here the eggs and frijoles are thrown together and scrambled. I use olive oil, but if you want a more authentic taste, use lard as they do in the state of Veracruz. You can make the refried beans here with canned black beans if you suddenly have a hankering for this dish. It'll still be good.

6	large eggs or 3 eggs plus 5 egg whites
6	heaped tablespoons black Refried Beans (page 193)
	salt to taste
1	tablespoon olive oil
½	small white onion, finely chopped (about ⅓ cup)
1	to 2 jalapeño chiles to taste, seeded and finely minced

Beat the eggs in a bowl. Add the beans and beat together to mix thoroughly. Add salt to taste.

Heat the oil in a large heavy nonstick skillet over medium heat and add the onion and chiles. Cook, stirring, until the onion is tender, about 5 minutes.

Add the egg mixture and cook, stirring constantly, until the eggs are scrambled. Remove from the heat and serve with hot corn tortillas.

Advance Preparation: The black beans can be made 3 or 4 days ahead of time and held in the refrigerator.

PER PORTION (WHOLE EGGS)

Calories	216	Protein	13 g
Fat	12 g	Carbohydrate	14 g
Saturated Fat	3 g	Fiber	3 g
Cholesterol	319 mg	Sodium	287 mg

PER PORTION (EGGS AND EGG WHITES)

Calories	185	Protein	14 g
Fat	8 g	Carbohydrate	14 g
Saturated Fat	2 g	Fiber	3 g
Cholesterol	159 mg	Sodium	322 mg

FRIED EGGS WITH
BLACK BEANS, TORTILLAS, AND SALSA
Makes 4 servings

I first ate the dish on which this one is based, huevos motuleños, not in the Yucatán, where it originates (in the town of Motul), but in one of Austin's best Mexican restaurants, Las Mañitas. Whenever I'm in Austin, I try to make at least one breakfast excursion to this wonderful restaurant, and the last time I was there a friend told me to make sure I had this dish. Classic huevos motuleños might include diced ham, deep-fried pork rind (chicharones), cheese, and often cream. I've made my own lighter version with the elements I like best: the black beans, eggs, tortillas, and salsa.

1½ pounds (6 medium or 3 large) tomatoes, peeled, seeded, and coarsely chopped

2 serrano or 1 jalapeño chile, seeded for a milder sauce and coarsely chopped, or 1 habanero chile, roasted, peeled, seeded, veined, and chopped for a very hot sauce*

1 garlic clove, minced or pressed

1 tablespoon canola oil

¼ small onion, coarsely chopped
salt to taste, about ½ teaspoon

2 cups cooked black beans with liquid (page 192)

4 large eggs

8 corn tortillas, heated*

1 ounce queso fresco, cotija, farmer's cheese, or feta, crumbled (about ¼ cup)

* *To roast chiles:* Roast the chiles either directly over a gas flame or under a broiler, turning often until uniformly charred. When the chiles are blackened on all sides, transfer to a plastic bag, seal, and cool. Remove the charred skin, rinse, and pat dry. Remove the seeds and veins (wear rubber gloves for hot chiles).

* *To heat tortillas:* Wrap in aluminum foil and heat through in a 350-degree oven for 15 minutes; or heat 1 or 2 at a time in a dry nonstick skillet over medium-high heat until flexible; or wrap in a clean kitchen towel and steam for 1 minute, then let sit for 10 minutes; or wrap in wax paper or a damp towel and heat in a microwave on HIGH (100%) power for 1 minute.

Place the tomatoes, chiles, and garlic in a blender and puree, retaining a bit of texture. `

Heat 2 teaspoons of the oil in a large heavy nonstick skillet over medium heat and add the onion. Cook, stirring, until tender, about 3 to 5 minutes. Add the tomato puree and cook, stirring, for about 10 to 15 minutes, until the sauce darkens, thickens, and begins to stick to the pan. Add salt and remove from the heat.

Heat the beans in a saucepan or a nonstick frying pan. The broth should be thick.

Heat the remaining teaspoon of oil in a nonstick skillet over medium-high heat and fry the eggs sunny side up. Turn off the heat as soon as the whites have set, in 2 to 3 minutes.

Place 2 hot tortillas on each plate, overlapping slightly, and spoon about $1/4$ cup of beans over each. Place a fried egg in the middle, on top of the beans, and spoon a generous spoonful of salsa over the egg. Sprinkle on the cheese and serve hot.

Advance Preparation: The beans and the cooked tomato sauce will hold for several days in the refrigerator. The final cooking and assembly should be done at the last minute.

PER PORTION

Calories	452	Protein	21 g
Fat	15 g	Carbohydrate	61 g
Saturated Fat	4 g	Fiber	11 g
Cholesterol	218 mg	Sodium	990 mg

Variation
QUICK VERSION USING CANNED BEANS: You will need two 15-ounce cans. Also use about $1^1/2$ cups prepared salsa.

RED CHILAQUILES WITH ZUCCHINI, TOMATO, AND EGG

Makes 4 servings

These creamy chilaquiles make great comfort food and are marvelous for brunch or supper.

1½   pounds (6 medium or 3 large) tomatoes, roasted* and peeled
1   red or white medium onion, half roughly chopped, half thinly sliced
2   large garlic cloves, 1 whole or roughly chopped, the other minced or pressed
1   to 3 serrano chiles to taste, seeded for a milder sauce and roughly chopped
1   tablespoon canola or sunflower oil
2   medium (about ¾ pound) zucchini, cut into ½-inch dice
     salt to taste, about ½ teaspoon or more
4   eggs or 2 whole eggs plus 4 egg whites, lightly beaten
6   corn tortillas, preferably stale, cut into ½-inch square pieces and toasted*
2   tablespoons chopped fresh cilantro
1   ounce queso fresco or feta cheese, crumbled (about ¼ cup)

Transfer the peeled tomatoes, along with any liquid that has accumulated in the bowl, to a blender. Add the chopped onion, the roughly chopped garlic clove, and the chile. Puree the mixture.

* *To roast tomatoes:* Preheat the broiler. Line a baking sheet with foil and place the tomatoes on it. Place under the broiler, about 2 to 3 inches from the heat (at the highest rack setting). Turn after 2 or 3 minutes, when the tomatoes have charred on one side (this may take longer in an electric oven), and repeat on the other side. Remove from the heat and transfer to a bowl. When the tomatoes are cool enough to handle, peel and core.

* *To toast tortilla chips:* To bake the chips, preheat the oven to 325 degrees. Place the tortilla pieces on a baking sheet and bake for 20 to 30 minutes, until light brown and crisp, shaking the baking sheet every 10 minutes. Allow to cool on a rack. To microwave the chips, place about 6 to 10 pieces at a time on a plate or on the plate in your microwave oven. Microwave on HIGH (100%) power for 1 minute. If the pieces are not crisp, turn them over and microwave for another 40 to 60 seconds. If they are still not crisp and are just beginning to brown, microwave for another 20 to 30 seconds, until crisp. Cool on a rack or in a basket.

Heat the oil in a large heavy nonstick skillet or saucepan over medium heat and add the sliced onion. Cook, stirring, until the onion begins to soften, about 3 to 5 minutes. Add the zucchini, remaining garlic, and a bit of salt (to draw out liquid from the zucchini so that the mixture won't stick). Cook, stirring, until the zucchini is tender but still bright green, about 5 to 8 minutes. Turn the heat to medium-high. Add the tomato puree and more salt and cook, stirring, until the sauce thickens and turns a brighter orange, about 10 to 15 minutes (the sauce may sputter, so take care not to let it burn your arm). The mixture should be thick.

Stir the eggs into the sauce. Cook, stirring, until the eggs just set and the mixture remains creamy. Stir in the toasted tortillas, cilantro, and cheese. Taste and add salt if necessary. Serve hot.

Advance Preparation: The chilaquiles can be made, through the cooking of the tomato sauce, an hour or so ahead. Reheat shortly before serving, and proceed with the recipe.

PER PORTION (WHOLE EGGS)

Calories	290	Protein	13 g
Fat	13 g	Carbohydrate	33 g
Saturated Fat	3 g	Fiber	5 g
Cholesterol	218 mg	Sodium	557 mg

PER PORTION (EGGS AND EGG WHITES)

Calories	273	Protein	14 g
Fat	10 g	Carbohydrate	33 g
Saturated Fat	3 g	Fiber	5 g
Cholesterol	111 mg	Sodium	594 mg

Variation: Strips of roasted poblano peppers (rajas) are excellent in this. Roast 1 large or 2 medium poblano peppers until charred (see page 348). Skin and remove the seeds and membranes. Cut into narrow strips. Throw them in when you add the eggs to the tomato sauce.

Scrambled Eggs with
Vegetables and Crisp Tortillas

Makes 6 servings

The authentic version of this dish, called *migas,* involves frying the tortilla strips in oil, then incorporating them into the eggs, as you would in traditional chilaquiles. I've altered my technique to bring the fat down here, crisping the tortillas in a microwave or an oven instead. As long as you serve the eggs right away, the dish will still taste like migas—which is to say fantastic. Serve the migas with hot corn tortillas.

1	tablespoon canola oil
1	small onion, chopped
2	to 4 serrano or jalapeño chiles, seeded for a milder dish and finely chopped
1	pound (4 medium or 2 large) tomatoes, seeded and chopped
10	large eggs or 5 eggs plus 8 egg whites
	salt, $1/2$ teaspoon or more, and freshly ground pepper to taste
6	corn tortillas, cut into $1/2$-inch-wide by 2-inch-long strips, toasted*
2	tablespoons chopped fresh cilantro

Heat the oil in a large heavy nonstick skillet over medium heat. Add the onion and chiles and cook, stirring, until the onion is tender, about 5 minutes. Add the tomatoes and cook for another minute. Turn the heat to medium-low.

Beat the eggs with the salt and pepper in a bowl, just enough to incorporate the yolks and the whites. Stir into the vegetables and cook, stirring over medium-low heat, until the mixture is just about set, about 8 to 10 minutes. Stir in the crisp tortilla strips and the cilantro and stir for another minute. Remove from the heat, taste, and adjust the seasoning. Serve piping hot, with fresh hot tortillas.

* *To toast tortilla chips:* To bake the chips, preheat the oven to 325 degrees. Place the tortilla pieces on a baking sheet and bake for 20 to 30 minutes, until light brown and crisp, shaking the baking sheet every 10 minutes. Allow to cool on a rack. To microwave the chips, place about 6 to 10 pieces at a time on a plate or on the plate in your microwave oven. Microwave on HIGH (100%) power for 1 minute. If the pieces are not crisp, turn them over and microwave for another 40 to 60 seconds. If they are still not crisp and are just beginning to brown, microwave for another 20 to 30 seconds, until crisp. Cool on a rack or in a basket.

Advance Preparation: The tortilla strips can be crisped a day ahead of time, and all of the vegetables prepared, but cooking should be done when you're ready to eat.

PER PORTION (WHOLE EGGS)

Calories	223	Protein	13 g
Fat	11 g	Carbohydrate	18 g
Saturated Fat	3 g	Fiber	3 g
Cholesterol	354 mg	Sodium	335 mg

PER PORTION (EGGS AND EGG WHITES)

Calories	183	Protein	12 g
Fat	7 g	Carbohydrate	18 g
Saturated Fat	2 g	Fiber	3 g
Cholesterol	177 mg	Sodium	355 mg

Chapter
Ten

Fish and Hearty Fish Soups

Cold Lime-Cooked Fish (Seviche)
Fish and Shellfish Soup from Veracruz
Veracruz-Style Crab Soup
Veracruz-Style Paella (Arroz a la Tumbada)
Veracruz-Style Fish
Grilled Tuna with Tomato and Corn Salsa
Tuna Steaks with Adobo Sauce
Pan-Cooked Salmon Fillets with Tomatillo Salsa
Green Tomatillo Mole with Salmon or Shrimp
Pan-Cooked Fish with Spicy Vegetable Salsa
Grilled Swordfish or Halibut with Mango Mint Salsa
Fish Fillets in Adobo, Cooked in Corn Husks
Shredded Shark or Mahimahi Salpicón from Veracruz
Empanadas
Crab Claws Bathed in Picante Chipotle Sauce
Shrimp with Garlic Sauce
Shrimp with Green Garlic Sauce

I had been a strict vegetarian for four years when I found myself on the blisteringly hot, sandy beach at Salina Cruz, in southern Oaxaca, for a week. We were sleeping in hammocks under thatch palapas, in a sort of open-air "hotel" run by an old woman named Marta. I had to make a choice about how I was going to eat. I could stick to my vegetarian diet and eat eggs cooked in quite a bit of oil at every meal, or I could partake of the fresh fish I watched the fishermen drag out of the sea every day. I opted for the fish and never looked back. Marta grilled the large whole sierras (a kind of mackerel) and snappers over coals, and we ate the incredibly fresh, succulent fish with nothing more than salt, lime, and hot corn tortillas. Twenty years later I remember that fish vividly. I've been an enthusiastic fish eater ever since.

Most of the traditional Mexican recipes in this chapter come from the state of Veracruz, a state with a long Gulf coastline where I ate some of the best fish dishes I've ever tasted. I've toned down the oil, but the flavors are authentic. Veracruz-style fish, usually made with red snapper, is probably Mexico's most well-known fish preparation. It is one of the great fish dishes of the world, with its picante-acid sauce of tomatoes, capers, olives, and pickled jalapeños. Other dishes from Veracruz, like crab soup and the shark or mahimahi salpicón (a salpicón is a shredded mixture) use the same combination of capers, olives, and chiles, resulting in flavors that always amaze and please my guests. The Spanish overtones in these dishes are quite distinctive, as they are in the rice and seafood dish called *arroz a la tumbada,* Mexico's paella. Other seafood dishes from Veracruz are as clearly Mexican as you can get. The chipotle chile is the defining ingredient in the chipotle-bathed crab claws and, in Chapter 8, the picante shrimp enchiladas.

Seviche—lime-marinated raw fish—is a perfect low-fat dish. The marvelous fresh-tasting dish can be made with lower-fat fish like snapper or cod (it is traditionally made with sierra, which is a fattier fish) and served as a first or a main course. I usually serve it as a first course at a dinner party, but for everyday eating I'd make a meal of it.

Salsas and fish go together so nicely, and the combinations can be easy to throw together, especially grilled or pan-cooked fish with fresh salsa. Fresh salsas neither overpower mild-flavored fish like snapper nor are overtaken by stronger-tasting fish like salmon or tuna. On the other hand, meaty fish like tuna can stand up to a rich adobo, which is like Mexican barbecue sauce.

The dishes in this chapter are great for entertaining. The crab soup is a winter favorite, and in summer I love the tuna steaks with adobo sauce or salsa. But don't wait for a dinner party to try these dishes. I hope the simpler ones will become regulars on your weekly menus.

COLD LIME-COOKED FISH (SEVICHE)

Makes 6 main-course servings or 8 to 10 first-course servings

There are many versions of seviche in my repertoire. This is the one I've been making the longest, and I never tire of it. Because the fish is uncooked, you must be very certain that it is utterly fresh. Go to the best fishmonger in town. I adore the fresh flavors here and the contrasting colors and textures that all of the vegetables bring to the dish. Obviously the avocado adds a lot of richness to the dish, so you might want to omit it, especially if the seviche is part of a larger menu.

1½	pounds very fresh white-fleshed fish fillets, such as cod, red snapper, halibut, bream, or sea bass
1½	to 2 cups fresh lime juice, from 7 large limes
1	medium red or white onion, sliced
2	large garlic cloves, minced or pressed
2	fresh or canned jalapeño or serrano chiles, seeded and chopped
2	medium tomatoes, chopped
	salt and freshly ground pepper to taste
1	medium avocado, peeled, pitted, and diced, optional
1	tablespoon olive oil
⅓	cup chopped fresh cilantro, plus sprigs for garnish
1	head of Boston lettuce or ½ pound fresh spinach for serving

Cut the fish into ½-inch cubes and place in a bowl. Pour on the lime juice and toss together well. Cover with plastic wrap and refrigerate. Marinate for 7 hours, tossing every once in a while to redistribute the lime juice.

Add the onion, garlic, chiles, tomatoes, salt, pepper, avocado, and olive oil to the bowl. Toss together, cover, and refrigerate for another hour. Stir in the chopped cilantro shortly before serving and adjust the seasonings.

To serve, drain off some of the marinade. Line a platter or salad bowl or individual serving plates with lettuce or spinach leaves and spoon on the seviche. The leaves will be dressed with the excess lime juice and will make a delicious finish to the dish. Garnish with cilantro sprigs and serve.

Advance Preparation: Seviche must be started 8 hours ahead, but the fish should be purchased and the seviche made on the day you are serving it.

PER PORTION

Calories	151	Protein	22 g
Fat	3 g	Carbohydrate	9 g
Saturated Fat	.47 g	Fiber	1 g
Cholesterol	49 mg	Sodium	72 mg

FISH AND SHELLFISH SOUP FROM VERACRUZ

Makes 6 to 8 servings

This sopa de mariscos is a classic from the state of Veracruz. The broth is an aromatic, tomatoey, masa-thickened fish broth. The soup I ate at Nico's Restaurant in Xalapa, on which this one is based, was infused with the flavor of field corn, which is cooked and served in the broth. Here we find sweet corn more readily than the starchy Mexican type, so my soup is sweeter than the one I had in Mexico. Serve this with lots of hot corn tortillas, which will be all the better if they're homemade.

4	dozen littleneck clams
1/2	cup dry white wine
2	quarts water, plus 1 cup (if using reconstituted masa to thicken the soup)
2	guajillo chiles, toasted*
8	plum tomatoes, roasted*
2	corn tortillas, toasted* and ground in a spice mill, or 1/4 cup masa harina dissolved in 3 tablespoons water
1	tablespoon olive oil

* *To toast chiles:* Wearing rubber gloves, tear the chiles into flat pieces and remove the seeds and veins. Heat a heavy skillet or comal over medium heat and toast the chiles on both sides, pressing them down with a metal spatula and turning them as soon as they sizzle and blister, in a matter of seconds. Remove from the heat at once and transfer to a bowl or plate.

* *To roast tomatoes:* Preheat the broiler. Line a baking sheet with foil and place the tomatoes on it. Place under the broiler, about 2 to 3 inches from the heat (at the highest rack setting). Turn after 2 or 3 minutes, when the tomatoes have charred on one side (this may take longer in an electric oven), and repeat on the other side. Remove from the heat and transfer to a bowl. When the tomatoes are cool enough to handle, peel and core.

$^1\!/_2$	small white onion, finely chopped
2	large garlic cloves, minced or pressed
1	bay leaf
2	fresh rosemary sprigs
	salt to taste, 2 teaspoons or more
6	ounces medium shrimp, peeled and deveined
6	ounces crabmeat or small bay shrimp
6	ounces squid, cleaned and cut into $^1\!/_4$-inch-thick slices
$^1\!/_2$	pound grouper, snapper, or other white-fleshed fish fillets, cut into 1-inch pieces
2	tablespoons chopped fresh epazote or cilantro
3	ears corn, broken or cut into thirds, or 2 cups frozen corn kernels
4	limes, quartered, for serving

Scrub the clams with a coarse brush or a toothbrush and rinse in several changes of water to remove sand. Combine the wine and 2 cups water in a large saucepan and bring to a boil. Add the clams and cover tightly. Steam for 5 minutes or until the shells open. Remove from the heat and remove the clams from the pot. When cool enough to handle, remove the clams from the shells and quickly rinse under cold water to rid them of any remaining sand. Discard any that have not opened. Strain the cooking water through a cheesecloth-lined strainer and set aside.

Pour boiling water over the toasted chiles to cover. Weight with a plate. Let sit for 30 minutes.

Transfer the peeled tomatoes to a blender along with any juice that has accumulated in the bowl. Drain the chiles and add to the blender. If you're using ground toasted tortillas, add to the blender as well. Puree until smooth.

Heat the oil in a large heavy soup pot over medium heat and add the onion. Cook, stirring, until tender, about 5 minutes. Add the garlic and cook, stirring, for another minute, until the garlic begins to color. Add the pureed tomato and chile, the bay leaf, and the rosemary. Cook, stirring, for 5 minutes,

* *To toast tortilla:* To bake the tortillas, preheat the oven to 325 degrees. Place the tortillas on a baking sheet and bake for 20 to 30 minutes, until light brown and crisp, shaking the baking sheet every 10 minutes. Allow to cool on a rack. To microwave, place about 1 or 2 tortillas on a plate or on the plate in your microwave oven. Microwave on HIGH (100%) power for 1 minute. If the tortillas are not crisp, turn them over and microwave for another 40 to 60 seconds. If they are still not crisp and are just beginning to brown, microwave for another 20 to 30 seconds, until crisp. Cool on a rack or in a basket.

until the mixture thickens. Turn the heat down to medium-low and continue to simmer for 5 to 10 minutes, stirring often, until thick and aromatic. Add the cooking liquid from the clams and 6 cups water. If you're using reconstituted masa, stir 1 cup water into the masa and stir well with a whisk or wooden spoon to dissolve the masa. Strain this mixture into the soup pot. Bring to a boil, add salt, reduce the heat, cover, and simmer for 15 minutes.

Add all of the seafood to the pot, along with the epazote and corn. Bring back to a simmer and simmer for 10 minutes, until all of the seafood is cooked through but tender. Taste, add salt as desired, and serve with the limes, making sure each person gets a piece of corn.

Advance Preparation: The soup base (up until the last paragraph, when you add the seafood) will keep for a day in the refrigerator. However, it is best, as all seafood dishes are served the day it is made.

PER PORTION

Calories	316	Protein	40 g
Fat	6 g	Carbohydrate	27 g
Saturated Fat	.84 g	Fiber	3 g
Cholesterol	181 mg	Sodium	974 mg

VERACRUZ-STYLE CRAB SOUP

Makes 6 to 8 servings

This is an incredibly rich-tasting soup. The slight acidity introduced by the combination of pickled capers, jalapeños, and olives gives the soup a depth that is more than just picante. This sharp note is softened by the sweet crabmeat, which is added at the last minute. I love the way crabmeat spreads through a soup so that you get sweet, luxurious strands in every bite. Although it isn't traditional, I like to add squash to this dish to make a heartier stewlike soup.

1½   pounds crabmeat
1   tablespoon olive oil
2   medium onions, chopped
3   large garlic cloves, minced or pressed
2   pounds (8 medium or 4 large) tomatoes, peeled, seeded, and
         chopped, or two 28-ounce cans, drained and chopped
      salt to taste, 1 to 2 teaspoons
1½   pounds (5 to 6 medium) waxy potatoes, scrubbed and diced
1   pound winter squash, pumpkin, or summer squash, peeled and
         diced (about 2 cups)
2   medium canned or homemade pickled jalapeño chiles, seeded
         and chopped (about 3 tablespoons)
¼   cup chopped pitted green olives
      scant ¼ cup drained capers, rinsed and chopped
2   fresh cilantro sprigs, plus ½ cup chopped for garnish
1   fresh mint sprig
½   teaspoon dried oregano, preferably Mexican
2   bay leaves
2   quarts water
3   limes, cut into wedges, for serving

Buy fresh crab that has already been cooked, shelled, and cleaned. Keep refrigerated while you prepare the soup base.

Heat the oil in a large heavy soup pot or Dutch oven over medium heat and add the onions. Cook, stirring, for 5 to 8 minutes, until tender. Add the garlic and continue to cook for another minute or two, until the garlic begins to color. Add the tomatoes and about ½ teaspoon salt and cook, stirring, for about 15 minutes, until the tomatoes are somewhat cooked down and the mixture smells fragrant. Add the potatoes, squash, chiles, olives, capers, cilantro, mint, oregano, and bay leaves and stir together for 5 minutes. Add the water and salt to taste and bring to a simmer. Simmer for 20 to 30 minutes, until the potatoes and squash are tender and the broth tastes marvelous. Adjust the salt and garlic. Remove from the heat if not serving right away.

Five minutes before serving, heat the soup to just below a simmer and stir in the crab. Heat through, stirring and being careful not to let the soup boil, or the crabmeat, which is already cooked, will become rubbery. Just before serving, stir in the chopped cilantro, and serve with lime wedges on the side.

Advance Preparation: The entire soup, up to adding the crabmeat, can be done a day ahead and held in the refrigerator.

PER PORTION

Calories	315	Protein	28 g
Fat	6 g	Carbohydrate	40 g
Saturated Fat	.71 g	Fiber	5 g
Cholesterol	113 mg	Sodium	1,236 mg

VERACRUZ-STYLE PAELLA
(ARROZ A LA TUMBADA)

Makes 8 servings

This dish is what paella has become over the centuries in Veracruz. It is a heady mixture of rice, fish, and shellfish. There is no saffron as there is in Spanish paella; instead there are jalapeños and epazote, giving the dish an incredibly deep, rich flavor. Although there are many steps here, several, such as cooking the crabs and clams, can be accomplished early in the day. This is definitely a meal in itself, requiring only the simplest of green salads as accompaniment and a light, fruity dessert.

4	dozen littleneck clams
4	soft-shell crabs, cleaned, or one 2-pound crab, cracked, cleaned, and broken into pieces, or 1 pound crab legs, cracked
6½	cups water
½	pound firm fish fillets, such as snapper, sea bass, mahimahi, or shark
½	teaspoon salt, plus up to 1 teaspoon to taste
1	pound (about 5 or 6) plum tomatoes, roasted*
2	medium onions, 1 cut in half and roasted,* 1 thinly sliced
3	tablespoons olive oil
1½	cups medium- or long-grain white rice
8	large garlic cloves, 4 crushed in a mortar and pestle, 4 minced or pressed
2	jalapeño chiles, sliced into crosswise rings
16	medium shrimp, peeled and deveined
3	Dublin bay prawns or crayfish, halved and cleaned, or 8 large shrimp
½	pound squid or octopus, cleaned and sliced into ½-inch pieces freshly ground pepper to taste

* *To roast tomatoes and onion:* Preheat the broiler. Line a baking sheet with foil and place the tomatoes and halved onion on it. Place under the broiler, about 2 to 3 inches from the heat (at the highest rack setting). Turn after 2 or 3 minutes, when the tomatoes have charred on one side (this may take longer in an electric oven), and repeat on the other side. Turn the onion halves every 2 or 3 minutes, until browned in spots and softened, 5 to 10 minutes. Remove from the heat and transfer to a bowl. When the tomatoes are cool enough to handle, peel and core.

2   large fresh epazote sprigs, coarsely chopped (about 2 tablespoons), or 2 tablespoons chopped cilantro

Rinse the clams in several changes of water. Brush well to rid the shells of sand.

Buy the crabs the day you are going to make this, have them cleaned and cracked, and refrigerate them as soon as you get home or, even better, cook them right away. Rinse the crabs thoroughly under cold water. Bring 1 quart water to a boil in a large pot and drop in the crabs. Cover tightly and cook for about 5 minutes, until the shells are pink and the crabmeat is opaque and tender. Remove from the heat. Remove the crabs from the water and strain the water into a bowl through a cheesecloth-lined strainer. If you're using soft-shell crabs, cut them in half. Set aside.

Return 2 cups water from the crabs to the pot and bring to a boil. Add the clams. Cover and steam for 5 minutes or until the clams open. Remove from the heat. Remove the clams from their shells and discard the shells. Discard any that have not opened. Transfer the clams to a bowl and rinse quickly to remove any remaining sand. Strain the cooking liquid through a cheesecloth-lined strainer. Set aside the clams and return the water from the clams and the water from the crabs to the pot. Bring back to a simmer and add the fish fillets. Cook for 5 minutes, until the fish flakes. Remove from the water and cut the fillets into 1-inch pieces or simply flake the fish using your fingers. Set aside with the clams. Taste the broth, add salt as desired, and strain again into a 1-quart measuring cup.

Transfer the tomatoes and the roasted onion and any liquid that has accumulated in the bowl to a blender. Blend until smooth.

Heat 1 tablespoon olive oil in a skillet over medium-high heat and add a bit of the puree. If it sizzles, add the rest (wait a few minutes if it doesn't). Cook, stirring, for 10 to 15 minutes, until the puree is thick and aromatic and beginning to stick to the pan. Remove from the heat and set aside.

Pour the remaining 2$^{1}/_{2}$ cups water into a saucepan and bring to a simmer. Heat another tablespoon of the olive oil in a heavy 1$^{1}/_{2}$- or 2-quart saucepan over medium heat and add the rice. Cook, stirring, until the rice begins to color and all of the grains are separate, about 5 minutes. Add the simmering water and $^{1}/_{2}$ teaspoon salt and bring to a boil. Reduce the heat, cover, and simmer for 15 minutes, until the water is absorbed. The rice will not be cooked through. Set aside.

In a large wide casserole, paella pan, or heavy nonstick skillet, heat the remaining oil over medium heat. Add the crushed garlic, sliced onion, and jalapeños and cook, stirring, for about 5 minutes, until the onion is tender and the garlic has colored slightly. Add the medium shrimp, crayfish, and squid, season with salt and pepper, and cook, stirring, for 1 minute. Add the minced garlic, cooked clams, and tomato-onion puree, stir together, and add 3 cups of the reserved fish and clam broth. Bring to a boil and cook for 5 minutes.

Add the rice and crab pieces to the fish mixture and stir together for about 3 minutes. Add the fish and epazote or cilantro, reduce the heat to medium-low, and simmer, stirring, for another 5 to 7 minutes, until the rice is cooked through. The dish should remain soupy. Adjust the seasoning, adding more salt, chile, or epazote if desired, and serve at once.

Advance Preparation: The crab, clams, and fish fillets can be cooked hours ahead on the day you are serving this. Refrigerate if not using within the hour. The tomato sauce can be prepared up to a day ahead and held in the refrigerator. The rice can be partially cooked hours ahead of finishing the dish.

PER PORTION

Calories	385	Protein	36 g
Fat	8 g	Carbohydrate	40 g
Saturated Fat	1 g	Fiber	2 g
Cholesterol	173 mg	Sodium	409 mg

VERACRUZ-STYLE FISH

Makes 6 servings

This is one of the best-known Mexican fish dishes. Its popularity is easy to understand, since it has so many wonderful savory/picante flavors. It couldn't be more Mediterranean—until it comes to the pickled jalapeño chiles. Red snapper is the fish used in Veracruz for this dish, but I have made it successfully with many different kinds of firm-fleshed fish. Serve this dish with rice; the rice will soak up the sauce.

6   firm-fleshed fish fillets, 5 to 6 ounces each, such as red snapper,
        sea bass, halibut, or cod
    juice of 2 limes
    salt to taste
2   tablespoons olive oil

8	garlic cloves, 5 minced or pressed, 3 left whole
2	medium onions, chopped or thinly sliced
3	pounds (about 12 medium or 6 large) tomatoes, peeled, seeded, juice reserved, and chopped, or 2½ 28-ounce cans, lightly drained and chopped
20	green olives, pitted, 10 chopped, 10 cut in half lengthwise
2	tablespoons drained capers, rinsed, 1 tablespoon chopped
2	to 3 pickled jalapeño chiles to taste, stemmed, seeded, and sliced into strips
1½	tablespoons pickling juice from the chiles
¼	cup chopped fresh parsley
4	bay leaves
1	inch cinnamon stick or ½ teaspoon ground cinnamon
2	fresh rosemary sprigs or 1 teaspoon dried
2	fresh marjoram or thyme sprigs or ½ teaspoon dried
½	teaspoon dried oregano, preferably Mexican
½	teaspoon coarsely crushed black peppercorns

Rinse the fish fillets, toss with the lime juice and a little salt, and refrigerate for 1 hour while you prepare the sauce.

Heat the oil over medium heat in a large heavy casserole that will hold the fish fillets. Add the whole garlic cloves and cook, stirring, until browned, about 5 minutes. Remove them from the heat and discard. Add the onions to the pot and cook, stirring, until they begin to color but not brown, about 5 to 8 minutes. Add the minced garlic and stir together for a minute, until the garlic smells fragrant.

Stir in the tomatoes and their juice and cook, stirring often, for 10 minutes, until they have cooked down slightly. Add the chopped olives, chopped capers, jalapeños and their pickling juice, 2 tablespoons of the chopped parsley, the bay leaves, cinnamon, rosemary, marjoram, and oregano (if you wish, you can tie the bay leaves, cinnamon, dried herbs, and peppercorns in cheesecloth; remove the cheesecloth at the end of cooking). Add about ½ teaspoon salt, reduce the heat to low, cover, and simmer, stirring occasionally, for 20 to 30 minutes. The tomatoes should cook down, but the sauce should not be so thick that it won't make a good poaching medium for the fish; it should be a little watery. Remove from the heat, taste, and adjust the salt.

Remove the fish from the refrigerator 15 minutes before cooking. Bring the sauce to a simmer over medium heat and add the fish fillets. Make sure they are covered with the sauce. Cover and simmer for 4 minutes. Turn the fillets over and simmer for another 3 to 4 minutes (depending on the thickness of the fish) or until the fish flakes easily when poked with a fork. Remove from the heat and serve, topping each fillet with a generous amount of sauce and garnishing with the remaining parsley, capers, and halved olives. Serve with rice, which will soak up some of the sauce.

NOTE: The fish can also be baked. Preheat the oven to 425 degrees. Lay the fillets in an oiled baking dish and spoon on the sauce. Cover with foil and bake for 10 minutes, or until the fish flakes. Serve as directed.

Advance Preparation: The sauce can be made hours or even a day ahead. Hold overnight in the refrigerator.

PER PORTION

Calories	291	Protein	35 g
Fat	9 g	Carbohydrate	18 g
Saturated Fat	1 g	Fiber	4 g
Cholesterol	58 mg	Sodium	811 mg

GRILLED TUNA WITH TOMATO AND CORN SALSA

Makes 6 servings

Grilled rare tuna is a perfect match for the salsa. Since precut tuna steaks are always larger than 4 or 5 ounces, you will have to ask your fishmonger to cut the slices into 4- or 5-ounce pieces. They may look small, but remember how thick they are. You can use a grill pan for cooking the steaks on top of the stove. Swordfish also works well here.

2 pounds (8 medium or 4 large) tomatoes, chopped
½ small red onion, minced and rinsed
2 to 3 jalapeño or serrano chiles to taste, seeded for a milder salsa and minced
¼ cup chopped fresh cilantro or more to taste
1 tablespoon red wine vinegar, balsamic vinegar, or lime juice, optional
1 ear white corn, steamed for 4 minutes and kernels removed

salt and freshly ground pepper to taste

6   4- to 5-ounce tuna or swordfish steaks, about ³/₄ to 1 inch thick

1   tablespoon olive oil

Mix together the tomatoes, red onion, chiles, cilantro, vinegar, and corn. Add salt and pepper. If you're not serving within the hour, refrigerate, but remove the salsa from the refrigerator at least a half hour before serving so that it isn't too cold.

Rinse the tuna steaks and pat dry. Salt and pepper lightly and brush with olive oil.

Prepare your grill or heat a nonstick grill pan over high heat. Grill the tuna steaks for 3 minutes on each side. The fish should remain pink in the middle. Transfer to a serving platter or plates and serve with the salsa.

NOTE: When corn is not in season, make the tomato salsa without it and pep up the tomatoes with the vinegar or lime juice.

Advance Preparation: The salsa will hold for several hours in the refrigerator.

PER PORTION

Calories	253	Protein	32 g
Fat	9 g	Carbohydrate	11 g
Saturated Fat	2 g	Fiber	3 g
Cholesterol	48 mg	Sodium	67 mg

Tuna Steaks with Adobo Sauce

Makes 8 servings

I had this dish at my favorite New York Mexican restaurant, El Teddy, and immediately wanted to include it in my repertoire. The beefy tuna steaks are a perfect match for the rich, picante, sweet and sour barbecue sauce. Of course if you keep adobo sauce in your refrigerator—and it keeps well—this is quite an easy dish to throw together.

1   recipe Adobo Sauce (page 75)
8   ³/₄-inch-thick tuna steaks, about 4 to 5 ounces each (you will probably have to buy larger boneless tuna steaks and cut them into pieces, since tuna steaks are usually larger)

Either the day before or early in the morning, make the sauce.

Marinate the fish about 2 hours before you wish to serve it. Divide the sauce into 2 equal portions and place 1 in a large bowl. Toss with the tuna steaks, cover, and marinate for 2 hours, turning the fish from time to time. Refrigerate for the first hour and a half, but let the fish come to room temperature for a half hour before you cook it.

Warm the remaining sauce in a heavy saucepan while you cook the fish. Prepare a grill or heat a grill pan or a nonstick skillet over medium-high heat. Grill the fish for 2¹/₂ to 3 minutes on each side; it should be pink in the middle. Remove from the heat and slice the tuna into thin slices.

Place 2 to 3 tablespoons of the warm sauce on each plate, lay the tuna slices over it, and serve.

Advance Preparation: The sauce will keep for at least 2 weeks in the refrigerator and can be frozen.

PER PORTION

Calories	278	Protein	29 g
Fat	12 g	Carbohydrate	16 g
Saturated Fat	2 g	Fiber	4 g
Cholesterol	43 mg	Sodium	411 mg

Pan-Cooked Salmon Fillets with Tomatillo Salsa

Makes 4 servings

I'm combining a French technique with a Mexican sauce here. The salmon fillets, with their skin on, are cooked on one side only—à l'unilatéral—and sauced with a pale green cooked tomatillo salsa. The colors of the fish and salsa are beautiful together, and the slightly acidic sauce is perfect with the rich salmon. Serve the fish with hot corn tortillas.

$^1/_2$ pound (about 4 large) fresh tomatillos, husked and rinsed, or one 13-ounce can, drained

1   to 2 jalapeño or serrano chiles to taste, stemmed and seeded for a milder salsa

1   slice of onion, $1^1/_2$ inches thick, roughly chopped (2 heaped tablespoons)

1   large garlic clove, roughly chopped
salt to taste, $^1/_4$ to $^1/_2$ teaspoon

10   fresh cilantro sprigs or more to taste, plus sprigs for garnish

2   teaspoons olive or canola oil

1   cup vegetable, garlic, or chicken stock (pages 158–160)

4   salmon fillets, about 5 ounces each, with skin attached

If you're using fresh tomatillos, simmer in water to cover for 10 minutes. Drain and place in a blender or a food processor fitted with the steel blade. If you're using canned tomatillos, place in the blender or food processor. Add the chile, onion, garlic, salt, and half the cilantro. Puree the mixture.

Heat 1 teaspoon of the oil in a heavy saucepan or nonstick skillet over medium heat. Drizzle a bit of the tomatillo mixture into the pan and, if it sizzles, add the rest (wait a bit if it doesn't). Cook the tomatillo puree, stirring, until it thickens and begins to stick to the pan, about 5 minutes. Add the stock, stir together, and bring to a simmer. Simmer for 15 to 20 minutes, until the mixture is slightly thick. Remove from the heat, taste, and adjust the salt. Place about $^1/_2$ cup of the sauce in a blender with the remaining 5 cilantro sprigs and blend the cilantro into the sauce. Stir back into the pan. This final addition of cilantro restores a bit of color to the sauce. Keep the sauce warm while you cook the fish.

Brush the salmon skin with the remaining oil. Heat a large nonstick skillet over medium-high heat. Add the salmon fillets, skin side down. Cook for 6 to 8 minutes on one side only, until the skin is brown and the salmon has begun to turn from translucent to pink. The top should remain quite rare. If you wish to cook the fish through, lower the heat after 6 minutes, put a lid over the pan, and continue to cook for 2 to 3 minutes. Remove the fish from the heat.

Place about ¼ cup of the salsa on each plate and top with the salmon. Garnish with cilantro and serve with hot tortillas.

Advance Preparation: The sauce will hold for 4 days in the refrigerator and can be frozen.

PER PORTION

Calories	244	Protein	29 g
Fat	12 g	Carbohydrate	4 g
Saturated Fat	2 g	Fiber	0
Cholesterol	78 mg	Sodium	390 mg

GREEN TOMATILLO MOLE WITH SALMON OR SHRIMP

Makes 6 servings

This rich, nutty mole is traditionally served with chicken or pork, but it also goes beautifully with fish. I like it with a pink fish, which is why I choose either salmon or shrimp. I particularly love the way the creamy texture of salmon melds into the creamy mole. If you'd like a leaner fish, try the sauce with halibut and cook the fish as you would a salmon steak. I recommend using fillets if you want to keep each serving to 5 ounces, since salmon steaks are usually bigger. Serve this sensational combination with rice.

1   **recipe Green Tomatillo Mole, page 70**

For Salmon:
6   **5-ounce salmon fillets with or without skin or 6 salmon steaks, about ¾ inch thick**
1   **teaspoon olive or canola oil**

For Shrimp:

1¾ **pounds medium or large shrimp, peeled and deveined**
   Cilantro sprigs and radishes for garnish

Make the mole and keep warm in a saucepan.

FOR SALMON FILLETS: Brush the salmon skin with olive or canola oil. Heat a large nonstick skillet over medium-high heat. Add the salmon fillets, skin side down. Cook on one side, until the skin is brown and the salmon has begun to turn from translucent to pink, about 6 minutes. Lower the heat, cover the pan, and cook for another 2 to 5 minutes, until the fillets are just cooked through. Or place the fillets in a lightly oiled baking dish, cover tightly, and bake in a preheated 425-degree oven for 10 to 15 minutes.

FOR SALMON STEAKS: Heat a nonstick skillet or grill pan over medium-high heat and brush with oil. Cook the steaks for 3 to 4 minutes per side, until cooked through but quite pink in the middle. Remove from the heat.

Bring the mole to a simmer. Spoon ⅓ cup mole onto each of 6 wide soup plates or dinner plates, top with a salmon fillet or steak, drizzle a spoonful of sauce over the fish, garnish with cilantro sprigs and radishes and serve.

FOR SHRIMP: Bring the mole to a simmer and drop the shrimp into the sauce. Simmer, stirring from time to time, for 5 minutes or until the shrimp are pink on both sides. Remove from the heat and serve in wide soup bowls, garnish with cilantro sprigs and radishes.

Advance Preparation: The mole will keep for 3 days in the refrigerator and can also be frozen. You will need to whisk it well when you thaw it to get the right texture.

PER PORTION (SALMON)

Calories	314	Protein	30 g
Fat	16 g	Carbohydrate	12 g
Saturated Fat	2 g	Fiber	2 g
Cholesterol	70 mg	Sodium	527 mg

PER PORTION (SHRIMP)

Calories	246	Protein	26 g
Fat	10 g	Carbohydrate	13 g
Saturated Fat	1 g	Fiber	2 g
Cholesterol	163 mg	Sodium	630 mg

Pan-Cooked Fish with
Spicy Vegetable Salsa

Makes 4 servings

This is inspired by a fantastic dish that I often order at my favorite L.A. Mexican restaurant, La Serenata de Garibaldi. There the sauce is called Oaxaqueña. The chile de árbol and the flavors evoked by the fennel and tarragon do indeed remind me of the flavors of Oaxacan chiles and hoja santa, an herb used widely in southern Mexico. This sauce is more of a salsa, really, consisting of very finely minced vegetables and just a bit of liquid. It goes well with a firm-fleshed white fish, salmon, grilled chicken, or even on its own with corn tortillas. I make tacos and quesadillas with the leftovers.

$\frac{1}{2}$ pound fresh spinach, cleaned and stemmed
    salt and freshly ground pepper to taste
4 teaspoons olive oil
$\frac{1}{2}$ medium or 1 small onion, minced
2 large garlic cloves, minced or pressed
1 dried chile de árbol, seeded and minced or crumbled
$\frac{1}{2}$ teaspoon fennel seeds, crushed in a mortar and pestle or cracked
    in a spice mill
3 large mushrooms, minced (about $\frac{2}{3}$ cup)
1 medium zucchini or green summer squash, minced
    (about $1\frac{1}{4}$ cups)
1 medium tomato, peeled, seeded, and minced
$\frac{1}{4}$ cup dry white wine
$\frac{1}{2}$ cup water
4 5-ounce halibut, mahimahi, sea bass, or salmon fillets or steaks
$\frac{1}{4}$ small avocado, peeled, pitted, and minced
1 tablespoon chopped fresh tarragon

Bring a large pot of water to a boil. Fill a large bowl with cold water. Add a tablespoon of salt to the boiling water, add the spinach, count to 10, and transfer the spinach to the bowl of cold water using a slotted spoon or a deep-frying skimmer. Drain and squeeze the water out of the spinach. Chop and set aside.

Heat 1 tablespoon of the oil in a heavy nonstick skillet over medium-low heat. Add the onion and cook, stirring, until tender, about 3 to 5 minutes. Add the garlic, chile, and fennel seeds and cook, stirring, for about 30 to 60 seconds, until the garlic is fragrant. Add the mushrooms, zucchini, and about

$^1/_2$ teaspoon salt. Turn the heat to medium and cook, stirring, for 5 minutes, until the squash is tender but still bright green and the mushrooms have released some fragrant liquid. Stir in the tomato and cook for about 2 minutes. Stir in the wine and $^1/_4$ cup water. Bring to a simmer and simmer for 2 minutes. Remove from the heat, taste, and adjust the salt.

Heat a nonstick skillet over medium-high heat. Brush the pan with the remaining teaspoon of oil and add the fish. Salt and pepper the side that isn't cooking. Cook for about 3 to 4 minutes per side, until just cooked through (it should flake when poked with a fork). Turn off the heat but leave the fish in the pan.

Bring the vegetable mixture back to a simmer and stir in the chopped spinach, avocado, tarragon, and remaining water. Stir for about a minute and remove from the heat.

Transfer the fish from the pan to individual plates or a platter and surround with the salsa, spooning a small amount over the top of the fish as well. Serve at once.

Advance Preparation: The salsa can be prepared several hours before serving. The spinach and tarragon shouldn't be added until just before serving, or they'll lose their vivid color and taste. The fish is cooked quickly at the last minute.

PER PORTION

Calories	299	Protein	33 g
Fat	13 g	Carbohydrate	11 g
Saturated Fat	2 g	Fiber	3 g
Cholesterol	45 mg	Sodium	673 mg

GRILLED SWORDFISH OR HALIBUT WITH MANGO MINT SALSA

Makes 4 servings

Sweet and picante mango salsa goes wonderfully with many different types of fish. Swordfish and halibut are my favorites. You can grill the fish over coals or a gas grill or in a grill pan.

	salt and freshly ground pepper to taste
4	4- to 6-ounce swordfish or halibut steaks
1	recipe Mango Salsa with 1 tablespoon chopped fresh mint added (page 72)
2	limes, cut into wedges, for serving

Prepare a grill or heat a nonstick grill pan over medium-high heat. Lightly salt and pepper the fish. Grill the fish for 3 to 4 minutes on each side, until just cooked through. Remove from the heat and serve with the salsa spooned partially over the fish, partially on the side. Pass the lime wedges for squeezing over the fish.

Advance Preparation: The salsa can be made a few hours before serving and held in the refrigerator.

PER PORTION

Calories	212	Protein	26 g
Fat	5 g	Carbohydrate	16 g
Saturated Fat	1 g	Fiber	1 g
Cholesterol	49 mg	Sodium	116 mg

FISH FILLETS IN ADOBO, COOKED IN CORN HUSKS

Makes 6 servings

When you grill fish in soaked corn husks, you get that wonderful aroma of tamales but no masa fat. You eat these like tamales—that is, you open up a toasty corn husk surprise package to find succulent fish bathed in adobo sauce or paste.

This dish requires 3 hours of advance time for making the sauce, marinating the fish, and soaking the corn husks. I have made the dish successfully with both the classic adobo sauce, the paste, and the quick adobo sauce made from adobo paste. The adobo sauce is sweeter than the paste.

> 1 cup Red Chile Paste (Adobo) (page 73) or Quick Adobo Sauce (page 74)
> 1½ pounds firm white-fleshed fish fillets such as shark, sea bass, snapper, or catfish
> ¼ pound corn husks
> salt to taste
> 4 or 5 limes, quartered
> 1 bunch of cilantro, chopped

First make the adobo (or sauce) if you don't have it on hand. Give yourself about 1 hour for this, since the chiles require toasting and soaking.

Cut the fish into strips about 3 inches long and ½ inch wide. Measure out ½ cup of the adobo paste or sauce and toss with the fish in a bowl. Refrigerate for 2 hours or longer.

Meanwhile, place the corn husks in a saucepan or pot and cover with water. Bring to a simmer and simmer for 10 minutes. Remove from the heat, weight with a plate to submerge them, and let soak for 2 hours, until the husks are pliable.

Separate out 18 of the largest husks. They should be about 5 or 6 inches across at the widest end. If they are too narrow, place 2 together, overlapping them by about 2 inches. From the remaining corn husks, tear off 24 thin strips about ¼ inch wide and tie them together in twos so that you have 12 long strips for securing the filled husks like tamales.

Divide the fish into 6 portions. Lay a corn husk out on your work surface and spread a teaspoon of adobo paste or sauce over a 2- by 3-inch area at the wide end of the corn husk. Lay half of one portion of fish over the paste, lightly salt the fish, and squeeze on a bit of lime juice. Lay the other half-portion of

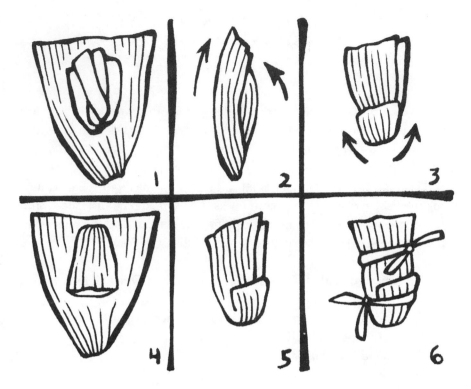

1. Spread the corn husk with adobo paste or sauce and top with the fish as directed.

2. Fold the sides of the corn husk up over the fish, trying to overlap at the middle.

3. Fold over the narrow end, so that three edges of the packet are enveloped in corn husk and the wider end is not.

4. Lay this package, seam-side down, on the wide end of another corn husk, with the open end of the package toward the center.

5. Wrap the long sides over the package, then fold the narrow end over so that the fish is entirely enveloped in a corn husk package.

6. Tie the package up with the strips of corn husk, wrapping a strip twice around each end.

fish on top, lightly salt, and squeeze on some lime juice. Spread with another teaspoon of the adobo paste or sauce. Fold the sides of the corn husk up over the fish, trying to overlap at the middle. Next fold over the narrow end so that three edges of the packet are enveloped in corn husk and the wider end is not. Lay this package, seam side down, on the wide end of another corn husk, with the open end of the package toward the center. Wrap the long sides over the package, then fold the narrow end over so that the fish is entirely enveloped in a corn husk package. Tie up the package with the strips of corn husk, wrapping a strip twice around each end.

To cook, either heat a griddle or heavy skillet over medium-high heat or preheat your broiler, with the rack about 4 inches from the heat. Cook on the griddle for about 6 minutes per side and 1 minute on each long edge. To broil, place on a baking sheet and cook for 6 minutes on one side and 5 minutes on the other. Remove from the heat, open one packet, and test with a fork for doneness: the fish should flake easily. If done, remove the outer corn husks and discard them. Place the packages on plates, open up the inner corn husk, being careful not to let the juice escape, squeeze on lime juice, and sprinkle on cilantro. Serve with plenty of hot corn tortillas and additional lime wedges.

Advance Preparation: The adobo paste or sauce will last for a couple of weeks in the refrigerator. The packets can be assembled hours before cooking and held in the refrigerator. They also hold well after cooking if you don't open them up.

PER PORTION

Calories	211	Protein	27 g
Fat	6 g	Carbohydrate	16 g
Saturated Fat	1 g	Fiber	1 g
Cholesterol	58 mg	Sodium	542 mg

SHREDDED SHARK OR MAHIMAHI SALPICÓN
FROM VERACRUZ

Makes 3 cups or enough for 32 small empanadas or
stuffed chiles or 16 quesadillas or soft tacos,
serving 6 to 8 as a main dish or 10 as an appetizer

This Veracruz salpicón is full of intriguing and wonderful flavors. Its Spanish origins are obvious—the combination of onion, garlic, tomatoes, olives, capers, and currants or raisins is as Mediterranean as you can get. But the chile makes it decidedly Mexican. Serve on hot tortillas, or fill empanadas.

1	quart water
2	bay leaves
2	fresh rosemary sprigs
2	fresh thyme sprigs
	salt to taste, about 1 teaspoon
1	pound shark or mahimahi fillets
2	tablespoons olive oil
1	medium onion, chopped
6	garlic cloves, chopped
6	medium plum tomatoes, peeled and chopped
1	serrano chile, chopped, or 1 pickled jalapeño, chopped
8	green olives, pitted and finely chopped
1	tablespoon drained capers, rinsed and finely chopped
1	tablespoon currants or coarsely chopped raisins
2	tablespoons chopped fresh flat-leaf parsley

Combine the water, bay leaves, rosemary, and thyme in a stockpot and bring to a boil. Add ½ teaspoon salt and the fish, turn the heat to low, and simmer for 10 minutes, until the fish flakes. Remove the fillets from the water with a slotted spatula and transfer to a bowl. Allow to cool, then pick out any bones and flake the fish by rubbing between your fingers or using a fork. Set aside.

Heat the olive oil in a large heavy nonstick skillet over medium heat. Add the onion and cook, stirring, until tender, about 3 to 5 minutes. Add the garlic and stir together for about a minute, just until the garlic begins to smell fragrant. Add the tomatoes, chile, olives, capers, currants, and salt. Cook, stirring, for 10 to 15 minutes, until the tomatoes have cooked down and the mixture smells fragrant. It should not be sticking to the pan. Stir in the fish and parsley and cook together for about 1 minute. Taste and adjust seasonings and remove from the heat.

Advance Preparation: This will hold for several hours in or out of the refrigerator.

PER PORTION

Calories	176	Protein	17 g
Fat	9 g	Carbohydrate	7 g
Saturated Fat	1 g	Fiber	1 g
Cholesterol	39 mg	Sodium	502 mg

EMPANADAS

Makes 32 4-inch empanadas

$2^2/_3$ **cups masa harina**
$1^3/_4$ **cups hot tap water or more as needed**

Combine the masa harina and the water in a bowl and knead together until smooth. You can also do this in a mixer, using the paddle attachment, or in a food processor. Knead for a couple of minutes. Wrap in a plastic bag and let stand for 20 to 30 minutes. The dough should be fairly moist but should not stick to your hands. Divide into 32 small balls, about $1^1/_4$ inches in diameter, and cover with plastic wrap. Using a tortilla press, press out a ball between two Ziploc bags or rounds of plastic wrap. Do not press too hard. Carefully peel back the top piece of plastic. Flip the tortilla over onto the plastic you peeled off and peel off the other piece of plastic. Lay the tortilla down and top the half nearest you with a tablespoon of the filling. Fold the tortilla over the filling, using the plastic to guide the tortilla over the filling. Peel back the plastic and gently press the edges of the tortilla together to seal. Continue to fill the remaining tortillas in this way.

TO TOAST THE EMPANADAS: Heat a large griddle or heavy skillet over medium heat for 10 minutes. Bake the empanadas on the griddle for 5 minutes on each side, until lightly browned. Keep warm on a rack in a low oven as you finish the remaining empanadas.

CRAB CLAWS BATHED IN PICANTE CHIPOTLE SAUCE

Makes 4 to 6 appetizer servings

These crab claws adobados are very rich tasting and picante—and also messy and fun to eat. Give your guests lots of paper napkins. The crab claws are slathered in the sauce, and there's no other way to eat them than with your hands. They make a great first course at a fish dinner.

1½   **pounds crab claws, cooked and cracked**
1   **small or ½ large head of garlic, peeled**
1   **pound tomatoes, roasted***
½   **small can chipotles en adobo (or less to taste)**
1   **tablespoon canola or olive oil**
   salt to taste
   lime wedges for serving

Place the cracked crab claws in a bowl and run under cold water for several minutes to remove sand and grit.

Pound the garlic to a paste in a mortar and pestle. You should have 2 tablespoons of puree.

* *To roast tomatoes:* Preheat the broiler. Line a baking sheet with foil and place the tomatoes on it. Place under the broiler, about 2 to 3 inches from the heat (at the highest rack setting). Turn after 2 or 3 minutes, when the tomatoes have charred on one side (this may take longer in an electric oven), and repeat on the other side. Remove from the heat and transfer to a bowl. When the tomatoes are cool enough to handle, peel and core.

Transfer the roasted tomatoes to a blender along with any juices that have accumulated in the bowl. Add the chipotles in their adobo sauce and blend until smooth. Strain into a bowl.

Heat the oil in a heavy saucepan or skillet over medium heat and add the garlic paste. Cook, stirring, for about 2 to 3 minutes, until the garlic paste colors. Add the chipotle mixture and cook, stirring, for 5 to 10 minutes, until it thickens slightly and begins to stick to the bottom of the pan. Taste and add salt if desired. Stir in the crab claws, heat through for about 1 minute, and serve, with lime wedges on the side.

Advance Preparation: The sauce will keep for 4 or 5 days in the refrigerator but will become hotter. It can be reheated just before adding the crab claws.

PER PORTION

Calories	170	Protein	18 g
Fat	6 g	Carbohydrate	10 g
Saturated Fat	.48 g	Fiber	2 g
Cholesterol	85 mg	Sodium	456 mg

SHRIMP WITH GARLIC SAUCE

Makes 4 servings

Most versions of this dish—which can also be made with Dublin Bay prawns or with fish—require copious amounts of oil in which a great deal of sliced garlic is cooked. But here the garlic is pounded and the shrimp are marinated in the paste. Using this method, it's easy to reduce the traditional amount of oil. Serve the shrimp with rice.

1   **small or ¹/₂ large head of garlic, peeled**
     salt to taste
1   **pound shrimp, peeled and deveined with tails left on**
¹/₄   **cup fresh lime juice**
1   **tablespoon olive oil**
2   **tablespoons chopped fresh parsley**
     Chipotle Salsa (page 76) as desired, optional

Combine the garlic and ¼ teaspoon salt in a mortar and pestle and pound until you have a smooth paste. You should have 2 heaped tablespoons or more. Toss with the shrimp and lime juice in a bowl. Cover and refrigerate for 1 hour.

Heat the oil in a heavy nonstick skillet over medium-high heat. Add the shrimp and its marinade and cook, stirring constantly, for 5 to 8 minutes, until the shrimp is cooked through, pink, and fragrant. Season with salt to taste.

Using a skimmer or a slotted spoon, transfer the shrimp to a warm serving dish. There will still be liquid and garlic in the pan. Turn the heat to medium and continue to cook, stirring, until the mixture in the pan thickens and colors slightly. Stir into the shrimp. Sprinkle with parsley and serve at once. If you wish, pass salsa as a condiment.

Advance Preparation: The shrimp can marinate for up to 2 hours in the garlic paste. The dish should be served as soon as it is ready.

PER PORTION

Calories	139	Protein	19 g
Fat	5 g	Carbohydrate	4 g
Saturated Fat	.75 g	Fiber	0
Cholesterol	140 mg	Sodium	273 mg

SHRIMP WITH GREEN GARLIC SAUCE

Makes 6 to 8 servings

This dish is just astounding. The beautiful pale green sauce that coats the shrimp combines the pungency of abundant garlic, the subtle heat of the parboiled chiles, and the sweetness and acidity of the fresh herbs and pale green tomatoes. The original recipe from Veracruz calls for six leaves of hoja santa, for which I have substituted a combination of fresh basil and mint. Hoja santa has a different, slightly sarsaparilla/anise flavor, but the basil and mint work beautifully. Serve the dish with rice or steamed potatoes.

10   **large garlic cloves, peeled**
½   **teaspoon salt**
2   **to 4 tablespoons water as needed**

6 ounces (about 4 medium) tomatillos
3 serrano chiles, stemmed
$^1/_2$ cup fresh basil leaves
2 tablespoons fresh mint leaves
1 tablespoon olive oil
2 pounds shrimp, peeled and deveined with tails left on, or crayfish tails

Place the garlic and salt in a mortar and pestle and pound to a paste. Add enough water to make a smooth paste.

Simmer the tomatillos in water to cover for 5 to 8 minutes. Add the chiles and continue to simmer for 5 minutes, until they have softened just a bit. Drain and transfer to a blender. Add the basil and mint and blend until smooth. Heat the oil in a large heavy nonstick skillet over medium-high heat and add the shrimp. Cook, stirring, for 2 minutes. Add the garlic paste and cook, stirring, another 2 minutes. Pour in the tomatillo mixture, stir together, and turn the heat to medium-low. Cook, stirring often, for 6 to 10 minutes, until the sauce coats the shrimp and the shellfish is tender. Taste, adjust salt, and serve.

Advance Preparation: The green puree can be prepared several hours before cooking this dish, but the rest should be done close to serving time.

PER PORTION

Calories	172	Protein	26 g
Fat	5 g	Carbohydrate	6 g
Saturated Fat	.70 g	Fiber	0
Cholesterol	186 mg	Sodium	366 mg

Chapter
Eleven

Poultry

Shredded Poached Chicken Breasts (Pollo Deshebrado)
Grilled or Panfried Chicken Breasts with Salsa
Veracruz-Style Chicken Picadillo
Ground Turkey Picadillo
Stewed Chicken with Chipotles and Prunes
Veracruz-Style Chicken Stew
Stuffed Poblano Chiles
Green Hominy Stew (Pozole) with Chicken
Red Hominy Stew (Pozole) with Chicken

Anyone who has ridden on local buses in Mexico knows how important chickens are. They ride the buses too, either on the laps of the people taking them to or from the market, on the luggage racks, or under the arms of passengers standing in the aisles. The first sounds of the day in rural Mexico are cocks crowing and donkeys braying.

More widely eaten than any other meat in Mexico, chickens are fed corn and run around, so they have very tasty meat that is lean and a bit too tough for baking or grilling. Instead the poultry is usually steamed or stewed, in wonderful, complex sauces. Our birds are fattier than the Mexican fowl, but by removing the skin we can cut down on the fat considerably.

Moist poached chicken breasts come up all the time in Mexican recipes, to be shredded and wrapped in salsa-drenched tortillas for enchiladas or piled onto crisp tostadas or soft tortillas along with other delicious ingredients; or cooked with a Spanish-style sofrito of onion, garlic, tomato, olives, and capers, for empanadas and stuffed chiles. You'll find these shredded chicken combinations in many of the tacos, enchiladas, and quesadillas in Chapter 8 and in the stuffed jalapeños and chipotles in Chapter 4.

The chicken picadillo (a picadillo is a mixture of finely chopped foods) and the ground turkey picadillo contrast savory meat and vegetables with sweet spices, raisins, and fruit. They make wonderful stuffings for squash and poblano chiles as well as fillings or toppings for empanadas, enchiladas, or soft tacos.

The stews have all become standbys at my house, both for entertaining and for one-dish family suppers. They get better overnight, since the flavors develop and mingle. The pozoles are incredibly hearty meals in a bowl, meant to be garnished with shredded lettuce, crisp tortillas, onions, and cilantro. These dishes are adapted from more authentic recipes made with pork and a lot more fat. There's so much flavor inherent in both the pozole and the meat and seasonings that the fat here is not missed.

The stuffed poblano chiles are filled with an amazing mixture of ground turkey and fruit. It's based on the picadillo used in a famous specialty from Puebla, chiles en nogada; those chiles are filled with a wonderful combination of meat, usually beef and pork, and fruit, then they're dipped in an egg batter and fried and topped with a very rich sauce made from fresh walnuts. Not exactly a dish for this book; but I love the combination of flavors in that dish, especially the picante chiles against the sweet and savory filling. So I decided to make a similar stuffed chile, do away with the sauce, and bake the chiles under the batter, rather than fry them in it. The finished dish is blanketed with a dramatic soufflélike topping and served with a tomato sauce.

As for a dish that you can put together in minutes, there's nothing simpler than a grilled chicken breast topped with salsa. The salsa can be fresh or cooked, and if you're short on time you can pick up a prepared salsa when you buy the chicken breasts. How much easier can a great dinner be?

SHREDDED POACHED CHICKEN BREAST

Makes about 1^1/$_2$ to 1^3/$_4$ cups

Shredded chicken—pollo deshebrado—comes up repeatedly in Mexican soups, tacos, enchiladas, and quesadillas. Here is a master recipe, which will be repeated in recipes for specific dishes. I buy whole chicken breasts on the bone and have them skinned and split. When you let them cool in the broth, the meat is very moist.

> 5   **cups water**
> 1   **onion, quartered**
> 2   **garlic cloves, peeled and crushed**
> 1   **whole chicken breast, skinned and split**
> ^{1}/$_2$ **teaspoon dried thyme or oregano or a combination**
>   **salt to taste, 1 to 1^1/$_2$ teaspoons**

Combine the water, onion, and garlic in a 2-quart saucepan and bring to a boil over medium heat. Add the chicken and bring back to a simmer. Skim off any foam that rises, then add the herbs. Cover partially, reduce the heat to low, and simmer for 13 to 15 minutes, until the chicken is cooked through. Add salt. Allow the chicken to cool in the broth if you have time. Remove the chicken from the broth when cool enough to handle, bone, and shred.

NOTE: The broth you get from this quick simmer is a mild chicken broth that I use in salsas for the recipes calling for the chicken.

Skinned and boned chicken breasts may cook a bit faster than breasts on the bone, so check carefully after 13 minutes. I cut them in half to see (since you're going to shred them anyway, it really doesn't matter).

Advance Preparation: The cooked chicken will keep for about 3 days in the refrigerator.

PER PORTION (¹/₂ CUP)

Calories	71	Protein	13 g
Fat	2 g	Carbohydrate	0
Saturated Fat	.43 g	Fiber	0
Cholesterol	37 mg	Sodium	305 mg

GRILLED OR PANFRIED CHICKEN BREASTS WITH SALSA

Makes 4 servings

Chicken breasts, cooked in a nonstick skillet, grill pan, or outdoor grill, make such an easy dinner. My choice for salsa would be any of the fresh ones, such as salsa fresca (page 61) or tomato, avocado, and corn salsa (page 62). You can also use a good commercial salsa for a quick, nourishing meal.

4 **boneless, skinless chicken breast halves**
2 **teaspoons olive oil**
 salt and freshly ground pepper to taste
1¹/₂ **cups homemade fresh or commercial salsa**

Toss the chicken with the olive oil, salt, and pepper.

FOR PANFRYING: Heat a nonstick skillet or grill pan over medium-high heat. Drop a bit of water onto it and, if it evaporates immediately, the pan is hot enough (if not, wait a minute or two). Cook the chicken breasts until golden, about 3 to 5 minutes per side. Transfer to plates or a platter and spoon on the salsa, partially but not totally covering the chicken breasts. Serve at once.

FOR GRILLING: Preheat the grill, set between medium and medium-high heat if you're using a gas grill. Grill the chicken breasts for 3 to 5 minutes per side, until just golden. Remove from the grill and proceed as directed.

Advance Preparation: See the salsa recipes in chapter 2 for advance preparation. The chicken breasts are cooked at the last minute.

PER PORTION

Calories	172	Protein	27 g
Fat	4 g	Carbohydrate	6 g
Saturated Fat	.72 g	Fiber	1 g
Cholesterol	66 mg	Sodium	289 mg

VERACRUZ-STYLE CHICKEN PICADILLO

Makes 3¹/₂ cups, serving 6 to 8

Like so many Veracruz dishes, this sweet and savory mixture reflects the culinary marriage of Spain, the Caribbean, and Mexico. Use the picadillo to fill enchiladas, quesadillas, chiles, and vegetables.

1   whole chicken breast, skinned and split
6   cups water
2   medium onions, 1 quartered, 1 finely chopped
4   garlic cloves, 2 peeled and slightly crushed, 2 minced or pressed
    pinch of dried thyme and/or oregano
4   fresh cilantro or parsley sprigs
1   bay leaf
1   tablespoon canola or olive oil
1   pound (4 medium or 2 large) tomatoes, peeled, seeded, and chopped
1   small ripe plantain, chopped
12 almonds, peeled and chopped
¹/₄ cup raisins
    salt to taste
2   tablespoons semidry sherry

Combine the chicken, water, quartered onion, and the whole crushed garlic cloves in a large saucepan or Dutch oven over medium heat and bring to a simmer. Skim off any foam that rises, then add the dried herbs, cilantro or parsley, and bay leaf. Cover partially, reduce the heat to low, and simmer for 13 to 15 minutes or until the chicken is cooked through. If you have time, allow the chicken to cool in the broth. Remove the chicken from the broth and, when cool enough to handle, bone and shred, then finely chop the meat.

Heat the oil in a large heavy nonstick skillet over medium heat and add the chopped onion. Cook, stirring, until tender, about 5 minutes. Add the minced garlic and cook, stirring, until it begins to color, about 1 minute. Add the tomatoes, plantain, almonds, raisins, and about 1/2 teaspoon salt. Cook, stirring often, for 10 minutes, until the tomatoes have cooked down and the mixture is fragrant. Stir in the chicken and sherry and heat through for another minute (the mixture will be dry). Taste, adjust the seasonings, and remove from the heat.

NOTE: For a lower-fat version, omit the almonds.

Advance Preparation: The cooked shredded chicken will keep for several days in the refrigerator. The picadillo will also keep for about 3 days in the refrigerator.

PER PORTION

Calories	167	Protein	11 g
Fat	4 g	Carbohydrate	22 g
Saturated Fat	.41 g	Fiber	3 g
Cholesterol	22 mg	Sodium	219 mg

GROUND TURKEY PICADILLO

Makes about 4 cups, serving 6 to 8

Most minced or ground meat fillings for tacos and chiles rellenos are made with ground pork or beef in Mexico and the Southwest, but I've substituted ground turkey in this typical Oaxacan recipe. The meat is much lower in fat and has good flavor, especially when enhanced as it is here, with spices, raisins, and other aromatics.

1½	pounds (6 medium or 3 large) tomatoes, roasted,* or
	one 28-ounce can
⅓	cup water
1	tablespoon canola oil
1	medium onion, finely chopped
2	large garlic cloves, minced or pressed
1½	pounds ground turkey
10	black peppercorns, ground in a spice mill
1	teaspoon ground cinnamon
5	cloves, ground in a spice mill, or ½ teaspoon ground cloves
¼	cup raisins
4	teaspoons rice wine vinegar or cider vinegar
	salt to taste, ½ to 1 teaspoon
1	tart apple, peeled, cored, and finely chopped

Transfer the roasted tomatoes to a blender along with any juice that has accumulated in the bowl, plus the water. If you're using canned tomatoes, simply transfer to the blender with their juice. Puree the tomatoes until smooth.

Heat the oil in a large heavy nonstick skillet over medium heat. Add the onion and cook, stirring, until tender, about 5 minutes. Add the garlic and cook, stirring, for about a minute, until the garlic just begins to color. Add the ground turkey and press it into a layer in the pan, then stir and cook until lightly browned, about 5 to 8 minutes. Pour off any liquid from the pan.

---

* *To roast tomatoes:* Preheat the broiler. Line a baking sheet with foil and place the tomatoes on it. Place under the broiler, about 2 to 3 inches from the heat (at the highest rack setting). Turn after 2 or 3 minutes, when the tomatoes have charred on one side (this may take longer in an electric oven), and repeat on the other side. Remove from the heat and transfer to a bowl. When the tomatoes are cool enough to handle, peel and core.

Add the remaining ingredients except the apple and bring to a simmer. Simmer for 20 minutes, stirring often, then stir in the apple and continue to simmer for 10 minutes or until the tomatoes have cooked down and the mixture is thick and somewhat homogenous. Taste and adjust the seasonings. Remove from the heat and use as a filling for soft tacos, enchiladas, or quesadillas or for vegetables.

Advance Preparation: This will keep for 3 or 4 days in the refrigerator.

PER PORTION

Calories	276	Protein	22 g
Fat	14 g	Carbohydrate	16 g
Saturated Fat	3 g	Fiber	3 g
Cholesterol	57 mg	Sodium	355 mg

STEWED CHICKEN WITH CHIPOTLES AND PRUNES

Makes 6 servings

This marvelous, complex (but simple to make) chicken stew comes from the state of Veracruz, where chipotle chiles are used widely. The chiles give the stew heat and depth, and the prunes, roasted tomatoes and garlic and cinnamon add more depth. I use fewer chiles than traditional recipes call for, and I like the resulting balance of flavors. The large quantity of salt called for draws some of the heat out of the chiles, and most of it goes out with the soaking water. Serve the chicken and its sauce over rice.

2½ quarts water
2 to 3 large or 4 smaller dried chipotle chiles
¼ cup salt for the chipotles, plus additional for the stew
1 medium onion, halved, 1 half roasted*
1 3-pound chicken, skinned and cut up
8 prunes, pitted
4 large garlic cloves, 2 minced or pressed, 2 unpeeled and toasted*
2 pounds (8 medium or 4 large) tomatoes, roasted,* or two
    28-ounce cans, drained
2 black peppercorns, ground in a spice mill (a pinch)
1 clove, ground in a spice mill (a pinch)
1 tablespoon canola or olive oil
3 inches cinnamon stick

Bring 2 cups water to a boil in a saucepan and add the chiles and the salt. Stir to dissolve the salt, remove from the heat, and let the chiles soak for 3 hours

* *To roast tomatoes and onion:* Preheat the broiler. Line a baking sheet with foil and place the tomatoes and onion on it. Place under the broiler, about 2 to 3 inches from the heat (at the highest rack setting). Turn after 2 or 3 minutes, when the tomatoes have charred on one side (this may take longer in an electric oven), and repeat on the other side. The onion will take longer. Turn it several times, until charred and softened, about 5 to 10 minutes. Remove from the heat and transfer to a bowl. When the tomatoes are cool enough to handle, peel and core.

* *To toast garlic:* Heat a heavy skillet or comal over medium-high heat and toast the garlic in its skin, turning or shaking the pan often, until it smells toasty and is blackened in several places, about 10 minutes. Remove from the heat and peel.

or longer. Flip the chiles over from time to time or weight with a plate so that they are soaked evenly.

Combine the raw onion half, the remaining water, the chicken, and 2 of the prunes in a large pot and bring to a simmer. Skim off any foam that rises. Add 1 teaspoon salt and the minced garlic. Simmer for 15 minutes while you prepare the ingredients for the sauce. Strain 2½ cups of the resulting stock through a cheesecloth-lined strainer into a measuring cup. Keep the chicken in the remaining stock while you cook the sauce.

Transfer the roasted or drained canned tomatoes and the roasted onion to a blender along with any juices that have accumulated in the bowl. Add the toasted garlic. Drain the chipotles and rinse thoroughly in several changes of water to rid them of the salt. Add to the blender along with the ground pepper and clove and the 2 prunes you simmered with the chicken. Blend until smooth. Strain into a bowl through a medium-mesh strainer.

Heat the oil in a large heavy casserole or large nonstick skillet over medium-high heat and add a bit of the tomato puree. If it sizzles loudly, add the rest (wait a couple of minutes if it doesn't). Stir together for about 3 to 5 minutes, until the sauce thickens slightly, and stir in ½ cup of the strained stock and about ½ teaspoon salt. Turn the heat to low and simmer, stirring often, for 20 minutes, until the sauce is fragrant and thick. Add the chicken pieces, the remaining prunes, the cinnamon, the remaining 2 cups of strained stock from the chicken, and more salt to taste (strain the remaining stock and freeze or use for cooking rice). Stir together, cover partially, and simmer over medium-low heat for 30 minutes, stirring from time to time, or until the chicken is tender. Taste and adjust salt. Serve hot.

Advance Preparation: This will keep for a few days in the refrigerator. The flavors will mature overnight. The tomato sauce can be made hours or even a day before you finish the dish.

PER PORTION

Calories	223	Protein	25 g
Fat	6 g	Carbohydrate	17 g
Saturated Fat	1 g	Fiber	3 g
Cholesterol	76 mg	Sodium	281 mg

VERACRUZ-STYLE CHICKEN STEW

Makes 6 servings

This is one of the few Mexican stews I've come across that calls for no chiles. More than any other Veracruzana dish, this one really has a Spanish flavor. The traditional recipe includes 2 tablespoons chopped peeled almonds, which I've omitted for this low-fat version. The stew is marvelous in its complexity of flavors and easy to make. Serve the dish with rice.

2	pounds (8 medium or 4 large) tomatoes, roasted,* or two 28-ounce cans, drained
1	medium onion, quartered, roasted*
4	large garlic cloves, unpeeled and toasted*
1	tablespoon olive oil
2½	cups chicken stock
	salt to taste
10	medium green olives, pitted and finely chopped (2 tablespoons)
1	tablespoon drained capers, rinsed and finely chopped
¼	cup raisins
1	fresh rosemary sprig
	pinch of dried marjoram
1	teaspoon dried oregano, preferably Mexican
3	bay leaves
2	inches cinnamon stick
1	3-pound chicken, skinned and cut up
¼	cup dry sherry

* *To roast tomatoes and onion:* Preheat the broiler. Line a baking sheet with foil and place the tomatoes and onion on it. Place under the broiler, about 2 to 3 inches from the heat (at the highest rack setting). Turn after 2 or 3 minutes, when the tomatoes have charred on one side (this may take longer in an electric oven), and repeat on the other side. The onion will take longer. Turn it several times, until charred and softened, about 5 to 10 minutes. Remove from the heat and transfer to a bowl. When the tomatoes are cool enough to handle, peel and core.

* *To toast garlic:* Heat a heavy skillet or comal over medium-high heat and toast the garlic in its skin, turning or shaking the pan often, until it smells toasty and is blackened in several places, about 10 minutes. Remove from the heat and peel.

Transfer the roasted or canned tomatoes and onion to a blender with any juices that have accumulated in the bowl. Add the toasted garlic and blend until smooth, then strain through a medium-mesh strainer into a bowl.

Heat the oil in a large heavy casserole or Dutch oven over medium-high heat and add a bit of the puree. If it sizzles loudly, add the rest (wait a few minutes if it doesn't). Cook, stirring, for 2 minutes, just to sear the sauce. Add $1/2$ cup of the stock and about $1/2$ teaspoon salt. Turn the heat to low and simmer, stirring from time to time, for 20 minutes.

Add the remaining ingredients except the sherry and bring to a simmer. Cover partially and simmer over low heat for 40 to 50 minutes, until the chicken is tender. Stir in the sherry. Taste and adjust seasonings. Serve hot.

Advance Preparation: This will keep for a day in the refrigerator. The flavors will mature overnight. The tomato sauce can be made hours before you finish the dish.

PER PORTION

Calories	246	Protein	25 g
Fat	7 g	Carbohydrate	18 g
Saturated Fat	1 g	Fiber	3 g
Cholesterol	76 mg	Sodium	435 mg

STUFFED POBLANO CHILES

Makes 6 servings

The sweet and savory filling for these incredibly complex stuffed chiles is inspired by the famous Puebla dish, chiles en nogada. I've never seen the dish made with ground turkey; traditionally the meat used is pork or beef or both, but turkey works quite well. Chiles en nogada are batter-fried (as are most other stuffed chiles), then topped with a very rich walnut sauce. I think a tomato sauce works marvelously. This memorable, impressive dish is time-consuming but well worth the effort.

For the Tomato Sauce:

2   teaspoons olive oil

3   to 4 large garlic cloves to taste, minced or pressed

3   pounds (12 medium or 6 large) tomatoes, peeled, seeded, and chopped, or three 28-ounce cans tomatoes, drained and chopped

1/4   teaspoon sugar

salt, preferably sea salt, to taste

1   teaspoon dried oregano and/or thyme

freshly ground pepper to taste

For the Chiles:

6   large or 12 small fresh poblano chiles, roasted*

2   tablespoons canola oil

1   small white onion, minced

1/2   pound ground turkey

2   garlic cloves, minced or pressed

2   pounds (8 medium or 4 large) tomatoes, 1 1/2 pounds pureed and strained (2 1/2 cups), 1/2 pound peeled, seeded, and diced

salt to taste

2   apples, peeled, cored, and diced

1   pear, peeled, cored, and diced

3   tablespoons raisins

1   ripe plantain, heart removed, diced

1   peach, peeled, pitted, and diced, optional

2   tablespoons sugar

2   to 4 tablespoons unbleached white flour, as needed

3   large eggs, separated, plus 1 egg white

Make the tomato sauce first. Heat the oil in a large heavy nonstick skillet over medium heat and add the garlic. When the garlic begins to color, add the tomatoes, sugar, salt, and dried herbs. Cook, stirring often, for 20 minutes or until the tomatoes are cooked down and beginning to stick to the pan. Add the pepper and remove from the heat. If you want your sauce to have a smooth, thick, uniform texture, transfer to a food processor fitted with the steel blade

* *To roast chiles:* Roast the chiles either directly over a gas flame or under a broiler, turning often until uniformly charred. When the chiles are blackened on all sides. As soon as they are charred, plunge into a bowl of cold water. Drain and remove the charred skin. Rinse and pat dry. Remove the seeds and veins (wear rubber gloves for hot chiles).

and blend for about 30 seconds. Transfer to a saucepan, taste and adjust the seasonings, and heat through just before serving.

Carefully slit the skinned chiles lengthwise down one side and open out flat. Remove the top stem and the seeds. Leave the veins in. Pat dry with paper towels and set aside.

Heat 1 tablespoon of the oil in a large heavy nonstick skillet over medium heat and add half the onion. Cook, stirring, until the onion begins to soften, about 3 minutes. Add the ground turkey and garlic and brown the meat, stirring constantly. Transfer to a bowl and pour off any fat that has accumulated in the pan.

Wipe the pan and heat the second tablespoon of oil. Add the remaining onion and cook, stirring, until it softens, about 5 minutes. Add the pureed and diced tomatoes, bring to a simmer, and cook over medium heat, stirring often, for about 10 minutes, until the tomatoes have cooked down and are beginning to smell fragrant. Turn the heat to low, add salt, and carefully stir in the fruit and sugar. Cook, stirring often and checking to make sure the mixture doesn't stick and burn, for about 15 minutes, until the mixture is thick and most of the liquid has evaporated. Stir in the meat, taste, and adjust the seasonings. Remove from the heat.

Preheat the oven to 400 degrees. Oil a gratin or baking dish large enough to hold all the chiles without squeezing them together too tightly.

Lightly salt the inside of the chiles. Place a heaped spoonful or two of the filling on the chiles and fold the sides over so that they overlap. They should be packed as full as you can get them. Sprinkle the flour on a plate and gently roll the chiles in the flour so they're lightly coated. Place the chiles side by side in the baking dish.

Beat the egg whites until they form stiff but not dry peaks. Beat the yolks and gently fold into the whites. Carefully spread this mixture over the chiles.

Bake for 10 to 15 minutes, until the top is browned. Meanwhile, warm the tomato sauce and spread a spoonful on each serving plate. When the peppers are done, place them on top of the tomato sauce and serve at once.

Advance Preparation: The filling and the tomato sauce will keep for a couple of days in the refrigerator.

PER PORTION

Calories	421	Protein	18 g
Fat	14 g	Carbohydrate	64 g
Saturated Fat	3 g	Fiber	8 g
Cholesterol	125 mg	Sodium	458 mg

GREEN HOMINY STEW (POZOLE)
WITH CHICKEN

Makes 8 generous servings

A friend who came to a pozole dinner party at my house summed up the difference between this pozole and the traditional Mexican dish: "In Mexico there would be lots of pork and a lot of fat floating on the top." This is definitely a toned-down pozole verde, made with chicken only, green tomatoes and sorrel but no pumpkin seeds, and lots of chile and garlic. Cook the chicken the day before so that you can skim the fat off the stock. Note that no salt is called for until the end of the recipe, even for the chicken stock. Pozole will toughen if exposed to salt too early on in the cooking. For a discussion of pozole, see the ingredients section.

For the Chicken and Stock:
- 1 medium chicken, plus 2 legs and thighs (about 4 pounds total), cut up and skinned
- 3 quarts water
- 1 onion, quartered
- 2 carrots, coarsely chopped
- 4 garlic cloves, peeled
- 1 bay leaf
- 2 fresh parsley sprigs
  pinch of dried thyme

For the Pozole:
- 1 pound (about 2¼ cups) pozole
- 4 quarts water
- 1 pound (about 8 large) fresh tomatillos, husked and rinsed, or two 13-ounce cans, drained
- 2 ounces (1 small bunch or 2 cups) sorrel leaves, stems removed and leaves washed and torn
- 5 fresh cilantro sprigs
- 6 to 8 serrano or 3 to 4 jalapeño chiles to taste, stemmed and coarsely chopped
- 1 tablespoon canola oil
- 1 large onion, chopped
- 6 large garlic cloves, minced or pressed

    salt to taste, about 1 tablespoon
2   large fresh epazote sprigs, chopped, optional
³/₄ cup chopped fresh cilantro

For Garnish:
1   small red onion, (about 1 tablespoon), preferably Mexican, finely
      chopped and rinsed
    dried oregano, preferably Mexican
1   small avocado, peeled, pitted, and minced, optional
6   tortillas, toasted* and crumbled
8   leaves romaine lettuce, cut crosswise into thin slivers

The day before you wish to make the pozole, cook the chicken. Combine all
the ingredients for the chicken and stock and bring to a simmer. Skim off any
foam that rises. Continue to skim for a few minutes, until there is no more
foam, then cover and simmer for 1 hour. Remove the chicken pieces and the
bay leaf from the broth and transfer the chicken to a bowl. Strain the broth
through a cheesecloth-lined strainer, cover, and refrigerate overnight. Allow
the chicken to cool until you can handle the meat, then remove the meat from
the bones and shred, discarding any fat. Transfer to a bowl, cover tightly, and
refrigerate overnight.

The next day, skim off and discard the fat from the top of the stock. Measure out 2 quarts of stock and set aside. Freeze whatever remains.

Rinse the pozole and combine with the water. Bring to a boil, reduce the
heat, and simmer for 1¹/₂ to 2 hours, until tender and the kernels have begun
to splay. Drain over a bowl and measure out 1 quart of cooking liquid.

Meanwhile, prepare the tomatillo mixture. Simmer fresh tomatillos in
water to cover for 10 to 15 minutes, until tender. Drain and place in a blender
(just transfer the canned tomatillos to the blender). Add the sorrel, cilantro,
and chiles and blend until smooth.

Heat the oil in a large heavy casserole or Dutch oven over medium heat.

* *To toast tortillas:* To bake the tortillas, preheat the oven to 325 degrees. Place the tortillas
on a baking sheet and bake for 20 to 30 minutes, until light brown and crisp, shaking the
baking sheet every 10 minutes. Allow to cool on a rack. To microwave, place about 1 or 2
at a time on a plate or on the plate in your microwave oven. Microwave on HIGH (100%)
power for 1 minute. If the tortillas are not crisp, turn them over and microwave for another
40 to 60 seconds. If they are still not crisp and are just beginning to brown, microwave for
another 20 to 30 seconds, until crisp. Cool on a rack or in a basket.

Add the onion and cook, stirring, until tender, about 5 minutes. Add half the garlic and cook for another 30 seconds or so, just until the garlic begins to color. Add the tomatillo mixture and stir together. Cook, stirring constantly with a long-handled spoon, for 5 minutes, until the mixture is thick and bright green. Stir in the remaining garlic, the pozole, the chicken broth, and the pozole broth and bring back to a simmer. Cover and simmer for 2 hours or until the pozole is tender and opened out like a flower. Add salt to taste—a tablespoon or even a bit more.

Fifteen minutes before serving, stir the shredded chicken into the broth along with the epazote. Simmer 15 minutes. Stir in the cilantro. Taste and adjust seasonings and serve with the garnishes sprinkled over each bowl.

Advance Preparation: The chicken stock should be made and the chicken shredded a day ahead of time. This is the most time-consuming task, so you'll be glad to get that out of the way. The entire dish, up until the last step (adding chicken to the broth), can be made a day ahead and kept in the refrigerator. The corn will become even more tender overnight.

PER PORTION

Calories	457	Protein	32 g
Fat	7 g	Carbohydrate	65 g
Saturated Fat	1 g	Fiber	3 g
Cholesterol	83 mg	Sodium	953 mg

RED HOMINY STEW (POZOLE) WITH CHICKEN

Makes 8 generous servings

This rich-tasting, hearty stew is indeed very light, with only 1 tablespoon of oil. The hominy (pozole) imparts a marvelous perfume to the broth. The chiles add just enough zest, and all of the garnishes add texture, flavor, and fun. This is a great dish for a Saturday night dinner party. Cook the chicken the night before. Or, even better, cook the chicken two nights before and make the pozole the day before; the dish is even better the next day.

1 recipe Chicken and Stock (see preceding recipe)

For the Pozole:
1 pound (about 2¹/₄ cups) pozole
3 quarts water

For the Chile and Tomato Flavoring:
3 large (about 1¹/₂ ounces) ancho chiles, stemmed and toasted*
4 large (about 1 ounce) guajillo chiles, stemmed and toasted*
1 pound (4 medium or 2 large) tomatoes, peeled and quartered, or one 28-ounce can, drained
4 large garlic cloves or more to taste, 2 coarsely chopped, 2 minced or pressed
1 tablespoon canola oil
1 large onion, chopped
   salt to taste, 4 teaspoons or more
2 large fresh epazote sprigs or ¹/₄ cup cilantro leaves

For Garnish:
1 small red onion, finely chopped and rinsed
   dried oregano, about 1 tablespoon, preferably Mexican
1 small avocado, peeled, pitted, and diced, optional
¹/₂ head of romaine or iceberg lettuce, shredded
10 tortillas, toasted (see previous recipe) and crumbled
   lime wedges
1 bunch of cilantro, chopped

The day before you wish to make the pozole, cook and shred the chicken as directed on page 325, strain the stock, transfer to a bowl, cover tightly, and refrigerate overnight.

The next day, skim off and discard the fat that has congealed at the top of the stock. Measure out 2 quarts of stock and set aside. Freeze whatever remains.

Rinse the pozole and combine with the water in a large pot. Bring to a boil, reduce the heat, and simmer for 1¹/₂ to 2 hours, until tender and the ker-

* *To toast chiles:* Wearing rubber gloves, tear the chiles into flat pieces and remove the seeds and veins. Heat a heavy skillet or comal over medium heat and toast the chiles on both sides, pressing them down with a metal spatula and turning them as soon as they sizzle and blister, in a matter of seconds. Remove from the heat at once and transfer to a bowl.

nels have begun to splay. Drain over a bowl and measure out 1 quart of cooking liquid.

Cover the toasted chiles with boiling water. Weight with a plate to submerge them and soak for 30 minutes.

Drain the chiles, rinse briefly, and transfer to a blender. Add the tomatoes and coarsely chopped garlic. Blend until smooth. Strain through a medium-mesh strainer.

Heat the oil in a large heavy casserole or Dutch oven over medium heat. Add the onion and cook, stirring, until tender, about 5 minutes. Add the minced garlic and cook for another 30 seconds or so, just until the garlic begins to color. Add the tomato-chile mixture and stir together. Cook, stirring constantly with a long-handled spoon, for 5 minutes, until the mixture begins to thicken. Stir in the pozole, chicken broth, and reserved pozole broth and bring back to a simmer. Cover and simmer for 2 hours or until the pozole is tender and opened out like a flower. Add salt to taste—4 teaspoons or even a bit more.

Fifteen minutes before serving, stir the shredded chicken into the broth along with the epazote. Simmer for 15 minutes. Taste and adjust the seasonings and serve with the garnishes sprinkled over each bowl.

Advance Preparation: The chicken stock should be made and the chicken shredded a day ahead of time. This is the most time-consuming task, so you'll be glad to get that out of the way. The entire dish, up until the chicken is added to the broth, can be made a day ahead and kept in the refrigerator. The hominy becomes even more tender and fragrant overnight.

Variation

RED POZOLE WITH RABBIT: Substitute 1 large (3-pound) or 2 medium rabbits, cut up, for the chicken. Following the directions for cooking the chicken, cook the rabbit until it is falling off the bone, which should take 1 hour or a bit more. If you wish, substitute chicken stock for the water (you will obtain a rich-tasting stock in any case with the rabbit, but an even richer one with chicken stock). Rabbit is not as fatty as chicken, so you don't need to cook it the day before to remove fat.

PER PORTION

Calories	501	Protein	34 g
Fat	9 g	Carbohydrate	74 g
Saturated Fat	1 g	Fiber	5 g
Cholesterol	83 mg	Sodium	1,256 mg

Chapter
Twelve

Vegetarian Stews

Black Bean Chili
Black Bean and Greens Stew
Green Hominy Stew (Pozole Verde)
Red Pozole with Beans
Chili sin Carne
Oaxacan Green Herb Mole with White Beans and Vegetables

I've collected these six recipes in one short chapter to make it easy to find these hearty main dishes—a vegetarian's dream. They are among my favorite meals in the book, and I wouldn't hesitate to serve any of them to the staunchest meat eater.

The chilis are the familiar dishes. The delicious black bean chili is a long-simmering dish, while the chili sin carne (without meat) is put together more quickly. Less familiar is the black bean and greens dish called *xonequi* (pronounced sho-*ne*-kee) in the highlands of Veracruz, after the greens used in this thick soup, which is more of a stew. First you make a savory pot of black beans, then you cook up a huge bunch of greens (spinach and chard here, since we can't get xonequi) right in the beans, and you get an amazing result.

The green pozole is a welcome dish for vegetarians who may have missed out on the wonders of hominy, which gives off a most marvelous, fragrant broth as it softens and opens up like a flower. Here it is cooked in a tart and savory stew whose main flavorings are tomatillos, chiles, and sorrel.

The green herb mole is a Oaxacan mole based on one that I learned from Chicago chef Rick Bayless. That mole had pork in it, but I find the basic mixture works beautifully in this vegetarian version. The white beans provide a marvelous savory stock, which gives the mole the depth it requires.

We may think of the cuisines of Mexico as meat and fish oriented, but I think that's mainly a function of the way the food has been presented in our restaurants. One close look at the variety of beans and grains and all of the wonderful produce that the country has to offer tells you that Mexico provides vegetarians with a wealth of possibilities.

Black Bean Chili

Makes 6 generous servings

I've published other recipes for black bean chili, but in my continuing effort to simplify dishes, I've come up with this version, a fantastic vegetarian main dish, which I think is the most delicious one yet. I hope it becomes a standby in your home. For best results, make it the day (or even two days) before you wish to serve. Serve the chili with hot corn tortillas or cornbread.

1	pound dried black beans, rinsed and picked over
14	cups water, if draining; 2 quarts if not
2	medium onions, chopped
6	large garlic cloves, minced or pressed
	salt to taste, 2 teaspoons or more
2	tablespoons canola or olive oil
$^1/_4$	cup pure ground chile powder, mild or $^1/_2$ hot and $^1/_2$ mild (page 81)
2	teaspoons ground cumin
1	28-ounce can crushed tomatoes in puree
1	teaspoon dried oregano, preferably Mexican
$^1/_2$	cup chopped fresh cilantro

For the Creamy Garnish:

1	cup nonfat cottage cheese
$^1/_4$	cup plain nonfat yogurt
2	ounces goat cheese, crumbled (about $^1/_2$ cup)

Soak the beans in 6 cups water for at least 6 hours. Drain if desired.

In a large soup pot, combine the beans, 1 onion, and 2 quarts water or enough to cover the beans by 1 inch. Bring to a boil, skim off any foam, and add 2 garlic cloves. Reduce the heat, cover, and simmer for 1 hour.

Add the salt and 2 more garlic cloves. Simmer for another hour, until the beans are tender and the broth is thick and fragrant. Let sit overnight for the best flavor.

Heat the oil in a heavy nonstick skillet over medium heat and add the remaining onion. Cook, stirring, until tender, about 5 minutes and add the ground chile and cumin. Cook, stirring, for 2 to 3 minutes, until the mixture begins to stick to the pan. Add the remaining 2 garlic cloves, stir together for about 30 seconds, and add 1 cup water. Stir together for 2 to 5 minutes, until the mixture is thick. Stir in the tomatoes and oregano. Add salt to taste. Bring to a simmer, reduce the heat, cover partially, and simmer for 45 to 60 minutes. The mixture should be thick and quite fragrant. Stir often, since the mixture tends to stick to the bottom of the pan.

Stir the tomato mixture into the beans and bring to a simmer. Simmer for 30 minutes. Taste and adjust the seasonings. Remove 2 cups of the chili and puree in a blender or food processor fitted with the steel blade. Stir back into the chili and mix well. Set aside until serving time.

In a food processor fitted with the steel blade, blend together the garnish ingredients until completely smooth. Transfer to a bowl. Just before serving, bring the chili back to a simmer and stir in the cilantro. Serve in wide soup bowls, topped with a generous dollop of the cottage cheese mixture, with corn bread or corn tortillas on the side.

Advance Preparation: This will have the best flavor if cooked a day ahead. The chili will keep for 3 to 4 days in the refrigerator and freezes well.

PER PORTION

Calories	449	Protein	26 g
Fat	10 g	Carbohydrate	68 g
Saturated Fat	3 g	Fiber	13 g
Cholesterol	11 mg	Sodium	1,191 mg

BLACK BEAN AND GREENS STEW

Makes 6 generous servings

This stew is based on a fantastic specialty of the Veracruz highlands. The dish is called *xonequi,* or *sopa de xonequi,* xonequi being an intriguing green that looks sort of ivylike and tastes like a cross between spinach, chard, and something a bit stronger like sorrel or mustard. Spinach and chard are a good substitute. The quantity of greens seems like quite a lot, but they cook down in the beans and add great depth of flavor.

This dish is incredibly rich tasting and nourishing. I served it to a friend who admitted afterward that she doesn't normally like black beans, but all the greens made this pot of beans an altogether different story. Traditionally the soup is served with masa dumplings. I serve it with toasted tortillas instead, because it's hard to make a good dumpling without fat.

- 1   pound dried black beans, rinsed and picked over
- 14   cups water if draining the beans, 2 quarts if not
- 1   medium onion, chopped, plus 1 slice of onion
- 5   garlic cloves, minced or pressed
-      salt to taste, 2 teaspoons or more
- 2   dried chipotle chiles
- 2   ancho chiles
- 1   tablespoon canola oil
- 2   pounds spinach, Swiss chard leaves, or, preferably, a combination, stemmed and coarsely chopped, plus a bunch of sorrel (sorrel is optional)
- $\frac{1}{4}$ cup chopped fresh cilantro
- 4   to 6 corn tortillas, cut into thin strips and toasted*

Soak the beans in 6 cups water for at least 6 hours. Drain if desired.

In a large soup pot, combine the beans, chopped onion, 2 garlic cloves, and 2 quarts water or enough to cover the beans by an inch. Bring to a boil, reduce the heat, cover, and simmer for 1 hour.

Add the salt and another 2 garlic cloves. Simmer for another hour, until the beans are tender and the broth is thick and fragrant. Let sit overnight for the best flavor.

Combine the chiles, remaining garlic clove, and slice of onion in a saucepan, cover with water, and bring to a boil. Reduce the heat and simmer for 20 minutes. Turn off the heat and weight the chiles with a small plate or bowl so that they are submerged. Let soak for 15 minutes. Drain, remove the stems and seeds, and rinse with cold water. Transfer the chiles, onion slice, and remaining garlic clove to a blender. Puree, adding $\frac{1}{4}$ cup water or more if necessary.

Heat the oil in a medium-size nonstick skillet over medium heat and add

---

* *To toast tortilla strips:* To bake the strips, preheat the oven to 325 degrees. Place the tortilla pieces on a baking sheet and bake for 20 to 30 minutes, until light brown and crisp, shaking the baking sheet every 10 minutes. Allow to cool on a rack. To microwave the strips, place about 6 to 10 pieces at a time on a plate or on the plate in your microwave oven. Microwave on HIGH (100%) power for 1 minute. If the pieces are not crisp, turn them over and microwave for another 40 to 60 seconds. If they are still not crisp and are just beginning to brown, microwave for another 20 to 30 seconds, until crisp. Cook on a rack or in a basket.

the chile paste. It should sizzle. Turn the heat to medium-low and cook, stirring often, for 15 minutes, until the puree is quite thick. Add to the beans and mix well. Bring the beans to a boil. Stir in a couple of large handfuls of the greens. Stir until they begin to cook down. Add another few handfuls and stir again until the leaves cook down a bit. Continue until all of the greens have been added. Bring back to a simmer and simmer for 10 to 15 minutes. The greens should be nicely amalgamated into the beans but should still have some color and body. Taste and add salt or garlic if desired.

Sprinkle with cilantro and serve, floating a handful of crisp tortilla strips on each bowl.

Advance Preparation: The beans are best if made a day ahead and will keep for 3 to 4 days in the refrigerator. The entire dish will keep for a couple of days in the refrigerator and can be frozen. However, it's best if you wait to add the greens until the serving day.

PER PORTION

Calories	377	Protein	22 g
Fat	4 g	Carbohydrate	67 g
Saturated Fat	.55 g	Fiber	14 g
Cholesterol	0	Sodium	861 mg

Variation

BLACK BEAN AND GREENS SOUP: This is more like the dish I ate in Veracruz, a soup rather than a stew. The recipe is exactly the same as the above, except it calls for half the quantity of beans, so the resulting dish is very brothy. Serve it as a first course or as a light supper. Follow the recipe above, substituting $1/2$ pound black beans for the pound. All other ingredients remain the same.

GREEN HOMINY STEW (POZOLE VERDE)

Makes 4 very generous main-course servings, 8 appetizer servings

There are meatless pozoles, but the most common pozole verde is a hearty stew of pork, sometimes chicken as well, and hominy. Traditional green pozole is green thanks to tomatillos and pumpkin seeds. Too high in fat for our purposes, the pumpkin seeds have been omitted in this version. I've added nontraditional potatoes for body and texture. The tomatillos and the starch from the pozole thicken the broth as it simmers, and the soup is a hearty, rich-tasting one-dish meal.

$\frac{1}{2}$ pound (about 1 cup plus 2 tablespoons) pozole or 4 cups drained canned hominy or thawed frozen pozole

2 quarts water (omit for canned hominy or frozen cooked pozole)

4 to 6 cups vegetable, garlic, or chicken stock as needed (pages 158–160) (2 quarts for frozen cooked pozole or canned hominy)

1 pound (about 8 large or 16 medium) fresh tomatillos, husked and rinsed, or two 13-ounce cans, drained

2 ounces (about 2 cups or 1 small bunch) sorrel leaves, stemmed and torn or coarsely chopped

6 serrano or 3 jalapeño chiles, stemmed, seeded for a milder soup, and coarsely chopped

1 tablespoon canola oil

1 medium onion, chopped

2 large garlic cloves, minced or pressed

1 pound (4 medium) potatoes, peeled if desired and diced
salt to taste, about 2 to 3 teaspoons

2 large fresh epazote sprigs, chopped, optional

$\frac{1}{2}$ cup chopped fresh cilantro

For Garnish:

6 tortillas, baked or microwaved until crisp* and crumbled

---

* *To toast tortillas:* To bake the tortillas, preheat the oven to 325 degrees. Place the tortillas on a baking sheet and bake for 20 to 30 minutes, until light brown and crisp, shaking the baking sheet every 10 minutes. Allow to cool on a rack. To microwave, place on a plate or on the plate in your microwave oven. Microwave on HIGH (100%) power for 1 minute. If the tortillas are not crisp, turn them over and microwave for another 40 to 60 seconds. If they are still not crisp and are just beginning to brown, microwave for another 20 to 30 seconds, until crisp. Cool on a rack or in a basket.

8 romaine lettuce leaves, cut crosswise into slivers
1 small red onion, finely chopped and rinsed
1 small avocado, minced, optional
2 tablespoons dried oregano, preferably Mexican
3 limes, cut into wedges

Rinse the pozole and combine with 2 quarts water. Bring to a boil, reduce the heat, and simmer for 1½ to 2 hours, until tender and some, if not all, of the kernels are splayed. Remove from the heat and drain over a bowl. Measure the cooking broth and add to it enough stock to measure 2 quarts. (For canned hominy or thawed frozen pozole you will need 2 quarts stock.)

Simmer fresh tomatillos in water to cover for 10 to 15 minutes, until tender. Drain and place in a blender (simply drain canned tomatillos). Add the sorrel leaves and chiles and blend until smooth.

Heat the oil in a large heavy soup pot or Dutch oven over medium heat and add the onion. Cook, stirring, until the onion is tender, about 5 minutes. Add the garlic and stir together for about 30 seconds, until the garlic just begins to color. Stir in the tomatillo mixture and cook, stirring constantly with a long-handled spoon, for 5 minutes, until the mixture is thick. Stir in the pozole, the reserved broth and stock, and the potatoes. Bring to a simmer, cover, and simmer for 1 hour, stirring every 15 minutes or so to be sure nothing is sticking to the bottom of the pan. The stock should be slightly thick and very fragrant. The pozole should be soft and splayed. If it is chewy, continue to simmer for 30 to 60 minutes. Add salt and the epazote and simmer for 15 minutes. Stir in the cilantro, taste, and adjust the seasonings.

Serve hot in wide bowls. Top each bowl with the garnishes—the crumbled tortilla chips first, then a generous handful of lettuce and a sprinkle of red onion and avocado and a pinch of oregano. Let guests squeeze a bit of lime over the top.

Advance Preparation: The pozole will keep for a few days in the refrigerator and can be frozen. It's even better the day after you make it, since the pozole kernels continue to soften, open out, and absorb flavor. But if you do make it a day ahead, don't add the cilantro until you reheat the soup. Bring to a simmer, stir in the cilantro, taste, adjust the seasonings, and serve.

PER PORTION

Calories	503	Protein	13 g
Fat	6 g	Carbohydrate	103 g
Saturated Fat	.45 g	Fiber	7 g
Cholesterol	0	Sodium	2,161 mg

RED POZOLE WITH BEANS

Makes 8 very generous servings

This rich-tasting vegetarian pozole is a chili of sorts. The chile and tomato flavoring is complex and aromatic and not particularly picante. You could add a chipotle or two if you want a hotter, smoky flavor. Be sure to wear rubber gloves when working with the chiles.

1   pound dried pinto or pink beans, rinsed and picked over
5   quarts water
1   pound (about 2½ cups) pozole
1   tablespoon canola oil
1   medium onion, chopped
4   large garlic cloves, minced or pressed
2   large (about 1 ounce) ancho chiles, stemmed and toasted*
2   to 4 (about ½ ounce) guajillo chiles, stemmed and toasted*
1   to 2 dried chipotle chiles, stemmed and toasted,* optional
1   pound (4 medium or 2 large) tomatoes, peeled and quartered, or
      one 28-ounce can, drained
2   large fresh epazote sprigs or ¼ cup chopped cilantro
      salt to taste, 2 to 3 teaspoons

For Garnish:
1   small red onion, finely chopped and rinsed
      dried oregano, preferably Mexican
½   head of iceberg or romaine lettuce, shredded
10 corn tortillas, toasted,* and crumbled
      lime wedges
      chopped cilantro

* *To toast chiles:* Wearing rubber gloves, tear the chiles into flat pieces and remove the seeds and veins. Heat a heavy skillet or comal over medium heat and toast the chiles on both sides, pressing them down with a metal spatula and turning them as soon as they sizzle and blister, in a matter of seconds. Remove from the heat at once and transfer to a bowl.

* *To toast tortillas:* To bake the tortillas, preheat the oven to 325 degrees. Place the tortillas on a baking sheet and bake for 20 to 30 minutes, until light brown and crisp, shaking the baking sheet every 10 minutes. Allow to cool on a rack. To microwave, place on a plate or on the plate in your microwave oven. Microwave on HIGH (100%) power for 1 minute. If the tortillas are not crisp, turn them over and microwave for another 40 to 60 seconds. If they are still not crisp and are just beginning to brown, microwave for another 20 to 30 seconds, until crisp. Cool on a rack or in a basket.

Soak the beans in 2 quarts water for 6 hours or overnight. Drain over a bowl.

Meanwhile, rinse the pozole and combine with 3 quarts water. Bring to a boil, reduce the heat, and simmer for 1½ to 2 hours, until tender and the kernels have opened out. Remove from the heat. Drain over a bowl. Measure the cooking liquid. Add either fresh water or the soaking water from the beans to measure 3 quarts.

Heat the oil in a large soup pot or Dutch oven over medium heat. Add the onion and cook, stirring, until the onion is just about tender. Add half the garlic and stir together for about 30 seconds, just until the garlic begins to color. Add the beans and the pozole and the 3 quarts cooking water. Bring to a boil, skim off any foam, cover, and reduce the heat. Simmer for 1 hour.

Meanwhile, cover the toasted chiles with boiling water. Weight with a plate to be sure they are submerged and soak for 30 minutes.

Drain the chiles, rinse briefly, and transfer to a blender. Add the tomatoes and remaining garlic, and puree until smooth. Strain through a medium-mesh strainer and stir into the beans and pozole. Add the epazote and salt, cover, and continue to cook for 1 hour. Taste, adjust the seasonings, and serve, passing the garnishes to sprinkle over each bowl.

Advance Preparation: This will only get better after a day in the refrigerator. It will keep for 3 or 4 days and can be frozen.

PER PORTION

Calories	535	Protein	21 g
Fat	5 g	Carbohydrate	105 g
Saturated Fat	.51 g	Fiber	11 g
Cholesterol	0	Sodium	755 mg

Chili sin Carne

Makes 4 servings

This is a rich-tasting, spicy, but simple vegetarian chili. Following the recipe is a version with turkey sausage added. Since the sausage is spicy already, it can be added to the chili at the end. That way you can make a large batch and add the turkey to it for the insistent meat eaters at the table. As for the chile powder, don't use the commercial product that has salt and other ingredients added; use pure powdered (ground) red chiles, which can be found in some Mexican and southwestern markets. There is also a recipe for it in Chapter 2. The chili benefits from sitting overnight in the refrigerator, so make it a day ahead of time if you can. Serve it with corn bread or hot corn tortillas.

2	tablespoons canola or olive oil
1	medium onion, chopped
1	large carrot, minced or grated
1	red bell pepper, chopped
	salt to taste
1/4	cup pure ground chile powder, 1/2 mild and 1/2 hot (page 81)
2	teaspoons ground cumin
2	garlic cloves, minced or pressed
3/4	cup water
1	28-ounce can crushed tomatoes
3/4	teaspoon dried oregano, preferably Mexican
1	medium zucchini, diced
1 1/2	cups cooked pinto or red beans or one 15-ounce can, drained
1/4	cup chopped fresh cilantro

Heat the oil in a heavy soup pot or Dutch oven over medium heat. Add the onion and cook, stirring, until just about tender, 3 to 5 minutes. Add the carrot, red pepper, and some salt and cook, stirring, for about 5 minutes. Add the chile powder and cumin and cook, stirring, for 2 to 3 minutes, until the mixture begins to stick to the pan. Add the garlic and stir together for about 30 seconds. Add the water and stir together for a minute or two, until the mixture is thick. Stir in the tomatoes, oregano, and zucchini. Add salt to taste. Bring to a simmer, reduce the heat, cover, and simmer for 45 to 60 minutes. Stir often, since the chili tends to stick. Stir in the beans, taste, and adjust the seasonings. Set aside until ready to serve.

Just before serving, bring back to a simmer and stir in the cilantro. Serve with corn bread or corn tortillas.

Advance Preparation: The chili will keep for 3 days in the refrigerator and can be frozen. Make it a day ahead for the best flavor.

CHILI CON CARNE: To the recipe, add ½ to 1 pound southwestern spiced turkey or turkey and chicken sausage (½ pound if you're dividing the chili into 2 portions, one for meat eaters and one for vegetarians). Place the sausages in a large heavy saucepan and add water to cover the sausages by about ½ inch. Bring to a simmer, reduce the heat, cover, and simmer for 20 minutes, turning the sausages from time to time. Cut the sausages in half and continue to simmer for 5 minutes. Pour off the cooking liquid, transfer the sausages to a cutting board, and cut into ¼-inch slices. Stir into the chili (or divide the chili in half and stir into the meat eaters' half) and serve.

PER PORTION

Calories	250	Protein	9 g
Fat	9 g	Carbohydrate	38 g
Saturated Fat	.63 g	Fiber	9 g
Cholesterol	0	Sodium	413 mg

OAXACAN GREEN HERB MOLE WITH WHITE BEANS AND VEGETABLES

Makes 6 servings

This is a vegetarian version of the traditional green Oaxacan mole made with white beans and pork. I've always liked the broth that results when white beans are cooked with lots of garlic, which serves here as a wonderful base for this delicious, thick vegetable stew.

½	pound dried white beans
3	quarts water
1	large onion, chopped
12	large garlic cloves or 1 small head, 8 minced or pressed, 4 unpeeled and toasted*
1	bay leaf
	salt to taste, 2 teaspoons or more
1	pound (8 large or 16 medium) tomatillos, husked, rinsed, and roasted*
3	serrano or 2 jalapeño chiles, toasted*
½	teaspoon ground cumin seeds
10	black peppercorns, ground (¼ teaspoon)
4	whole cloves, ground (¼ teaspoon)
6	romaine lettuce leaves, washed and broken into pieces
1	tablespoon canola or olive oil
2	medium (½ to ¾ pound) red potatoes, scrubbed and diced
1	medium (about 1 pound) chayote, peeled, seeded, and cut into ½-inch dice (about 2 cups)

* *To toast garlic and chiles:* Heat a heavy skillet over medium-high heat and toast the garlic and chiles, turning or shaking the pan often, until the chiles are blackened and blistered, about 5 minutes, and the garlic smells toasty and is blackened in several places, about 10 minutes. Remove from the heat, peel the garlic, and skin the chiles.

* *To roast tomatillos:* Preheat the broiler. Line a baking sheet with foil and place the tomatillos on it. Place under the broiler, about 2 to 3 inches from the heat (at the highest rack setting). Turn after 2 or 3 minutes, when the tomatillos have charred on one side (this may take longer in an electric oven), and repeat on the other side. Remove from the heat and transfer to a bowl.

½	pound green beans, trimmed and cut in half (about 2 cups)
2	ears of fresh corn, shucked and broken or cut into thirds
2	(about ½ pound) yellow squash, scrubbed and diced
⅔	cup fresh masa or ½ cup masa harina mixed with 6 tablespoons hot water or broth
8	large fresh flat-leaf parsley sprigs, plus chopped parsley for garnish
2	small fresh epazote sprigs
2	hoja santa leaves or 4 fresh basil sprigs, 2 fennel sprigs, and 2 fresh tarragon sprigs

Soak the beans in 6 cups water overnight or for at least 6 hours. Drain.

Combine the beans, onion, minced garlic, bay leaf, and remaining 6 cups water in a large pot and bring to a boil. Reduce the heat, cover, and simmer for 1 hour. Add salt and simmer for another 30 minutes or until the beans are tender. Taste and adjust the seasonings. The broth should be aromatic. Add garlic and salt if it is at all bland. Remove and set aside 1½ cups broth.

Transfer the roasted tomatillos to a blender or a food processor fitted with the steel blade. Add the toasted garlic, chiles, and ground cumin, peppercorns, and cloves. Add the lettuce leaves. Puree until smooth.

Heat the oil in a heavy nonstick skillet over medium-high heat and add a bit of the tomatillo puree. If it sizzles, add the rest (wait a bit if it doesn't). Cook, stirring, for 5 minutes, until the mixture thickens and begins to stick to the pan. Stir into the beans and mix well. Bring to a simmer and simmer, covered, for 15 minutes, stirring occasionally. Add the potatoes and chayote and simmer for 20 minutes, or until tender. Add the remaining vegetables and simmer for 10 minutes, uncovered, until they are just tender. Taste and adjust the seasonings.

Gradually stir ¾ cup of the reserved broth into the masa or moistened masa harina. Strain this into the simmering stew and stir or whisk well until the stew is thickened.

Place the parsley, epazote, and hoja santa (or basil, fennel, and tarragon) in a blender or food processor. Add the remaining reserved broth and puree. Stir into the stew. Thin out if desired with water or broth. Taste and adjust the salt. Serve garnished with chopped parsley.

Advance Preparation: The mole, without the final herbal addition, will keep for a couple of days in the refrigerator and can be frozen. The pureed herbs should be added just before serving.

PER PORTION

Calories	342	Protein	16 g
Fat	4 g	Carbohydrate	65 g
Saturated Fat	.38 g	Fiber	8 g
Cholesterol	0	Sodium	942 mg

Chapter
Thirteen

Vegetables

Roasted Poblano Strips (Rajas)
Potato Gratin with Red and Green Rajas
Potatoes with Rajas
Corn Pudding with Toasted Garlic
Corn off the Cob with Mexican Herbs
Grilled Corn with Chipotle Salsa or Dip
Pan-Cooked Cactus Paddles with Tomatoes and Chiles
Baked Sweet Potatoes with Lime
Sweet Potato and Chayote Stew
Plantain Pancakes
Wild Mushroom Stew
Panfried Mushrooms with Guajillo Chiles and Epazote
Cooked Butternut Squash with Onion and Salsa
Squash Simmered with Tomatoes, Onion, and Garlic
Squash Blossoms Stuffed with Refried Black Beans
Summer Vegetable Stew with Roasted Poblano Chiles

Cuando menos burros, más elotes.
The fewer the donkeys, the more ears of corn.

I get hungry just looking at the list of dishes in this chapter. It's the way I feel whenever I walk through a Mexican market—or any great produce market for that matter. Vegetables really get me going.

I decided to concentrate here on the vegetables that most evoke Mexico for me. Many of them—squash, corn, potatoes, chiles—are native to the Americas, which is probably why I want to cook them up into dishes with Mexican flavors. Every once in a while you'll see a marriage of the European and the Mexican, though; the beautiful potato gratin with its red and green lattice of roasted pepper rajas immediately comes to mind.

Before I began work on this book, I didn't know how extensively wild mushrooms are used in Mexican cuisine. It's an ingredient that evokes Mediterranean flavors in my gastronomic imagination. Now my wild mushroom repertoire has expanded in the most wonderful directions, as the vegetables are paired with chipotle chiles, guajillo chiles, epazote, and other seasonings.

Many of the dishes in this chapter can double as toppings for soft tacos or fillings for quesadillas. For example, you might want to serve the squash simmered with tomatoes, onion, and garlic as a side dish with fish or chicken one night and the next night pile the leftovers onto hot tortillas. Sprinkle on a bit of fresh or dried Mexican cheese or Parmesan, and you've made two distinct meals out of one dish.

Roasted Poblano Strips (Rajas)

Makes 4 to 8 servings

These mildly picante, earthy-flavored peppers are the same roasted chiles called for in many other recipes in the book. They're tossed with scrambled eggs or with potatoes for delicious quesadilla fillings, they're mixed into vegetable soups and stews, and they can add a new dimension to a corn pudding, a taco topping, or a potato gratin. What makes them rajas is that they are cut into strips. The broiler will be faster for four chiles and will cook the peppers more thoroughly; flame roasting is simpler for a single pepper and produces firmer rajas.

4   medium poblano chiles, roasted*

Slice the chiles into lengthwise strips about ¼ inch wide and proceed with the recipe.

Advance Preparation: These will keep for about 5 days in the refrigerator. Cover them with olive oil and they'll keep for a couple of weeks.

PER PORTION

Calories	34	Protein	2 g
Fat	.17 g	Carbohydrate	8 g
Saturated Fat	.02 g	Fiber	0
Cholesterol	0	Sodium	6 mg

* *To roast chiles:* Roast the peppers either directly over a gas flame or under a broiler, turning often until uniformly charred. When the chiles are blackened on all sides, transfer to a plastic bag or bowl, seal or cover, and cool. Remove the charred skin, rinse, and pat dry. Remove the seeds and veins (wear rubber gloves for hot chiles).

POTATO GRATIN WITH RED AND GREEN RAJAS

Makes 8 servings

This gratin, with its Mexican flag colors, is a marvelous dinner party dish. The recipe is not traditional Mexican by any means, but the rajas—picante roasted green poblano strips and sweet roasted red bell pepper strips, which are latticed across the top of the gratin toward the end of the baking—give it a decidedly south-of-the-border flavor. The gratin goes well with fish or chicken, or it can be part of a vegetarian menu.

> **Rajas made from ¾ pound (about 6 small or 3 large) poblano chiles (see previous recipe)**
> **Rajas made from 1 pound (2 large) red bell peppers (see previous recipe)**
> 2 **large garlic cloves, halved lengthwise**
> 3 **pounds waxy potatoes, such as Yukon Gold, scrubbed and sliced about ¼ inch thick**
> 3½ **cups skim milk**
> 2 **large eggs, lightly beaten**
> ¾ **to 1 teaspoon salt to taste**
> **freshly ground pepper to taste**
> 2 **ounces fresh goat cheese, crumbled (about ½ cup)**

Set aside two thirds of the rajas in separate bowls, one for the green and one for the red.

Preheat the oven to 400 degrees. Rub the inside of a large (at least 3-quart) gratin dish with garlic. Slice the remaining garlic and toss with the potatoes and the other third of the rajas. Place in an even layer in the gratin dish.

Beat together the milk, eggs, salt, pepper, and goat cheese. Stir in any liquid from the peppers. Pour over the potatoes.

Bake for 1 hour, removing the gratin from the oven every 15 to 20 minutes to break up the potatoes on the top with a wooden spoon and stir. After 1 hour, arrange the remaining pepper strips over the top in a lattice, alternating colors. Bake for another 30 minutes, or until the gratin is browned on top and the potatoes are tender. Remove from the oven and serve.

Advance Preparation: The rajas will keep for 3 or 4 days in the refrigerator. The gratin can be assembled a couple of hours before baking.

PER PORTION

Calories	237	Protein	11 g
Fat	3 g	Carbohydrate	42 g
Saturated Fat	2 g	Fiber	4 g
Cholesterol	58 mg	Sodium	352 mg

POTATOES WITH RAJAS

Makes 4 side-dish servings, 6 to 8 as a first-course taco filling

This luscious combination can fill or top tacos or quesadillas or stand alone. The traditional version might not include the tomatoes, but with so little oil the dish needs something moist.

2   pounds red or white new potatoes, scrubbed and cut into $\frac{1}{2}$-inch dice
1   tablespoon canola oil
1   small white onion, thinly sliced
1   or 2 garlic cloves to taste, minced or pressed
    Rajas (page 348) made from 2 medium or large poblano chiles
    salt to taste, $\frac{1}{4}$ to $\frac{1}{2}$ teaspoon
$\frac{1}{2}$ pound (2 medium or 1 large) tomatoes, chopped
2   ounces queso fresco or fresh goat or farmer's cheese, crumbled (about $\frac{1}{2}$ cup)

Steam the potatoes until tender, about 10 minutes. Remove from the heat.

Heat the oil in a large heavy nonstick skillet over medium heat and add the onion. Cook, stirring, until translucent, about 5 minutes. Add the potatoes and garlic and cook, stirring, until the edges of the potatoes begin to brown, about 5 to 10 minutes. Stir in the rajas, salt, and tomatoes and stir together for a few minutes, until the tomatoes cook down slightly. Stir in the cheese and stir together until the cheese just begins to melt. Remove from the heat and serve on or in warm tortillas or as a side dish.

Advance Preparation: You can roast and peel the peppers and dice and steam the potatoes hours ahead of cooking this dish. The entire dish, up to the adding of the cheese, will hold for several hours at room temperature or a day or two in the refrigerator. Reheat in a nonstick skillet and add the cheese just before serving.

PER PORTION

Calories	300	Protein	9 g
Fat	8 g	Carbohydrate	50 g
Saturated Fat	3 g	Fiber	5 g
Cholesterol	10 mg	Sodium	336 mg

CORN PUDDING WITH TOASTED GARLIC

Makes 6 servings

A summer dish to make when corn is sweet enough to make you swoon. The toasted garlic flavor is infused throughout this rich-tasting pudding. It can be eaten as a main dish or a side dish. For a marvelous variation, try it with roasted poblano chiles.

	kernels from 5 ears corn (about 4 cups)
4	**garlic cloves, unpeeled and toasted***
2/3	**cup low-fat (1%) milk**
3	**large eggs**
1/2	**teaspoon salt**
	freshly ground pepper to taste

Preheat the oven to 350 degrees. Oil a 2-quart soufflé or gratin dish.

Set aside 1 cup of the corn kernels. Combine the remaining kernels with the toasted garlic and milk in a blender and blend until very smooth.

Beat together the eggs, salt, and pepper. Stir in the pureed corn and the

---

* *To toast garlic:* Heat a heavy skillet or comal over medium-high heat and toast the garlic in its skin, turning or shaking the pan often, until it smells toasty and is blackened in several places, about 10 minutes. Remove from the heat and peel.

corn kernels. Turn into the prepared baking dish. Place the baking dish in a pan and fill the pan with water to reach halfway up the sides of the baking dish. Place in the oven and bake for 1 hour or until the pudding is firm and the top is just beginning to brown. Serve hot.

Advance Preparation: The ingredients can be prepared hours before assembling and baking, but the pudding should be eaten shortly after it leaves the oven.

LEFTOVERS: I have filled squash flowers with leftover corn pudding with great results. Prepare the squash blossoms as directed for squash blossoms stuffed with refried black beans (page 366) and fill with leftover corn pudding. Make the cooked tomato sauce on page 322 and heat the stuffed squash blossoms in the sauce in a 350-degree oven for 20 minutes.

PER PORTION

Calories	116	Protein	7 g
Fat	4 g	Carbohydrate	17 g
Saturated Fat	1 g	Fiber	2 g
Cholesterol	107 mg	Sodium	239 mg

Variation

CORN PUDDING WITH TOASTED GARLIC AND POBLANO CHILES: Add to the rajas (page 348) made from 2 medium poblano chiles, cut into small dice. Prepare the pudding as directed and stir in the diced peppers along with the corn kernels.

PER PORTION

Calories	128	Protein	7 g
Fat	4 g	Carbohydrate	19 g
Saturated Fat	1 g	Fiber	3 g
Cholesterol	107 mg	Sodium	241 mg

CORN OFF THE COB WITH MEXICAN HERBS

Makes 4 to 6 servings

This dish is just amazing; it's incredibly simple but tastes complex. I love the texture of corn off the cob, and the fresh herbs here give it an unforgettable flavor. Try to find fresh epazote for a really surprising taste.

1	tablespoon olive or canola oil
1	small onion, chopped
	kernels from 6 ears corn
½	cup water
	salt and freshly ground pepper to taste
2	tablespoons chopped fresh cilantro or 1 tablespoon chopped fresh epazote, or 1 tablespoon each

Heat the oil in a heavy skillet over medium heat. Add the onion and cook, stirring, until the onion is tender, about 5 minutes. Add the corn and stir together for a minute, then add the water and turn up the heat. When the water comes to a boil, add a bit of salt and pepper and cook, stirring, until it has just about evaporated. This should take no more than 4 or 5 minutes. If there is still a lot of liquid in the pan, pour some of it off. You don't want to overcook the corn. Stir in the cilantro, stir together, taste and adjust salt, and serve.

Advance Preparation: This should be served right away, but the corn can be cut from the cobs hours before cooking the dish.

PER PORTION

Calories	157	Protein	5 g
Fat	5 g	Carbohydrate	28 g
Saturated Fat	.63 g	Fiber	5 g
Cholesterol	0	Sodium	22 mg

GRILLED CORN WITH CHIPOTLE SALSA OR DIP

Makes 6 servings

This is a marvelous way to cook corn. You soak the ears, husks still on, in water for an hour, then throw them directly onto a grill. The flavor is incredible, and it's even better when served with creamy chipotle dip, or a more brazen, picante salsa. The sweet, juicy corn contrasts beautifully with the smoke and heat of chipotle chiles. You could simply boil or steam the corn and serve it with the same accompaniments, but if you're lighting a grill anyway, throw the corn on and serve with either of the sauces, spread in a very thin layer over the kernels. The dip is a richer spread, more like butter (with hardly any fat).

6   to 12 ears fresh corn in their husks
1   recipe Chipotle Salsa (page 76) or Creamy Chipotle Dip
     (page 78)

About 1 hour before serving, place the corn in a huge bowl or pot of water or in a sink full of water and weight with heavy pans to keep them submerged.

Prepare a grill (set a gas grill between medium and medium-high). When the coals are medium-hot, lay the corn on the grill, about 4 inches from the coals. Turn the corn after 10 minutes and grill for another 10 minutes, until the outer leaves are blackened (it should cook for about 20 minutes; some of the kernels should be lightly browned). Remove from the grill and let sit until you can handle it, then remove the leaves and silk. Wrap in a towel to keep warm and serve, passing the salsa or dip.

If you're using the chipotle salsa, just spread it in a very thin layer over strips of the corn; it's very hot. If you're serving the dip, spoon a generous dollop onto your plate and roll the corn in it or spread it on the corn with a knife.

Advance Preparation: The chipotle salsa keeps for weeks in the refrigerator, and the dip keeps for a few days.

PER PORTION

Calories	172	Protein	5 g
Fat	7 g	Carbohydrate	28 g
Saturated Fat	.78 g	Fiber	4 g
Cholesterol	0	Sodium	21 mg

PAN-COOKED CACTUS PADDLES
WITH TOMATOES AND CHILES

Makes 4 servings

The flavors of the picante chiles, sweet tomatoes, and tart cactus are marvelous together here. Serve this dish as a filling for quesadillas or soft tacos, with rice or tortillas, or as a side dish with fish or chicken.

1	pound (3 large) cactus paddles
	salt to taste
1/4	teaspoon baking soda
1	tablespoon canola or olive oil
1/2	medium white onion, finely chopped
2	large garlic cloves, minced or pressed
2	jalapeño or 3 to 4 serrano chiles to taste, thinly sliced
1/2	pound (2 medium or 1 large) tomatoes, finely chopped
2	fresh epazote sprigs, chopped, or 2 tablespoons chopped fresh cilantro

Clean the cactus paddles. Hold the end where the paddle has been cut from the plant carefully, looking out for spines, and, using a sharp paring knife, trim off the outer edge of the paddle. Using a potato peeler or a sharp knife, scrape off all of the spiny nodes. Cut into 1/2-inch dice.

Bring a large pot of water to a rolling boil and add a tablespoon of salt and the baking soda. Add the diced cactus and boil uncovered until tender, about 15 minutes. Drain.

Heat the oil in a large heavy nonstick skillet over medium heat. Add the onion and cook, stirring, until tender, about 4 to 5 minutes. Add the garlic and cook, stirring, for about 30 seconds, until the garlic begins to color. Add the cactus, chiles, tomatoes, epazote, and about 1/2 teaspoon salt or to taste. Stir together for another 2 minutes, stir in the cilantro if you're using it instead of epazote, and remove from the heat. Taste and adjust the seasoning. Serve warm.

Advance Preparation: The dish can be completed hours before serving and reheated gently in the pan.

BAKED SWEET POTATOES WITH LIME

Makes 6 servings

Sweet potatoes and lime go wonderfully together, and they're often paired in the cuisines of the Gulf Coast and the Yucatán. The honey rounds out the flavors, as does the optional butter.

2   to 2½ pounds (2 very large or 3 medium-large) sweet potatoes
    or yams
3   to 4 tablespoons fresh lime juice to taste
1   tablespoon mild-flavored honey, such as clover or acacia
1   tablespoon unsalted butter, melted, optional
    pinch of salt

Preheat the oven to 425 degrees. Line a baking sheet with foil. Scrub the sweet potatoes or yams and pierce in several places with a sharp knife. Place on the baking sheet and bake for 45 minutes to 1½ hours, depending on the size of the sweet potatoes, until they are thoroughly soft and a sweet, sugary syrup is beginning to ooze onto the foil.

Remove the potatoes from the oven and peel when cool enough to handle. Mash with a fork or potato masher or puree in a food processor along with the lime juice, honey, butter, and salt. Serve at once or transfer to a lightly buttered baking dish and heat through for 20 minutes in a 350-degree oven.

Advance Preparation: The potatoes can be baked a day or two ahead. The puree will hold for a day or two in the refrigerator, but it's best if you squeeze and add the lime juice no more than a few hours before serving.

Calories	142	Protein	2 g
Fat	.36 g	Carbohydrate	33 g
Saturated Fat	.07 g	Fiber	4 g
Cholesterol	0	Sodium	38 mg

SWEET POTATO AND CHAYOTE STEW

Makes 4 servings

Oddly enough, the idea of combining sweet potatoes and chayote squash comes from a Frenchman, Roger Vergé. This spicy cazuela, a sort of New World ratatouille, makes a great side dish with fish, poultry, or meat dishes. It also makes a meal in itself, served with rice. For a vegetarian main dish, add the chickpeas to the stew.

1   large (about ³/₄ pound) chayote, peeled, cored, and cut into strips about ¹/₂ inch wide by 2 inches long

1¹/₂   pounds (2 large) sweet potatoes, peeled and cut into strips about ¹/₂ inch wide by 2 inches long

1   tablespoon canola oil

1   medium onion, finely chopped

2   large garlic cloves, minced or pressed

2   teaspoons ground cumin

1   serrano chile, finely chopped

2   large or 3 medium tomatoes, peeled, seeded, and coarsely chopped

   salt to taste, ¹/₂ to 1 teaspoon

1¹/₃   cups chicken stock, vegetable stock, or water

1   cup cooked or drained canned chickpeas, optional

Bring a large pot of salted water to a boil and add the chayote and sweet potatoes. Boil for 5 minutes and transfer, using a slotted spoon or deep-frying skimmer, to a bowl. Do not rinse with cold water. Set aside.

     Heat the oil in a heavy casserole over medium-low heat and add the onion. Cook, stirring, until tender, about 5 to 8 minutes. Add the garlic, cumin, and chile, stir together for about 1 to 2 minutes, until the mixture begins to smell fragrant, and add the tomatoes and about $1/4$ to $1/2$ teaspoon salt. Stir together over medium heat for about 5 minutes, until the tomatoes just begin to cook down. Add the blanched chayote and sweet potato and stock, stir together, cover, turn the heat to low, and simmer for 30 minutes, stirring occasionally, until the vegetables are tender and the mixture is fragrant. Stir in the chickpeas and heat through. Taste, adjust the seasonings, and serve.

Advance Preparation: This will keep for about 4 days in the refrigerator. The sweet potatoes will actually become sweeter. Reheat gently in a heavy casserole.

PER PORTION

Calories	231	Protein	4 g
Fat	5 g	Carbohydrate	44 g
Saturated Fat	.35 g	Fiber	5 g
Cholesterol	0	Sodium	625 mg

PLANTAIN PANCAKES

Makes 2 to 4 servings

Plantains are used widely along the Gulf Coast of Mexico, bringing a Caribbean flavor to its cuisines. They are almost always fried. Green plantains are sliced paper-thin and deep-fried, and the resulting tostones are very much like potato chips. Ripe plantains are thickly sliced and fried once, then the slices are flattened and refried. I base my plantain pancakes on this second ripe plantain preparation (called *plátanos machucos*). If you have a good-quality large heavy nonstick pan, you can do it. One tablespoon of oil will suffice for 1 plantain if you can fit all of the slices in a layer in your pan. First I brown them, then I flatten the rounds into very thin pancakes, using a tortilla press, then I brown them again. They are fantastic with black beans and rice and with the shredded shark or mahimahi salpicón on page 302. I think they are especially delicious spread with a very thin film of chipotle salsa. The smoky heat against the sweetness is just wonderful.

juice of 1 lemon or lime
1   **large ripe plantain**
1   **tablespoon canola oil**
    Chipotle Salsa (page 76)

Fill a bowl with water and add the lemon juice. Peel the plantain—an easy way to do this neatly is to cut through the skin lengthwise down the plantain, using the tip of a sharp knife, and cut off the tips. Cut the plantain in half crosswise, then open up the slit and peel off the skin. Immediately slice the plantain into $1/3$-inch-thick rounds and place them in the bowl of acidulated water.

Heat the oil in a large nonstick skillet over medium-high heat. Remove the rounds of plantain from the water and blot dry on both sides with paper towels. Place the rounds in a single layer in the skillet and brown lightly on both sides, about 2 to 3 minutes per side. Drain again on paper towels and turn the heat to medium.

Place 3 rounds on a Ziploc bag, leaving 1 to 2 inches of space between them. Top with another Ziploc bag. Place on a tortilla press and, with one quick but not hard movement, press out the plantain rounds so that they are a little less than $1/8$ inch thick. Use a rolling pin if you don't have a tortilla press. Carefully peel the top bag off, then reverse the bottom bag onto the peeled-off top bag and peel that off. Carefully transfer the pancakes to the skillet and brown for 1 minute on each side. Because there is no oil left in the pan, they will brown quickly, but they won't burn or stick if you watch closely. Transfer to a plate and keep warm in a low oven while you make the remaining pancakes. Serve warm and pass the chipotle salsa to serve as a condiment.

Advance Preparation: These will keep for several days in the refrigerator, wrapped in plastic. They reheat well in a microwave or in the oven. Rewrap in foil and reheat in a low oven for 15 minutes or wrap in plastic and reheat in the microwave for 1 minute.

PER PORTION

Calories	197	Protein	1 g
Fat	7 g	Carbohydrate	36 g
Saturated Fat	.48 g	Fiber	3 g
Cholesterol	0	Sodium	5 mg

WILD MUSHROOM STEW

Makes 6 servings

This intense wild mushroom cazuela is inspired by a dish I ate at Topolobampo in Chicago. It was the earthy taste of the mushrooms seasoned with epazote that stuck in my mind. This dish is different, but it has that same meaty-earthy quality. I love it with the chipotles, which make the dish quite picante and add a smoky flavor. But I also like to leave the chiles out and let the mushroom flavor dominate this marvelous stew. Serve this over warm tortillas or rice or as a side dish with chicken or turkey.

1	ounce (about 1 cup) dried cèpes or porcini
2	cups boiling water
1	tablespoon olive oil or canola oil
3	medium shallots or 1 medium onion, minced
2	pounds fresh wild mushrooms or 1 pound wild mushrooms mixed with 1 pound cultivated, trimmed, cleaned, and cut into quarters or thick slices
	salt to taste, about 1 teaspoon
4	large garlic cloves, minced or pressed
½	cup red wine
1¼	pounds (5 medium) tomatoes, peeled, seeded, and pureed, or one 15-ounce can with the juice, pureed (about 2 cups)
1	teaspoon fresh thyme or ½ teaspoon dried
½	teaspoon dried oregano, preferably Mexican
1	to 2 canned chipotles en adobo, seeded and chopped, optional
2	fresh epazote sprigs or 2 tablespoons chopped fresh cilantro

Put the dried mushrooms in a bowl or pyrex measuring cup and pour on the boiling water. Let sit for 20 to 30 minutes, until softened. Drain through a cheesecloth- or paper towel–lined strainer set over bowl, squeeze the mushrooms over the strainer, and rinse in several changes of water. Set aside. Measure the strained soaking liquid and add water if necessary to make 2 cups.

Heat the oil in a large heavy casserole over medium-low heat and add the shallots. Cook, stirring often, for 8 to 10 minutes, until they are thoroughly tender and light brown. Add the fresh mushrooms and about ½ teaspoon salt and turn the heat up to medium. Cook, stirring, until the mushrooms begin to release water. Stir for about 5 minutes and add half the garlic. Continue to cook, stirring, for another 5 to 10 minutes, until most of the liquid has evaporated. Add the wine and dried mushrooms and cook together for 5 minutes or until most of the liquid has evaporated.

Stir in the tomato puree and remaining garlic, as well as a little more salt if desired, and cook, stirring often, for 8 to 10 minutes, until the tomatoes have cooked down a bit and the sauce smells fragrant. Stir in the mushroom-soaking broth, thyme, oregano, chipotles, and epazote. Bring to a simmer, stir, reduce the heat to low, cover, and simmer for 20 minutes, stirring from time to time.

Taste and adjust the seasonings. If the sauce is not thick enough to coat a spoon, remove the lid and turn the heat up to high. Boil until the sauce has reduced by about a third and is thick. Stir in the cilantro if you're using it instead of epazote. Remove from the heat and serve.

Advance Preparation: This will keep for a couple of days in the refrigerator.

PER PORTION

Calories	99	Protein	5 g
Fat	3 g	Carbohydrate	16 g
Saturated Fat	.43 g	Fiber	4 g
Cholesterol	0	Sodium	385 mg

PANFRIED MUSHROOMS WITH
GUAJILLO CHILES AND EPAZOTE

Makes 4 servings

This easy dish makes a marvelous topping for soft tacos or a vegetable side dish. Strips of guajillo chiles are crisp-fried in olive oil, and the now-spicy oil becomes a cooking medium for the mushrooms. The dish works equally well with wild or cultivated mushrooms. If you can't find epazote, make the dish without it; it'll still be good.

1	tablespoon olive oil
2	guajillo chiles, seeded and cut crosswise with scissors into thin rings
1	medium onion, sliced
4	garlic cloves, minced or pressed
2	pounds wild or cultivated mushrooms, trimmed, cleaned, and cut into $1/2$-inch slices
	salt to taste, about $1/2$ teaspoon
1	large fresh epazote sprig, chopped
2	tablespoons chopped fresh parsley for garnish

Heat the olive oil in a large nonstick skillet over medium-high heat and add the sliced chiles. Cook, stirring, until crisp, about 1 to 2 minutes. Remove the peppers from the oil, leaving the oil in the pan, and drain on paper towels. Turn the heat down to medium and add the onion to the oil. Cook, stirring, until tender, about 5 minutes. Add half the garlic and cook, stirring, until the garlic begins to color, about 1 minute. Add the mushrooms and salt and cook, stirring occasionally, until they begin to release their liquid, about 5 to 6 minutes.

Stir in the remaining garlic and the epazote, reduce the heat to medium-low, and cook for 15 minutes, until the mushrooms are cooked through and glazed. Taste and adjust the seasonings. Turn onto a platter or into a bowl, sprinkle on the crisp guajillo chiles and the parsley, and serve.

Advance Preparation: This will keep for a day or two in the refrigerator, without the crisped chiles and parsley sprinkled on. Reheat the mushrooms, sprinkle on the chiles and parsley, and serve.

COOKED BUTTERNUT SQUASH WITH ONION AND SALSA

Makes 4 servings

Butternut squash has a sweet, nutty flavor that is set off by the cooked tomato salsa. You can use salsa ranchera or a prepared salsa, but it should be a cooked, not an uncooked, one. In this case, substitute 1 cup of salsa for the tomato and serrano chile listed in the ingredients and omit the second paragraph of the directions. Serve the squash as a side dish or pile it onto warm tortillas for a delicious winter taco.

2   pounds (1 large) butternut squash, quartered, seeds and
     membranes scraped away
½   pound (2 medium or 1 large) tomatoes, roasted*
1   small or ½ medium serrano chile
1   tablespoon canola oil
1   medium onion, chopped
2   teaspoons ground cumin
2   large garlic cloves, minced or pressed
     salt to taste
1   ounce Parmesan cheese, freshly grated, or queso fresco,
     crumbled (¼ cup)

Steam the squash for 15 to 20 minutes above 1 inch of boiling water, until the squash is tender when pierced with a knife. The quarters from the narrower

---

* *To roast tomatoes:* Preheat the broiler. Line a baking sheet with foil and place the tomatoes on it. Place under the broiler, about 2 to 3 inches from the heat (at the highest rack setting). Turn after 2 or 3 minutes, when the tomatoes have charred on one side (this may take longer in an electric oven), and repeat on the other side. Remove from the heat and transfer to a bowl. When the tomatoes are cool enough to handle, peel and core.

part of the squash will be cooked before the larger, bulbous bottom pieces. Remove the pieces from the heat as they are done and allow to cool. Peel away the skin and cut into ½-inch dice. You should have about 4 cups squash. Set aside.

While the squash is cooking, place the roasted tomatoes in a blender with the chile and blend until smooth.

Heat the oil in a large heavy nonstick skillet over medium heat and add the onion and cumin. Cook, stirring, until tender and beginning to color, about 5 to 8 minutes. Add the steamed squash, garlic, and salt and stir together for about 3 minutes, until the mixture begins to smell fragrant. Stir in the tomato puree or salsa and cook, stirring, for about 5 to 8 minutes for tomato puree, until the mixture thickens and coats the squash. For salsa, stir together for 1 minute and remove from the heat. Some of the squash will fall apart in the pan, thickening the mixture. This is fine. Taste and adjust the seasoning.

Just before serving, heat through, sprinkle with the cheese, and serve.

Advance Preparation: The squash and onion mixture can be made a day ahead and reheated in a nonstick skillet over medium heat. Or transfer to a lightly oiled gratin dish, sprinkle with the cheese, cover, and heat through for 30 minutes in a 350-degree oven.

PER PORTION

Calories	178	Protein	6 g
Fat	6 g	Carbohydrate	30 g
Saturated Fat	1 g	Fiber	5 g
Cholesterol	5 mg	Sodium	129 mg

SQUASH SIMMERED WITH TOMATOES, ONION, AND GARLIC

Makes 4 to 6 servings

This savory dish makes a perfect side dish with fish or chicken, or it can top tortillas or rice for an easy vegetarian meal.

1   tablespoon olive oil
1   medium onion, chopped
4   large garlic cloves, minced or pressed

1½	pounds zucchini or mixed summer squashes, cut into ½-inch dice (about 5 cups)
½	teaspoon salt or more to taste
2	serrano chiles, finely chopped
1½	pounds (6 medium or 3 large) tomatoes, seeded and chopped, or one 28-ounce can, drained and chopped
1	teaspoon dried oregano, preferably Mexican
2	tablespoons chopped fresh epazote or cilantro freshly ground pepper to taste

Heat the oil in a large nonstick skillet over medium heat. Add the onion and cook, stirring, until tender, about 5 minutes. Add one of the garlic cloves and stir together for another minute, until the garlic begins to color. Add the squash and ½ teaspoon salt. Stir together and continue to cook for about 5 minutes, until the squash is beginning to soften. Add a couple of tablespoons of water if the vegetables begin to stick to the pan. Add the chiles, tomatoes, oregano, and remaining garlic. Stir together, turn the heat down to medium-

---

10 EASY PIECES

Mexican food isn't always time-consuming to prepare, even when you make your own salsas. Here are 10 easy dinners.

Mexican-Style Gazpacho
Soft Tacos with Chicken, Corn, and Avocado
Quesadillas with Broccoli and Garlic
Quesadillas with Potatoes and Sorrel
Shrimp and Lime Nachos (Tostadas) (quick version)
Scrambled Eggs with Onion, Chile, and Tomato
Grilled Tuna with Tomato and Corn Salsa (or use a commercial salsa)
Grilled Swordfish or Halibut with Mango Mint Salsa
Grilled or Panfried Chicken Breasts with Salsa
Chili sin Carne

---

low, and cook, stirring often, for about 15 minutes, until the tomatoes have cooked down and the vegetables are tender and aromatic. Stir in the epazote or cilantro, add pepper, taste, and adjust the seasonings. Serve warm.

Advance Preparation: Although best at its freshest, this keeps well for a few days in the refrigerator. I've enjoyed terrific quick quesadilla lunches using the leftovers. Or use leftovers as a pasta topping—not exactly Mexican, but good!

PER PORTION

Calories	111	Protein	4 g
Fat	4 g	Carbohydrate	18 g
Saturated Fat	.59 g	Fiber	4 g
Cholesterol	0	Sodium	295 mg

SQUASH BLOSSOMS STUFFED WITH REFRIED BLACK BEANS

Makes 4 to 6 servings

I would never have thought of stuffing squash blossoms with black beans if I hadn't seen and tasted the dish at El Bajio Restaurant in Mexico City. It's such a simple combination, beautiful to look at, as squash blossoms always are, and absolutely delicious. This is a quick dish to prepare if you use canned beans. If you don't have a garden with squash blossoms, look for them at farmer's markets or ethnic markets.

20 good-size squash blossoms
1½ cups black Refried Beans (page 193) or the quick version made with canned beans (page 195)
½ cup water, vegetable stock, or chicken stock
1 cup any red or green salsa

Prepare the squash blossoms. Cut down the middle of one side of the flower and gently open it up, then remove the stamen from the inside of the blossom. Trim off the green base (calyx). Rinse the flowers if sandy and gently pat dry. Fill the flowers with 2 heaped teaspoons of refried black beans. Close them up and twist the tips around to enclose the filling tightly.

Place the squash flowers in a lightly oiled nonstick skillet and add ½ cup water. Bring to a simmer over medium heat. Cover, reduce the heat to medium-low, and simmer for 10 minutes. Remove from the heat and transfer the flowers to a serving dish, using a slotted spoon. Serve with the salsa of your choice.

Advance Preparation: The filled squash flowers will keep for a day in the refrigerator. It's best to fill the flowers on the day you buy them. Refried beans will keep for 3 days in the refrigerator and can be frozen.

PER PORTION

Calories	189	Protein	8 g
Fat	7 g	Carbohydrate	25 g
Saturated Fat	.56 g	Fiber	5 g
Cholesterol	0	Sodium	463 mg

SUMMER VEGETABLE STEW WITH ROASTED POBLANO CHILES

Makes 6 servings

This summer stew is a colorful succotash made with squash, beans, corn, peas, potatoes, tomatoes, and roasted poblano chiles—mostly New World vegetables. Serve it as a main dish with grains and/or corn tortillas, as a starter, or as a side dish.

1½	pounds (6 medium or 3 large) tomatoes, roasted*
2	medium poblano chiles, roasted*
½	pound (2 medium) waxy potatoes, such as Yukon Gold, cut into ½-inch pieces
1	tablespoon olive oil
1	medium onion, sliced
	salt to taste, about ½ to 1 teaspoon
¾	pound mixed green and yellow summer squash, cut into ¼-inch dice (about 2½ cups)
4	large garlic cloves, minced or pressed
¼	pound green beans, trimmed and broken into 1-inch lengths (about 1 cup)
1	pound fresh peas in pods, shucked (1 cup), or another ¼ pound green beans
	kernels from 2 ears corn
1	teaspoon dried oregano, preferably Mexican
½	cup chopped fresh cilantro

While the tomatoes and chiles are cooling, steam the potatoes until crisp-tender, about 6 to 8 minutes. Refresh under cold water and set aside.

Peel the cooled tomatoes and transfer to a blender along with any juice that has accumulated in the bowl. Blend until smooth and strain through a medium-mesh strainer. Peel the poblanos, rinse briefly, and cut in half. Re-

---

* *To roast tomatoes and chiles:* Preheat the broiler. Line a baking sheet with foil and place the tomatoes and chiles on it. Place under the broiler, about 2 to 3 inches from the heat (at the highest rack setting). Turn after 2 or 3 minutes, when the tomatoes and chiles have charred on one side (this may take longer in an electric oven), and repeat on the other side. Remove from the heat and transfer to separate bowls, covering the chile bowl with a plate.

move the seeds and membranes (wear rubber gloves to avoid irritating your hands) and cut into thin strips about 2 inches long. Set aside.

Heat the oil in a large nonstick skillet over medium heat. Add the onion and cook until tender, about 5 minutes. Add a couple of pinches of salt and the squash. Stir together and continue to cook for about 5 minutes, until the squash is beginning to soften. Add a couple of tablespoons of water if the vegetables begin to stick to the pan. Add the garlic and stir together for about 1 minute, until the garlic begins to smell fragrant. Add the pureed tomatoes, beans, peas, corn, steamed potatoes, and oregano. Stir together, add about $1/2$ teaspoon salt, turn the heat down to medium-low, and cook, stirring often, for about 15 to 20 minutes, until the tomato puree has thickened and the vegetables are tender and aromatic. Stir in the poblanos and cilantro, simmer for another minute, taste, and adjust salt. Serve hot or warm.

Advance Preparation: This can be made hours or even a day ahead and reheated in the pan. It will keep for 3 or 4 days in the refrigerator. If you make it ahead, don't add the poblanos or cilantro until you reheat the dish.

PER PORTION

Calories	163	Protein	6 g
Fat	3 g	Carbohydrate	31 g
Saturated Fat	.43 g	Fiber	6 g
Cholesterol	0	Sodium	298 mg

Chapter
Fourteen

Desserts

Strawberries in a Sea of Mango
Blueberries in a Sea of Papaya
Ice-Cold Pineapple Doused with Tequila
Fruit Ambrosia with Lime-Honey Dressing
Melon Balls with Mint and Cointreau
Poached Fruit Compote
Grapefruit Ice
Mango Ice
Lime Ice with a Splash of Tequila
Mexican Chocolate Ice
Coffee-Cinnamon Granita with Kahlúa
Almond Rice Ice
Little Almond Cookies
Chocolate Meringue Cookies
Cinnamon Sugar Cookies
Sweet Potato Soufflé
Baked Plantains with Prunes
Vanilla Flan
Mexican Rice Pudding

Mientras dura, vida y dulzura.
While life yet lasts, laughter and molasses.

I've let the fruits of Mexico (and a few North American berries) inspire me in this chapter. Most of the traditional Mexican sweets are too sugary for my taste, and many are too rich for this lightened collection. No matter. What I really want after a Mexican meal is a refreshing, fruity dessert, like strawberries floating on a luxurious sea of pureed mango or juicy pineapple doused with a little tequila and pepped up with fresh mint.

Fruit ices like the tangy lime and tequila ice or the vivid grapefruit ice also provide memorable finales to Mexican dinners. These do have their roots in Mexico; specifically, they're inspired by the ices I ate at the Chagüita nieve (ice cream) stand in the Oaxaca market and the ice cream stand in the main square in Coatepec, a colorful town in the Veracruz highlands. I've let my imagination go with three of the frozen desserts here, all of them based on Mexican drinks. The Mexican chocolate ice is rich, a real splurge, and wonderful. The almond rice ice is an offshoot of the milky almond and rice drink called *horchata.* And the coffee-cinnamon granita is a refreshing, icy version of the pot-brewed café de olla.

When I serve a fruity dessert, I always like to pass some cookies, and you'll have a few to choose from here. My favorite new cookies are the little, very light chocolate meringues.

There are a few traditional Mexican desserts here. The baked plantains with prunes are popular in the state of Veracruz, where plantains represent the Caribbean influence on the cuisine. I didn't want to omit flan, the most classic Mexican dessert, so I worked out a recipe that calls for fewer eggs than a traditional flan and uses low-fat milk. The caramel is still there, providing a sugary contrast to the mildly sweet, delicate custard.

Of course I couldn't leave out one of the most comforting sweet dishes in the world, arroz con leche, Mexican rice pudding. My taste for this dish is partly sentimental. During my early days in the Rio Grande Valley, when I first fell in love with the Mexican culture, I worked for a short time in a day-care center. We taught Chicano children (or, truthfully, they taught me) Spanish songs, among other things. One of my favorites was called "Arroz con Leche." That song and those adorable children, who are now in their late twenties, come back to me every time I make this dessert.

STRAWBERRIES IN A SEA OF MANGO

Makes 4 servings

This sensuous, beautiful dessert gets the biggest raves of all whenever I give a Mexican dinner party. It's incredibly easy to throw together.

1   large mango, peeled and pitted
2   tablespoons fresh lime juice
1   tablespoon sugar
1   pint strawberries, hulled and quartered
    fresh mint leaves for garnish

Place the mango, 1 tablespoon lime juice, and 1 teaspoon sugar in a food processor fitted with the steel blade or in a blender and puree. You should have approximately 1 cup of puree.

Toss the strawberries with the remaining lime juice and sugar and let sit for 15 to 30 minutes if possible to draw out their juices.

Spoon about ¼ cup mango puree onto a dessert plate or into a dessert bowl and top with strawberries. Garnish with mint and serve.

Advance Preparation: The mango puree can be made a day ahead and held in the refrigerator. The strawberries can be prepared a few hours before serving.

PER PORTION

Calories	80	Protein	1 g
Fat	.46 g	Carbohydrate	20 g
Saturated Fat	.05 g	Fiber	3 g
Cholesterol	0	Sodium	2 mg

BLUEBERRIES IN A SEA OF PAPAYA

Makes 6 servings

The taste of papaya, the first bite, transports me to Mexico—a beach in the Yucatán, a resort in Acapulco, Oaxaca in the springtime. It doesn't matter where. When I'm at home, I don't often think to buy papaya; when I'm in Mexico, it's one of the first fruits I pile onto my plate every morning. The subtle, rich fruit is dessert here, a gorgeous puree topped with juicy blueberries (a North American touch).

2   medium (about 2 pounds) papayas
2   tablespoons plus 1 teaspoon sugar
¼   cup fresh lime juice
¾   cup blueberries
      lime wedges and fresh mint leaves for garnish

Cut the papayas in half and scoop out all the seeds. Cut the halves in half again, then peel away the skin. Cut into chunks and transfer to a food processor fitted with the steel blade. Add the sugar and lime juice and puree until completely smooth. Transfer to a wide serving bowl. Chill.

Just before serving, float the blueberries on top of the papaya puree. Garnish with mint leaves and lime wedges and serve.

Advance Preparation: The puree will keep for a day in the refrigerator. Stir well before adding the blueberries.

PER PORTION

Calories	71	Protein	1 g
Fat	.21 g	Carbohydrate	18 g
Saturated Fat	.04 g	Fiber	1 g
Cholesterol	0	Sodium	4 mg

ICE-COLD PINEAPPLE DOUSED WITH TEQUILA

Makes 6 servings

I could eat pineapple after any meal. The juicy, ripe fruit is incredibly refreshing. Here it's enhanced with mint and a splash of tequila. Serve it with a
cookie for a perfect dessert.

   1   **large ripe pineapple**
   2   **tablespoons slivered fresh mint leaves, plus mint sprigs for**
         garnish
¼   **cup tequila**

Quarter the pineapple, then run a sharp knife down the inside of the peels, to
separate the pulp. Cut away any spiny bits remaining on the outside and cut
away the core. Cut each quarter lengthwise into thirds, then slice thinly and
transfer to a bowl. Toss with the mint and tequila and chill for several hours.

Just before serving, stir again, garnish with mint, and serve.

Advance Preparation: You can prepare the pineapple hours ahead,
but don't let it sit for more than a couple of hours with the mint, or the mint
will discolor.

PER PORTION

Calories	76	Protein	.41 g
Fat	.44 g	Carbohydrate	13 g
Saturated Fat	.03 g	Fiber	1 g
Cholesterol	0	Sodium	1 mg

FRUIT AMBROSIA WITH
LIME-HONEY DRESSING

Makes 6 servings

I love the mixture of ripe acidic pineapple and subtle papaya here. Coconut, an ingredient that conjures up Mexico as much as pineapple and papaya, is what defines this fruit salad as ambrosia; however, because coconut is also high in fat, I've made it optional. For a special treat, serve this refreshing dessert with chocolate meringue cookies.

2	cups (about $1/2$ large) chopped ripe pineapple
1	small ripe papaya, peeled, seeded, and chopped
1	pint strawberries, hulled and quartered
2	ripe peaches or nectarines, peeled, pitted, and chopped
$1/4$	cup grated unsweetened coconut, optional
2	to 3 tablespoons mild-flavored honey, such as clover or acacia, to taste
$1/4$	cup kirsch or tequila
$1/4$	cup fresh lime juice
	fresh mint leaves for garnish

Toss together the fruit and coconut in a bowl. Mix together 2 tablespoons honey, the kirsch, and the lime juice. Toss with the fruit. Cover and refrigerate for 1 hour or longer. Taste and add more honey if desired. Garnish with mint leaves and serve.

Advance Preparation: The fruit can be prepared hours before serving and kept in the refrigerator. The dressing should not be made too many hours before serving, or the lime juice will become too acidic, but it will hold up for 2 or 3 hours.

PER PORTION

Calories	132	Protein	1 g
Fat	.50 g	Carbohydrate	30 g
Saturated Fat	.03 g	Fiber	3 g
Cholesterol	0	Sodium	3 mg

MELON BALLS WITH MINT AND COINTREAU

Makes 6 servings

Melon, especially watermelon (sandía), is such a treat in Mexico. There it is always breakfast food for me. Here it is often dessert, a refreshing finish to a lively Mexican meal. This is as simple as can be, yet I've served it at the most elegant dinner parties. It depends on ripe, sweet, juicy melons. Serve one of the cookies in this book along with it.

¼	**watermelon**
½	**good-size cantaloupe**
½	**good-size green melon, such as honeydew or muskmelon**
¼	**cup slivered mint leaves, plus sprigs for garnish**
¼	**cup Cointreau or triple sec**

Scoop out the watermelon with a melon baller and place the balls in a large, attractive serving bowl. Tilt the watermelon over the bowl to get all of the juice that has accumulated in the melon.

Remove and discard the seeds from the orange and green melons and scoop out balls with the melon baller. Toss with the watermelon.

Add the mint and liqueur, cover, and chill for an hour before serving. Garnish with mint sprigs and serve.

Advance Preparation: You can prepare the melon balls a day ahead, but don't add the mint or liqueur more than an hour or two before serving.

PER PORTION

Calories	102	Protein	1 g
Fat	.57 g	Carbohydrate	21 g
Saturated Fat	0	Fiber	2 g
Cholesterol	0	Sodium	15 mg

POACHED FRUIT COMPOTE

Makes 6 servings

This recipe is inspired by Rick Bayless's poached guavas in spicy syrup, from *Authentic Mexican* (William Morrow, 1987). Guavas have a marvelous appley perfume and, when really ripe, a pale pink color. They are not particularly easy to find, so use quince or apples instead if you must.

	juice of 1 lemon or lime
3	**pounds guavas, quinces, or tart apples such as Granny Smith or Gravenstein**
1	**quart water**
4	**inches cinnamon stick**
6	**cloves**
1	**vanilla bean, split in half lengthwise, or ½ teaspoon vanilla extract**
1	**tablespoon fresh lime juice**
½	**cup sugar**

Fill a large bowl with water and add the lemon juice. Prepare the fruit. Peel the guavas, cut in half, and scoop out the seed pods using a teaspoon, then quarter the guavas. Transfer to the bowl of water. Peel, core, and slice the quinces or the apples and transfer to the acidulated water.

Combine the remaining ingredients in a large heavy nonreactive saucepan and bring to a boil. Stir until the sugar is dissolved, reduce the heat, cover, and simmer over medium heat for 20 minutes.

Remove the cinnamon stick and cloves with a slotted spoon and add the fruit. When the syrup comes back to a simmer, cover partially. Simmer guavas for about 10 minutes, until tender but still firm; simmer quinces for 25 to 30 minutes, apples for 15 to 20 minutes. Remove from the heat, uncover, and allow the fruit to cool in the syrup.

Transfer the fruit to a serving dish using a slotted spoon. Remove the vanilla bean. If you would like a thicker syrup, bring it back to a boil and reduce by half. Whether thickened or not, pour the syrup over the fruit. Cool and serve, either cold or at room temperature.

Advance Preparation: This will hold for about 3 days in the refrigerator.

GRAPEFRUIT ICE

Makes 4 to 6 servings

I think I prefer grapefruit ice to any other. The vivid grapefruit flavor rings true and clear here, making a perfect finish to any spicy meal. For the right texture, the ice should soften in the refrigerator for 20 to 30 minutes before serving. When I serve it at a dinner party, I always transfer it from the freezer to the refrigerator just before sitting down to the main course.

½   **cup sugar**
1   **cup water**
    zest of 1 grapefruit
1   **tablespoon fresh lemon juice**
2   **cups fresh grapefruit juice, strained**

Combine the sugar, water, and grapefruit zest in a saucepan. Bring to a boil and stir to dissolve the sugar. Reduce the heat and simmer for 10 minutes, until slightly thickened. Remove from the heat and allow to cool.

Strain the syrup and lemon juice into the grapefruit juice, discarding the zest. Freeze in an ice cream freezer according to the manufacturer's directions. Or transfer to a bowl or ice cube trays and freeze.

When the mixture is frozen solid, transfer to the refrigerator for 30 minutes. Cut into 3 or 4 sections with a sharp knife and process one section at a time using the pulse action in a food processor fitted with the steel blade until you have a smooth, fluffy mixture (keep the remaining grapefruit mixture in the refrigerator or freezer as you process each portion). Spoon into individual serving dishes, cover with plastic wrap, then with foil to secure, and quickly transfer to the freezer.

Allow the ices to soften in the refrigerator for 20 to 30 minutes before serving.

Advance Preparation: The ice will keep for weeks in the freezer.

MANGO ICE

Makes 4 generous or 5 slightly smaller servings

This is heavenly. The mango is seasoned with lime and a not-too-sweet sugar syrup to which a whisper of triple sec is added. The texture is voluptuous.

- 1   **cup water**
- ½   **cup sugar**
- 1   **tablespoon finely minced or grated lime zest**
- 2   **large or 4 small mangoes**
- ¼   **cup fresh lime juice**
- 2   **teaspoons triple sec**
    fresh mint sprigs and/or 4 or 5 sliced strawberries for garnish

Combine the water and sugar in a saucepan and bring to a boil. Add the lime zest, turn the heat to very low, and simmer for 10 minutes while you prepare the mangoes.

Holding the mangoes over a bowl to catch their juice, cut them down the 4 sides of the pits, then peel away the skin. Place the pulp in a food processor fitted with the steel blade and puree until completely smooth. Transfer to the bowl with the juice and stir in the lime juice and triple sec. Strain the syrup into the mango mixture and mix well. Freeze in an ice cream freezer following the manufacturer's instructions, or cover and place in the freezer until just about frozen solid, about 3 to 4 hours.

If you're not using an ice cream freezer, chill 4 or 5 individual ramekins or small bowls. Remove the lime mixture from the freezer and cut with a sharp knife into 2 portions. Place one portion in a food processor fitted with the steel blade and set the bowl with the remaining puree back in the freezer. Break up the mixture using the pulse action. Turn on the machine and blend thoroughly until the mixture is uniform and fluffy. Transfer to 2 individual dishes and place the dishes directly in the freezer. Repeat this step with the remaining portion. When all of the dishes are filled, cover each one with plastic wrap, then with foil to secure.

Twenty minutes before serving, place the ices in your refrigerator. Serve, garnishing each bowl with a sprig of mint and/or a sliced strawberry.

Advance Preparation: This will keep for weeks in the freezer.

PER PORTION

Calories	193	Protein	1 g
Fat	.35 g	Carbohydrate	49 g
Saturated Fat	.09 g	Fiber	1 g
Cholesterol	0	Sodium	3 mg

LIME ICE WITH A SPLASH OF TEQUILA

Makes 8 servings

My earliest Tex-Mex meals, at restaurants all over the Rio Grande Valley and Austin, Texas, invariably ended with a lime sherbet. They were always very sweet and often unnaturally green. But they did make a cooling finish to a rich, spicy meal. This one has just a splash of tequila, which helps give the ice a smooth texture and a whisper of margarita flavor.

2   **cups water**
2   **cups sugar**
2   **cups fresh lime juice, from about 15 limes**
2   **tablespoons finely chopped or grated lime zest**
2   **tablespoons plus 2 teaspoons tequila**
     fresh mint sprigs and/or thin slices of lime for garnish

Bring the water to a boil in a 2- or 3-quart saucepan and add the sugar. Stir to dissolve, then turn the heat to very low and simmer for 10 minutes while you squeeze the limes. It will thicken slightly.

Remove the sugar syrup from the heat and stir in the lime juice and zest. Let sit for 1 hour.

Strain the lime mixture into a bowl and press all the zest against the strainer to extract all the juice. Stir in the tequila. Freeze in an ice cream freezer following the manufacturer's instructions or cover and place in the freezer until just about frozen solid, about 6 hours.

If you're not using an ice cream freezer, chill 8 individual ramekins or small bowls. Remove the lime mixture from the freezer and cut with a sharp knife into 4 portions. Place one portion in a food processor fitted with the steel blade and return the bowl with the lime mixture to the freezer. Break up the mixture in the food processor using the pulse action. Turn on the machine and blend thoroughly until the mixture is uniform and fluffy. It will be almost white. Transfer to 2 individual dishes and place the dishes directly in the freezer. Repeat this step with the remaining 3 portions. When all of the dishes are filled, cover each one with plastic wrap, then with foil to secure.

Twenty minutes before serving, place the ices in your refrigerator. Serve, garnishing each bowl with a thin slice of lime and/or a sprig of mint.

Advance Preparation: This will keep for weeks in the freezer.

PER PORTION

Calories	224	Protein	0
Fat	.06 g	Carbohydrate	56 g
Saturated Fat	0	Fiber	0
Cholesterol	0	Sodium	1 mg

MEXICAN CHOCOLATE ICE

Makes 8 servings

If you ever go to Oaxaca, don't miss visiting the chocolate shops around the central market. The chocolate in Mexico is blended with cinnamon, almonds, and sugar, and it is one of the great gastronomic delights of that country. At the mills, roasted cocoa beans, cinnamon, sugar, and almonds are weighed out and ground together, and the aroma is overwhelming. Hot Mexican chocolate is made by dissolving tablets of chocolate in hot water and whisking with a special wooden beater called a *molinillo* until a froth is achieved on the surface. This ice is sweet, intense, and as rich a dish as you'll find in this book. Serve it on special occasions.

- 3 cups water
- ⅓ cup sugar
- ¾ pound Mexican chocolate, roughly chopped or broken into pieces
- ½ teaspoon vanilla extract
- 4 large egg whites

Bring the water to a simmer in a saucepan and add the sugar. Stir to dissolve. Remove from the heat and add the chocolate. Stir with a wooden spoon or a whisk until the chocolate has melted. Stir in the vanilla. Allow to cool to warm or lukewarm.

Beat the egg whites to stiff but not dry peaks. Quickly whisk in the chocolate mixture and combine well. Freeze in an ice cream maker according to the manufacturer's directions. Or transfer to a bowl or a baking dish, cover with plastic wrap, and freeze until just about solid, about 4 hours. Remove from the freezer and cut the mixture into 4 pieces. Keep the pieces you aren't working with in the freezer while one at a time you transfer the pieces to a food processor. Blend, using the pulse action, until you get an icy, smooth mixture. The mixture may ball up into fudgy bits at first, but keep the pulse action going until the mixture smooths out, being careful not to allow the mixture to melt. Immediately transfer to an attractive serving dish or to individual dishes or ramekins and place in the coldest part of your freezer. Repeat with the remaining portions. When all the ices have been in the freezer for about 30 minutes, cover each one with plastic wrap, then with foil to secure.

Twenty minutes before serving, transfer the ices to the refrigerator.

Advance Preparation: This will keep for days, even weeks, in the freezer.

PER PORTION

Calories	245	Protein	2 g
Fat	6 g	Carbohydrate	42 g
Saturated Fat	.92 g	Fiber	0
Cholesterol	0	Sodium	27 mg

COFFEE-CINNAMON GRANITA WITH KAHLÚA

Makes 6 servings

One of my favorite Mexican after-meal drinks is café de olla, pot-brewed coffee sweetened with Mexican dark brown sugar (*piloncillo*) and cinnamon. I've transposed the drink here and made a sort of granita, an iced dessert that resembles a snow cone more than a sorbet and is very refreshing. Traditionally café de olla is made like campfire coffee, brewed in a pot of boiled water (the *olla* is the pot), then strained. I found the texture of café de olla a bit too grainy for the ice using this method, so I brew extra-strength coffee in a drip pot, then stir in a syrup. This dessert melts quickly, which is fine, because it's very thirst-quenching. Serve it in chilled wineglasses.

- ²/₃ **cup Italian roast decaffeinated coffee, ground for a drip coffee pot**
- 1 **quart water**
- ¼ **pound Mexican piloncillo sugar, roughly chopped, or ¹/₂ cup dark brown sugar**
- 4 **inches cinnamon stick**
- ¼ **cup Kahlúa for serving, optional**

Place the coffee in a filter above a pot. Bring the water to a boil and pour 2 cups over the coffee.

Add the sugar and cinnamon to the remaining water in a saucepan and stir to melt the sugar. Turn the heat to low and simmer gently for 10 minutes. Remove from the heat and remove the cinnamon stick. Stir in the coffee. Allow the mixture to cool to lukewarm.

Transfer to a shallow pan, such as a pie pan or ice cube trays, and freeze for 1 hour, until the edges are frozen and the rest of the mixture is beginning to crystallize. Using a fork or 2 knives, break up the ice crystals by mashing and stirring the mixture. Return to the freezer and freeze for another 30 minutes. Again, break up the ice crystals with a fork or 2 knives. Repeat every 30 minutes (about twice more), until the mixture is just about set. The mixture should be crystallized throughout but not frozen solid when you serve it (if it is, allow it to soften in the refrigerator for 20 to 40 minutes).

Chill 6 wineglasses in the freezer. Just before serving, cut the mixture into cubes or break up with a knife one more time and spoon into large wineglasses. Add 2 teaspoons of Kahlúa to each serving if you wish, and serve.

Advance Preparation: This should be made about 4 hours before serving. However, if you make it in advance and freeze it solid, you can allow it to soften in the refrigerator as directed.

PER PORTION

Calories	74	Protein	0
Fat	.02 g	Carbohydrate	19 g
Saturated Fat	0	Fiber	0
Cholesterol	0	Sodium	10 mg

ALMOND RICE ICE

Makes 8 servings

This ice is based on the delicious rich drink called *horchata* made from ground rice and almonds. Horchata is quite sweet and very refreshing, and it translates well into an ice. I subtract some of the almonds that an authentic horchata would have by substituting almond extract. Give the ice at least 30 minutes to soften in the refrigerator before you serve it.

1/3	**cup long-grain white rice**
2/3	**cup almonds**
1	**inch cinnamon stick, crumbled**
1	**quart water**
2/3	**cup sugar**
1/2	**teaspoon almond extract**

Grind the rice in a spice mill until you have a powder. Transfer to a bowl.

Blanch and peel the almonds by dropping them into a pan of boiling water, boiling for 1 minute, then transferring them immediately to a bowl of cold water. Pop off the skins and transfer to the bowl with the rice. Add the cinnamon stick.

Heat 2 cups of the water to a simmer and pour over the rice and almonds. Stir together. Let sit for 8 hours or overnight.

Transfer the mixture to a blender and blend until completely smooth, about 3 to 4 minutes. Add another cup of water to the blender. Blend again for a minute or so. Line a large strainer with 3 layers of dampened cheesecloth and set over a bowl. Pour in the mixture and press it through the strainer with the back of a spoon. Then take up the cheesecloth and squeeze out every bit of liquid that you can.

Heat the remaining cup of water to a simmer and stir in the sugar. Stir until the sugar is dissolved, remove from the heat, and stir into the almond mixture. Add the almond extract. Taste and add more sugar if the mixture doesn't taste sweet enough. Transfer to an ice cream freezer and freeze according to the manufacturer's instructions. Or transfer to a bowl or ice cube trays, cover, and place in the freezer until just about frozen solid, about 3 to 4 hours.

If you're not using an ice cream freezer, chill 8 individual ramekins or small bowls. Remove the mixture from the freezer and cut with a sharp knife into 3 or 4 portions. Place one portion in a food processor fitted with the steel blade and set the bowl with the remaining puree back in the freezer. Break up the mixture using the pulse action. Turn on the machine and blend thoroughly until the mixture is uniform and fluffy. Transfer to the individual dishes and place the dishes directly in the freezer. Repeat with the remaining portions. When all of the dishes are filled, cover each one with plastic wrap, then with foil to secure.

Thirty to 40 minutes before serving, place the ices in the refrigerator to soften the mixture.

Advance Preparation: This will keep in the freezer for a few weeks.

PER PORTION

Calories	158	Protein	3 g
Fat	6 g	Carbohydrate	25 g
Saturated Fat	.54 g	Fiber	1 g
Cholesterol	0	Sodium	2 mg

LITTLE ALMOND COOKIES

Makes about 60 cookies

Everybody likes a cookie with a fruit dessert; just a little sweet nibble, not a huge cakelike thing. These nutty bite-size gems couldn't be easier to make (you will need a pastry bag with a star tip); they're simple and light, always a crowd pleaser.

> **scant 2 cups almonds**
> ²/₃ **cup dark brown sugar**
> 6 **large egg whites**
> ¼ **teaspoon almond extract or a drop more to taste**

Preheat the oven to 350 degrees and toast the almonds on a baking sheet for 10 to 15 minutes, just until they begin to brown and smell toasty. Remove from the oven and allow to cool.

Put the toasted almonds and 2 tablespoons of the sugar in a food processor fitted with the steel blade. Pulse until finely ground but don't turn them to butter. Add the remaining sugar and process until the mixture is uniform. Add the egg whites and almond extract and blend together. Scrape the mixture into a bowl, cover, and refrigerate overnight or for several hours to stiffen up the batter.

Preheat the oven to 350 degrees. Butter 2 nonstick baking sheets or cover baking sheets with buttered parchment. Transfer the batter to a pastry bag fitted with a star-shaped nozzle and pipe the batter in ³/₄- to 1-inch stars onto your baking sheets. Bake the cookies for 12 to 15 minutes or until lightly browned around the bottom edge and top ridges. Cool on racks.

Advance Preparation: These will keep for a couple of days in an airtight box.

PER PORTION

Calories	36	Protein	1 g
Fat	2 g	Carbohydrate	3 g
Saturated Fat	.27 g	Fiber	0
Cholesterol	0	Sodium	8 mg

CHOCOLATE MERINGUE COOKIES

Makes about 70 little cookies

These adorable little cookies, called *besitos,* "little kisses" in Spanish, are very easy to make and make a beautiful light treat. Serve them with fruit or ice.

- 3 **ounces Mexican or semisweet chocolate**
- 4 **large egg whites**
- 1/4 **teaspoon cream of tartar**
- **pinch of salt**
- 1/8 **teaspoon ground cinnamon if using semisweet chocolate**
- 1/2 **teaspoon vanilla extract**
- 1/2 **cup sugar**

Preheat the oven to 300 degrees. Butter 2 nonstick baking sheets or cover 2 baking sheets with buttered parchment (I tend to use the parchment even on nonstick sheets).

Grate the chocolate using a Mouli cheese grater if you have one or the small side of a box grater or blend to a powder in a food processor fitted with the steel blade. Sift through a medium-mesh strainer so no pieces will block the tip of your pastry bag.

Beat the egg whites until they begin to foam. Add the cream of tartar and salt and continue to beat until the egg whites form stiff peaks. Continue to beat on medium speed while you gradually add the cinnamon, vanilla, and sugar, a tablespoon at a time. Gradually add the chocolate, still beating. When all of the ingredients have been added, you should have a shiny meringue.

Spoon or pipe teaspoonsful of the meringue onto the prepared baking sheet and place in the preheated oven. Bake for 25 to 30 minutes, until the cookies are just beginning to brown around the edges and can easily be removed from the baking sheets. Remove from the heat and cool on racks. Keep in a covered container.

Advance Preparation: If you can resist eating them, the cookies will keep for at least a week if well sealed.

PER PORTION

Calories	13	Protein	0
Fat	.46 g	Carbohydrate	2 g
Saturated Fat	.27 g	Fiber	0
Cholesterol	0	Sodium	6 mg

Cinnamon Sugar Cookies

Makes 3¹/₂ to 4 dozen cookies

These cookies have a nice crumbly texture and a fine cinnamon flavor. They're easy to make and great to have around to serve with fruity desserts.

6	ounces (1¹/₂ sticks) unsalted butter
¹/₂	cup sugar
1	large egg
1	teaspoon vanilla extract
2¹/₂	to 3 cups all-purpose flour as needed
1	tablespoon ground cinnamon
1	teaspoon baking powder
¹/₂	teaspoon salt
1	egg beaten with 2 tablespoons water for glazing the cookies, optional

Cream the butter and sugar in an electric mixer or in a food processor fitted with the steel blade. Beat in the egg and vanilla.

Sift together 2¹/₂ cups flour, the cinnamon, baking powder, and salt. Add to the butter mixture. Mix together and, if the mixture is quite sticky and moist, add additional flour. Gather into a ball. Divide into 2 pieces and roll out to log shapes about 2 inches in diameter. Wrap in wax paper or plastic, seal in a plastic bag, and place in the refrigerator overnight or in the freezer for 1 or 2 hours.

Preheat the oven to 350 degrees. Butter cookie sheets. Remove one of the logs from the refrigerator or freezer and slice into ¹/₈- to ¹/₄-inch-thick rounds. Keep the remaining dough in the refrigerator or freezer. Place on cookie sheets. If you want a shiny surface, brush the cookies with the egg beaten with water.

Bake for 10 to 15 minutes, until lightly browned around the edges. Allow to cool for 2 minutes on the cookie sheets, then transfer to wire racks and allow to cool. Keep in a well-sealed tin.

Advance Preparation: These cookies keep well for at least a week if sealed.

PER PORTION

Calories	70	Protein	1 g
Fat	3 g	Carbohydrate	9 g
Saturated Fat	2 g	Fiber	0
Cholesterol	13 mg	Sodium	40 mg

Sweet Potato Soufflé

Makes 6 servings

Although I've never seen a sweet potato soufflé in Mexico, sweet potatoes are used widely for candies and desserts. I like this creamy dish much better than the cloying Mexican sweet potato preparations I've had. It's not nearly as decadent as it seems. Mashed sweet potatoes are spiced up with cinnamon, nutmeg, and ginger, lightened with beaten egg whites, and baked until puffy and slightly browned on the outside. The soufflé is easier than pie and makes an impressive dessert.

1	**pound (1 large or 2 small) sweet potatoes**
1	**tablespoon unsalted butter**
1	**tablespoon sugar**
3	**tablespoons mild-flavored honey, such as clover or acacia**
1/2	**teaspoon ground cinnamon**
1/4	**teaspoon ground nutmeg**
1/4	**teaspoon ground ginger**
1/8	**teaspoon salt**
1/4	**cup plain nonfat yogurt**
5	**large egg whites at room temperature**

Preheat the oven to 425 degrees. Scrub the sweet potatoes and pierce in several places with a sharp knife. Line a baking sheet with foil and place the potatoes on it. Bake for 45 to 60 minutes, depending on the size of the sweet potatoes, until they are thoroughly soft and beginning to ooze. Remove from the heat and allow the potatoes to cool. Turn the oven down to 400 degrees.

Meanwhile, rub the inside of a 2-quart soufflé dish with the butter and sprinkle with the sugar. Tilt the dish to distribute the sugar evenly over the surfaces.

Peel the potatoes and mash through a potato ricer or strainer or in a food processor fitted with the steel blade. Add the honey, cinnamon, nutmeg, ginger, salt, and yogurt and combine well.

Beat the egg whites to stiff but not dry peaks. Stir a quarter of the egg whites into the sweet potato mixture. Gently fold in the rest until thoroughly combined. Carefully pour into the prepared soufflé dish and bake for 20 minutes, until puffed and just beginning to brown on the surface. Remove from the heat and serve at once. The soufflé should be runny on the inside.

Advance Preparation: The sweet potato mixture, without the egg whites, will hold for a couple of days in the refrigerator. Bring to room temperature before proceeding with the recipe.

PER PORTION

Calories	135	Protein	4 g
Fat	2 g	Carbohydrate	25 g
Saturated Fat	1 g	Fiber	2 g
Cholesterol	5 mg	Sodium	126 mg

BAKED PLANTAINS WITH PRUNES

Makes 6 servings

Afro-Caribbean and Spanish ingredients—plantains, rum, and prunes—come together here, sweetened and moistened with orange juice and sugar and baked until tender. Make sure your plantains are ripe, or they will be too starchy for the dessert to work.

- 3   large or 4 medium-size ripe plantains
- ¼   pound prunes, pitted and chopped
- ½   cup fresh orange juice
- 1   tablespoon fresh lime juice
- 3   tablespoons dark rum
- ¼   cup sugar
- 2   tablespoons unsalted butter

For the Topping:
- ½   cup plain nonfat yogurt
- 2   tablespoons low-fat (1%) or skim milk
- 2   to 3 teaspoons mild-flavored honey, such as clover or acacia, to
       taste

Preheat the oven to 350 degrees. Butter a baking dish large enough to hold the plantains. Without peeling, place them in the baking dish and bake for 30 minutes, until blackened and the skin has split.

Remove the plantains from the oven and peel when cool enough to handle. Cut the tough ends off and cut in half lengthwise. Remove the tough inner core and cut the plantains into 2-inch pieces. Return to the baking dish and toss with the chopped prunes.

Combine the orange juice, lime juice, and rum and stir in the sugar. Stir to dissolve, then spoon over the plantains. Dot with butter.

Cover the dish with lightly buttered foil. Bake for 20 minutes or until the plantains are tender. Meanwhile, whisk together the yogurt, milk, and honey in a bowl, until the mixture is smooth and creamy.

Serve the plantains and prunes warm, spooning the syrup in the pan over the fruit, then topping with a spoonful of the yogurt mixture.

Advance Preparation: Although these can be made ahead of time and reheated, the plantains tend to absorb much of the syrup if they sit too long. So it's best to bake them close to serving time. However, you can bake the plantains in their skins hours ahead.

PER PORTION

Calories	295	Protein	3 g
Fat	5 g	Carbohydrate	61 g
Saturated Fat	3 g	Fiber	4 g
Cholesterol	13 mg	Sodium	68 mg

VANILLA FLAN

Makes 8 servings

Flan—the Spanish or Mexican version of crème caramel—is the most classic of Mexican desserts. Mine is not at all classic, because it isn't rich; I use 1% low-fat milk and fewer egg yolks than normal. This means that the flan takes a bit longer to set—very long in fact—but when it does, it has a heavenly, creamy texture. This is also not a very sweet custard, but the caramel syrup makes up for that, and the contrast of the silky, not-too-sweet flan against the sweet caramel is very nice indeed, a perfect balance.

For the Custard:

3½   cups low-fat (1%) milk
1   vanilla bean, split in half lengthwise, or 1 teaspoon vanilla extract
⅔   cup sugar
4   large eggs
2   large egg yolks

For the Caramel:

1   cup sugar
¼   cup water

Before you begin, bring a kettle of water to a simmer. Preheat the oven to 350 degrees with the rack in the middle and set an 8-inch 2½-quart soufflé dish or 8 custard cups in a baking pan deep enough to hold 2 inches of water.

Pour the milk into a saucepan and scrape in the seeds from the vanilla pod if you're using it. Add the vanilla pod to the milk and bring the milk to a simmer. Stir in the sugar. When the sugar has dissolved, remove from the heat and let the milk steep with the vanilla pods for 15 minutes. Remove the vanilla pods from the milk (rinse and allow to dry, then cover with sugar to make vanilla sugar). If you're not using vanilla beans, simply bring the milk to a simmer, dissolve the sugar, and remove from the heat.

If you're using vanilla extract, beat the eggs with the vanilla in a large bowl. Beat in the hot sweet milk, stir the mixture well, and set aside while you prepare the caramel.

Make the caramel. Measure the sugar for the caramel into a small heavy saucepan and add the water. Stir well and bring to a boil over high heat. Dip a pastry brush in water and brush down the sides of the pan, then turn the heat to medium and simmer without stirring until the syrup begins to color. If crystals form on the sides of the pan, cover the pan for 30 seconds to a few minutes, until the steam melts the sugar and it flows back into the syrup. Simmer until the syrup is a dark amber color, like iced tea. Swirl the pan to even the color. Remove from the heat and pour immediately into the mold or custard cups, then tilt the mold or custard cups to distribute the caramel over the bottom and sides.

Pour the custard mixture into the mold or custard cups and set them back in the baking pan. Pour in 2 inches of simmering water. Cover lightly with foil and bake individual servings for about 30 to 45 minutes, the large mold for $1^1/_2$ to 2 hours, until the mixture has just set and a knife inserted in the center comes out clean. Remove from the heat and allow to cool in the water bath. Transfer to a refrigerator and chill for several hours or overnight.

To unmold, run a knife around the edges of the flan(s) and rotate the mold quickly, holding it flat against the counter, to loosen the sides. Invert a deep serving plate over the top of the mold and invert the flan onto the plate. The syrup will run in a pool around the sides of the flan, which is why you need a deep serving dish. Serve, spooning some of the syrup onto each plate.

Advance Preparation: The flan can be made several days ahead of time and kept, without unmolding, in the refrigerator. Even unmolded I have kept a flan for a day in the refrigerator. The caramel topping can be made and poured into the mold or molds hours before you make the custard.

PER PORTION

Calories	260	Protein	7 g
Fat	5 g	Carbohydrate	47 g
Saturated Fat	2 g	Fiber	0
Cholesterol	164 mg	Sodium	87 mg

MEXICAN RICE PUDDING

Makes 6 to 8 servings

Arroz con leche is one of Mexico's most popular desserts. Children love it so much that they sing songs about it in nursery school. While this low-fat version is not as creamy as the authentic rice pudding, it's comforting and delicious. If you bring home coffee honey from Mexico, try it here.

2   cups water
1   cup white rice
1/4   teaspoon salt
2   inches cinnamon stick
1   quart low-fat (1%) or nonfat milk
1/2   cup sugar or 1/3 cup plus 1 tablespoon mild honey, such as clover, acacia, or coffee
1/2   cup raisins, optional
    freshly grated nutmeg to taste

Bring the water to a boil in a medium-size heavy saucepan. Add the rice, salt, and cinnamon stick. When the mixture comes back to a boil, stir the mixture once, cover, reduce the heat to medium-low, and simmer for 15 minutes or until the liquid is absorbed and the rice is tender.

Stir the milk, sugar, and raisins into the rice and bring back to a simmer over medium heat, stirring. Turn the heat back to medium-low and continue to simmer, stirring often, until the mixture has thickened but is still soupy, about 20 to 25 minutes. Remove from the heat, sprinkle with freshly grated nutmeg, and serve hot.

Advance Preparation: This can be made hours ahead of serving, but you should take it off the heat 5 minutes earlier. You will have to thin out the mixture with additional hot milk when you are ready to serve.

PER PORTION

Calories	246	Protein	8 g
Fat	2 g	Carbohydrate	49 g
Saturated Fat	1 g	Fiber	0
Cholesterol	6 mg	Sodium	173 mg

Suggested Menus

The menus that follow are 3- or 4-course menus, plus hors d'oeuvres for entertaining. I've listed vegetarian menus separately, but feel free to replace a fish or chicken dish with a vegetarian dish where you wish and vice versa. For simpler meals you can use these suggestions and eliminate starters and a first course. See more about menu planning in the "Introduction to the Recipes."

Griddle-Toasted Fava Beans
Chips Without Oil with Assorted Salsas
Cold Lime-Cooked Fish (Seviche) or Spinach Salad with
      Lime-Marinated Fish
Black Bean Tostadas (aka Chalupas)
Red Rice with Peas and Carrots
Ice-Cold Pineapple Doused with Tequila
Little Almond Cookies

Nachos (Tostadas) with Tomatillo Guacamole
Garlicky Zucchini Quesadillas
Tuna Steaks with Adobo Sauce
Grilled Corn with Chipotle Salsa or Dip
Nasturtium and Watercress Salad
Strawberries in a Sea of Mango

Jícama Slices with Lime Juice and Chile Powder
Shrimp Chilpachol
Soft Tacos with Shredded Shark or Mahimahi Salpicón from Veracruz
Refried Black Beans with Plantain Pancakes
Baby Lettuces with Lime and Balsamic Vinaigrette
Vanilla Flan

Black Bean Nachos (Tostadas)
Cactus, Avocado, and Tomato Salad
Green or Red Hominy Stew (Pozole) with Chicken
Mexican Chocolate Ice

Light and Fragrant Corn Soup or Crab Claws Bathed in Picante
    Chipotle Sauce
Veracruz-Style Fish
Plain white rice or White Rice with Herbs
Baby Lettuces with Lime and Balsamic Vinaigrette
Baked Plantains with Prunes

Picante Shrimp Enchiladas with Chipotle Sauce
Veracruz-Style Chicken Stew
Plain white (or brown) rice or White Rice with Herbs
Baby Lettuces with Lime and Balsamic Vinaigrette
Mango Ice

Green Bean Salad
Grilled Tuna with Tomato and Corn Salsa
Potato Gratin with Red and Green Rajas
Grapefruit Ice
Chocolate Meringue Cookies

Filled Masa Cups
Black Bean Salad
Veracruz-Style Crab Soup
Corn Bread
Lime Ice with a Splash of Tequila
Chocolate Meringue Cookies

Jícama Slices with Lime Juice and Chile Powder
Vinegared Oyster Mushrooms with Onions, Carrots, and Chiles
Green Tomatillo Mole with Salmon or Shrimp
Plain white rice or White Rice with Herbs
Simply steamed summer squash or broccoli
Poached Fruit Compote

Shrimp and Lime Nachos (Tostadas)
Roasted Yellow Tomato Soup
Quesadillas with Oyster Mushrooms and Chipotles
Corn Pudding with Toasted Garlic
Nasturtium and Watercress Salad
Blueberries in a Sea of Papaya

Vinegar-Bathed Shrimp
Corn, Tomato, and Poblano Soup
Grilled Swordfish or Halibut with Mango Mint Salsa
Baked Sweet Potatoes with Lime
Coffee-Cinnamon Granita with Kahlúa

Vegetable Tostadas with Red Chile Sauce
Mixed Greens Salad with Sweet Potatoes and Crumbly Cheese
Stewed Chicken with Chipotles and Prunes
White Rice with Herbs or Plain White Rice
Mango Ice
Cinnamon Sugar Cookies

Soft Tacos with Oyster Mushrooms and Tomatoes
Stuffed Poblano Chiles
Green Rice with Cilantro and Spinach or Parsley (Arroz Verde)
Baby Lettuces with Lime and Balsamic Vinaigrette
Ice-Cold Pineapple Doused with Tequila
Chocolate Meringue Cookies

Shrimp and Crudités with Creamy Chipotle Dip
Corn and Potato Salad with Tomatillo Dressing *or* Cactus, Avocado,
    and Tomato Salad
Black Bean Chili
Corn Tortillas or Corn Bread
Lime Ice with a Splash of Tequila

Swiss Chard Quesadillas
Veracruz-Style Fava Bean Soup
Shrimp with Green Garlic Sauce
Green Rice with Cilantro and Spinach or Parsley (Arroz Verde) or
    plain rice
Melon Balls with Mint and Cointreau

Mexican-Style Gazpacho
Veracruz-Style Paella (Arroz a la Tumbada)
Baby Lettuces with Lime and Balsamic Vinaigrette
Grapefruit Ice

Vegetarian Dinner Party Menus

Griddle-Toasted Fava Beans
Chips Without Oil with Assorted Dips and/or Salsas
Tortilla Soup
Mushroom and Garlic Enchiladas with Chipotle Tomato Sauce
Refried Black Beans with Plantain Pancakes
Mango Ice

Black Bean Nachos (Tostadas)
Jícama Slices with Lime Juice and Chile Powder
Green Hominy Stew (Pozole Verde)
Mexican Chocolate Ice

Mexican-Style Gazpacho
Black Bean Tostadas (aka Chalupas)
Squash Simmered with Tomatoes, Onion, and Garlic *or* Corn off the
        Cob with Mexican Herbs
Strawberries in a Sea of Mango
Chocolate Meringue Cookies

Green Bean Salad
Veracruz-Style Fava Bean Soup
Grilled Corn with Chipotle Salsa or Creamy Chipotle Dip
Quesadillas with Oyster Mushrooms and Chipotles
Grapefruit Ice

Squash Blossom Quesadillas
Cactus, Avocado, and Tomato Salad
Black Bean and Greens Stew
Vanilla Flan

Vegetable Tostadas with Red Chile Sauce
Jícama and Orange Salad (Pico de Gallo)
Oaxacan Green Herb Mole with White Beans and Vegetables
Corn Tortillas
Almond Rice Ice
Chocolate Meringue Cookies

Vinegared Oyster Mushrooms with Onions, Carrots, and Chiles
Vegetable Chilpachol
Enfrijoladas
Green Rice with Cilantro and Spinach or Parsley (Arroz Verde)
Poached Fruit Compote

Crusty Hard Bread with Pickled Vegetables (Pedrazos)
Creamy Corn and Poblano Soup
Garlicky Zucchini Quesadillas
Refried Black Beans with Plantain Pancakes
Lime Ice with a Splash of Tequila

Bite-Size Cornmeal Pancakes with Tomato-Corn Salsa
Lentil Soup with Chipotles and Plantain Garnish
Squash Blossom Quesadillas
White Rice with Herbs
Wild Mushroom Stew
Almond Rice Ice

A Mexican Cocktail Party

Mexican Sangria
Margaritas
Sparkling Limeade
Iced Hibiscus Tea
Cantaloupe Water
Crudités and Shrimp with Creamy Chipotle Dip
Black Bean Nachos (Tostadas)
Stuffed Jalapeño Peppers
Bite-Size Cornmeal Pancakes with Tomato-Corn Salsa
Mussels on the Half-Shell with Salsa Fresca
Tomatillo Guacamole
Tostadas with Chicken, Corn, and Avocado

A Mexican Buffet Feast

Margaritas
Sparkling Limeade
Crudités with Creamy Chipotle Dip
Mussels on the Half-Shell with Salsa Fresca
Cactus, Avocado, and Tomato Salad
Rice Salad with Roasted Poblanos and Cumin Vinaigrette
Empanadas with Shredded Shark or Mahimahi Salpicón
Quesadillas with Oyster Mushrooms and Chipotles
Fish Fillets in Adobo, Cooked in Corn Husks
A Great Pot of Beans: Black Beans with Epazote
Hot Corn Tortillas
Corn off the Cob with Mexican Herbs *or* Sweet Potato and Chayote
    Stew
Strawberries in a Sea of Mango
Vanilla Flan
Assorted cookies

A Mexican Buffet Brunch

Pot-brewed Coffee with Cinnamon and Brown Sugar
Banana-Strawberry Licuados
Cantaloupe-Seed Horchata
Pineapple Water
Mexican Sangria
Fruit Ambrosia with Lime-Honey Dressing
Black Bean Nachos (Tostadas)
Green Chilaquiles
Scrambled Eggs with Vegetables and Crisp Tortillas (Migas)
Filled Masa Cups
Squash Blossom Quesadillas
Wild Mushroom Stew

A Summer Picnic

Hard-Crusted Sandwiches from Puebla (Cemitas)
Filled Pambazos
Chicken Salad with Chipotle Chiles
Crusty Hard Bread with Marinated Vegetables (Pedrazos)
Black Bean Salad or Rice Salad with Roasted Poblanos and Cumin
     Vinaigrette
Vegetable Tostadas with Red Chile Sauce
Ice-Cold Pineapple Doused with Tequila
Melon Balls with Mint and Cointreau

A Summer Barbecue

Cactus, Avocado, and Tomato Salad
Tostadas with Tomatillo Guacamole
Tostadas with Salsa Fresca
Grilled Tuna Steaks with Adobo Sauce
Fish Fillets in Adobo, Cooked in Corn Husks
Grilled Corn with Chipotle Salsa or Creamy Chipotle Dip
Potatoes with Rajas
Fruit Ambrosia with Lime-Honey Dressing
Cinnamon Sugar Cookies

Selected Bibliography

Andrews, Jean. *Red Hot Peppers.* New York: Macmillan Publishing Co., 1993.

Bayless, Rick, with Deann Groen Bayless. *Authentic Mexican.* New York: William Morrow and Co., Inc., 1987.

de Araza Campos, Laura B. *El Libro Clásico de la Cocina Mexicana.* México, D.F.: Promexa, 1991.

Dent, Huntley. *The Feast of Santa Fe.* New York: Simon & Schuster, 1985.

Fernández, Adela. *La Tradicional Cocina Mexicana y sus Mejores Recetas.* México, D.F.: Panorama Editorial, 1989.

Hutson, Lucinda. *Tequila! Cooking with the Spirit of Mexico.* Berkeley: 10-Speed Press, 1995.

Kennedy, Diana. *The Cuisines of Mexico.* New York: Harper & Row, Publishers, 1972.

———. *The Tortilla Book.* New York: Harper & Row, Publishers, 1975.

———. *Mexican Regional Cooking* (originally published as *Recipes from the Regional Cooks of Mexico*). New York: Harper Perennial, 1978, 1984, 1990.

———. *The Art of Mexican Cooking.* New York: Bantam Books, 1989.

Lara, Silvia Luz Carillo. *Cocina Yucateca Tradicional.* México, D.F.: Editorial Diana, 1994.

Lomelí, Arturo. *El Chile y Otros Picantes.* México, D.F.: Asociación Mexicana de Estudios para la Defensa del Consumidor, A.C., 1987.

Madison, Deborah, with Edward Espe Brown. *The Greens Cookbook.* New York: Bantam Books, 1987.

Madison, Deborah. *The Savory Way.* New York: Bantam Books, 1990.

Margen, Sheldon, M.D., and the Editors of the UC Berkeley Wellness Letter. *The Wellness Encyclopedia of Food and Nutrition.* New York: Health Letter Associates, 1992.

Miller, Mark. *The Great Chile Book.* Berkeley: 10-Speed Press, 1991.

Milliken, Mary Sue, and Feniger, Susan, with Helene Siegel. *Mesa Mexicana.* New York: William Morrow and Co., Inc., 1994.

Molinar, Rita. *Dulces Mexicanos.* México, D.F.: Editorial Pax-Mexico, 1969.

Peyton, James W. *La Cocina de la Frontera: Mexican-American Cooking from the Southwest.* Santa Fe: Red Crane Books, 1994.

Sax, Richard, and Simmons, Marie. *Lighter Quicker Better.* New York: William Morrow and Co., Inc., 1995.

Sellers, Jeff M. *Folk Wisdom of Mexico.* San Francisco: Chronicle Books, 1994.

Shulman, Martha Rose. *Entertaining Light.* New York: Bantam Books, 1991.

———. *Main Dish Salads.* New York: Bantam Books, 1992.

Stoopen, María; Delgado, Ana Laura; Ramírez Delgollado, Carmen; Villalobos de Arenas, Carmen. *La Cocina Veracruzana.* Gobierno del Estado de Veracruz, 1992.

Vergé, Roger. *Les Légumes de Mon Moulin.* Paris: Flammarion, 1992.

Index